Hands-On Machine Learning for Algorithmic Trading

Design and implement investment strategies based on smart algorithms that learn from data using Python

Stefan Jansen

BIRMINGHAM - MUMBAI

Hands-On Machine Learning for Algorithmic Trading

Commissioning Editor: Sunith Shetty
Acquisition Editor: Joshua Nadar
Content Development Editor: Snehal Kolte
Technical Editor: Sayli Nikalje
Copy Editor: Safis Editing
Project Coordinator: Manthan Patel
Proofreader: Safis Editing
Indexer: Rekha Nair
Graphics: Jisha Chirayil
Production Coordinator: Arvindkumar Gupta

First published: December 2018

Production reference: 1311218

Published by Packt Publishing Ltd.
Livery Place
35 Livery Street
Birmingham
B3 2PB, UK.

ISBN 978-1-78934-641-1

www.packtpub.com

`mapt.io`

Mapt is an online digital library that gives you full access to over 5,000 books and videos, as well as industry leading tools to help you plan your personal development and advance your career. For more information, please visit our website.

Why subscribe?

- Spend less time learning and more time coding with practical eBooks and Videos from over 4,000 industry professionals

- Improve your learning with Skill Plans built especially for you

- Get a free eBook or video every month

- Mapt is fully searchable

- Copy and paste, print, and bookmark content

Packt.com

Did you know that Packt offers eBook versions of every book published, with PDF and ePub files available? You can upgrade to the eBook version at `www.packt.com` and as a print book customer, you are entitled to a discount on the eBook copy. Get in touch with us at `customercare@packtpub.com` for more details.

At `www.packt.com`, you can also read a collection of free technical articles, sign up for a range of free newsletters, and receive exclusive discounts and offers on Packt books and eBooks.

Contributors

About the author

Stefan Jansen, CFA is Founder and Lead Data Scientist at Applied AI where he advises Fortune 500 companies and startups across industries on translating business goals into a data and AI strategy, builds data science teams and develops ML solutions. Before his current venture, he was Managing Partner and Lead Data Scientist at an international investment firm where he built the predictive analytics and investment research practice.

He was also an executive at a global fintech startup operating in 15 markets, worked for the World Bank, advised Central Banks in emerging markets, and has worked in 6 languages on four continents. Stefan holds Master's from Harvard and Berlin University and teaches data science at General Assembly and Datacamp.

I thank Packt for this opportunity and the team who made the result possible, esp Snehal Kolte for facilitating the editing process. Many supporters deserve mention but Prof Zeckhauser at Harvard stands out for inspiring interest in the creative use of quantitative methods to solve problems. I am indebted to my parents for encouraging curiosity and supporting me throughout. Above all, however, I am grateful for Mariana who makes it all worthwhile.

About the reviewers

Doug Ortiz is an experienced enterprise cloud, big data, data analytics, and solutions architect who has architected, designed, developed, re-engineered, and integrated enterprise solutions. His other expertise includes Amazon Web Services, Azure, Google Cloud platform, business intelligence, Hadoop, Spark, NoSQL databases, and SharePoint.

He is the founder of Illustris.

> *Huge thanks to my wonderful wife, Milla, as well as Maria, Nikolay, and our children for all their support.*

Sandipan Dey is a data scientist with a wide range of interests, including topics such as machine learning, deep learning, image processing, and computer vision. He has worked in numerous data science fields, including recommender systems, predictive models for the events industry, sensor localization models, sentiment analysis, and device prognostics. He earned his master's degree in computer science from the University of Maryland, Baltimore County, and has published in a few IEEE data mining conferences and journals.

He has earned certifications from 100+ MOOCs on data science, machine learning, deep learning, image processing, and related courses/specializations. He is a regular blogger on his blog (`sandipanweb`) and is a machine learning education enthusiast.

Packt is searching for authors like you

If you're interested in becoming an author for Packt, please visit `authors.packtpub.com` and apply today. We have worked with thousands of developers and tech professionals, just like you, to help them share their insight with the global tech community. You can make a general application, apply for a specific hot topic that we are recruiting an author for, or submit your own idea.

Table of Contents

Preface

The availability of diverse data has increased the demand for expertise in algorithmic trading strategies. With this book, you will select and apply **machine learning (ML)** to a broad range of data sources and create powerful algorithmic strategies.

This book will start by introducing you to essential elements, such as evaluating datasets, accessing data APIs using Python, using Quandl to access financial data, and managing prediction errors. We then cover various machine learning techniques and algorithms that can be used to build and train algorithmic models using pandas, Seaborn, StatsModels, and sklearn. We will then build, estimate, and interpret AR(p), MA(q), and ARIMA (p, d, q) models using StatsModels. You will apply Bayesian concepts of prior, evidence, and posterior, in order to distinguish the concept of uncertainty using PyMC3. We will then utilize NLTK, sklearn, and spaCy to assign sentiment scores to financial news and classify documents to extract trading signals. We will learn to design, build, tune, and evaluate feed forward neural networks, **recurrent neural networks (RNNs)**, and **convolutional neural networks (CNNs)**, using Keras to design sophisticated algorithms. You will apply transfer learning to satellite image data to predict economic activity. Finally, we will apply reinforcement learning for optimal trading results.

By the end of the book, you will be able to adopt algorithmic trading to implement smart investing strategies.

Who this book is for

The book is for data analysts, data scientists, and Python developers, as well as investment analysts and portfolio managers working within the finance and investment industry. If you want to perform efficient algorithmic trading by developing smart investigating strategies using ML algorithms, this is the book you need! Some understanding of Python and ML techniques is mandatory.

What this book covers

Chapter 1, *Machine Learning for Trading*, identifies the focus of the book by outlining how ML matters in generating and evaluating signals for the design and execution of a trading strategy. It outlines the strategy process from hypothesis generation and modeling, data selection, and backtesting to evaluation and execution in a portfolio context, including risk management.

Chapter 2, *Market and Fundamental Data*, covers sources and working with original exchange-provided tick and financial reporting data, as well as how to access numerous open-source data providers that we will rely on throughout this book.

Chapter 3, *Alternative Data for Finance*, provides categories and criteria to assess the exploding number of sources and providers. It also demonstrates how to create alternative data sets by scraping websites, for example to collect earnings call transcripts for use with **natural language processing (NLP)** and sentiment analysis algorithms in the second part of the book.

Chapter 4, *Alpha Factor Research*, provides a framework for understanding how factors work and how to measure their performance, for example using the **information coefficient (IC)**. It demonstrates how to engineer alpha factors from data using Python libraries offline and on the Quantopian platform. It also introduces the `zipline` library to backtest factors and the `alphalens` library to evaluate their predictive power.

Chapter 5, *Strategy Evaluation*, introduces how to build, test and evaluate trading strategies using historical data with `zipline` offline and on the Quantopian platform. It presents and demonstrates how to compute portfolio performance and risk metrics using the `pyfolio` library. It also addresses how to manage methodological challenges of strategy backtests and introduce methods to optimize a strategy from a portfolio risk perspective.

Chapter 6, *Machine Learning Workflow*, sets the stage by outlining how to formulate, train, tune and evaluate the predictive performance of ML models as a systematic workflow.

Chapter 7, *Linear Models*, it shows how to use linear and logistic regression for inference and prediction and how to use regularization to manage the risk of overfitting. It presents the Quantopian trading platform and demonstrates how to build factor models and predict asset prices.

Chapter 8, *Time Series Models*, covers univariate and multivariate time series, including vector autoregressive models and cointegration tests, and how they can be applied to pairs trading strategies.

Chapter 9, *Bayesian Machine Learning*, presents how to formulate probabilistic models and how **Markov Chain Monte Carlo (MCMC)** sampling and Variational Bayes facilitate approximate inference. It also illustrates how to use PyMC3 for probabilistic programming to gain deeper insights into parameter and model uncertainty.

Chapter 10, *Decision Trees and Random Forests,* shows how to build, train and tune non-linear tree-based models for insight and prediction. It introduces tree-based ensemble models and shows how random forests use bootstrap aggregation to overcome some of the weaknesses of decision trees. Chapter 11, *Gradient Boosting Machines* ensemble models and demonstrates how to use the libraries xgboost, lightgbm, and catboost for high-performance training and prediction, and reviews in depth how to tune the numerous hyperparameters.

Chapter 11, *Gradient Boosting Machines,* demonstrates how to use the libraries xgboost, lightgbm, and catboost for high-performance training and prediction, and reviews in depth how to tune the numerous hyperparameters.

Chapter 12, *Unsupervised Learning,* introduces how to use dimensionality reduction and clustering for algorithmic trading. It uses principal and independent component analysis to extract data-driven risk factors. It presents several clustering techniques and demonstrates the use of hierarchical clustering for asset allocation.

Chapter 13, *Working with Text Data,* demonstrates how to convert text data into a numerical format and applies the classification algorithms from *part two* for sentiment analysis to large datasets.

Chapter 14, *Topic Modeling,* applies Bayesian unsupervised learning to extract latent topics that can summarize a large number of documents and offer more effective ways to explore text data or use topics as features for a classification model. It demonstrates how to apply this technique to earnings call transcripts sourced in Chapter 3, *Alternative Data for Finance,* and to annual reports filed with the **Securities and Exchange Commission (SEC)**.

Chapter 15, *Word Embeddings,* uses neural networks to learn state-of-the-art language features in the form of word vectors that capture semantic context much better than traditional text features and represent a very promising avenue for extracting trading signals from text data.

Chapter 16, *Next Steps,* is a summary of all the previous chapters.

Chapter 17, *Deep Learning,* introduces Keras, TensorFlow and PyTorch, the most popular deep learning frameworks that we will use throughout part four. It also presents techniques for training and tuning, including regularization and provides an overview of common architectures. To read this chapter, go to the link https://www.packtpub.com/sites/default/files/downloads/Deep_Learning.pdf.

Chapter 18, *Recurrent Neural Networks*, shows how RNNs are useful for sequence-to-sequence modeling, including for time series. It demonstrates how RNN capture non-linear patterns over longer periods. To read this chapter, go to the link https://www.packtpub.com/sites/default/files/downloads/Recurrent_Neural_Networks.pdf.

Chapter 19, *Convolutional Neural Networks*, covers CNNs that are very powerful for classification tasks with unstructured data at scale. We will introduce successful architectural designs, train a CNN on satellite data, for example, to predict economic activity, and use transfer learning to speed up training. To read this chapter, go to the link https://www.packtpub.com/sites/default/files/downloads/Convolutions_Neural_Networks.pdf.

Chapter 20, *Autoencoders and Generative Adversarial Nets*, addresses unsupervised deep learning including autoencoders for non-linear compression of high-dimensional data and **Generative Adversarial Networks (GANs)**, one of the most important recent innovations to generate synthetic data. To read this chapter, go to the link https://www.packtpub.com/sites/default/files/downloads/Autoencoders_and_Generative_Adversarial_Nets.pdf.

Chapter 21, *Reinforcement Learning*, presents reinforcement learning that permits the design and training of agents that learn to optimize decisions over time in response to their environment. You will see how build an agent that responds to market signals using the Open AI gym. To read this chapter, go to the link https://www.packtpub.com/sites/default/files/downloads/Reinforcement_Learning.pdf.

To get the most out of this book

All you need for this book is a basic understanding of Python and machine learning techniques.

Download the example code files

You can download the example code files for this book from your account at www.packt.com. If you purchased this book elsewhere, you can visit www.packt.com/support and register to have the files emailed directly to you.

You can download the code files by following these steps:

1. Log in or register at `www.packt.com`.
2. Select the **SUPPORT** tab.
3. Click on **Code Downloads & Errata**.
4. Enter the name of the book in the **Search** box and follow the onscreen instructions.

Once the file is downloaded, please make sure that you unzip or extract the folder using the latest version of:

- WinRAR/7-Zip for Windows
- Zipeg/iZip/UnRarX for Mac
- 7-Zip/PeaZip for Linux

The code bundle for the book is also hosted on GitHub at `https://github.com/PacktPublishing/Hands-On-Machine-Learning-for-Algorithmic-Trading`. In case there's an update to the code, it will be updated on the existing GitHub repository.

We also have other code bundles from our rich catalog of books and videos available at `https://github.com/PacktPublishing/`. Check them out!

Download the color images

We also provide a PDF file that has color images of the screenshots/diagrams used in this book. You can download it here: `https://www.packtpub.com/sites/default/files/downloads/9781789346411_ColorImages.pdf`.

Conventions used

There are a number of text conventions used throughout this book.

`CodeInText`: Indicates code words in text, database table names, folder names, filenames, file extensions, pathnames, dummy URLs, user input, and Twitter handles. Here is an example: "The algorithm continues to execute after calling the `run_algorithm()` function and returns the same backtest performance `DataFrame`."

A block of code is set as follows:

```
interesting_times = extract_interesting_date_ranges(returns=returns)
interesting_times['Fall2015'].to_frame('pf') \
    .join(benchmark_rets) \
    .add(1).cumprod().sub(1) \
    .plot(lw=2, figsize=(14, 6), title='Post-Brexit Turmoil')
```

Bold: Indicates a new term, an important word, or words that you see onscreen.

 Warnings or important notes appear like this.

 Tips and tricks appear like this.

Get in touch

Feedback from our readers is always welcome.

General feedback: If you have questions about any aspect of this book, mention the book title in the subject of your message and email us at customercare@packtpub.com.

Errata: Although we have taken every care to ensure the accuracy of our content, mistakes do happen. If you have found a mistake in this book, we would be grateful if you would report this to us. Please visit www.packt.com/submit-errata, selecting your book, clicking on the Errata Submission Form link, and entering the details.

Piracy: If you come across any illegal copies of our works in any form on the Internet, we would be grateful if you would provide us with the location address or website name. Please contact us at copyright@packt.com with a link to the material.

If you are interested in becoming an author: If there is a topic that you have expertise in and you are interested in either writing or contributing to a book, please visit authors.packtpub.com.

Reviews

Please leave a review. Once you have read and used this book, why not leave a review on the site that you purchased it from? Potential readers can then see and use your unbiased opinion to make purchase decisions, we at Packt can understand what you think about our products, and our authors can see your feedback on their book. Thank you!

For more information about Packt, please visit `packt.com`.

Machine Learning for Trading 1

Algorithmic trading relies on computer programs that execute algorithms to automate some, or all, elements of a trading strategy. Algorithms are a sequence of steps or rules to achieve a goal and can take many forms. In the case of **machine learning** (**ML**), algorithms pursue the objective of learning other algorithms, namely rules, to achieve a target based on data, such as minimizing a prediction error.

These algorithms encode various activities of a portfolio manager who observes market transactions and analyzes relevant data to decide on placing buy or sell orders. The sequence of orders defines the portfolio holdings that, over time, aim to produce returns that are attractive to the providers of capital, taking into account their appetite for risk.

Ultimately, the goal of active investment management consists in achieving alpha, that is, returns in excess of the benchmark used for evaluation. The fundamental law of active management applies the **information ratio** (**IR**) to express the value of active management as the ratio of portfolio returns above the returns of a benchmark, usually an index, to the volatility of those returns. It approximates the information ratio as the product of the **information coefficient** (**IC**), which measures the quality of forecast as their correlation with outcomes, and the breadth of a strategy expressed as the square root of the number of bets.

Hence, the key to generating alpha is forecasting. Successful predictions, in turn, require superior information or a superior ability to process public information. Algorithms facilitate optimization throughout the investment process, from asset allocation to idea-generation, trade execution, and risk management. The use of ML for algorithmic trading, in particular, aims for more efficient use of conventional and alternative data, with the goal of producing both better and more actionable forecasts, hence improving the value of active management.

Historically, algorithmic trading used to be more narrowly defined as the automation of trade execution to minimize costs as offered by the sell side, but we will take a more comprehensive perspective since the use of algorithms, and ML, in particular, has come to impact a broader range of activities from idea generation and alpha factor design to asset allocation, position sizing, and the testing and evaluation of strategies.

This chapter looks at the bigger picture of how the use of ML has emerged as a critical source of competitive advantage in the investment industry and where it fits into the investment process to enable algorithmic trading strategies.

We will be covering the following topics in the chapter:

- How this book is organized and who should read it
- How ML has come to play a strategic role in algorithmic trading
- How to design and execute a trading strategy
- How ML adds value to an algorithmic trading strategy

How to read this book

If you are reading this, then you are probably aware that ML has become a strategic capability in many industries, including the investment industry. The explosion of digital data that drives much of the rise of ML is having a particularly powerful impact on investing, which already has a long history of using sophisticated models to process information. The scope of trading across asset classes implies that a vast range of new, alternative data may be relevant in addition to the market and fundamental data that used to be the focus of the analytical efforts.

You may have also come across the insight that the successful application of ML or data science requires the integration of statistical knowledge, computational skills, and domain expertise at the individual or team level. In other words, it is essential to ask the right questions, identify and understand the data that may provide the answers, deploy a broad range of tools to obtain results, and interpret them in a way that leads to the right decisions.

Consequently, this book takes an integrated perspective on the application of ML to the domain of investment and trading. In this section, we will lay out what to expect, how it goes about achieving its objectives, and what you need to both meet your goals and have fun in the process.

What to expect

This book aims to equip you with the strategic perspective, conceptual understanding, and practical tools to add value from applying ML to the trading and investment process. To this end, it covers ML as an important element in a process rather than a standalone exercise.

First and foremost, it covers a broad range of supervised, unsupervised, and reinforcement learning algorithms useful for extracting signals from the diverse data sources relevant to different asset classes. It introduces a ML workflow and focuses on practical use cases with relevant data and numerous code examples. However, it also develops the mathematical and statistical background to facilitate the tuning of an algorithm or the interpretation of the results.

The book recognizes that investors can extract value from third-party data more than other industries. As a consequence, it covers not only how to work with market and fundamental data but also how to source, evaluate, process, and model alternative data sources such as unstructured text and image data.

It relates the use of ML to research and evaluate alpha factors to quantitative and factor-based strategies and introduces portfolio management as the context for the deployment of strategies that combine multiple alpha factors. It also highlights that ML can add value beyond predictions relevant to individual asset prices, for example to asset allocation and addresses the risks of false discoveries from using ML with large datasets to develop a trading strategy.

It should not be a surprise that this book does not provide investment advice or ready-made trading algorithms. Instead, present building blocks required to identify, evaluate, and combine datasets that suitable for any given investment objective, select and apply ML algorithms to this data, and develop and test algorithmic trading strategies based on the results.

Who should read this book

You should find the book informative if you are an analyst, data scientist, or ML engineer with an understanding of financial markets and interest in trading strategies. You should also find value as an investment professional who aims to leverage ML to make better decisions.

If your background is software and ML, you may be able to just skim or skip some introductory material on ML. Similarly, if your expertise is in investment, you will likely be familiar with some or all of the financial context. You will likely find the book most useful as a survey of key algorithms, building blocks and use cases than for specialized coverage of a particular algorithm or strategy. However, the book assumes you are interested in continuing to learn about this very dynamic area. To this end, it references numerous resources to support your journey towards customized trading strategies that leverage and build on the fundamental methods and tools it covers.

You should be comfortable using Python 3 and various scientific computing libraries like `numpy`, `pandas`, or `scipy` and be interested in picking up numerous others along the way. Some experience with ML and scikit-learn would be helpful, but we briefly cover the basic workflow and reference various resources to fill gaps or dive deeper.

How the book is organized

The book provides a comprehensive introduction to how ML can add value to the design and execution of trading strategies. It is organized in four parts that cover different aspects of the data sourcing and strategy development process, as well as different solutions to various ML challenges.

Part I – the framework – from data to strategy design

The first part provides a framework for the development of algorithmic trading strategies. It focuses on the data that power the ML algorithms and strategies discussed in this book, outlines how ML can be used to derive trading signals, and how to deploy and evaluate strategies as part of a portfolio.

The remainder of this chapter summarizes how and why ML became central to investment, describes the trading process and outlines how ML can add value. Chapter 2, *Market and Fundamental Data*, covers sources and working with original exchange-provided tick and financial reporting data, as well as how to access numerous open-source data providers that we will rely on throughout this book.

Chapter 3, *Alternative Data for Finance*, provides categories and criteria to assess the exploding number of sources and providers. It also demonstrates how to create alternative data sets by scraping websites, for example to collect earnings call transcripts for use with **natural language processing** (**NLP**) and sentiment analysis algorithms in the second part of the book.

Chapter 4, *Alpha Factor Research*, provides a framework for understanding how factors work and how to measure their performance, for example using the **information coefficient (IC)**. It demonstrates how to engineer alpha factors from data using Python libraries offline and on the Quantopian platform. It also introduces the `zipline` library to backtest factors and the `alphalens` library to evaluate their predictive power.

Chapter 5, *Strategy Evaluation*, introduces how to build, test and evaluate trading strategies using historical data with `zipline` offline and on the Quantopian platform. It presents and demonstrates how to compute portfolio performance and risk metrics using the `pyfolio` library. It also addresses how to manage methodological challenges of strategy backtests and introduce methods to optimize a strategy from a portfolio risk perspective.

Part 2 – ML fundamentals

The second part covers the fundamental supervised and unsupervised learning algorithms and illustrates their application to trading strategies. It also introduces the Quantopian platform where you can leverage and combine the data and ML techniques developed in this book to implement algorithmic strategies that execute trades in live markets.

Chapter 6, The *Machine Learning Process*, sets the stage by outlining how to formulate, train, tune and evaluate the predictive performance of ML models as a systematic workflow.

Chapter 7, *Linear Models*, it shows how to use linear and logistic regression for inference and prediction and how to use regularization to manage the risk of overfitting. It presents the Quantopian trading platform and demonstrates how to build factor models and predict asset prices.

Chapter 8, *Time Series Models*, covers univariate and multivariate time series, including vector autoregressive models and cointegration tests, and how they can be applied to pairs trading strategies. Chapter 9, *Bayesian Machine Learning*, presents how to formulate probabilistic models and how **Markov Chain Monte Carlo (MCMC)** sampling and Variational Bayes facilitate approximate inference. It also illustrates how to use PyMC3 for probabilistic programming to gain deeper insights into parameter and model uncertainty.

Chapter 10, *Decision Trees and Random Forests*, shows how to build, train and tune non-linear tree-based models for insight and prediction. It introduces tree-based ensemble models and shows how random forests use bootstrap aggregation to overcome some of the weaknesses of decision trees. Chapter 11, *Gradient Boosting Machines* ensemble models and demonstrates how to use the libraries `xgboost`, `lightgbm`, and `catboost` for high-performance training and prediction, and reviews in depth how to tune the numerous hyperparameters.

Chapter 12, *Unsupervised Learning* introduces how to use dimensionality reduction and clustering for algorithmic trading. It uses principal and independent component analysis to extract data-driven risk factors. It presents several clustering techniques and demonstrates the use of hierarchical clustering for asset allocation.

Part 3 – natural language processing

Part three focuses on text data and introduces state-of-the-art unsupervised learning techniques to extract high-quality signals from this key source of alternative data.

Chapter 13, *Working with Text Data*, demonstrates how to convert text data into a numerical format and applies the classification algorithms from *part two* for sentiment analysis to large datasets. Chapter 14, *Topic Modeling*, applies Bayesian unsupervised learning to extract latent topics that can summarize a large number of documents and offer more effective ways to explore text data or use topics as features for a classification model. It demonstrates how to apply this technique to earnings call transcripts sourced in Chapter 3, *Alternative Data for Finance*, and to annual reports filed with the **Securities and Exchange Commission (SEC)**.

Chapter 15, *Word Embeddings*, uses neural networks to learn state-of-the-art language features in the form of word vectors that capture semantic context much better than traditional text features and represent a very promising avenue for extracting trading signals from text data.

Part 4 – deep and reinforcement learning

Part 4 introduces deep learning and reinforcement learning.

- Chapter 17, *Deep Learning*, introduces Keras, TensorFlow and PyTorch, the most popular deep learning frameworks and illustrates how to train and tune various architectures.
- Chapter 18, *Recurrent Neural Networks*, presents RNNs for time series data

- Chapter 19, *Convolutional Neural Networks*, illustrates how to use CNNs with image and text data
- Chapter 20, *Autoencoders and Generative Adversarial Nets*, shows how to use deep neural networks for unsupervised learning with autoencoders and presents GANs that produce synthetic data
- Chapter 21, *Reinforcement Learning,* demonstrates the use of reinforcement learning to build dynamic agents that learn a policy function based on rewards using the OpenAI gym platform

What you need to succeed

The book content revolves around the application of ML algorithms to different datasets. Significant additional content is hosted on GitHub to facilitate review and experiments with the examples discussed in the book. It contains additional detail and instructions as well as numerous references.

Data sources

We will use freely available historical data from market, fundamental and alternative sources. Chapter 2, *Market and Fundamental Data* and Chapter 3, *Alternative Data for Finance* cover characteristics and access to these data sources and introduce key providers that we will use throughout the book. The companion GitHub repository (see beneath) contains instructions on how to obtain or create some of the datasets that we will use throughout and includes some smaller datasets.

A few sample data sources that we will source and work with include, but are not limited to:

- NASDAQ ITCH order book data
- Electronic Data Gathering, Analysis, and Retrieval (EDGAR) SEC filings
- Earnings call transcripts from Seeking Alpha
- Quandl daily prices and other data points for over 3,000 US stocks
- Various macro fundamental data from the Federal Reserve and others
- Large Yelp business reviews and Twitter datasets
- Image data on oil tankers

Some of the data is several GB large (e.g. the NASDAQ and SEC filings). The notebooks indicate when that is the case.

GitHub repository

The GitHub repository contains Jupyter Notebooks that illustrate many of the concepts and models in more detail. The Notebooks are referenced throughout the book where used. Each chapter has its own directory with separate instructions where needed, as well as reference specific to the chapter's content.

Jupyter Notebooks is a great tool for creating reproducible computational narratives, and it enables users to create and share documents that combine live code with narrative text, mathematical equations, visualizations, interactive controls, and other rich output. It also provides building blocks for interactive computing with data, such as a file browser, terminals, and a text editor.

 You can find the code files placed at:
`https://github.com/PacktPublishing/Hands-On-Machine-Learning-for-Algorithmic-Trading`.

Python libraries

The book uses Python 3.7, and recommends `miniconda` to install the `conda` package manager and to create a `conda` environment to install the the requisite libraries. To this end, the GitHub repo contains an `environment.yml` file. Please refer to the installation instructions referenced in the GitHub repo's `README` file.

The rise of ML in the investment industry

The investment industry has evolved dramatically over the last several decades and continues to do so amid increased competition, technological advances, and a challenging economic environment. This section will review several key trends that have shaped the investment environment in general, and the context for algorithmic trading more specifically, and related themes that will recur throughout this book.

The trends that have propelled algorithmic trading and ML to current prominence include:

- Changes in the market microstructure, such as the spread of electronic trading and the integration of markets across asset classes and geographies
- The development of investment strategies framed in terms of risk-factor exposure, as opposed to asset classes

- The revolutions in computing power, data-generation and management, and analytic methods
- The outperformance of the pioneers in algorithmic traders relative to human, discretionary investors

In addition, the financial crises of 2001 and 2008 have affected how investors approach diversification and risk management and have given rise to low-cost passive investment vehicles in the form of **exchange-traded funds** (**ETFs**). Amid low yield and low volatility after the 2008 crisis, cost-conscious investors shifted $2 trillion from actively-managed mutual funds into passively managed ETFs. Competitive pressure is also reflected in lower hedge fund fees that dropped from the traditional 2% annual management fee and 20% take of profits to an average of 1.48% and 17.4%, respectively, in 2017.

From electronic to high-frequency trading

Electronic trading has advanced dramatically in terms of capabilities, volume, coverage of asset classes, and geographies since networks started routing prices to computer terminals in the 1960s.

Equity markets have led this trend worldwide. The 1997 order-handling rules by the SEC introduced competition to exchanges through **electronic communication networks** (**ECN**). ECNs are automated **Alternative Trading Systems** (**ATS**) that match buy-and-sell orders at specified prices, primarily for equities and currencies and are registered as broker-dealers. It allows significant brokerages and individual traders in different geographic locations to trade directly without intermediaries, both on exchanges and after hours. Dark pools are another type of ATS that allow investors to place orders and trade without publicly revealing their information, as in the order book maintained by an exchange. Dark pools have grown since a 2007 SEC ruling, are often housed within large banks, and are subject to SEC regulation.

With the rise of electronic trading, algorithms for cost-effective execution have developed rapidly and adoption has spread quickly from the sell side to the buy side and across asset classes. Automated trading emerged around 2000 as a sell-side tool aimed at cost-effective trade execution that spread orders over time to limit the market impact. These tools spread to the buy side and became increasingly sophisticated by taking into account, for example, transaction costs and liquidity, as well as short-term price and volume forecasts.

Direct Market Access (**DMA**) gives a trader greater control over execution by allowing it to send orders directly to the exchange using the infrastructure and market participant identification of a broker who is a member of an exchange. Sponsored access removes pre-trade risk controls by the brokers and forms the basis for **high-frequency trading** (**HFT**).

HFT refers to automated trades in financial instruments that are executed with extremely low latency in the microsecond range and where participants hold positions for very short periods. The goal is to detect and exploit inefficiencies in the market microstructure, the institutional infrastructure of trading venues. HFT has grown substantially over the past ten years and is estimated to make up roughly 55% of trading volume in US equity markets and about 40% in European equity markets. HFT has also grown in futures markets to roughly 80% of foreign-exchange futures volumes and two-thirds of both interest rate and Treasury 10 year futures volumes (FAS 2016).

HFT strategies aim to earn small profits per trade using passive or aggressive strategies. Passive strategies include arbitrage trading to profit from very small price differentials for the same asset, or its derivatives, traded on different venues. Aggressive strategies include order anticipation or momentum ignition. Order anticipation, also known as **liquidity detection**, involves algorithms that submit small exploratory orders to detect hidden liquidity from large institutional investors and trade ahead of a large order to benefit from subsequent price movements. Momentum ignition implies an algorithm executing and canceling a series of orders to spoof other HFT algorithms into buying (or selling) more aggressively and benefit from the resulting price changes.

Regulators have expressed concern over the potential link between certain aggressive HFT strategies and increased market fragility and volatility, such as that experienced during the May 2010 Flash Crash, the October 2014 Treasury Market volatility, and the sudden crash by over 1,000 points of the Dow Jones Industrial Average on August 24, 2015. At the same time, market liquidity has increased with trading volumes due to the presence of HFT, which has lowered overall transaction costs.

The combination of reduced trading volumes amid lower volatility and rising costs of the technology and access to both data and trading venues has led to financial pressure. Aggregate HFT revenues from US stocks have been estimated to drop beneath $1 billion for the first time since 2008, down from $7.9 billion in 2009.

This trend has led to industry consolidation with various acquisitions by, for example, the largest listed proprietary trading firm Virtu Financial, and shared infrastructure investments, such as the new Go West ultra-low latency route between Chicago and Tokyo. Simultaneously, startups such as Alpha Trading Lab make HFT trading infrastructure and data available to democratize HFT by crowdsourcing algorithms in return for a share of the profits.

Factor investing and smart beta funds

The return provided by an asset is a function of the uncertainty or risk associated with the financial investment. An equity investment implies, for example, assuming a company's business risk, and a bond investment implies assuming default risk.

To the extent that specific risk characteristics predict returns, identifying and forecasting the behavior of these risk factors becomes a primary focus when designing an investment strategy. It yields valuable trading signals and is the key to superior active-management results. The industry's understanding of risk factors has evolved very substantially over time and has impacted how ML is used for algorithmic trading.

Modern Portfolio Theory (**MPT**) introduced the distinction between idiosyncratic and systematic sources of risk for a given asset. Idiosyncratic risk can be eliminated through diversification, but systematic risk cannot. In the early 1960s, the **Capital Asset Pricing Model (CAPM)** identified a single factor driving all asset returns: the return on the market portfolio in excess of T-bills. The market portfolio consisted of all tradable securities, weighted by their market value. The systematic exposure of an asset to the market is measured by beta, which is the correlation between the returns of the asset and the market portfolio.

The recognition that the risk of an asset does not depend on the asset in isolation, but rather how it moves relative to other assets, and the market as a whole, was a major conceptual breakthrough. In other words, assets do not earn a risk premium because of their specific, idiosyncratic characteristics, but because of their exposure to underlying factor risks.

However, a large body of academic literature and long investing experience have disproved the CAPM prediction that asset risk premiums depend only on their exposure to a single factor measured by the asset's beta. Instead, numerous additional risk factors have since been discovered. A factor is a quantifiable signal, attribute, or any variable that has historically correlated with future stock returns and is expected to remain correlated in future.

These risk factors were labeled anomalies since they contradicted the **Efficient Market Hypothesis (EMH)**, which sustained that market equilibrium would always price securities according to the CAPM so that no other factors should have predictive power. The economic theory behind factors can be either rational, where factor risk premiums compensate for low returns during bad times, or behavioral, where agents fail to arbitrage away excess returns.

Well-known anomalies include the value, size, and momentum effects that help predict returns while controlling for the CAPM market factor. The size effect rests on small firms systematically outperforming large firms, discovered by Banz (1981) and Reinganum (1981). The value effect (Basu 1982) states that firms with low valuation metrics outperform. It suggests that firms with low price multiples, such as the price-to-earnings or the price-to-book ratios, perform better than their more expensive peers (as suggested by the inventors of value investing, Benjamin Graham and David Dodd, and popularized by Warren Buffet).

The momentum effect, discovered in the late 1980s by, among others, Clifford Asness, the founding partner of AQR, states that stocks with good momentum, in terms of recent 6-12 month returns, have higher returns going forward than poor momentum stocks with similar market risk. Researchers also found that value and momentum factors explain returns for stocks outside the US, as well as for other asset classes, such as bonds, currencies, and commodities, and additional risk factors.

In fixed income, the value strategy is called **riding the yield curve** and is a form of the duration premium. In commodities, it is called the **roll return**, with a positive return for an upward-sloping futures curve and a negative return otherwise. In foreign exchange, the value strategy is called **carry**.

There is also an illiquidity premium. Securities that are more illiquid trade at low prices and have high average excess returns, relative to their more liquid counterparts. Bonds with higher default risk tend to have higher returns on average, reflecting a credit risk premium. Since investors are willing to pay for insurance against high volatility when returns tend to crash, sellers of volatility protection in options markets tend to earn high returns.

Multifactor models define risks in broader and more diverse terms than just the market portfolio. In 1976, Stephen Ross proposed arbitrage pricing theory, which asserted that investors are compensated for multiple systematic sources of risk that cannot be diversified away. The three most important macro factors are growth, inflation, and volatility, in addition to productivity, demographic, and political risk. In 1992, Eugene Fama and Kenneth French combined the equity risk factors' size and value with a market factor into a single model that better explained cross-sectional stock returns. They later added a model that also included bond risk factors to simultaneously explain returns for both asset classes.

A particularly attractive aspect of risk factors is their low or negative correlation. Value and momentum risk factors, for instance, are negatively correlated, reducing the risk and increasing risk-adjusted returns above and beyond the benefit implied by the risk factors. Furthermore, using leverage and long-short strategies, factor strategies can be combined into market-neutral approaches. The combination of long positions in securities exposed to positive risks with underweight or short positions in the securities exposed to negative risks allows for the collection of dynamic risk premiums.

As a result, the factors that explained returns above and beyond the CAPM were incorporated into investment styles that tilt portfolios in favor of one or more factors, and assets began to migrate into factor-based portfolios. The 2008 financial crisis underlined how asset-class labels could be highly misleading and create a false sense of diversification when investors do not look at the underlying factor risks, as asset classes came crashing down together.

Over the past several decades, quantitative factor investing has evolved from a simple approach based on two or three styles to multifactor smart or exotic beta products. Smart beta funds have crossed $1 trillion AUM in 2017, testifying to the popularity of the hybrid investment strategy that combines active and passive management. Smart beta funds take a passive strategy but modify it according to one or more factors, such as cheaper stocks or screening them according to dividend payouts, to generate better returns. This growth has coincided with increasing criticism of the high fees charged by traditional active managers as well as heightened scrutiny of their performance.

The ongoing discovery and successful forecasting of risk factors that, either individually or in combination with other risk factors, significantly impact future asset returns across asset classes is a key driver of the surge in ML in the investment industry and will be a key theme throughout this book.

Algorithmic pioneers outperform humans at scale

The track record and growth of **Assets Under Management (AUM)** of firms that spearheaded algorithmic trading has played a key role in generating investor interest and subsequent industry efforts to replicate their success. Systematic funds differ from HFT in that trades may be held significantly longer while seeking to exploit arbitrage opportunities as opposed to advantages from sheer speed.

Systematic strategies that mostly or exclusively rely on algorithmic decision-making were most famously introduced by mathematician James Simons who founded Renaissance Technologies in 1982 and built it into the premier quant firm. Its secretive Medallion Fund, which is closed to outsiders, has earned an estimated annualized return of 35% since 1982.

DE Shaw, Citadel, and Two Sigma, three of the most prominent quantitative hedge funds that use systematic strategies based on algorithms, rose to the all-time top-20 performers for the first time in 2017 in terms of total dollars earned for investors, after fees, and since inception.

DE Shaw, founded in 1988 with $47 billion AUM in 2018 joined the list at number 3. Citadel started in 1990 by Kenneth Griffin, manages $29 billion and ranks 5, and Two Sigma started only in 2001 by DE Shaw alumni John Overdeck and David Siegel, has grown from $8 billion AUM in 2011 to $52 billion in 2018. Bridgewater started in 1975 with over $150 billion AUM, continues to lead due to its Pure Alpha Fund that also incorporates systematic strategies.

Similarly, on the Institutional Investors 2017 Hedge Fund 100 list, five of the top six firms rely largely or completely on computers and trading algorithms to make investment decisions—and all of them have been growing their assets in an otherwise challenging environment. Several quantitatively-focused firms climbed several ranks and in some cases grew their assets by double-digit percentages. Number 2-ranked **Applied Quantitative Research (AQR)** grew its hedge fund assets 48% in 2017 to $69.7 billion and managed $187.6 billion firm-wide.

Among all hedge funds, ranked by compounded performance over the last three years, the quant-based funds run by Renaissance Technologies achieved ranks 6 and 24, Two Sigma rank 11, D.E. Shaw no 18 and 32, and Citadel ranks 30 and 37. Beyond the top performers, algorithmic strategies have worked well in the last several years. In the past five years, quant-focused hedge funds gained about 5.1% per year while the average hedge fund rose 4.3% per year in the same period.

ML driven funds attract $1 trillion AUM

The familiar three revolutions in computing power, data, and ML methods have made the adoption of systematic, data-driven strategies not only more compelling and cost-effective but a key source of competitive advantage.

As a result, algorithmic approaches are not only finding wider application in the hedge-fund industry that pioneered these strategies but across a broader range of asset managers and even passively-managed vehicles such as ETFs. In particular, predictive analytics using machine learning and algorithmic automation play an increasingly prominent role in all steps of the investment process across asset classes, from idea-generation and research to strategy formulation and portfolio construction, trade execution, and risk management.

Estimates of industry size vary because there is no objective definition of a quantitative or algorithmic fund, and many traditional hedge funds or even mutual funds and ETFs are introducing computer-driven strategies or integrating them into a discretionary environment in a human-plus-machine approach.

Morgan Stanley estimated in 2017 that algorithmic strategies have grown at 15% per year over the past six years and control about $1.5 trillion between hedge funds, mutual funds, and smart beta ETFs. Other reports suggest the quantitative hedge fund industry was about to exceed $1 trillion AUM, nearly doubling its size since 2010 amid outflows from traditional hedge funds. In contrast, total hedge fund industry capital hit $3.21 trillion according to the latest global Hedge Fund Research report.

The market research firm Preqin estimates that almost 1,500 hedge funds make a majority of their trades with help from computer models. Quantitative hedge funds are now responsible for 27% of all US stock trades by investors, up from 14% in 2013. But many use data scientists—or quants—which, in turn, use machines to build large statistical models (WSJ).

In recent years, however, funds have moved toward true ML, where artificially-intelligent systems can analyze large amounts of data at speed and improve themselves through such analyses. Recent examples include Rebellion Research, Sentient, and Aidyia, which rely on evolutionary algorithms and deep learning to devise fully-automatic **Artificial Intelligence (AI)**-driven investment platforms.

From the core hedge fund industry, the adoption of algorithmic strategies has spread to mutual funds and even passively-managed exchange-traded funds in the form of smart beta funds, and to discretionary funds in the form of quantamental approaches.

The emergence of quantamental funds

Two distinct approaches have evolved in active investment management: systematic (or quant) and discretionary investing. Systematic approaches rely on algorithms for a repeatable and data-driven approach to identify investment opportunities across many securities; in contrast, a discretionary approach involves an in-depth analysis of a smaller number of securities. These two approaches are becoming more similar as fundamental managers take more data-science-driven approaches.

Even fundamental traders now arm themselves with quantitative techniques, accounting for $55 billion of systematic assets, according to Barclays. Agnostic to specific companies, quantitative funds trade patterns and dynamics across a wide swath of securities. Quants now account for about 17% of total hedge fund assets, data compiled by Barclays shows.

Point72 Asset Management, with $12 billion in assets, has been shifting about half of its portfolio managers to a man-plus-machine approach. Point72 is also investing tens of millions of dollars into a group that analyzes large amounts of alternative data and passes the results on to traders.

Investments in strategic capabilities

Rising investments in related capabilities—technology, data and, most importantly, skilled humans—highlight how significant algorithmic trading using ML has become for competitive advantage, especially in light of the rising popularity of passive, indexed investment vehicles, such as ETFs, since the 2008 financial crisis.

Morgan Stanley noted that only 23% of its quant clients say they are not considering using or not already using ML, down from 44% in 2016.

Guggenheim Partners LLC built what it calls a supercomputing cluster for $1 million at the Lawrence Berkeley National Laboratory in California to help crunch numbers for Guggenheim's quant investment funds. Electricity for the computers costs another $1 million a year.

AQR is a quantitative investment group that relies on academic research to identify and systematically trade factors that have, over time, proven to beat the broader market. The firm used to eschew the purely computer-powered strategies of quant peers such as Renaissance Technologies or DE Shaw. More recently, however, AQR has begun to seek profitable patterns in markets using ML to parse through novel datasets, such as satellite pictures of shadows cast by oil wells and tankers.

The leading firm BlackRock, with over $5 trillion AUM, also bets on algorithms to beat discretionary fund managers by heavily investing in SAE, a systematic trading firm it acquired during the financial crisis. Franklin Templeton bought Random Forest Capital, a debt-focused, data-led investment company for an undisclosed amount, hoping that its technology can support the wider asset manager.

ML and alternative data

Hedge funds have long looked for alpha through informational advantage and the ability to uncover new uncorrelated signals. Historically, this included things such as proprietary surveys of shoppers, or voters ahead of elections or referendums. Occasionally, the use of company insiders, doctors, and expert networks to expand knowledge of industry trends or companies crosses legal lines: a series of prosecutions of traders, portfolio managers, and analysts for using insider information after 2010 has shaken the industry.

In contrast, the informational advantage from exploiting conventional and alternative data sources using ML is not related to expert and industry networks or access to corporate management, but rather the ability to collect large quantities of data and analyze them in real-time.

Three trends have revolutionized the use of data in algorithmic trading strategies and may further shift the investment industry from discretionary to quantitative styles:

- The exponential increase in the amount of digital data
- The increase in computing power and data storage capacity at lower cost
- The advances in ML methods for analyzing complex datasets

Conventional data includes economic statistics, trading data, or corporate reports. Alternative data is much broader and includes sources such as satellite images, credit card sales, sentiment analysis, mobile geolocation data, and website scraping, as well as the conversion of data generated in the ordinary course of business into valuable intelligence. It includes, in principle, any data source containing trading signals that can be extracted using ML.

For instance, data from an insurance company on sales of new car-insurance policies proxies not only the volumes of new car sales but can be broken down into brands or geographies. Many vendors scrape websites for valuable data, ranging from app downloads and user reviews to airlines and hotel bookings. Social media sites can also be scraped for hints on consumer views and trends.

Typically, the datasets are large and require storage, access, and analysis using scalable data solutions for parallel processing, such as Hadoop and Spark; there are more than 1 billion websites with more than 10 trillion individual web pages, with 500 exabytes (or 500 billion gigabytes) of data, according to Deutsche Bank. And more than 100 million websites are added to the internet every year.

Real-time insights into a company's prospects, long before their results are released, can be gleaned from a decline in job listings on its website, the internal rating of its chief executive by employees on the recruitment site Glassdoor, or a dip in the average price of clothes on its website. This could be combined with satellite images of car parks and geolocation data from mobile phones that indicate how many people are visiting stores. On the other hand, strategic moves can be learned from a jump in job postings for specific functional areas or in certain geographies.

Among the most valuable sources is data that directly reveals consumer expenditures, with credit card information as a primary source. This data only offers a partial view of sales trends, but can offer vital insights when combined with other data. Point72, for instance, analyzes 80 million credit card transactions every day. We will explore the various sources, their use cases, and how to evaluate them in detail in Chapter 3, *Alternative Data for Finance*.

Investment groups have more than doubled their spending on alternative sets and data scientists in the past two years, as the asset management industry has tried to reinvigorate its fading fortunes. In December 2018, there were 375 alternative data providers listed on `alternativedata.org` (sponsored by provider Yipit).

Asset managers last year spent a total of $373 million on datasets and hiring new employees to parse them, up 60% on 2016, and will probably spend a total of $616 million this year, according to a survey of investors by `alternativedata.org`. It forecasts that overall expenditures will climb to over $1 billion by 2020. Some estimates are even higher: Optimus, a consultancy, estimates that investors are spending about $5 billion per year on alternative data, and expects the industry to grow 30% per year over the coming years.

As competition for valuable data sources intensifies, exclusivity arrangements are a key feature of data-source contracts, to maintain an informational advantage. At the same time, privacy concerns are mounting and regulators have begun to start looking at the currently largely unregulated data-provider industry.

Crowdsourcing of trading algorithms

More recently, several algorithmic trading firms have begun to offer investment platforms that provide access to data and a programming environment to crowd-source risk factors that become part of an investment strategy, or entire trading algorithms. Key examples include WorldQuant, Quantopian, and, launched in 2018, Alpha Trading Labs.

WorldQuant managed more than $5 billion for Millennium Management with $34.6 billion AUM since 2007 and announced in 2018 that it would launch its first public fund. It employs hundreds of scientists and many more part-time workers around the world in its alpha factory that organizes the investment process as a quantitative assembly line. This factory claims to have produced 4 million successfully tested alpha factors for inclusion in more complex trading strategies and is aiming for 100 million. Each alpha factor is an algorithm that seeks to predict a future asset price change. Other teams then combine alpha factors into strategies and strategies into portfolios, allocate funds between portfolios, and manage risk while avoiding strategies that cannibalize each other.

Design and execution of a trading strategy

ML can add value at multiple steps in the lifecycle of a trading strategy, and relies on key infrastructure and data resources. Hence, this book aims to addresses how ML techniques fit into the broader process of designing, executing, and evaluating strategies.

An algorithmic trading strategy is driven by a combination of alpha factors that transform one or several data sources into signals that in turn predict future asset returns and trigger buy or sell orders. Chapter 2, *Market and Fundamental Data* and Chapter 3, *Alternative Data for Finance* cover the sourcing and management of data, the raw material and the single most important driver of a successful trading strategy.

Chapter 4, *Alpha Factor Research* outlines a methodologically sound process to manage the risk of false discoveries that increases with the amount of data. Chapter 5, *Strategy Evaluation* provides the context for the execution and performance measurement of a trading strategy:

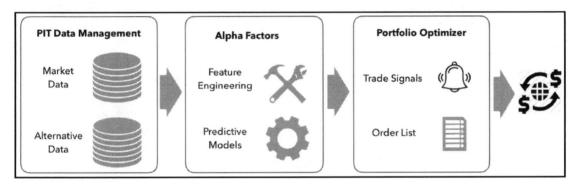

Let's take a brief look at these steps, which we will discuss in depth in the following chapters.

Sourcing and managing data

The dramatic evolution of data in terms of volume, variety, and velocity is both a necessary condition for and driving force of the application of ML to algorithmic trading. The proliferating supply of data requires active management to uncover potential value, including the following steps:

1. Identify and evaluate market, fundamental, and alternative data sources containing alpha signals that do not decay too quickly.
2. Deploy or access cloud-based scalable data infrastructure and analytical tools like Hadoop or Spark Sourcing to facilitate fast, flexible data access
3. Carefully manage and curate data to avoid look-ahead bias by adjusting it to the desired frequency on a **point-in-time** (PIT) basis. This means that data may only reflect information available and know at the given time. ML algorithms trained on distorted historical data will almost certainly fail during live trading.

Alpha factor research and evaluation

Alpha factors are designed to extract signals from data to predict asset returns for a given investment universe over the trading horizon. A factor takes on a single value for each asset when evaluated, but may combine one or several input variables. The process involves the steps outlined in the following figure:

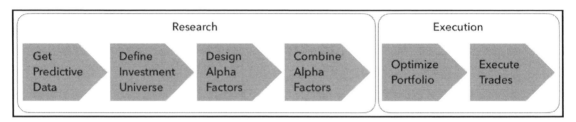

The **Research phase** of the trading strategy workflow includes the design, evaluation, and combination of alpha factors. ML plays a large role in this process because the complexity of factors has increased as investors react to both the signal decay of simpler factors and the much richer data available today.

The development of predictive alpha factors requires the exploration of relationships between input data and the target returns, creative feature-engineering, and the testing and fine-tuning of data transformations to optimize the predictive power of the input.

The data transformations range from simple non-parametric rankings to complex ensemble models or deep neural networks, depending on the amount of signal in the inputs and the complexity of the relationship between the inputs and the target. Many of the simpler factors have emerged from academic research and have been increasingly widely used in the industry over the last several decades.

To minimize the risks of false discoveries due to data mining and because finance has been subject to decades of research that has resulted in several Nobel prizes, investors prefer to rely on factors that align with theories about financial markets and investor behavior. Laying out these theories is beyond the scope of this book, but the references will highlight avenues to dive deeper into this important framing aspect of algorithmic trading strategies.

To validate the signal content of an alpha factor candidate, it is necessary to obtain a robust estimate of its predictive power in environments representative of the market regime during which the factor would be used in a strategy. Reliable estimates require avoiding numerous methodological and practical pitfalls, including the use of data that induces survivorship or look-ahead biases by not reflecting realistic PIT information, or the failure to correct for bias due to multiple tests on the same data.

Signals derived from alpha factors are often individually weak, but sufficiently powerful when combined with other factors or data sources, for example, to modulate the signal as a function of the market or economic context.

Portfolio optimization and risk management

Alpha factors emit entry and exit signals that lead to buy or sell orders, and order execution results in portfolio holdings. The risk profiles of individual positions interact to create a specific portfolio risk profile. Portfolio management involves the optimization of position weights to achieve the desired portfolio risk and return a profile that aligns with the overall investment objectives. This process is highly dynamic to incorporate continuously-evolving market data.

The execution of trades during this process requires balancing the trader's dilemma: fast execution tends to drive up costs due to market impact, whereas slow execution may create implementation shortfall when the realized price deviates from the price that prevailed when the decision was taken. Risk management occurs throughout the portfolio-management process to adjust holdings or assume hedges, depending on observed or predicted changes in the market environment that impact the portfolio risk profile.

Strategy backtesting

The incorporation of an investment idea into an algorithmic strategy requires extensive testing with a scientific approach that attempts to reject the idea based on its performance in alternative out-of-sample market scenarios. Testing may involve simulated data to capture scenarios deemed possible but not reflected in historic data.

A strategy-backtesting engine needs to simulate the execution of a strategy realistically to achieve unbiased performance and risk estimates. In addition to the potential biases introduced by the data or a flawed use of statistics, the backtest engine needs to accurately represent the practical aspects of trade-signal evaluation, order placement, and execution in line with market conditions.

ML and algorithmic trading strategies

Quantitative strategies have evolved and become more sophisticated in three waves:

1. In the 1980s and 1990s, signals often emerged from academic research and used a single or very few inputs derived from market and fundamental data. These signals are now largely commoditized and available as ETF, such as basic mean-reversion strategies.

2. In the 2000s, factor-based investing proliferated. Funds used algorithms to identify assets exposed to risk factors like value or momentum to seek arbitrage opportunities. Redemptions during the early days of the financial crisis triggered the quant quake of August 2007 that cascaded through the factor-based fund industry. These strategies are now also available as long-only smart-beta funds that tilt portfolios according to a given set of risk factors.

3. The third era is driven by investments in ML capabilities and alternative data to generate profitable signals for repeatable trading strategies. Factor decay is a major challenge: the excess returns from new anomalies have been shown to drop by a quarter from discovery to publication, and by over 50% after publication due to competition and crowding.

There are several categories of trading strategies that use algorithms to execute trading rules:

- Short-term trades that aim to profit from small price movements, for example, due to arbitrage
- Behavioral strategies that aim to capitalize on anticipating the behavior of other market participants
- Programs that aim to optimize trade execution, and
- A large group of trading based on predicted pricing

The HFT funds discussed above most prominently rely on short holding periods to benefit from minor price movements based on bid-ask arbitrage or statistical arbitrage. Behavioral algorithms usually operate in lower liquidity environments and aim to anticipate moves by a larger player likely to significantly impact the price. The expectation of the price impact is based on sniffing algorithms that generate insights into other market participants' strategies, or market patterns such as forced trades by ETFs.

Trade-execution programs aim to limit the market impact of trades and range from the simple slicing of trades to match **time-weighted average pricing (TWAP)** or **volume-weighted average pricing (VWAP)**. Simple algorithms leverage historical patterns, whereas more sophisticated algorithms take into account transaction costs, implementation shortfall or predicted price movements. These algorithms can operate at the security or portfolio level, for example, to implement multileg derivative or cross-asset trades.

Use Cases of ML for Trading

ML extracts signals from a wide range of market, fundamental, and alternative data, and can be applied at all steps of the algorithmic trading-strategy process. Key applications include:

- Data mining to identify patterns and extract features
- Supervised learning to generate risk factors or alphas and create trade ideas
- Aggregation of individual signals into a strategy
- Allocation of assets according to risk profiles learned by an algorithm
- The testing and evaluation of strategies, including through the use of synthetic data
- The interactive, automated refinement of a strategy using reinforcement learning

We briefly highlight some of these applications and identify where we will demonstrate their use in later chapters.

Data mining for feature extraction

The cost-effective evaluation of large, complex datasets requires the detection of signals at scale. There are several examples throughout the book:

- Information theory is a useful tool to extract features that capture potential signals and can be used in ML models. In Chapter 4, *Alpha Factor Research* we use mutual information to assess the potential values of individual features for a supervised learning algorithm to predict asset returns.
- In Chapter 12, *Unsupervised Learning*, we introduce various techniques to create features from high-dimensional datasets. In Chapter 14, *Topic Modeling*, we apply these techniques to text data.

- We emphasize model-specific ways to gain insights into the predictive power of individual variables. We use a novel game-theoretic approach called **SHapley Additive exPlanations** (**SHAP**) to attribute predictive performance to individual features in complex Gradient Boosting machines with a large number of input variables.

Supervised learning for alpha factor creation and aggregation

The main rationale for applying ML to trading is to obtain predictions of asset fundamentals, price movements or market conditions. A strategy can leverage multiple ML algorithms that build on each other. Downstream models can generate signals at the portfolio level by integrating predictions about the prospects of individual assets, capital market expectations, and the correlation among securities. Alternatively, ML predictions can inform discretionary trades as in the quantamental approach outlined above. ML predictions can also target specific risk factors, such as value or volatility, or implement technical approaches, such as trend following or mean reversion:

- In Chapter 3, *Alternative Data for Finance*, we illustrate how to work with fundamental data to create inputs to ML-driven valuation models
- In Chapter 13, *Working with Text Data*, Chapter 14, *Topic Modeling*, and Chapter 15, *Word Embeddings* we use alternative data on business reviews that can be used to project revenues for a company as an input for a valuation exercise.
- In Chapter 8, *Time Series Models*, we demonstrate how to forecast macro variables as inputs to market expectations and how to forecast risk factors such as volatility
- In Chapter 18, *Recurrent Neural Networks* we introduce **recurrent neural networks** (**RNNs**) that achieve superior performance with non-linear time series data.

Asset allocation

ML has been used to allocate portfolios based on decision-tree models that compute a hierarchical form of risk parity. As a result, risk characteristics are driven by patterns in asset prices rather than by asset classes and achieve superior risk-return characteristics.

In Chapter 5, *Strategy Evaluation* and Chapter 12, *Unsupervised Learning*, we illustrate how hierarchical clustering extracts data-driven risk classes that better reflect correlation patterns than conventional asset class definition.

Testing trade ideas

Backtesting is a critical step to select successful algorithmic trading strategies. Cross-validation using synthetic data is a key ML technique to generate reliable out-of-sample results when combined with appropriate methods to correct for multiple testing. The time series nature of financial data requires modifications to the standard approach to avoid look-ahead bias or otherwise contaminate the data used for training, validation, and testing. In addition, the limited availability of historical data has given rise to alternative approaches that use synthetic data:

- We will demonstrate various methods to test ML models using market, fundamental, and alternative that obtain sound estimates of out-of-sample errors.
- In Chapter 20, *Autoencoders and Generative Adversarial Nets*, we present GAN that are capable of producing high-quality synthetic data.

Reinforcement learning

Trading takes place in a competitive, interactive marketplace. Reinforcement learning aims to train agents to learn a policy function based on rewards.

- In Chapter 21, *Reinforcement Learning* we present key reinforcement algorithms like Q-Learning and the Dyna architecture and demonstrate the training of reinforcement algorithms for trading using OpenAI's gym environment.

Summary

In this chapter, we introduced algorithmic trading strategies and how ML has become a key ingredient for the design and combination of alpha factors, which in turn are the key drivers of portfolio performance. We covered various industry trends around algorithmic trading strategies, the emergence of alternative data, and the use of ML to exploit these new sources of informational advantages.

Furthermore, we introduced the algorithmic-trading-strategy design process, important types of alpha factors, and how we will use ML to design and execute our strategies. In the next two chapters, we will take a closer look at the oil that fuels any algorithmic trading strategy—the market, fundamental, and alternative data sources—using ML.

Market and Fundamental Data

2

Data has always been an essential driver of trading, and traders have long made efforts to gain an advantage by having access to superior information. These efforts date back at least to the rumors that the House Rothschild benefited handsomely from bond purchases upon advance news about the British victory at Waterloo carried by pigeons across the channel.

Today, investments in faster data access take the shape of the Go West consortium of leading **high-frequency trading (HFT)** firms that connects the **Chicago Mercantile Exchange (CME)** with Tokyo. The round-trip latency between the CME and the BATS exchange in New York has dropped to close to the theoretical limit of eight milliseconds as traders compete to exploit arbitrage opportunities.

Traditionally, investment strategies mostly relied on publicly available data, with limited efforts to create or acquire private datasets. In the case of equities, fundamental strategies used financial models built on reported financials, possibly combined with industry or macro data. Strategies motivated by technical analysis extract signals from market data, such as prices and volumes.

Machine learning (ML) algorithms can exploit market and fundamental data more efficiently, in particular when combined with alternative data, which is the topic of the next chapter. We will address several techniques that focus on market and fundamental data in later chapters, such as classic and modern time-series techniques, including **recurrent neural networks (RNNs)**.

This chapter introduces market and fundamental data sources and the environment in which they are created. Familiarity with various types of orders and the trading infrastructure matters because they affect backtest simulations of a trading strategy. We also illustrate how to use Python to access and work with trading and financial statement data.

In particular, this chapter will cover the following topics:

- How market microstructure shapes market data
- How to reconstruct the order book from tick data using Nasdaq ITCH

- How to summarize tick data using various types of bars
- How to work with **eXtensible Business Reporting Language** (**XBRL**)-encoded electronic filings
- How to parse and combine market and fundamental data to create a P/E series
- How to access various market and fundamental data sources using Python

How to work with market data

Market data results from the placement and processing of buy and sell orders in the course of the trading of financial instruments on the many marketplaces. The data reflects the institutional environment of trading venues, including the rules and regulations that govern orders, trade execution, and price formation.

Algorithmic traders use ML algorithms to analyze the flow of buy and sell orders and the resulting volume and price statistics to extract trade signals or features that capture insights into, for example, demand-supply dynamics or the behavior of certain market participants.

We will first review institutional features that impact the simulation of a trading strategy during a backtest. Then, we will take a look at how tick data can be reconstructed from the order book source. Next, we will highlight several methods that regularize tick data and aim to maximize the information content. Finally, we will illustrate how to access various market data provider interfaces and highlight several providers.

Market microstructure

Market microstructure is the branch of financial economics that investigates the trading process and the organization of related markets. The institutional details are quite complex and diverse across asset classes and their derivatives, trading venues, and geographies. We will only give a brief overview of key concepts before we dive into the data generated by trading. The references on GitHub link to several sources that treat this subject in great detail.

Marketplaces

Trading in financial instruments occurs in organized, mostly electronic exchanges, and over the counter. An exchange is a central marketplace where buyers and sellers meet, and buyers compete with each other for the highest bid while sellers compete for the lowest offer.

There are many exchanges and alternative trading venues across the US and abroad. The following table lists some of the larger global exchanges and the trading volumes for the 12 months concluded 03/2018 in various asset classes, including derivatives. Typically, a minority of financial instruments accounts for most trading:

| Exchange | Stocks | | | | |
	Market Cap (USD mn)	# Listed Companies	Volume / Day (USD mn)	# Shares / Day ('000)	# Options / Day ('000)
NYSE	23,138,626	2,294	78,410	6,122	1,546
Nasdaq-US	10,375,718	2,968	65,026	7,131	2,609
Japan Exchange Group Inc.	6,287,739	3,618	28,397	3,361	1
Shanghai Stock Exchange	5,022,691	1,421	34,736	9,801	
Euronext	4,649,073	1,240	9,410	836	304
Hong Kong Exchanges and Clearing	4,443,082	2,186	12,031	1,174	516
LSE Group	3,986,413	2,622	10,398	1,011	
Shenzhen Stock Exchange	3,547,312	2,110	40,244	14,443	
Deutsche Boerse AG	2,339,092	506	7,825	475	
BSE India Limited	2,298,179	5,439	602	1,105	
National Stock Exchange of India Limited	2,273,286	1,952	5,092	10,355	
BATS Global Markets – US					1,243
Chicago Board Options Exchange					1,811
International Securities Exchange					1,204

Exchanges may rely on bilateral trading or order-driven systems, where buy and sell orders are matched according to certain rules. Price formation may occur through auctions, such as in the **New York Stock Exchange (NYSE)**, where the highest bid and lowest offer are matched, or through dealers who buy from sellers and sell to buyers.

Many exchanges use intermediaries that provide liquidity, that is, the ability to trade, by making markets in certain securities. The NYSE, for example, usually has a single designated market maker who ensures orderly trading for each security, while the **National Association of Securities Dealers Automated Quotations (Nasdaq)** has several. Intermediaries can act as dealers that trade as principals on their own behalf, or brokers that trade as agents on behalf of others.

Exchanges used to be member-owned but have often moved to corporate ownership as market reforms have increased competition. The NYSE dates back to 1792, whereas the Nasdaq started 1971 as the world's first electronic stock market and took over most stock trades that had been executed OTC. In US equity markets alone, trading is fragmented across 13 exchanges and over 40 alternative trading venues, each reporting trades to the consolidated tape, but at different latencies.

Types of orders

Traders can place various types of buy or sell orders. Some orders guarantee immediate execution, while others may state a price threshold or other conditions that trigger execution. Orders are typically valid for the same trading day unless specified otherwise.

A market order guarantees immediate execution of the order upon arrival to the trading venue, at the price that prevails at that moment. In contrast, a limit order only executes if the market price is higher (lower) than the limit for a sell (buy) limit order. A stop order, in turn, only becomes active when the market price rises above (falls below) a specified price for a buy (sell) stop order. A buy stop order can be used to limit losses of short sales. Stop orders may also have limits.

Numerous other conditions can be attached to orders—all or none orders prevent partial execution and are only filled if a specified number of shares is available, and can be valid for the day or longer. They require special handling and are not visible to market participants. Fill or kill orders also prevent partial execution but cancel if not executed immediately. Immediate or cancel orders immediately buy or sell the number of shares that are available and cancel the remainder. Not-held orders allow the broker to decide on the time and price of execution. Finally, the market on open/close orders executes on or near the opening or closing of the market. Partial executions are allowed.

Working with order book data

The primary source of market data is the order book, which is continuously updated in real-time throughout the day to reflect all trading activity. Exchanges typically offer this data as a real-time service and may provide some historical data for free.

The trading activity is reflected in numerous messages about trade orders sent by market participants. These messages typically conform to the electronic **Financial Information eXchange (FIX)** communications protocol for real-time exchange of securities transactions and market data or a native exchange protocol.

The FIX protocol

Just like SWIFT is the message protocol for back-office (example, for trade-settlement) messaging, the FIX protocol is the de facto messaging standard for communication before and during, trade execution between exchanges, banks, brokers, clearing firms, and other market participants. Fidelity Investments and Salomon Brothers introduced FIX in 1992 to facilitate electronic communication between broker-dealers and institutional clients who by then exchanged information over the phone.

It became popular in global equity markets before expanding into foreign exchange, fixed income and derivatives markets, and further into post-trade to support straight-through processing. Exchanges provide access to FIX messages as a real-time data feed that is parsed by algorithmic traders to track market activity and, for example, identify the footprint of market participants and anticipate their next move.

The sequence of messages allows for the reconstruction of the order book. The scale of transactions across numerous exchanges creates a large amount (~10 TB) of unstructured data that is challenging to process and, hence, can be a source of competitive advantage.

The FIX protocol, currently at version 5.0, is a free and open standard with a large community of affiliated industry professionals. It is self-describing like the more recent XML, and a FIX session is supported by the underlying **Transmission Control Protocol (TCP)** layer. The community continually adds new functionality.

The protocol supports pipe-separated key-value pairs, as well as a tag-based FIXML syntax. A sample message that requests a server login would look as follows:

```
8=FIX.5.0|9=127|35=A|59=theBroker.123456|56=CSERVER|34=1|32=20180117-
08:03:04|57=TRADE|50=any_string|98=2|108=34|141=Y|553=12345|554=passw0rd!|1
0=131|
```

There are a few open source FIX implementations in python that can be used to formulate and parse FIX messages. Interactive Brokers offer a FIX-based **computer-to-computer interface (CTCI)** for automated trading (see the resources section for this chapter in the GitHub repo).

Nasdaq TotalView-ITCH Order Book data

While FIX has a dominant large market share, exchanges also offer native protocols. The Nasdaq offers a TotalView ITCH direct data-feed protocol that allows subscribers to track individual orders for equity instruments from placement to execution or cancellation.

As a result, it allows for the reconstruction of the order book that keeps track of the list of active-limit buy and sell orders for a specific security or financial instrument. The order book reveals the market depth throughout the day by listing the number of shares being bid or offered at each price point. It may also identify the market participant responsible for specific buy and sell orders unless it is placed anonymously. Market depth is a key indicator of liquidity and the potential price impact of sizable market orders.

In addition to matching market and limit orders, the Nasdaq also operates auctions or crosses that execute a large number of trades at market opening and closing. Crosses are becoming more important as passive investing continues to grow and traders look for opportunities to execute larger blocks of stock. TotalView also disseminates the **Net Order Imbalance Indicator** (**NOII**) for the Nasdaq opening and closing crosses and Nasdaq IPO/Halt cross.

Parsing binary ITCH messages

The ITCH v5.0 specification declares over 20 message types related to system events, stock characteristics, the placement and modification of limit orders, and trade execution. It also contains information about the net order imbalance before the open and closing cross.

The Nasdaq offers samples of daily binary files for several months. The GitHub repository for this chapter contains a notebook, `build_order_book.ipynb` that illustrates how to parse a sample file of ITCH messages and reconstruct both the executed trades and the order book for any given tick.

The following table shows the frequency of the most common message types for the sample file date March 29, 2018:

Message type	Order book impact	Number of messages
A	New unattributed limit order	136,522,761
D	Order canceled	133,811,007
U	Order canceled and replaced	21,941,015
E	Full or partial execution; possibly multiple messages for the same original order	6,687,379

X	Modified after partial cancellation	5,088,959
F	Add attributed order	2,718,602
P	Trade Message (non-cross)	1,120,861
C	Executed in whole or in part at a price different from the initial display price	157,442
Q	Cross Trade Message	17,233

For each message, the specification lays out the components and their respective length and data types:

Name	Offset	Length	Value	Notes
Message type	0	1	F	Add Order MPID attribution message
Stock locate	1	2	Integer	Locate code identifying the security
Tracking number	3	2	Integer	Nasdaq internal tracking number
Timestamp	5	6	Integer	Nanoseconds since midnight
Order reference number	11	8	Integer	Unique reference number of the new order
Buy/sell indicator	19	1	Alpha	The type of order: B = Buy Order, S = Sell Order
Shares	20	4	Integer	Number of shares for the order being added to the book
Stock	24	8	Alpha	Stock symbol, right-padded with spaces
Price	32	4	Price (4)	The display price of the new order
Attribution	36	4	Alpha	Nasdaq Market participant identifier associated with the order

Python provides the `struct` module to parse binary data using format strings that identify the message elements by indicating length and type of the various components of the byte string as laid out in the specification.

Let's walk through the critical steps to parse the trading messages and reconstruct the order book:

1. The ITCH parser relies on the message specifications provided as a `.csv` file (created by `create_message_spec.py`) and assembles format strings according to the `formats` dictionary:

```
formats = {
    ('integer', 2): 'H',  # int of length 2 => format string 'H'
    ('integer', 4): 'I',
    ('integer', 6): '6s', # int of length 6 => parse as string,
        convert later
    ('integer', 8): 'Q',
    ('alpha', 1)  : 's',
    ('alpha', 2)  : '2s',
    ('alpha', 4)  : '4s',
    ('alpha', 8)  : '8s',
    ('price_4', 4): 'I',
```

```
('price_8', 8): 'Q',
}
```

2. The parser translates the message specs into format strings and `namedtuples` that capture the message content:

```
# Get ITCH specs and create formatting (type, length) tuples
specs = pd.read_csv('message_types.csv')
specs['formats'] = specs[['value', 'length']].apply(tuple,
                            axis=1).map(formats)

# Formatting for alpha fields
alpha_fields = specs[specs.value == 'alpha'].set_index('name')
alpha_msgs = alpha_fields.groupby('message_type')
alpha_formats = {k: v.to_dict() for k, v in alpha_msgs.formats}
alpha_length = {k: v.add(5).to_dict() for k, v in
alpha_msgs.length}

# Generate message classes as named tuples and format strings
message_fields, fstring = {}, {}
for t, message in specs.groupby('message_type'):
    message_fields[t] = namedtuple(typename=t,
field_names=message.name.tolist())
    fstring[t] = '>' + ''.join(message.formats.tolist())
```

3. Fields of the `alpha` type require post-processing as defined in the `format_alpha` function:

```
def format_alpha(mtype, data):
    for col in alpha_formats.get(mtype).keys():
        if mtype != 'R' and col == 'stock': # stock name only in
                                        summary message 'R'
            data = data.drop(col, axis=1)
            continue
        data.loc[:, col] = data.loc[:, col].str.decode("utf-
                                8").str.strip()
        if encoding.get(col):
            data.loc[:, col] = data.loc[:,
                    col].map(encoding.get(col)) # int encoding
    return data
```

4. The binary file for a single day contains over 300,000,000 messages worth over 9 GB. The script appends the parsed result iteratively to a file in the fast HDF5 format to avoid memory constraints (see last section in this chapter for more on this format). The following (simplified) code processes the binary file and produces the parsed orders stored by message type:

```python
with (data_path / file_name).open('rb') as data:
    while True:
        message_size = int.from_bytes(data.read(2),
byteorder='big',
                            signed=False)
        message_type = data.read(1).decode('ascii')
        message_type_counter.update([message_type])
        record = data.read(message_size - 1)
        message =
message_fields[message_type]._make(unpack(fstring[message_type],
                            record))
        messages[message_type].append(message)
        # deal with system events like market open/close
        if message_type == 'S':
            timestamp = int.from_bytes(message.timestamp,
                                byteorder='big')
            if message.event_code.decode('ascii') == 'C': # close
                store_messages(messages)
                break
```

5. As expected, a small number of the over 8,500 equity securities traded on this day account for most trades:

```python
with pd.HDFStore(hdf_store) as store:
    stocks = store['R'].loc[:, ['stock_locate', 'stock']]
    trades = store['P'].append(store['Q'].rename(columns=
                        {'cross_price': 'price'}).merge(stocks)
trades['value'] = trades.shares.mul(trades.price)
trades['value_share'] = trades.value.div(trades.value.sum())
trade_summary =
    trades.groupby('stock').value_share.sum().sort_values
                        (ascending=False)
trade_summary.iloc[:50].plot.bar(figsize=(14, 6), color='darkblue',
                        title='% of Traded Value')
plt.gca().yaxis.set_major_formatter(FuncFormatter(lambda y, _:
                        '{:.0%}'.format(y)))
```

We get the following plot for the graph:

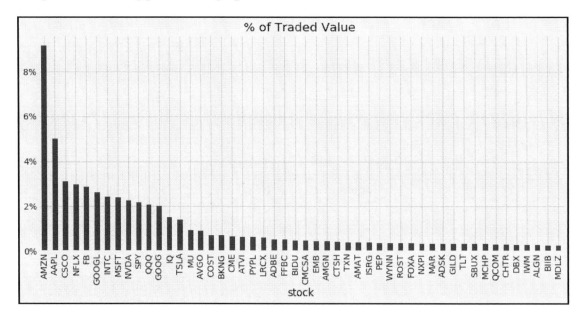

Reconstructing trades and the order book

The parsed messages allow us to rebuild the order flow for the given day. The `'R'` message type contains a listing of all stocks traded during a given day, including information about **initial public offerings (IPOs)** and trading restrictions.

Throughout the day, new orders are added, and orders that are executed and canceled are removed from the order book. The proper accounting for messages that reference orders placed on a prior date would require tracking the order book over multiple days, but we are ignoring this aspect here.

The `get_messages()` function illustrates how to collect the orders for a single stock that affects trading (refer to the ITCH specification for details about each message, slightly simplified, see notebook):

```
def get_messages(date, stock=stock):
    """Collect trading messages for given stock"""
    with pd.HDFStore(itch_store) as store:
        stock_locate = store.select('R', where='stock =
                                    stock').stock_locate.iloc[0]
        target = 'stock_locate = stock_locate'

        data = {}
```

```
    # relevant message types
    messages = ['A', 'F', 'E', 'C', 'X', 'D', 'U', 'P', 'Q']
    for m in messages:
        data[m] = store.select(m,
            where=target).drop('stock_locate', axis=1).assign(type=m)

order_cols = ['order_reference_number', 'buy_sell_indicator',
              'shares', 'price']
orders = pd.concat([data['A'], data['F']], sort=False,
                    ignore_index=True).loc[:, order_cols]

for m in messages[2: -3]:
    data[m] = data[m].merge(orders, how='left')

data['U'] = data['U'].merge(orders, how='left',
                            right_on='order_reference_number',
                            left_on='original_order_reference_number',
                            suffixes=['', '_replaced'])

data['Q'].rename(columns={'cross_price': 'price'}, inplace=True)
data['X']['shares'] = data['X']['cancelled_shares']
data['X'] = data['X'].dropna(subset=['price'])

data = pd.concat([data[m] for m in messages], ignore_index=True,
                 sort=False)
```

Reconstructing successful trades, that is, orders that are executed as opposed to those that were canceled from trade-related message types, C, E, P, and Q, is relatively straightforward:

```
def get_trades(m):
    """Combine C, E, P and Q messages into trading records"""
    trade_dict = {'executed_shares': 'shares', 'execution_price':
                  'price'}
    cols = ['timestamp', 'executed_shares']
    trades = pd.concat([m.loc[m.type == 'E', cols +
            ['price']].rename(columns=trade_dict),
            m.loc[m.type == 'C', cols +
            ['execution_price']].rename(columns=trade_dict),
            m.loc[m.type == 'P', ['timestamp', 'price', 'shares']],
            m.loc[m.type == 'Q', ['timestamp', 'price',
            'shares']].assign(cross=1),
            ], sort=False).dropna(subset=['price']).fillna(0)
    return trades.set_index('timestamp').sort_index().astype(int)
```

The order book keeps track of limit orders, and the various price levels for buy and sell orders constitute the depth of the order book. To reconstruct the order book for a given level of depth requires the following steps:

1. The `add_orders()` function accumulates sell orders in ascending, and buy orders in descending order for a given timestamp up to the desired level of depth:

```
def add_orders(orders, buysell, nlevels):
    new_order = []
    items = sorted(orders.copy().items())
    if buysell == -1:
        items = reversed(items)
    for i, (p, s) in enumerate(items, 1):
        new_order.append((p, s))
        if i == nlevels:
            break
    return orders, new_order
```

2. We iterate over all ITCH messages and process orders and their replacements as required by the specification:

```
for message in messages.itertuples():
    i = message[0]
    if np.isnan(message.buy_sell_indicator):
        continue
    message_counter.update(message.type)

    buysell = message.buy_sell_indicator
    price, shares = None, None

    if message.type in ['A', 'F', 'U']:
        price, shares = int(message.price), int(message.shares)

        current_orders[buysell].update({price: shares})
        current_orders[buysell], new_order =
          add_orders(current_orders[buysell], buysell, nlevels)
        order_book[buysell][message.timestamp] = new_order

    if message.type in ['E', 'C', 'X', 'D', 'U']:
        if message.type == 'U':
            if not np.isnan(message.shares_replaced):
                price = int(message.price_replaced)
                shares = -int(message.shares_replaced)
        else:
            if not np.isnan(message.price):
                price = int(message.price)
```

```
                shares = -int(message.shares)

        if price is not None:
            current_orders[buysell].update({price: shares})
            if current_orders[buysell][price] <= 0:
                current_orders[buysell].pop(price)
            current_orders[buysell], new_order =
              add_orders(current_orders[buysell], buysell, nlevels)
            order_book[buysell][message.timestamp] = new_order
```

The number of orders at different price levels, highlighted in the following screenshot using different intensities for buy and sell orders, visualizes the depth of liquidity at any given point in time. The left panel shows how the distribution of limit order prices was weighted toward buy orders at higher prices. The right panel plots the evolution of limit orders and prices throughout the trading day: the dark line tracks the prices for executed trades during market hours, whereas the red and blue dots indicate individual limit orders on a per-minute basis (see notebook for details):

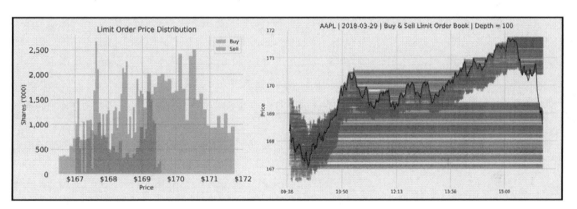

Regularizing tick data

The trade data is indexed by nanoseconds and is very noisy. The bid-ask bounce, for instance, causes the price to oscillate between the bid and ask prices when trade initiation alternates between buy and sell market orders. To improve the noise-signal ratio and improve the statistical properties, we need to resample and regularize the tick data by aggregating the trading activity.

We typically collect the open (first), low, high, and closing (last) price for the aggregated period, alongside the **volume-weighted average price** (**VWAP**), the number of shares traded, and the timestamp associated with the data.

See the `normalize_tick_data.ipynb` notebook in the folder for this chapter on GitHub for additional detail.

Tick bars

A plot of the raw tick price and volume data for `AAPL` looks as follows:

```
stock, date = 'AAPL', '20180329'
title = '{} | {}'.format(stock, pd.to_datetime(date).date()

with pd.HDFStore(itch_store) as store:
    s = store['S'].set_index('event_code') # system events
    s.timestamp = s.timestamp.add(pd.to_datetime(date)).dt.time
    market_open = s.loc['Q', 'timestamp']
    market_close = s.loc['M', 'timestamp']

with pd.HDFStore(stock_store) as store:
    trades = store['{}/trades'.format(stock)].reset_index()
trades = trades[trades.cross == 0] # excluding data from open/close
crossings
trades.price = trades.price.mul(1e-4)

trades.price = trades.price.mul(1e-4) # format price
trades = trades[trades.cross == 0]     # exclude crossing trades
trades = trades.between_time(market_open, market_close) # market hours only

tick_bars = trades.set_index('timestamp')
tick_bars.index = tick_bars.index.time
tick_bars.price.plot(figsize=(10, 5), title=title), lw=1)
```

We get the following plot for the preceding code:

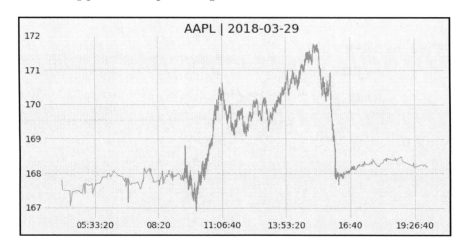

The tick returns are far from normally distributed, as evidenced by the low p-value of `scipy.stats.normaltest`:

```
from scipy.stats import normaltest
normaltest(tick_bars.price.pct_change().dropna())

NormaltestResult(statistic=62408.76562431228, pvalue=0.0)
```

Time bars

Time bars involve trade aggregation by period:

```
def get_bar_stats(agg_trades):
    vwap = agg_trades.apply(lambda x: np.average(x.price,
            weights=x.shares)).to_frame('vwap')
    ohlc = agg_trades.price.ohlc()
    vol = agg_trades.shares.sum().to_frame('vol')
    txn = agg_trades.shares.size().to_frame('txn')
    return pd.concat([ohlc, vwap, vol, txn], axis=1)

resampled = trades.resample('1Min')
time_bars = get_bar_stats(resampled)
```

We can display the result as a price-volume chart:

```
def price_volume(df, price='vwap', vol='vol', suptitle=title):
    fig, axes = plt.subplots(nrows=2, sharex=True, figsize=(15, 8))
    axes[0].plot(df.index, df[price])
    axes[1].bar(df.index, df[vol], width=1 / (len(df.index)),
                color='r')

    xfmt = mpl.dates.DateFormatter('%H:%M')
    axes[1].xaxis.set_major_locator(mpl.dates.HourLocator(interval=3))
    axes[1].xaxis.set_major_formatter(xfmt)
    axes[1].get_xaxis().set_tick_params(which='major', pad=25)
    axes[0].set_title('Price', fontsize=14)
    axes[1].set_title('Volume', fontsize=14)
    fig.autofmt_xdate()
    fig.suptitle(suptitle)
    fig.tight_layout()
    plt.subplots_adjust(top=0.9)

price_volume(time_bars)
```

We get the following plot for the preceding code:

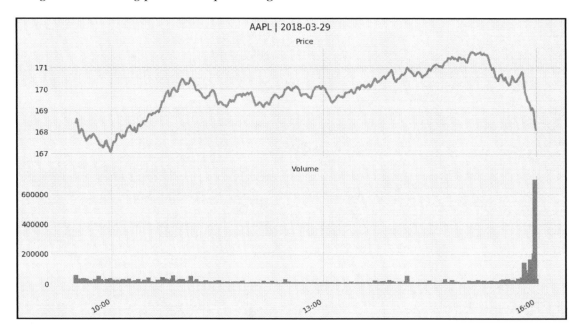

Or as a candlestick chart using the bokeh plotting library:

```
resampled = trades.resample('5Min') # 5 Min bars for better print
df = get_bar_stats(resampled)

increase = df.close > df.open
decrease = df.open > df.close
w = 2.5 * 60 * 1000 # 2.5 min in ms

WIDGETS = "pan, wheel_zoom, box_zoom, reset, save"

p = figure(x_axis_type='datetime', tools=WIDGETS, plot_width=1500, title =
"AAPL Candlestick")
p.xaxis.major_label_orientation = pi/4
p.grid.grid_line_alpha=0.4

p.segment(df.index, df.high, df.index, df.low, color="black")
p.vbar(df.index[increase], w, df.open[increase], df.close[increase],
fill_color="#D5E1DD", line_color="black")
p.vbar(df.index[decrease], w, df.open[decrease], df.close[decrease],
fill_color="#F2583E", line_color="black")
show(p)
```

Take a look at the following screenshot:

Plotting AAPL Candlestick

Volume bars

Time bars smooth some of the noise contained in the raw tick data but may fail to account for the fragmentation of orders. Execution-focused algorithmic trading may aim to match the **volume weighted average price (VWAP)** over a given period, and will divide a single order into multiple trades and place orders according to historical patterns. Time bars would treat the same order differently, even though no new information has arrived in the market.

Volume bars offer an alternative by aggregating trade data according to volume. We can accomplish this as follows:

```
trades_per_min = trades.shares.sum()/(60*7.5) # min per trading day
trades['cumul_vol'] = trades.shares.cumsum()
df = trades.reset_index()
by_vol =
    df.groupby(df.cumul_vol.div(trades_per_min).round().astype(int))
vol_bars = pd.concat([by_vol.timestamp.last().to_frame('timestamp'),
                      get_bar_stats(by_vol)], axis=1)
price_volume(vol_bars.set_index('timestamp'))
```

We get the following plot for the preceding code:

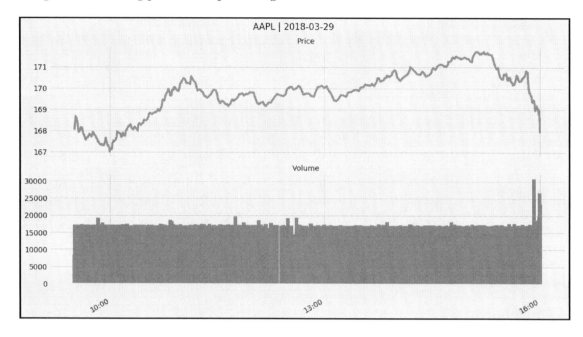

Dollar bars

When asset prices change significantly or after stock splits, the value of a given amount of shares changes. Volume bars do not correctly reflect this and can hamper the comparison of trading behavior for different periods that reflect such changes. In these cases, the volume bar method should be adjusted to utilize the product of shares and price to produce dollar bars.

API access to market data

There are several options to access market data via API using Python. We first present a few sources built into the `pandas` library. Then we briefly introduce the trading platform Quantopian, the data provider Quandl and the backtesting library that we will use later in the book, and list several additional options to access various types of market data. The folder directory `data_providers` on GitHub contains several notebooks that illustrate the usage of these options.

Remote data access using pandas

The `pandas` library enables access to data displayed on websites using the `read_html` function and access to the API endpoints of various data providers through the related `pandas-datareader` library.

Reading html tables

The download of the content of one or more `html` tables works as follows, for instance for the constituents of the `S&P500` index from Wikipedia:

```
sp_url = 'https://en.wikipedia.org/wiki/List_of_S%26P_500_companies'
sp = pd.read_html(sp_url, header=0)[0] # returns a list for each table
sp.info()

RangeIndex: 505 entries, 0 to 504
Data columns (total 9 columns):
Ticker symbol              505 non-null object
Security                   505 non-null object
SEC filings                505 non-null object
GICS Sector                505 non-null object
GICS Sub Industry          505 non-null object
Location                   505 non-null object
Date first added[3][4]     398 non-null object
CIK                        505 non-null int64
Founded                    139 non-null object
```

pandas-datareader for market data

pandas used to facilitate access to data providers' APIs directly, but this functionality has moved to the related `pandas-datareader` library. The stability of the APIs varies with provider policies, and as of June 2o18 at version 0.7, the following sources are available:

Source	Scope	Comment
Yahoo! Finance	EOD price, dividends, split data for stock and FX pairs	Unstable
Tiingo	EOD prices on equities, mutual funds, and ETFs	Free registration required
The **Investors Exchange (IEX)**	Historical stock prices, order-book data	Limited to five years
Robinhood	EOD equity prices	Limited to one year
Quandl	Marketplace for a broad range of asset prices	Premium data require a subscription

Nasdaq	Latest ticker symbols traded on Nasdaq with some additional info	
Stooq	Some stock market index data	
MOEX	Moscow Stock Exchange Data	
Alpha Vantage	EOD stock prices and FX pairs	
Fama/French	Factor returns and research portfolios from the FF Data Library	

Access and retrieval of data follow a similar API for all sources, as illustrated for Yahoo! Finance:

```python
import pandas_datareader.data as web
from datetime import datetime

start = '2014'                # accepts strings
end = datetime(2017, 5, 24)  # or datetime objects

yahoo= web.DataReader('FB', 'yahoo', start=start, end=end)
yahoo.info()

DatetimeIndex: 856 entries, 2014-01-02 to 2017-05-25
Data columns (total 6 columns):
High        856 non-null float64
Low         856 non-null float64
Open        856 non-null float64
Close       856 non-null float64
Volume      856 non-null int64
Adj Close   856 non-null float64

dtypes: float64(5), int64(1)
```

The Investor Exchange

IEX is an alternative exchange started in response to the HFT controversy and portrayed in Michael Lewis' controversial Flash Boys. It aims to slow down the speed of trading to create a more level playing field and has been growing rapidly since launch in 2016 while still small with a market share of around 2.5% in June 2018.

In addition to historical EOD price and volume data, IEX provides real-time depth of book quotations that offer an aggregated size of orders by price and side. This service also includes last trade price and size information:

```
book = web.get_iex_book('AAPL')
orders = pd.concat([pd.DataFrame(book[side]).assign(side=side) for side in
['bids', 'asks']])
orders.sort_values('timestamp').head()

   price  size timestamp       side
4 140.00   100 1528983003604 bids
3 175.30   100 1528983900163 bids
3 205.80   100 1528983900163 asks
1 187.00   200 1528996876005 bids
2 186.29   100 1528997296755 bids
```

See additional examples in the `datareader.ipynb` notebook.

Quantopian

Quantopian is an investment firm that offers a research platform to crowd-source trading algorithms. Upon free registration, it enables members to research trading ideas using a broad variety of data sources. It also offers an environment to backtest the algorithm against historical data, as well forward-test it out-of-sample with live data. It awards investment allocations for top-performing algorithms whose authors are entitled to a 10% (at time of writing) profit share.

The Quantopian research platform consists of a Jupyter Notebook environment for research and development for alpha factor research and performance analysis. There is also an **Interactive Development Environment (IDE)** for coding algorithmic strategies and backtesting the result using historical data since 2002 with minute-bar frequency.

Users can also simulate algorithms with live data, which is known as paper trading. Quantopian provides various market datasets, including US equity and futures price and volume data at a one-minute frequency, as well as US equity corporate fundamentals, and integrates numerous alternative datasets.

We will dive into the Quantopian platform in much more detail in Chapter 4, *Alpha Factor Research* and rely on its functionality throughout the book, so feel free to open an account right away (see GitHub repo for more details).

Zipline

Zipline is the algorithmic trading library that powers the Quantopian backtesting and live-trading platform. It is also available offline to develop a strategy using a limited number of free data bundles that can be ingested and used to test the performance of trading ideas before porting the result to the online Quantopian platform for paper and live trading.

The following code illustrates how `zipline` permits us to access daily stock data for a range of companies. You can run `zipline` scripts in the Jupyter Notebook using the magic function of the same name.

First, you need to initialize the context with the desired security symbols. We'll also use a counter variable. Then `zipline` calls `handle_data`, where we use the `data.history()` method to look back a single period and append the data for the last day to a `.csv` file:

```
%load_ext zipline
%%zipline --start 2010-1-1 --end 2018-1-1 --data-frequency daily
from zipline.api import order_target, record, symbol

def initialize(context):
 context.i = 0
 context.assets = [symbol('FB'), symbol('GOOG'), symbol('AMZN')]

def handle_data(context, data):
 df = data.history(context.assets, fields=['price', 'volume'],
                   bar_count=1, frequency="1d")
 df = df.to_frame().reset_index()

 if context.i == 0:
 df.columns = ['date', 'asset', 'price', 'volumne']
 df.to_csv('stock_data.csv', index=False)
 else:
     df.to_csv('stock_data.csv', index=False, mode='a', header=None)
             context.i += 1

df = pd.read_csv('stock_data.csv')
df.date = pd.to_datetime(df.date)
df.set_index('date').groupby('asset').price.plot(lw=2, legend=True,
        figsize=(14, 6));
```

We get the following plot for the preceding code:

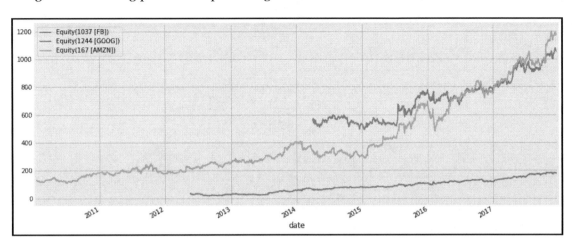

We will explore the capabilities of `zipline`, and, in particular, the online Quantopian platform, in more detail in the coming chapters.

Quandl

Quandl provides a broad range of data sources, both free and as a subscription, using a Python API. Register and obtain a free API key to make more than 50 calls/day. Quandl data covers multiple asset classes beyond equities and includes FX, fixed income, indexes, futures and options, and commodities.

API usage is straightforward, well-documented, and flexible, with numerous methods beyond single-series downloads, for example, including bulk downloads or metadata searches. The following call obtains the oil prices since 1986 as quoted by the US Department of Energy:

```
import quandl
oil = quandl.get('EIA/PET_RWTC_D').squeeze()
oil.plot(lw=2, title='WTI Crude Oil Price')
```

We get this plot for the preceding code:

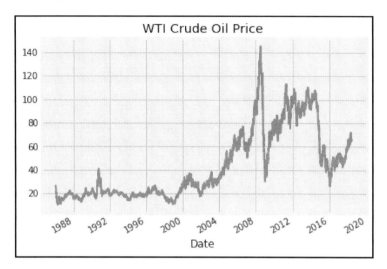

Other market-data providers

A broad variety of providers offer market data for various asset classes. Examples in relevant categories include:

- Exchanges derive a growing share of their revenues from an ever broader range of data services, typically using subscription.
- Bloomberg and Thomson Reuters have long been the leading data aggregators with a combined share of over 55% in the $28.5 billion financial data market. Smaller rivals, such as FactSet, are growing, or emerging, such as money.net and Quandl as well as Trading Economics or Barchart.
- Specialist data providers abound. One example is LOBSTER, which aggregates Nasdaq order-book data in real-time.
- Free data providers include Alpha Vantage that offers Python APIs for real-time equity, FX, and crypto-currency market data, as well as technical indicators.
- Crowd-sourced investment firms that provide research platforms with data access include, in addition to Quantopian, the Alpha Trading Labs, launched in March 2018, which provide HFT infrastructure and data.

How to work with fundamental data

Fundamental data pertains to the economic drivers that determine the value of securities. The nature of the data depends on the asset class:

- For equities and corporate credit, it includes corporate financials as well as industry and economy-wide data.
- For government bonds, it includes international macro-data and foreign exchange.
- For commodities, it includes asset-specific supply-and-demand determinants, such as weather data for crops.

We will focus on equity fundamentals for the US, where data is easier to access. There are some 13,000+ public companies worldwide that generate 2 million pages of annual reports and 30,000+ hours of earnings calls. In algorithmic trading, fundamental data and features engineered from this data may be used to derive trading signals directly, for example as value indicators, and are an essential input for predictive models, including machine learning models.

Financial statement data

The **Securities and Exchange Commission** (SEC) requires US issuers, that is, listed companies and securities, including mutual funds to file three quarterly financial statements (Form 10-Q) and one annual report (Form 10-K), in addition to various other regulatory filing requirements.

Since the early 1990s, the SEC made these filings available through its **Electronic Data Gathering, Analysis, and Retrieval** (**EDGAR**) system. They constitute the primary data source for the fundamental analysis of equity and other securities, such as corporate credit, where the value depends on the business prospects and financial health of the issuer.

Automated processing – XBRL

Automated analysis of regulatory filings has become much easier since the SEC introduced the XBRL, a free, open, and global standard for the electronic representation and exchange of business reports. XBRL is based on XML; it relies on **taxonomies** that define the meaning of the elements of a report and map to tags that highlight the corresponding information in the electronic version of the report. One such taxonomy represents the US **Generally Accepted Accounting Principles** (**GAAP**).

The SEC introduced voluntary XBRL filings in 2005 in response to accounting scandals before requiring this format for all filers since 2009 and continues to expand the mandatory coverage to other regulatory filings. The SEC maintains a website that lists the current taxonomies that shape the content of different filings and can be used to extract specific items.

The following datasets provide information extracted from EX-101 attachments submitted to the Commission in a flattened data format to assist users in consuming the data for analysis. The data reflects selected information from the XBRL-tagged financial statements. It currently includes numeric data from the quarterly and annual financial statements, as well as certain additional fields (for example, **Standard Industrial Classification (SIC)**).

There are several avenues to track and access fundamental data reported to the SEC:

- As part of the EDGAR **Public Dissemination Service (PDS)**, electronic feeds of accepted filings are available for a fee.
- The SEC updates **RSS** feeds every 10 minutes, which list structured disclosure submissions.
- There are public index files for the retrieval of all filings through FTP for automated processing.
- The financial statement (and notes) datasets contain parsed XBRL data from all financial statements and the accompanying notes.

The SEC also publishes log files containing the internet search traffic for EDGAR filings through SEC.gov, albeit with a six-month delay.

Building a fundamental data time series

The scope of the data in the financial statement and notes datasets consists of numeric data extracted from the primary financial statements (Balance sheet, income statement, cash flows, changes in equity, and comprehensive income) and footnotes on those statements. The data is available as early as 2009.

Extracting the financial statements and notes dataset

The following code downloads and extracts all historical filings contained in the **Financial Statement and Notes (FSN)** datasets for the given range of quarters (see `edgar_xbrl.ipynb` for addition details):

```
SEC_URL =
'https://www.sec.gov/files/dera/data/financial-statement-and-notes-data-set
s/'
```

```
first_year, this_year, this_quarter = 2014, 2018, 3
past_years = range(2014, this_year)
filing_periods = [(y, q) for y in past_years for q in range(1, 5)]
filing_periods.extend([(this_year, q) for q in range(1, this_quarter +
                                                            1)])
for i, (yr, qtr) in enumerate(filing_periods, 1):
    filing = f'{yr}q{qtr}_notes.zip'
    path = data_path / f'{yr}_{qtr}' / 'source'
    response = requests.get(SEC_URL + filing).content
    with ZipFile(BytesIO(response)) as zip_file:
        for file in zip_file.namelist():
            local_file = path / file
            with local_file.open('wb') as output:
                for line in zip_file.open(file).readlines():
                    output.write(line)
```

The data is fairly large and to enable faster access than the original text files permit, it is better to convert the text files to binary, columnar parquet format (see *Efficient data storage with pandas* section in this chapter for a performance comparison of various data-storage options compatible with pandas DataFrames):

```
for f in data_path.glob('**/*.tsv'):
    file_name = f.stem  + '.parquet'
    path = Path(f.parents[1]) / 'parquet'
    df = pd.read_csv(f, sep='\t', encoding='latin1', low_memory=False)
    df.to_parquet(path / file_name)
```

For each quarter, the FSN data is organized into eight file sets that contain information about submissions, numbers, taxonomy tags, presentation, and more. Each dataset consists of rows and fields and is provided as a tab-delimited text file:

File	Dataset	Description
SUB	Submission	Identifies each XBRL submission by company, form, date, and so on
TAG	Tag	Defines and explains each taxonomy tag
DIM	Dimension	Adds detail to numeric and plain text data
NUM	Numeric	One row for each distinct data point in filing
TXT	Plain text	Contains all non-numeric XBRL fields
REN	Rendering	Information for rendering on SEC website
PRE	Presentation	Detail on the tag and number presentation in primary statements
CAL	Calculation	Shows arithmetic relationships among tags

Retrieving all quarterly Apple filings

The submission dataset contains the unique identifiers required to retrieve the filings: the **Central Index Key (CIK)** and the Accession Number (`adsh`). The following shows some of the information about Apple's 2018Q1 10-Q filing:

```
apple = sub[sub.name == 'APPLE INC'].T.dropna().squeeze()
key_cols = ['name', 'adsh', 'cik', 'name', 'sic', 'countryba',
            'stprba', 'cityba', 'zipba', 'bas1', 'form', 'period',
            'fy', 'fp', 'filed']
apple.loc[key_cols]

name                    APPLE INC
adsh                    0000320193-18-000070
cik                     320193
name                    APPLE INC
sic                     3571
countryba               US
stprba                  CA
cityba                  CUPERTINO
zipba                   95014
bas1                    ONE APPLE PARK WAY
form                    10-Q
period                  20180331
fy                      2018
fp                      Q2
filed                   20180502
```

Using the central index key, we can identify all historical quarterly filings available for `Apple`, and combine this information to obtain 26 Forms `10-Q` and nine annual Forms `10-K`:

```
aapl_subs = pd.DataFrame()
for sub in data_path.glob('**/sub.parquet'):
    sub = pd.read_parquet(sub)
    aapl_sub = sub[(sub.cik.astype(int) == apple.cik) &
(sub.form.isin(['10-Q', '10-K']))]
    aapl_subs = pd.concat([aapl_subs, aapl_sub])

aapl_subs.form.value_counts()
10-Q     15
10-K      4
```

With the Accession Number for each filing, we can now rely on the taxonomies to select the appropriate XBRL tags (listed in the `TAG` file) from the `NUM` and `TXT` files to obtain the numerical or textual/footnote data points of interest.

First, let's extract all numerical data available from the 19 Apple filings:

```
aapl_nums = pd.DataFrame()
for num in data_path.glob('**/num.parquet'):
    num = pd.read_parquet(num)
    aapl_num = num[num.adsh.isin(aapl_subs.adsh)]
    aapl_nums = pd.concat([aapl_nums, aapl_num])

aapl_nums.ddate = pd.to_datetime(aapl_nums.ddate, format='%Y%m%d')
aapl_nums.shape
(28281, 16)
```

Building a price/earnings time series

In total, the nine years of filing history provide us with over 28,000 numerical values. We can select a useful field, such as **Earnings per Diluted Share** (EPS), that we can combine with market data to calculate the popular **Price/Earnings** (P/E) valuation ratio.

We do need to take into account, however, that Apple split its stock 7:1 on June 4, 2014, and Adjusted Earnings per Share before the split to make earnings comparable, as illustrated in the following code block:

```
field = 'EarningsPerShareDiluted'
stock_split = 7
split_date = pd.to_datetime('20140604')

# Filter by tag; keep only values measuring 1 quarter
eps = aapl_nums[(aapl_nums.tag == 'EarningsPerShareDiluted')
                & (aapl_nums.qtrs == 1)].drop('tag', axis=1)

# Keep only most recent data point from each filing
eps = eps.groupby('adsh').apply(lambda x: x.nlargest(n=1,
columns=['ddate']))

# Adjust earnings prior to stock split downward
eps.loc[eps.ddate < split_date,'value'] = eps.loc[eps.ddate <
        split_date, 'value'].div(7)
eps = eps[['ddate', 'value']].set_index('ddate').squeeze()
eps = eps.rolling(4, min_periods=4).sum().dropna() # create trailing
                    12-months eps from quarterly data
```

We can use Quandl to obtain Apple stock price data since 2009:

```
import pandas_datareader.data as web
symbol = 'AAPL.US'
aapl_stock = web.DataReader(symbol, 'quandl', start=eps.index.min())
aapl_stock = aapl_stock.resample('D').last() # ensure dates align with
                                               eps data
```

Now we have the data to compute the trailing 12-month P/E ratio for the entire period:

```
pe = aapl_stock.AdjClose.to_frame('price').join(eps.to_frame('eps'))
pe = pe.fillna(method='ffill').dropna()
pe['P/E Ratio'] = pe.price.div(pe.eps)
axes = pe.plot(subplots=True, figsize=(16,8), legend=False, lw=2);
```

We get the following plot for the preceding code:

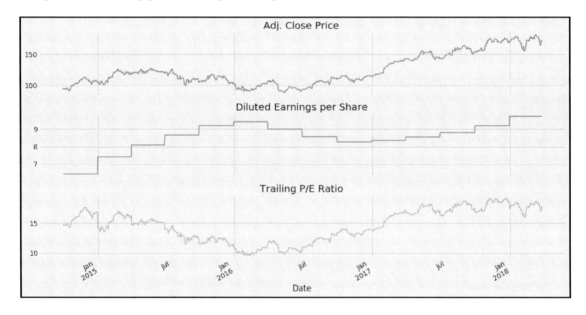

Other fundamental data sources

There are numerous other sources for fundamental data. Many are accessible using the `pandas_datareader` module introduced earlier. Additional data is available from certain organizations directly, such as the IMF, World Bank, or major national statistical agencies around the world (see references on GitHub).

pandas_datareader – macro and industry data

The pandas_datareader library facilitates access according to the conventions introduced at the end of the preceding section on market data. It covers APIs for numerous global fundamental macro and industry-data sources, including the following:

- **Kenneth French's data library**: Market data on portfolios capturing size, value, and momentum factors, disaggregated industry
- **St.Louis FED (FRED)**: Federal Reserve data on the US economy and financial markets
- **World Bank**: Global database on long-term, lower-frequency economic and social development and demographics
- **OECD**: Similar for OECD countries
- **Enigma**: Various datasets, including alternative sources
- **Eurostat**: EU-focused economics, social and demographic data

Efficient data storage with pandas

We'll be using many different data sets in this book, and it's worth comparing the main formats for efficiency and performance. In particular, we compare the following:

- **CSV**: Comma-separated, standard flat text file format.
- **HDF5**: Hierarchical data format, developed initially at the National Center for Supercomputing, is a fast and scalable storage format for numerical data, available in pandas using the PyTables library.
- **Parquet**: A binary, columnar storage format, part of the Apache Hadoop ecosystem, that provides efficient data compression and encoding and has been developed by Cloudera and Twitter. It is available for pandas through the pyarrow library, led by Wes McKinney, the original author of pandas.

The storage_benchmark.ipynb notebook compares the performance of the preceding libraries using a test DataFrame that can be configured to contain numerical or text data, or both. For the HDF5 library, we test both the fixed and table format. The table format allows for queries and can be appended to.

The following charts illustrate the read and write performance for 100,000 rows with either 1,000 columns of random floats and 1,000 columns of a random 10-character string, or just 2,000 float columns:

- For purely numerical data, the HDF5 format performs best, and the table format also shares with CSV the smallest memory footprint at 1.6 GB. The fixed format uses twice as much space, and the parquet format uses 2 GB.
- For a mix of numerical and text data, `parquet` is significantly faster, and HDF5 uses its advantage on reading relative to CSV (which has very low write performance in both cases):

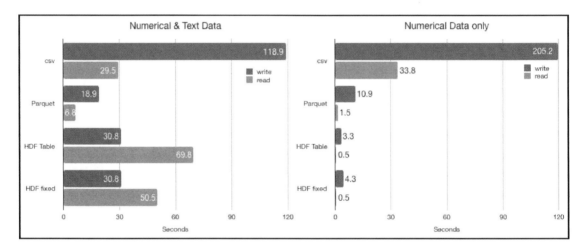

The notebook illustrates how to configure, test, and collect the timing using the `%%timeit` cell magic, and at the same time demonstrates the usage of the related pandas commands required to use these storage formats.

Summary

This chapter introduced the market and fundamental data sources that form the backbone of most trading strategies. You learned about numerous ways to access this data, and how to preprocess the raw information so that you can begin extracting trading signals using the machine learning techniques that we will be introducing shortly.

Before we move onto the design and evaluation of trading strategies and the use of ML models, we need to cover alternative datasets that have emerged in recent years and have been a significant driver of the popularity of ML for algorithmic trading.

3
Alternative Data for Finance

Propelled by the explosive growth of the internet and mobile networks, digital data continues to grow exponentially amid advances in the technology to process, store, and analyze new data sources. The exponential growth in the availability of and ability to manage more diverse digital data, in turn, has been a critical force behind the dramatic performance improvements of **machine learning** (**ML**) that are driving innovation across industries, including the investment industry.

The scale of the data revolution is extraordinary: the past two years alone have witnessed the creation of 90% of all data that exists in the world today, and by 2020, each of the 7.7 billion people worldwide is expected to produce 1.7 MB of new information every second of every day. On the other hand, back in 2012, only 0.5% of all data was ever analyzed and used, whereas 33% is deemed to have value by 2020. The gap between data availability and usage is likely to narrow quickly as global investments in analytics are set to rise beyond $210 billion by 2020, while the value creation potential is a multiple higher.

This chapter explains how individuals, business processes, and sensors produce alternative data. It also provides a framework to navigate and evaluate the proliferating supply of alternative data for investment purposes. It demonstrates the workflow, from acquisition to preprocessing and storage using Python for data obtained through web scraping to set the stage for the application of ML. It concludes by providing examples of sources, providers, and applications.

This chapter will cover the following topics:

- How the alternative data revolution has unleashed new sources of information
- How individuals, business processes, and sensors generate alternative data
- How to evaluate the proliferating supply of alternative data used for algorithmic trading
- How to work with alternative data in Python, such as by scraping the internet
- Important categories and providers of alternative data

The alternative data revolution

The data deluge driven by digitization, networking, and plummeting storage costs has led to profound qualitative changes in the nature of information available for predictive analytics, often summarized by the five Vs:

- **Volume**: The amount of data generated, collected, and stored is orders of magnitude larger as the byproduct of online and offline activity, transactions, records, and other sources and volumes continue to grow with the capacity for analysis and storage.
- **Velocity**: Data is generated, transferred, and processed to become available near, or at, real-time speed.
- **Variety**: Data is organized in formats no longer limited to structured, tabular forms, such as CSV files or relational database tables. Instead, new sources produce semi-structured formats, such as JSON or HTML, and unstructured content, including raw text, image, and audio or video data, adding new challenges to render data suitable for ML algorithms.
- **Veracity**: The diversity of sources and formats makes it much more difficult to validate the reliability of the data's information content.
- **Value**: Determining the value of new datasets can be much more time—and resource-consuming, as well as more uncertain than before.

For algorithmic trading, new data sources offer an informational advantage if they provide access to information unavailable from traditional sources, or provide access sooner. Following global trends, the investment industry is rapidly expanding beyond market and fundamental data to alternative sources to reap alpha through an informational edge. Annual spending on data, technological capabilities, and related talent are expected to increase from the current $3 billion by 12.8% annually through 2020.

Today, investors can access macro or company-specific data in real-time that historically has been available only at a much lower frequency. Use cases for new data sources include the following:

- Online price data on a representative set of goods and services can be used to measure inflation
- The number of store visits or purchases permits real-time estimates of company or industry-specific sales or economic activity
- Satellite images can reveal agricultural yields, or activity at mines or on oil rigs before this information is available elsewhere

As the standardization and adoption of big datasets advances, the information contained in conventional data will likely lose most of its predictive value.

Furthermore, the capability to process and integrate diverse datasets and apply ML allows for complex insights. In the past, quantitative approaches relied on simple heuristics to rank companies using historical data for metrics such as the price-to-book ratio, whereas ML algorithms synthesize new metrics, and learn and adapt such rules taking into account evolving market data. These insights create new opportunities to capture classic investment themes such as value, momentum, quality, or sentiment:

- **Momentum**: ML can identify asset exposures to market price movements, industry sentiment, or economic factors
- **Value**: Algorithms can analyze large amounts of economic and industry-specific structured and unstructured data, beyond financial statements, to predict the intrinsic value of a company
- **Quality**: The sophisticated analysis of integrated data allows for the evaluation of customer or employee reviews, e-commerce, or app traffic to identify gains in market share or other underlying earnings quality drivers

In practice, however, useful data is often not freely available and alternative datasets instead require thorough evaluation, costly acquisition, careful management, and sophisticated analysis to extract tradable signals.

Sources of alternative data

Alternative datasets are generated by many sources but can be classified at a high-level as predominantly produced by:

- **Individuals** who post on social media, review products, or use search engines
- **Businesses** that record commercial transactions, in particular, credit card payments, or capture supply-chain activity as intermediaries
- **Sensors** that, among many other things, capture economic activity through images such as satellites or security cameras, or through movement patterns such as cell phone towers

The nature of alternative data continues to evolve rapidly as new data sources become available while sources previously labeled alternative become part of the mainstream. The **Baltic Dry Index (BDI)**, for instance, assembles data from several hundred shipping companies to approximate the supply/demand of dry bulk carriers and is now available on the Bloomberg Terminal.

Alternative data includes raw data as well as data that is aggregated or has been processed in some form to add value. For instance, some providers aim to extract tradeable signals, such as sentiment scores. We will address the various types of providers in `Chapter 4,` *Alpha Factor Research*.

Alternative data sources differ in crucial respects that determine their value or signal content for algorithmic trading strategies. We will address these aspects in the next section on *Evaluating alternative datasets*.

Individuals

Individuals automatically create electronic data through online activities, as well as through their offline activity as the latter is captured electronically and often linked to online identities. Data generated by individuals is frequently unstructured in text, image, or video formats, disseminated through multiple platforms and includes:

- Social media posts, such as opinions or reactions on general-purpose sites such as Twitter, Facebook, or LinkedIn, or business-review sites such as Glassdoor or Yelp
- E-commerce activity that reflects an interest in or the perception of products on sites such as Amazon or Wayfair
- Search engine activity using platforms such as Google or Bing
- Mobile app usage, downloads, and reviews
- Personal data such as messaging traffic

The analysis of social media sentiment has become very popular because it can be applied to individual stocks, industry baskets, or market indices. The most common source is Twitter, followed by various news vendors and blog sites. Supply is competitive, and prices are lower because it is often obtained through increasingly commoditized web scraping. Reliable social media datasets that include blogs, tweets, or videos have typically less than five years of history, given how recently consumers have adopted these tools at scale. Search history, in contrast, is available from 2004.

Business processes

Businesses and public entities produce and collect many valuable sources of alternative data. Data that results from business processes has often more structure than that generated by individuals. It is very effective as a leading indicator for activity that is otherwise available at a much lower frequency.

Data generated by business processes include:

- Payment card transaction data made available by processors and financial institutions
- Company exhaust data produced by ordinary digitized activity or record-keeping, such as banking records, cashier scanner data, or supply chain orders
- Trade flow and market microstructure data (such as L-2 and L-3 order book data, illustrated in Chapter 2, *Market and Fundamental Data*)
- Company payments monitored by credit rating agencies or financial institutions to assess liquidity and creditworthiness

Credit card transactions and company exhaust data, such as point-of-sale data, are among the most reliable and predictive datasets. Credit card data is available with around ten years of history and, at different lags, almost up to real time, while corporate earnings are reported quarterly with a 2.5-week lag. The time horizon and reporting lag for company exhaust data varies widely depending on the source. Market microstructure datasets have over 15 years of history compared to sell-side flow data, which typically has fewer than five years of consistent history.

Sensors

Data generated by networked sensors embedded in a broad range of devices are among the most rapidly growing data sources, driven by the proliferation of smartphones and the reduction in the cost of satellite technologies.

This category of alternative data is typically very unstructured and often significantly larger in volume than data generated by individuals or business processes, and poses much higher processing challenges. Key alternative data sources in this category include:

- Satellite imaging to monitor economic activity, such as construction, shipping, or commodity supply
- Geolocation data to track traffic in retail stores, such as using volunteered smartphone data, or on transport routes, such as on ships or trucks
- Cameras positioned at a location of interest
- Weather and pollution sensors

The **Internet of Things (IoT)** will further accelerate the large-scale collection of this type of alternative data by embedding networked microprocessors into personal and commercial electronic devices such as home appliances, public spaces, and industrial production processes.

Sensor-based alternative data that contains satellite images, mobile app usage, or cellular-location tracking is typically available with a three to four-year history.

Satellites

The resources and timelines required to launch a geospatial imaging satellite have dropped dramatically; instead of tens of millions of dollars and years of preparation, the cost has fallen to around $100,000 to place a small satellite as a secondary payload into a low-earth orbit. Hence, companies can obtain much higher-frequency coverage (currently about daily) of specific locations using entire fleets of satellites.

Use cases include the monitoring of economic and commercial activity that can be captured using aerial coverage, such as agricultural and mineral production and shipments, construction of real estates or ships, industrial incidents such as a fire, or car, and foot traffic at locations of interest. Related sensor data is contributed by drones that are used in agriculture to monitor crops using infrared light.

Several challenges may need to be addressed before satellite image data can be reliably used in ML models. These include accounting for weather conditions and in particular, cloud cover and seasonal effects, around holidays, and the irregular coverage of specific locations that may affect the quality of the predictive signals.

Geolocation data

Geolocation data is another rapidly-growing category of alternative data generated by sensors. A familiar source is smartphones with which individuals voluntarily share their geographic location through an application or from wireless signals such as GPS, CDMA, or WiFi measure foot traffic around places of interest, such as stores, restaurants, or event venues.

Furthermore, an increasing number of airports, shopping malls, and retail stores have installed sensors that track the number and movements of customers. While the original motivation to deploy these sensors often was to measure the impact of marketing activity, the resulting data can also be used to estimate foot traffic or sales. Sensors to capture geolocation include 3D stereo video and thermal imaging, which lowers privacy concerns but works well with moving objects. There are also sensors attached to ceilings as well as pressure-sensitive mats. Some providers use multiple sensors in combination, including vision, audio, and cellphone location for a comprehensive account of the shopper journey, which includes not only the count and duration of visits but extends to conversion and measurement of repeat visits.

Evaluating alternative datasets

The ultimate objective of alternative data is to provide an informational advantage in the competitive search for trading signals that produce alpha, namely positive, uncorrelated investment returns. In practice, the signals extracted from alternative datasets can be used on a standalone basis or combined with other signals as part of a quantitative strategy. Independent usage is viable if the Sharpe ratio generated by a strategy based on a single dataset is sufficiently high, but is rare in practice (see `Chapter 4`, *Alpha Factor Research* for details on signal measurement and evaluation).

Quant firms are building libraries of alpha factors that may be weak signals individually but can produce attractive returns in combination. As highlighted in `Chapter 1`, *Machine Learning for Trading*, investment factors should be based on a fundamental and economic rationale, otherwise, they are more likely the result of overfitting to historical data than to persist and generate alpha on new data.

Signal decay due to competition is a serious concern, and as the alternative data ecosystem evolves, it is unlikely that many datasets will retain meaningful Sharpe ratio signals. Effective strategies to extend the half-life of the signal content of an alternative dataset include exclusivity agreements or a focus on datasets that pose processing challenges to raise the barriers to entry.

Evaluation criteria

An alternative dataset can be evaluated based on the quality of its signal content, qualitative aspects of the data, and various technical aspects.

Quality of the signal content

The signal content can be evaluated with respect to the target asset class, the investment style, the relation to conventional risk premiums, and most importantly, its alpha content.

Asset classes

Most alternative datasets contain information directly relevant to equities and commodities. Interesting datasets targeting investments in real estate have also multiplied after Zillow successfully pioneered price estimates in 2006.

Alternative data on corporate credit is growing as alternative sources for monitoring corporate payments, including for smaller businesses, are being developed. Data on fixed income and around interest-rate projections is a more recent phenomenon but continues to increase as more product sales and price information are being harvested at scale.

Investment style

The majority of datasets focus on specific sectors and stocks, and as such naturally appeal to long-short equity investors. As the scale and scope of alternative data collection continue to rise, alternative data will likely also become relevant for investors in macro themes, such as consumer credit, activity in emerging markets, and commodity trends.

Some alternative datasets can be used as proxies for traditional measures of market risk, while other signals are more relevant for high-frequency traders that use quantitative strategies over a brief time horizon.

Risk premiums

Some alternative datasets, such as credit card payments or social media sentiment, have been shown to produce signals that have a low correlation (lower than 5%) with traditional risk premiums in equity markets, such as value, momentum, and quality of volatility. As a result, combining signals derived from such alternative data with an algorithmic trading strategy based on traditional risk factors can be an important building block toward a more diversified risk premiums portfolio.

Alpha content and quality

The signal strength required to justify the investment in an alternative dataset naturally depends on its costs, and alternative data prices vary widely. Data that scores social sentiment can be acquired for a few thousand dollars or less, while the cost of a dataset on comprehensive and timely credit card payments can cost several million per year.

We will explore in detail how to evaluate trading strategies driven by alternative data using historical data, so-called **backtests**, to estimate the amount of alpha contained in a dataset. In isolated cases, a dataset may contain sufficient alpha signal to drive a strategy on a standalone basis, but more typical is the combined use of various alternative and other sources of data. In these cases, a dataset permits the extraction of weak signals that produce a small positive Sharpe ratio that would not receive a capital allocation on its own but can deliver a portfolio-level strategy when integrated with similar other signals. This is not guaranteed, however, as there are also many alternative datasets that do not contain any alpha content.

Besides evaluating a dataset's alpha content, it is also important to assess to which extent a signal is incremental or orthogonal, that is, unique to a dataset, or already captured by other data, and in the latter case compare the costs for this type of signal.

Finally, it is essential to evaluate the potential capacity of a strategy that relies on a given, that is, the amount of capital that can be allocated without undermining its success because a capacity limit will make it more difficult to recover the cost of the data.

Quality of the data

The quality of a dataset is another important criterion because it impacts the effort required to analyze and monetize it, and the reliability of the predictive signal it contains. Quality aspects include the data frequency and the length of its available history, the reliability or accuracy of the information it contains, the extent to which it complies with current or potential future regulations, and how exclusive its use is.

Legal and reputational risks

The use of alternative datasets may carry legal or reputational risk, in particular when they include the following items:

- **Material Non-Public Information (MNPI)** because it implies infringement of insider trading regulations
- **Personally Identifiable Information (PII)**, primarily since the European Union has enacted the **General Data Protection Regulation (GDPR)**

Accordingly, legal and compliance requirements require thorough review. There could also be conflicts of interest when the provider of the data is also a market participant who is actively trading based on the dataset.

Exclusivity

The likelihood that an alternative dataset contains a signal that is sufficiently predictive to drive a strategy on a stand-alone basis with a high Sharpe ratio for a meaningful period is inversely related to its availability and ease of processing. In other words, the more exclusive, and the harder to process the data, the better the chances that a dataset with alpha content can drive a strategy without suffering rapid signal decay.

Public fundamental data that provides standard financial ratios contains little alpha and is not attractive for a standalone strategy, but may help diversify a portfolio of risk factors. Large, complex datasets will take more time to be absorbed by the market, and new datasets continue to emerge on a frequent basis. Hence, it is essential to assess how familiar other investors already are with a dataset, and whether the provider is the best source for this type of information.

Additional benefits to exclusivity or being an early adopter of a new dataset may arise when a business just begins to sell exhaust data that it generated for other purposes because it may be possible to influence how the data is collected or curated, or to negotiate conditions that limit access for competitors at least for a certain time period.

Time horizon

More extensive history is highly desirable to test the predictive power of a dataset under different scenarios. The availability varies greatly between several months and several decades and has important implications for the scope of the trading strategy that can be built and tested based on the data. We mentioned some ranges for time horizons for different datasets when introducing the main types of sources.

Frequency

The frequency of the data determines how often new information becomes available and how differentiated a predictive signal can be over a given period. It also impacts the time horizon of the investment strategy and ranges from intra-day, to daily, weekly, or an even lower frequency.

Reliability

Naturally, the degree to which the data accurately reflects what it intends to measure or how well this can be verified is of significant concern and should be validated by means of a thorough audit. This applies to both raw and processed data where the methodology used to extract or aggregate information needs to be analyzed, taking into account the cost-benefit ratio for the proposed acquisition.

Technical aspects

Technical aspects concern the latency or delay of reporting, and the format in which the data is made available.

Latency

Data providers often provide resources in batches, and a delay can result from how the data is collected, subsequent processing and transmission, as well as regulatory or legal constraints.

Format

The data is made available in a broad range of formats, depending on the source. Processed data will be in user-friendly formats and easily integrated into existing systems or queries via a robust API. On the other end of the spectrum are voluminous data sources, such as video, audio, or image data, or a proprietary format, that require more skills to be prepared for analysis, but also provide higher barriers to entry for potential competitors.

The market for alternative data

The investment industry is going to spend an estimated to $2,000,000,000-3,000,000,000 on data services in 2018, and this number is expected to grow at double digits per year in line with other industries. This expenditure includes the acquisition of alternative data, investments in related technology, and the hiring of qualified talent.

A survey by Ernst and Young shows significant adoption of alternative data in 2017; 43% of funds are using scraped web data, for instance, and almost 30% are experimenting with satellite data. Based on the experience so far, fund managers considered scraped web data and credit card data to be most insightful, in contrast to geolocation and satellite data, which around 25% considered to be less informative:

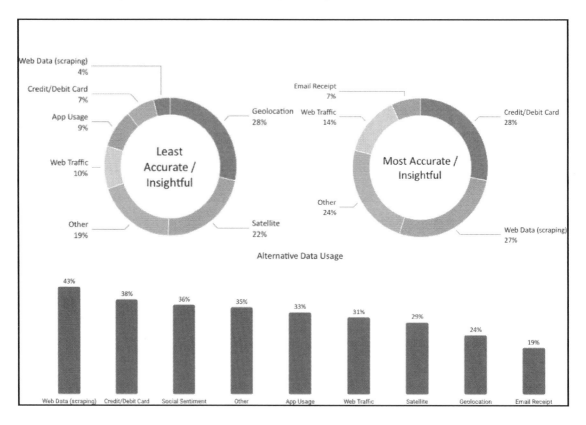

Reflecting the rapid growth of this new industry, the market for alternative data providers is quite fragmented. J.P. Morgan lists over 500 specialized data firms, while AlternativeData.org lists over 300. Providers play numerous roles, including intermediaries such as consultants, aggregators, and tech solutions; sell-side supports deliver data in various formats, ranging from raw to semi-processed data or some form of a signal extracted from one or more sources.

We will highlight the size of the main categories and profile a few prominent examples to illustrate their diversity.

Data providers and use cases

`AlternativeData.org` (supported by provider Yipit) lists several categories that can serve as a rough proxy for activity in various data-provider segments. Social sentiment analysis is by far the largest category, while satellite and geolocation data have been growing rapidly in recent years:

Product category	Number of providers	Goals
Social sentiment	48	Raw or processed social media data; short-term trends
Satellite	26	Aerial monitoring of medium-term economic activity
Geolocation	22	Track retail, commercial real estate, or event foot traffic
Web data and traffic	22	Monitor search interest, brand popularity, and events
Credit and debit card usage	14	Track near-term consumer spend and business revenues
App usage	7	Monitor app sales or collect secondary data
Email and consumer receipts	6	Track consumer spend by chain, brand, sector, or geography
Weather	4	Crop and commodity-related longer-term trends
Other	87	

The following brief examples aim to illustrate the broad range of service providers and potential use cases.

Social sentiment data

Social sentiment analysis is most closely associated with Twitter data. Gnip was an early social-media aggregator that provided data from numerous sites using an API and was acquired by Twitter in 2014 for $134 million. Search engines are another source that became prominent when researchers published in nature that investment strategies based on Google Trends for terms such as debt could be used for a profitable trading strategy over an extended period (see the GitHub repo `https://github.com/PacktPublishing/Hands-On-Machine-Learning-for-Algorithmic-Trading` for references).

Dataminr

Dataminr was founded in 2009 and provides social-sentiment and news analysis based on an exclusive agreement with Twitter. The company is one of the larger alternative providers and raised an additional $392 million in funding in June 2018 led by Fidelity at a $1,6 billion valuation, bringing total funding to $569 billion. It emphasizes real-time signals extracted from social media feeds using machine learning and serves a wide range of clients, including not only buy and sell-side investment firms but also news organizations and the public sector.

StockTwits

StockTwits is a social network and micro-blogging platform where several hundred thousand investment professionals share information and trading ideas in the form of StockTwits that are viewed by a large audience across the financial web and social media platforms. This data can be exploited because it may reflect investor sentiment or itself drive trades that, in turn, impact prices. The references on GitHub contain a link to a paper that builds a trading strategy on selected features.

RavenPack

RavenPack analyzes a large number of diverse, unstructured, text-based data to produce structured indicators, including sentiment scores, that aim to contain information relevant to investors. The underlying data sources range from premium newswires and regulatory information to press releases and over 19,000 web publications. J.P. Morgan tested a long-short sovereign bond and equity strategies based on sentiment scores and achieved positive results with low correlation to conventional risk premiums (see references).

Satellite data

RS Metrics, founded in 2010, triangulates geospatial data from satellites, drones, and airplanes with a focus on metals and commodities, as well as real-estate and industrial applications. The company offers signals, predictive analytics, alerts, and end-user applications based on its own high-resolution satellites. Use cases include the estimation of retail traffic targeting certain chains or commercial real estate, as well as the production and storage of certain common metals or employment at related production locations.

Geolocation data

Advan, founded in 2015, serves hedge fund clients with signals derived from mobile phone traffic data, targeting 1,600 tickers across various sectors in the US and EU. The company collects data using apps that install geolocation codes on smartphones with explicit user consent and track location using several channels (such as WiFi, Bluetooth, and cellular signal) for enhanced accuracy. The uses cases include estimates of customer traffic at physical store locations, which in turn can be used as input to models that predict top-line revenues of traded companies.

Email receipt data

Eagle Alpha provides, among other services, data on a large set of online transactions using email receipts, covering over 5000 retailers, including item—and SKU-level transaction data categorized in 53 product groups. J.P. Morgan analyzed a time series dataset, starting in 2013, that covered a constant group of users active throughout the entire sample period. The dataset contained total aggregate spend, number of orders, and the number of unique buyers per period.

Working with alternative data

We will illustrate the acquisition of alternative data using web scraping, targeting first OpenTable restaurant data, and then move to earnings call transcripts hosted by Seeking Alpha.

Scraping OpenTable data

Typical sources of alternative data are review websites such as Glassdoor or Yelp that convey insider insights using employee comments or guest reviews. This data provides valuable input for ML models that aim to predict a business' prospects or directly its market value to obtain trading signals.

The data needs to be extracted from the HTML source, barring any legal obstacles. To illustrate the web scraping tools that Python offers, we'll retrieve information on restaurant bookings from OpenTable. Data of this nature could be used to forecast economic activity by geography, real estate prices, or restaurant chain revenues.

Extracting data from HTML using requests and BeautifulSoup

In this section, we will request and parse HTML source code. We will be using the `requests` library to make **Hyper Text Transfer Protocol** (**HTTP**) requests and retrieve the HTML source code, and `BeautifulSoup` to parse and extract the text content.

We will, however, encounter a common obstacle: websites may request certain information from the server only after initial page-load using JavaScript. As a result, a direct HTTP request will not be successful. To sidestep this type of protection, we will use a headless browser that retrieves the website content as a browser would:

```
from bs4 import BeautifulSoup
import requests

# set and request url; extract source code
url = "https://www.opentable.com/new-york-restaurant-listings"
html = requests.get(url)
html.text[:500]

' <!DOCTYPE html><html lang="en"><head><meta charset="utf-8"/><meta http-
equiv="X-UA-Compatible" content="IE=9; IE=8; IE=7; IE=EDGE"/>
<title>Restaurant Reservation Availability</title> <meta name="robots"
content="noindex" > </meta> <link rel="shortcut icon"
href="//components.otstatic.com/components/favicon/1.0.4/favicon/favicon.ic
o" type="image/x-icon"/><link rel="icon"
href="//components.otstatic.com/components/favicon/1.0.4/favicon/favicon-16
.png" sizes="16x16"/><link rel='
```

Now we can use `BeautifulSoup` to parse the HTML content, and then look for all `span` tags with the class associated with the restaurant names that we obtain by inspecting the source code, `rest-row-name-text` (see GitHub repo for linked instructions to examine website source code):

```
# parse raw html => soup object
soup = BeautifulSoup(html.text, 'html.parser')

# for each span tag, print out text => restaurant name
for entry in soup.find_all(name='span', attrs={'class':'rest-row-name-
```

```
text'}):
    print(entry.text)

Wade Coves
Alley
Dolorem Maggio
Islands
...
```

Once you have identified the page elements of interest, BeautifulSoup makes it easy to retrieve the contained text. If you want to get the price category for each restaurant, you can use:

```
# get the number of dollars signs for each restaurant
for entry in soup.find_all('div', {'class':'rest-row-pricing'}):
    price = entry.find('i').text
```

When you try to get the number of bookings, however, you just get an empty list because the site uses JavaScript code to request this information after the initial loading is complete:

```
soup.find_all('div', {'class':'booking'})
[]
```

Introducing Selenium – using browser automation

We will use the browser automation tool Selenium to operate a headless FireFox browser that will parse the HTML content for us.

The following code opens the FireFox browser:

```
from selenium import webdriver

# create a driver called Firefox
driver = webdriver.Firefox()
```

Let's close the browser:

```
# close it
driver.close()
```

To retrieve the HTML source code using selenium and Firefox, do the following:

```
import time, re

# visit the opentable listing page
driver = webdriver.Firefox()
driver.get(url)
```

```
time.sleep(1) # wait 1 second

# retrieve the html source
html = driver.page_source
html = BeautifulSoup(html, "lxml")

for booking in html.find_all('div', {'class': 'booking'}):
    match = re.search(r'\d+', booking.text)
    if match:
        print(match.group())
```

Building a dataset of restaurant bookings

Now you only need to combine all the interesting elements from the website to create a feature that you could use in a model to predict economic activity in geographic regions or foot traffic in specific neighborhoods.

With Selenium, you can follow the links to the next pages and quickly build a dataset of over 10,000 restaurants in NYC that you could then update periodically to track a time series. First, we set up a function that parses the content of the pages that we plan on crawling:

```
def parse_html(html):
    data, item = pd.DataFrame(), {}
    soup = BeautifulSoup(html, 'lxml')
    for i, resto in enumerate(soup.find_all('div', class_='rest-row-
            info')):
        item['name'] = resto.find('span', class_='rest-row-name-
                                text').text

        booking = resto.find('div', class_='booking')
        item['bookings'] = re.search('\d+', booking.text).group() if
                                booking else 'NA'

        rating = resto.select('div.all-stars.filled')
        item['rating'] = int(re.search('\d+',
                rating[0].get('style')).group()) if rating else 'NA'

        reviews = resto.find('span', class_='star-rating-text--review-
                            text')
        item['reviews'] = int(re.search('\d+', reviews.text).group()) if
reviews else 'NA'

        item['price'] = int(resto.find('div', class_='rest-row-
                            pricing').find('i').text.count('$'))
        item['cuisine'] = resto.find('span', class_='rest-row-meta--
```

```
                                        cuisine').text
        item['location'] = resto.find('span', class_='rest-row-meta--
                                  location').text
        data[i] = pd.Series(item)
    return data.T
```

Then, we start a headless browser that continues to click on the **Next** button for us and capture the results displayed on each page:

```
restaurants = pd.DataFrame()
driver = webdriver.Firefox()
url = "https://www.opentable.com/new-york-restaurant-listings"
driver.get(url)
while True:
    sleep(1)
    new_data = parse_html(driver.page_source)
    if new_data.empty:
        break
    restaurants = pd.concat([restaurants, new_data], ignore_index=True)
    print(len(restaurants))
    driver.find_element_by_link_text('Next').click()
driver.close()
```

Websites continue to change, so this code may stop working at some point and will require updating to follow the latest site navigation and bot detection.

One step further – Scrapy and splash

Scrapy is a powerful library to build bots that follow links, retrieve the content, and store the parsed result in a structured way. In combination with the headless browser splash, it can also interpret JavaScript and becomes an efficient alternative to Selenium. You can run the spider using the `scrapy crawl opentable` command in the `01_opentable` directory where the results are logged to `spider.log`:

```
from opentable.items import OpentableItem
from scrapy import Spider
from scrapy_splash import SplashRequest

class OpenTableSpider(Spider):
    name = 'opentable'
    start_urls = ['https://www.opentable.com/new-york-restaurant-
                  listings']

    def start_requests(self):
        for url in self.start_urls:
            yield SplashRequest(url=url,
```

```
                                        callback=self.parse,
                                        endpoint='render.html',
                                        args={'wait': 1},
                                        )

    def parse(self, response):
        item = OpentableItem()
        for resto in response.css('div.rest-row-info'):
            item['name'] = resto.css('span.rest-row-name-
                                    text::text').extract()
            item['bookings'] =
                resto.css('div.booking::text').re(r'\d+')
            item['rating'] = resto.css('div.all-
                stars::attr(style)').re_first('\d+')
            item['reviews'] = resto.css('span.star-rating-text--review-
                                        text::text').re_first(r'\d+')
            item['price'] = len(resto.css('div.rest-row-pricing >
                                i::text').re('\$'))
            item['cuisine'] = resto.css('span.rest-row-meta--
                                        cuisine::text').extract()
            item['location'] = resto.css('span.rest-row-meta--
                                location::text').extract()
            yield item
```

There are numerous ways to extract information from this data beyond the reviews and bookings of individual restaurants or chains.

We could further collect and geo-encode the restaurants' addresses, for instance, to link the restaurants' physical location to other areas of interest, such as popular retail spots or neighborhoods to gain insights into particular aspects of economic activity. As mentioned before, such data will be most valuable in combination with other information.

Earnings call transcripts

Textual data is an essential alternative data source. One example of textual information is transcripts of earnings calls where executives do not only present the latest financial results, but also respond to questions by financial analysts. Investors utilize transcripts to evaluate changes in sentiment, emphasis on particular topics, or style of communication.

We will illustrate the scraping and parsing of earnings call transcripts from the popular trading website www.seekingalpha.com:

```
import re
from pathlib import Path
from time import sleep
```

```
from urllib.parse import urljoin
from bs4 import BeautifulSoup
from furl import furl
from selenium import webdriver

transcript_path = Path('transcripts')

SA_URL = 'https://seekingalpha.com/'
TRANSCRIPT = re.compile('Earnings Call Transcript')

next_page = True
page = 1
driver = webdriver.Firefox()
while next_page:
    url = f'{SA_URL}/earnings/earnings-call-transcripts/{page}'
    driver.get(urljoin(SA_URL, url))
    response = driver.page_source
    page += 1
    soup = BeautifulSoup(response, 'lxml')
    links = soup.find_all(name='a', string=TRANSCRIPT)
    if len(links) == 0:
        next_page = False
    else:
        for link in links:
            transcript_url = link.attrs.get('href')
            article_url = furl(urljoin(SA_URL,
                            transcript_url)).add({'part': 'single'})
            driver.get(article_url.url)
            html = driver.page_source
            meta, participants, content = parse_html(html)
            meta['link'] = link

driver.close()
```

Parsing HTML using regular expressions

To collect structured data from the unstructured transcripts, we can use regular expressions in addition to BeautifulSoup.

They allows us to collect detailed information not only about the earnings call company and timing but also capture who was present and attribute the statements to analysts and company representatives:

```
def parse_html(html):
    date_pattern = re.compile(r'(\d{2})-(\d{2})-(\d{2})')
    quarter_pattern = re.compile(r'(\bQ\d\b)')
```

```
soup = BeautifulSoup(html, 'lxml')

meta, participants, content = {}, [], []
h1 = soup.find('h1', itemprop='headline').text
meta['company'] = h1[:h1.find('(')].strip()
meta['symbol'] = h1[h1.find('(') + 1:h1.find(')')]

title = soup.find('div', class_='title').text
match = date_pattern.search(title)
if match:
    m, d, y = match.groups()
    meta['month'] = int(m)
    meta['day'] = int(d)
    meta['year'] = int(y)

match = quarter_pattern.search(title)
if match:
    meta['quarter'] = match.group(0)

qa = 0
speaker_types = ['Executives', 'Analysts']
for header in [p.parent for p in soup.find_all('strong')]:
    text = header.text.strip()
    if text.lower().startswith('copyright'):
        continue
    elif text.lower().startswith('question-and'):
        qa = 1
        continue
    elif any([type in text for type in speaker_types]):
        for participant in header.find_next_siblings('p'):
            if participant.find('strong'):
                break
            else:
                participants.append([text, participant.text])
    else:
        p = []
        for participant in header.find_next_siblings('p'):
            if participant.find('strong'):
                break
            else:
                p.append(participant.text)
        content.append([header.text, qa, '\n'.join(p)])
return meta, participants, content
```

We store the result in several `.csv` files for easy access when we use ML to process natural language:

```
def store_result(meta, participants, content):
    path = transcript_path / 'parsed' / meta['symbol']
    if not path.exists():
        path.mkdir(parents=True, exist_ok=True)
    pd.DataFrame(content, columns=['speaker', 'q&a',
            'content']).to_csv(path / 'content.csv', index=False)
    pd.DataFrame(participants, columns=['type', 'name']).to_csv(path /
            'participants.csv', index=False)
    pd.Series(meta).to_csv(path / 'earnings.csv'
```

See README in the GitHub repo for additional details and references for further resources to develop web-scraping applications.

Summary

In this chapter, we introduced new sources of alternative data made available as a result of the big data revolution, including individuals, business processes, and sensors, such as satellites or GPS location devices. We presented a framework to evaluate alternative datasets from an investment perspective and laid out key categories and providers to help you navigate this vast and quickly-expanding area that provides critical inputs for algorithmic trading strategies that use ML.

We explored powerful Python tools to collect your own datasets at scale so that you can potentially work on getting your private informational edge as an algorithmic trader using web scraping.

We will now proceed, in the following chapter, to the design and evaluation of alpha factors that produce trading signals, and look at how to combine them in a portfolio context.

4
Alpha Factor Research

Algorithmic trading strategies are driven by signals that indicate when to buy or sell assets to generate positive returns relative to a benchmark. The portion of an asset's return that is not explained by exposure to the benchmark is called **alpha**, and hence these signals are also called **alpha factors**.

Alpha factors aim to predict the price movements of assets in the investment universe based on the available market, fundamental, or alternative data. A factor may combine one or several input variables, but assumes a single value for each asset every time the strategy evaluates the factor. Trade decisions typically rely on relative values across assets. Trading strategies are often based on signals emitted by multiple factors, and we will see that **machine learning (ML)** models are particularly well suited to integrate the various signals efficiently to make more accurate predictions.

The design, evaluation, and combination of alpha factors are critical steps during the research phase of the algorithmic trading strategy workflow, as shown in the following diagram. We will focus on the research phase in this Chapter 4, *Strategy Evaluation*, and the execution phase in the next chapter. The remainder of this book will then focus on the use of ML to discover and combine alpha factors. Take a look at the following figure:

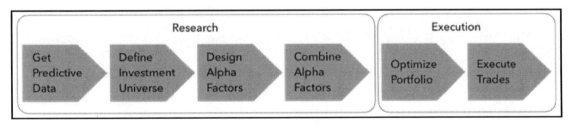

This chapter will use a simple mean-reversal factor to introduce the algorithmic trading simulator `zipline` that is written in Python and facilitates the testing of alpha factors for a given investment universe. We will also use `zipline` when we backtest trading strategies in a portfolio context in the next chapter. Next, we will discuss key metrics to evaluate the predictive performance of alpha factors, including the information coefficient and the information ratio, which leads to the fundamental law of active management.

In particular, this chapter will address the following topics:

- How to characterize, justify and measure key types of alpha factors
- How to create alpha factors using financial feature engineering
- How to use `zipline` offline to test individual alpha factors
- How to use `zipline` on Quantopian to combine alpha factors and identify more sophisticated signals
- How the **information coefficient** (**IC**) measures an alpha factor's predictive performance
- How to use `alphalens` to evaluate predictive performance and turnover

Engineering alpha factors

Alpha factors are transformations of market, fundamental, and alternative data that contain predictive signals. They are designed to capture risks that drive asset returns. One set of factors describes fundamental, economy-wide variables such as growth, inflation, volatility, productivity, and demographic risk. Another set consists of tradeable investment styles such as the market portfolio, value-growth investing, and momentum investing.

There are also factors that explain price movements based on the economics or institutional setting of financial markets, or investor behavior, including known biases of this behavior. The economic theory behind factors can be rational, where the factors have high returns over the long run to compensate for their low returns during bad times, or behavioral, where factor risk premiums result from the possibly biased, or not entirely rational behavior of agents that is not arbitraged away.

There is a constant search for and discovery of new factors that may better capture known or reflect new drivers of returns. Jason Hsu, the co-founder of Research Affiliates which manages close to $200 Bn, identified some 250 factors that had been published with empirical evidence in reputable journals by 2015 and estimated that this number was likely to increase by 40 factors per year. To avoid false discoveries and ensure a factor delivers consistent results, it should have a meaningful economic intuition that makes it plausible that it reflects risks that the market would compensate.

The data transformations include simple arithmetic such as absolute or relative changes of a variable over time, ratios between data series, or aggregations over a time window such as a simple or exponential moving average. They also include calculations that have emerged from the technical analysis of price patterns such as the relative strength index of demand versus supply and numerous metrics familiar from the fundamental analysis of securities.

Important factor categories

In an idealized world, categories of risk factors should be independent of each other (orthogonal), yield positive risk premia, and form a complete set that spans all dimensions of risk and explains the systematic risks for assets in a given class. In practice, these requirements will hold only approximately. We will address how to derive synthetic, data-driven risk factors using unsupervised learning, in particular principal and independent component analysis in Chapter 12, *Unsupervised Learning*.

We will review the key categories for factors derived from market, fundamental, and alternative data, and typical metrics used to capture them. We will also demonstrate how to implement these factors for algorithms tested on the Quantopian platform using built-in factors, custom computations using numpy and pandas, or the talib library for technical analysis.

Momentum and sentiment factors

Momentum investing follows the adage: the trend is your friend or let your winners run. Momentum risk factors are designed to go long assets that have performed well while going short assets with poor performance over a certain period.

The premise of strategies relying on this factor is that asset prices exhibit a trend, reflected in positive serial correlations. Such price momentum would defy the hypothesis of efficient markets which states that past price returns alone cannot predict future performance. Despite theoretical arguments to the contrary, price momentum strategies have produced positive returns across asset classes and are an important part of many trading strategies.

Rationale

Reasons for the momentum effect point to investor behavior, persistent supply, and demand imbalances, a positive feedback loop between risk assets and the economy, or the market microstructure.

The behavioral reasons reflect biases of under-reaction and over-reaction to market news as investors process new information at different speeds. After an initial under-reaction to news, investors often extrapolate past behavior and create price momentum. The technology stocks rally during the late 90s market bubble was an extreme example. A fear and greed psychology also motivates investors to increase exposure to winning assets and continue selling losing assets.

Momentum can also have fundamental drivers such as a positive feedback loop between risk assets and the economy. Economic growth boosts equities, and the resulting wealth effect feeds back into the economy through higher spending, again fueling growth. Positive feedback between prices and the economy often extends momentum in equities and credit to longer horizons than for bonds, FX, and commodities, where negative feedback creates reversals, requiring a much shorter investment horizon. Another cause of momentum can be persistent demand-supply imbalances due to market frictions, for example, when commodity production takes significant amounts of time to adjust to demand trends. Oil production may lag increased demand from a booming economy for years, and persistent supply shortages can trigger and support upward price momentum.

Market microstructure effects can also create price momentum related to behavioral patterns that motivate investors to buy products and implement strategies that mimic their biases. For example, the trading wisdom to cut losses and let profits run has investors use trading strategies such as stop loss, **constant proportion portfolio insurance (CPPI)**, dynamical delta hedging, or option-based strategies such as protective puts. These strategies create momentum because they imply an advance commitment to sell when an asset underperforms and buy when it outperforms. Similarly, risk parity strategies (see the next chapter) tend to buy low-volatility assets that often exhibit positive performance and sell high-volatility assets that often had negative performance. The automatic rebalancing of portfolios using these strategies tends to reinforce price momentum.

Key metrics

Momentum factors are typically derived from changes in price time series by identifying trends and patterns. They can be constructed based on absolute or relative return, by comparing a cross-section of assets or analyzing an asset's time series, within or across traditional asset classes, and at different time horizons.

A few popular illustrative indicators are listed in the following table:

Factor	Description
Relative Strength Indicator (RSI)	The RSI compares recent price changes across stocks to identify stocks as overbought or oversold. A high RSI (example, above 70) indicates overbought, and a low RSI (example below 30) indicates oversold. It uses the average price change for a given number of prior trading days with positive price changes $\tilde{\Delta p}^{up}$ and negative prices changes $\tilde{\Delta p}^{down}$ to compute: $$RSI = 100 - \frac{100}{1 + \tilde{\Delta p}^{up}/\tilde{\Delta p}^{down}}$$
Price momentum	This factor computes the total return for a given number of prior trading days. In the academic literature, it is common to use the last 12 months but exclude the most recent month because of a short-term reversal effect frequently observed in most recent price movements, but shorter periods have also been widely used.
12-month price momentum Vol Adj	The 12-month price momentum adjusted for volatility factor normalizes the total return over the previous 12 months by dividing it by the standard deviation of these returns.
Price acceleration	Price acceleration calculates the gradient of the trend (adjusted for volatility) using a linear regression on daily prices for a longer and a shorter period, e.g., a one year and three months of trading days and compares the change in the slope as a measure of price acceleration.
Percent Off 52 week high	This factor uses the percent difference between the most recent and the highest price for the last 52 weeks.

Additional sentiment indicators include the following:

Factor	Description
Earnings estimates count	This metric ranks stocks by the number of consensus estimates as a proxy for analyst coverage and information uncertainty. A higher value is more desirable.

N month change in recommendation	This factor ranks stocks by the change in consensus recommendation over the prior N month, where improvements are desirable (regardless of whether they have moved from strong sell to sell or buy to strong buy and so on).
12-month change in shares outstanding	This factor measures the change in a company's split-adjusted share count over the last 12 months, where a negative change implies share buybacks and is desirable because it signals that management views the stock as cheap relative to its intrinsic and, hence, future value.
6-month change in target price	The metric tracks the 6-month change in mean analyst target price and a higher positive change is naturally more desirable.
Net earnings revisions	This factor expresses the difference between upward and downward revisions to earnings estimates as a percentage of the total number of revisions.
Short interest to shares outstanding	This measure is the percentage of shares outstanding currently being sold short, that is, sold by an investor who has borrowed the share and needs to repurchase it at a later day while speculating that its price will fall. Hence, a high level of short interest indicates negative sentiment and is expected to signal poor performance going forward.

Value factors

Stocks with low prices relative to their fundamental value tend to deliver returns in excess of a capitalization-weighted benchmark. Value factors reflect this correlation and are designed to provide signals to buy undervalued assets, that is, those that are relatively cheap and sell those that are overvalued and expensive. For this reason, at the core of any value strategy is a valuation model that estimates or proxies the asset's fair or fundamental value. Fair value can be defined as an absolute price level, a spread relative to other assets, or a range in which an asset should trade (for example, two standard deviations).

Value strategies rely on mean-reversion of prices to the asset's fair value. They assume that prices only temporarily move away from fair value due to either behavioral effects, such as overreaction or herding, or liquidity effects such as temporary market impact or long-term supply/demand frictions. Since value factors rely on mean-reversion, they often exhibit properties opposite to those of momentum factors. For equities, the opposite to value stocks are growth stocks with a high valuation due to growth expectations.

Value factors enable a broad array of systematic strategies including fundamental and market valuation, statistical arbitrage, and cross-asset relative value. They are often implemented as long/short portfolios without exposure to other traditional or alternative risk factors.

Fundamental value strategies derive fair asset values from economic and fundamental indicators that depend on the target asset class. In fixed income, currencies, and commodities, indicators include, for example, levels and changes in the capital account balance, economic activity, inflation, or fund flows. In equities and corporate credit, value factors go back to Graham and Dodd's Security Analysis in the 1930s, since made famous by Warren Buffet. Equity value approaches compare a stock price to fundamental metrics such as book value, top line sales, bottom line earnings, or various cash-flow metrics.

Market value strategies use statistical or machine learning models to identify mispricing due to inefficiencies in liquidity provision. Statistical and Index Arbitrage are prominent examples that capture the reversion of temporary market impacts over short time horizons (we will cover pairs trading in the next chapter). Over longer time horizons, market value trades also leverage seasonal effects in equities and commodities.

Cross-asset relative value strategies focus on the relative mispricing of different assets. For example, convertible bond arbitrage involves trades on the relative value between the stock, credit, and volatility of a single company. Relative value also includes trades between credit and equity volatility, using credit signals to trade equities or relative value trades between commodities and equities.

Rationale

There are both rational and behavioral explanations for the existence of the value effect. We will cite a few prominent examples from a wealth of research with further references listed in the GitHub repository.

In the rational, efficient markets view, the value premium compensates for higher real or perceived risks. Researchers have presented evidence that value firms have less flexibility to adapt to the unfavorable economic environments than leaner and more flexible growth companies, or that value stock risks relate to high financial leverage and more uncertain future earnings. Value and small-cap portfolios have also been shown to be more sensitive to macro shocks than growth and large-cap portfolios.

From a behavioral perspective, the value premium can be explained by loss aversion and mental accounting biases. Investors may be less concerned about losses on assets with a strong recent performance due to the cushions offered by prior gains. This loss aversion bias induces investors to perceive the stock as less risky than before and discount its future cash flows at a lower rate. Conversely, poor recent performance may lead investors to raise the asset's discount rate. The differential return expectations result in a value premium since growth stocks with a high price multiple relative to fundamentals have done well in the past but, going forward, investors will require a lower average return due to their biased perception of lower risks, while the inverse is true for value stocks.

Key metrics

There is a large number of valuation proxies computed from fundamental data. These factors can be combined as inputs into a machine learning valuation model to predict prices. We will see examples of how some of these factors are used in practice in the following chapters:

Factor	Description
Cash flow yield	The ratio divides the operational cash flow per share by the share price. A higher ratio implies better cash returns for shareholders (if paid out using dividends or share buybacks, or profitably reinvested in the business).
Free cash flow yield	The ratio divides the free cash flow per share, which reflects the amount of cash available for distribution after necessary expenses and investments, by the share price. Higher and growing free cash flow yield is commonly viewed as a signal of outperformance.
Cash flow return on invested capital (CFROIC)	CFROIC measures a company's cash flow profitability. It divides operating cash flow by invested capital, defined as total debt plus net assets. A higher return means the business has more cash for a given amount of invested capital, generating more value for shareholders.
Cash flow to total assets	This ratio divides operational cash flow by total assets and indicates how much cash a company can generate relative to its assets, where a higher ratio is better similar as for CFROIC.
Free cash flow to enterprise value	This ratio measures the free cash flow that a company generates relative to its enterprise value, measured as the combined value of equity and debt.
EBITDA to enterprise value	This ratio measures a company's EBITDA (Earnings before interest, taxes, depreciation, and amortization), which is a proxy for cash flow relative to its enterprise value.

Earnings yield (1 Yr trailing)	This ratio divides the sum of earnings for the past 12 months by the last market (close) price.
Earnings yield (1 Yr forward)	Instead of actual historical earnings, this ratio divides a rolling 12 month forward consensus analyst earnings estimate by the last price, where consensus consists in a (possibly weighted) average of forecasts.
PEG ratio	The Price/Earnings to Growth (PEG) ratio divides a stock's price-to-earnings (P/E) ratio by the earnings growth rate for a given period. The ratio adjusts the price paid for a dollar of earnings (measured by the P/E ratio) by the company's earnings growth.
P/E 1 Yr Forward Relative to sector	Forecast P/E ratio relative to the corresponding sector P/E. It aims to alleviate the sector bias of the generic P/E ratio by accounting for sector differences in valuation.
Sales yield	The ratio measures the valuation of a stock relative to its ability to generate revenues. All else equal, stocks with higher historical sales to price ratios are expected to outperform.
Sales yield FY1	The forward sales to price ratio uses analyst sales forecast, combined to a (weighted) average.
Book value yield	The ratio divides the historical book value by the share price.
Dividend yield	The current annualized dividend divided by the last close price. Discounted cash flow valuation assumes a company's market value equates to the present value of its future cash flows.

Volatility and size factors

The low volatility factor captures excess returns on stocks with volatility, beta or idiosyncratic risk below average. Stocks with a larger market capitalization tend to have lower volatility so that the traditional *size* factor is often combined with the more recent volatility factor.

The low volatility anomaly is an empirical puzzle that is at odds with basic principles of finance. The **Capital Asset Pricing Model (CAPM)** and other asset pricing models assert that higher risk should earn higher returns, but in numerous markets and over extended periods, the opposite has been true with less risky assets outperforming their riskier peers.

Rationale

The low volatility anomaly contradicts the hypothesis of efficient markets and the CAPM assumptions. Instead, several behavioral explanations have been advanced.

The lottery effect builds on empirical evidence that individuals take on bets that resemble lottery tickets with a small expected loss but a large potential win, even though this large win may have a fairly low probability. If investors perceive the risk-return profile of a low price, volatile stock as similar to a lottery ticket, then it could be an attractive bet. As a result, investors may overpay for high volatility stocks and underpay for low volatility stocks due to their biased preferences. The representativeness bias suggests that investors extrapolate the success of a few, well-publicized volatile stocks to all volatile stocks while ignoring the speculative nature of such stocks.

Investors may also be overconfident in their ability to forecast the future, and their differences in opinions are higher for volatile stocks with more uncertain outcomes. Since it is easier to express a positive view by going long, that is, owning an asset than a negative view by going short, optimists may outnumber pessimists and keep driving up the price of volatile stocks, resulting in lower returns.

Furthermore, investors behave differently in bull markets and during crises. During bull markets, the dispersion of betas is much lower so that low volatility stocks do not underperform much if at all, whereas, during crises, investors seek or keep low-volatility stocks and the beta dispersion increases. As a result, lower volatility assets and portfolios do better over the long term.

Key metrics

Metrics used to identify low volatility stocks cover a broad spectrum, with realized volatility (standard deviation) on one end, and forecast (implied) volatility and correlations on the other end. Some operationalize low volatility as low beta. The evidence in favor of the volatility anomaly appears robust for different metrics.

Quality factors

The quality factor aims to capture the excess return on companies that are highly profitable, operationally efficient, safe, stable and well-governed, in short, high quality, versus the market. The markets also appear to reward relative earnings certainty and penalize stocks with high earnings volatility. A portfolio tilt towards businesses with high quality has been long advocated by stock pickers that rely on fundamental analysis but is a relatively new phenomenon in quantitative investments. The main challenge is how to define the quality factor consistently and objectively using quantitative indicators, given the subjective nature of quality.

Strategies based on standalone quality factors tend to perform in a counter-cyclical way as investors pay a premium to minimize downside risks and drive up valuations. For this reason, quality factors are often combined with other risk factors in a multi-factor strategy, most frequently with value to produce the quality at a reasonable price strategy. Long-short quality factors tend to have negative market beta because they are long quality stocks that are also low volatility, and short more volatile, low-quality stocks. Hence, quality factors are often positively correlated with low volatility and momentum factors, and negatively correlated with value and broad market exposure.

Rationale

Quality factors may signal outperformance because superior fundamentals such as sustained profitability, steady growth in cash flow, prudent leveraging, a low need for capital market financing or low financial risk underpin the demand for equity shares and support the price of such companies in the long run. From a corporate finance perspective, a quality company often manages its capital carefully and reduces the risk of over-leveraging or over-capitalization.

A behavioral explanation suggests that investors under-react to information about quality, similar to the rationale for momentum where investors chase winners and sell losers. Another argument for quality premia is a herding argument similar to growth stocks. Fund managers may find it easier to justify buying a company with strong fundamentals even when it is getting expensive rather than a more volatile (risky) value stock.

Key metrics

Quality factors rely on metrics computed from the balance sheet and income statement that indicate profitability reflected in high profit or cash flow margins, operating efficiency, financial strength, and competitiveness more broadly because it implies the ability to sustain a profitability position over time.

Hence, quality has been measured using gross profitability (which has been recently added to the Fama—French factor model, see `Chapter 7`, *Linear Models*), return on invested capital, low earnings volatility, or a combination of various profitability, earnings quality, and leverage metrics, with some options listed in the following table.

Earnings management is mainly exercised by manipulating accruals. Hence, the size of accruals is often used as a proxy for earnings quality: higher total accruals relative to assets make low earnings quality more likely. However, this is not unambiguous as accruals can reflect earnings manipulation just as well as accounting estimates of future business growth:

Factor	Description
Asset turnover	This factor measures how efficiently a company uses its assets, which require capital, to produce revenue and is calculated by dividing sales by total assets; higher turnover is better.
Asset turnover 12 month change	This factor measures a change in management's efficiency in using assets to produce revenue over the last year. Stocks with the highest level of efficiency improvements are typically expected to outperform.
Current Ratio	The current ratio is a liquidity metric that measures a company's ability to pay short-term obligations. It compares a company's current assets to its current liabilities, and a higher current ratio is better from a quality perspective.
Interest coverage	This factor measures how easily a company will be able to pay interest on its debt. It is calculated by dividing a company's EBIT (Earnings before interest and taxes) by its interest expense. A higher ratio is desirable.
Leverage	A firm with significantly more debt than equity is considered to be highly leveraged. The debt-to-equity ratio is typically inversely related to prospects, with lower leverage being better.
Payout ratio	The amount of earnings paid out in dividends to shareholders. Stocks with higher payout ratios were allocated to the top decile while those with lower payout ratios to the bottom decile.
Return on equity (ROE)	Ranks stocks based on their historical return on equity and allocates those with the highest ROE to the top decile.

How to transform data into factors

Based on a conceptual understanding of key factor categories, their rationale and popular metrics, a key task is to identify new factors that may better capture the risks embodied by the return drivers laid out previously, or to find new ones. In either case, it will be important to compare the performance of innovative factors to that of known factors to identify incremental signal gains.

Useful pandas and NumPy methods

NumPy and pandas are the key tools for custom factor computations. The Notebook `00-data-prep.ipynb` in the data directory contains examples of how to create various factors. The notebook uses data generated by the `get_data.py` script in the data folder in the root directory of the GitHub repo and stored in HDF5 format for faster access. See the notebook `storage_benchmarks.ipynb` in the directory for Chapter 2, *Market and Fundamental Data*, on the GitHub repo for a comparison of `parquet`, HDF5, and `csv` storage formats for pandas `DataFrames`.

The following illustrates some key steps in computing selected factors from raw stock data. See the Notebook for additional detail and visualizations that we have omitted here to save some space.

Loading the data

We load the Quandl stock price datasets covering the US equity markets 2000-18 using `pd.IndexSlice` to perform a slice operation on the `pd.MultiIndex`, select the adjusted close price and unpivot the column to convert the DataFrame to wide format with tickers in the columns and timestamps in the rows:

```
idx = pd.IndexSlice
with pd.HDFStore('../../data/assets.h5') as store:
    prices = store['quandl/wiki/prices'].loc[idx['2000':'2018', :],
                    'adj_close'].unstack('ticker')

prices.info()
DatetimeIndex: 4706 entries, 2000-01-03 to 2018-03-27
Columns: 3199 entries, A to ZUMZ
```

Resampling from daily to monthly frequency

To reduce training time and experiment with strategies for longer time horizons, we convert the business-daily data to month-end frequency using the available adjusted close price:

```
monthly_prices = prices.resample('M').last()
```

Computing momentum factors

To capture time series dynamics that capture, for example, momentum patterns, we compute historical returns using the `pct_change(n_periods)`, that is, returns over various monthly periods as identified by `lags`. We then convert the wide result back to long format using `.stack()`, use `.pipe()` to apply the `.clip()` method to the resulting `DataFrame` and winsorize returns at the [1%, 99%] levels; that is, we cap outliers at these percentiles.

Finally, we normalize returns using the geometric average. After using `.swaplevel()` to change the order of the `MultiIndex` levels, we obtain compounded monthly returns for six periods ranging from 1 to 12 months:

```
outlier_cutoff = 0.01
data = pd.DataFrame()
lags = [1, 2, 3, 6, 9, 12]
for lag in lags:
    data[f'return_{lag}m'] = (monthly_prices
                              .pct_change(lag)
                              .stack()
                              .pipe(lambda x:
x.clip(lower=x.quantile(outlier_cutoff),
                         upper=x.quantile(1-outlier_cutoff)))
                              .add(1)
                              .pow(1/lag)
                              .sub(1)
                              )
data = data.swaplevel().dropna()
data.info()

MultiIndex: 521806 entries, (A, 2001-01-31 00:00:00) to (ZUMZ, 2018-03-
                   31 00:00:00)
Data columns (total 6 columns):
return_1m 521806 non-null float64
return_2m 521806 non-null float64
return_3m 521806 non-null float64
return_6m 521806 non-null float64
return_9m 521806 non-null float64
return_12m 521806 non-null float6
```

We can use these results to compute momentum factors based on the difference between returns over longer periods and the most recent monthly return, as well as for the difference between 3 and 12 month returns as follows:

```
for lag in [2,3,6,9,12]:
    data[f'momentum_{lag}'] = data[f'return_{lag}m'].sub(data.return_1m)
data[f'momentum_3_12'] = data[f'return_12m'].sub(data.return_3m)
```

Using lagged returns and different holding periods

To use lagged values as input variables or features associated with the current observations, we use the `.shift()` method to move historical returns up to the current period:

```
for t in range(1, 7):
    data[f'return_1m_t-{t}'] =
data.groupby(level='ticker').return_1m.shift(t)
```

Similarly, to compute returns for various holding periods, we use the normalized period returns computed previously and shift them back to align them with the current financial features:

```
for t in [1,2,3,6,12]:
    data[f'target_{t}m'] =
data.groupby(level='ticker')[f'return_{t}m'].shift(-t)
```

Compute factor betas

We will introduce the Fama—French data to estimate the exposure of assets to common risk factors using linear regression in `Chapter 8`, *Time Series Models*. The five Fama—French factors, namely market risk, size, value, operating profitability, and investment have been shown empirically to explain asset returns and are commonly used to assess the risk/return profile of portfolios. Hence, it is natural to include past factor exposures as financial features in models that aim to predict future returns.

We can access the historical factor returns using the pandas-datareader and estimate historical exposures using the `PandasRollingOLS` rolling linear regression functionality in the `pyfinance` library as follows:

```
factors = ['Mkt-RF', 'SMB', 'HML', 'RMW', 'CMA']
factor_data = web.DataReader('F-F_Research_Data_5_Factors_2x3',
            'famafrench', start='2000')[0].drop('RF', axis=1)
factor_data.index = factor_data.index.to_timestamp()
factor_data = factor_data.resample('M').last().div(100)
factor_data.index.name = 'date'
```

```
factor_data = factor_data.join(data['return_1m']).sort_index()

T = 24
betas = (factor_data
          .groupby(level='ticker', group_keys=False)
          .apply(lambda x: PandasRollingOLS(window=min(T, x.shape[0]-1),
y=x.return_1m, x=x.drop('return_1m', axis=1)).beta))
```

We will explore both the Fama—French factor model and linear regression in `Chapter 7`, *Linear Models* in more detail. See the notebook for additional examples.

Built-in Quantopian factors

The accompanying notebook `factor_library.ipynb` contains numerous example factors that are either provided by the Quantopian platform or computed from data sources available using the research API from a Jupyter Notebook.

There are built-in factors that can be used, in combination with quantitative Python libraries, in particular `numpy` and `pandas`, to derive more complex factors from a broad range of relevant data sources such as US Equity prices, Morningstar fundamentals, and investor sentiment.

For instance, the price-to-sales ratio, the inverse of the sales yield introduce preceding, is available as part of the Morningstar fundamentals dataset. It can be used as part of a pipeline that is further described as we introduce the `zipline` library.

TA-Lib

The TA-Lib library includes numerous technical factors. A Python implementation is available for local use, for example, with `zipline` and `alphalens`, and it is also available on the Quantopian platform. The notebook also illustrates several technical indicators available using TA-Lib.

Seeking signals – how to use zipline

Historically, alpha factors used a single input and simple heuristics, thresholds or quantile cutoffs to identify buy or sell signals. ML has proven quite effective in extracting signals from a more diverse and much larger set of input data, including other alpha factors based on the analysis of historical patterns. As a result, algorithmic trading strategies today leverage a large number of alpha signals, many of which may be weak individually but can yield reliable predictions when combined with other model-driven or traditional factors by an ML algorithm.

The open source `zipline` library is an event-driven backtesting system maintained and used in production by the crowd-sourced quantitative investment fund Quantopian (`https://www.quantopian.com/`) to facilitate algorithm-development and live-trading. It automates the algorithm's reaction to trade events and provides it with current and historical point-in-time data that avoids look-ahead bias.

You can use it offline in conjunction with data bundles to research and evaluate alpha factors. When using it on the Quantopian platform, you will get access to a wider set of fundamental and alternative data. We will also demonstrate the Quantopian research environment in this chapter, and the backtesting IDE in the next chapter. The code for this section is in the `01_factor_research_evaluation` sub-directory of the GitHub repo folder for this chapter.

After installation and before executing the first algorithm, you need to ingest a data bundle that by default consists of Quandl's community-maintained data on stock prices, dividends and splits for 3,000 US publicly-traded companies. You need a Quandl API key to run the following code that stores the data in your home folder under `~/.zipline/data/<bundle>`:

```
$ QUANDL_API_KEY=<yourkey> zipline ingest [-b <bundle>]
```

The architecture – event-driven trading simulation

A `zipline` algorithm will run for a specified period after an initial setup and executes its trading logic when specific events occur. These events are driven by the trading frequency and can also be scheduled by the algorithm, and result in `zipline` calling certain methods. The algorithm maintains state through a `context` dictionary and receives actionable information through a `data` variable containing **point-in-time** (**PIT**) current and historical data. The algorithm returns a `DataFrame` containing portfolio performance metrics if there were any trades, as well as user-defined metrics that can be used to record, for example, the factor values.

You can execute an algorithm from the command line, in a Jupyter Notebook, and by using the `run_algorithm()` function.

An algorithm requires an `initialize()` method that is called once when the simulation starts. This method can be used to add properties to the `context` dictionary that is available to all other algorithm methods or register `pipelines` that perform more complex data processing, such as filtering securities based, for example, on the logic of alpha factors.

Algorithm execution occurs through optional methods that are either scheduled automatically by `zipline` or at user-defined intervals. The method `before_trading_start()` is called daily before the market opens and serves primarily to identify a set of securities the algorithm may trade during the day. The method `handle_data()` is called every minute.

The `Pipeline API` facilitates the definition and computation of alpha factors for a cross-section of securities from historical data. A pipeline defines computations that produce columns in a table with PIT values for a set of securities. It needs to be registered with the `initialize()` method and can then be executed on an automatic or custom schedule. The library provides numerous built-in computations such as moving averages or Bollinger Bands that can be used to quickly compute standard factors but also allows for the creation of custom factors as we will illustrate next.

Most importantly, the `Pipeline API` renders alpha factor research modular because it separates the alpha factor computation from the remainder of the algorithm, including the placement and execution of trade orders and the bookkeeping of portfolio holdings, values, and so on.

A single alpha factor from market data

We are first going to illustrate the `zipline` alpha factor research workflow in an offline environment. In particular, we will develop and test a simple mean-reversion factor that measures how much recent performance has deviated from the historical average. Short-term reversal is a common strategy that takes advantage of the weakly predictive pattern that stock price increases are likely to mean-revert back down over horizons from less than a minute to one month. See the Notebook `single_factor_zipline.ipynby` for details.

To this end, the factor computes the z-score for the last monthly return relative to the rolling monthly returns over the last year. At this point, we will not place any orders to simply illustrate the implementation of a `CustomFactor` and record the results during the simulation.

After some basic settings, `MeanReversion` subclasses `CustomFactor` and defines a `compute()` method. It creates default inputs of monthly returns over an also default year-long window so that the `monthly_return` variable will have 252 rows and one column for each security in the Quandl dataset on a given day.

The `compute_factors()` method creates a `MeanReversion` factor instance and creates `long`, `short`, and `ranking` pipeline columns. The former two contain Boolean values that could be used to place orders, and the latter reflects that overall ranking to evaluate the overall factor performance. Furthermore, it uses the built-in `AverageDollarVolume` factor to limit the computation to more liquid stocks:

```
from zipline.api import attach_pipeline, pipeline_output, record
from zipline.pipeline import Pipeline, CustomFactor
from zipline.pipeline.factors import Returns, AverageDollarVolume
from zipline import run_algorithm

MONTH, YEAR = 21, 252
N_LONGS = N_SHORTS = 25
VOL_SCREEN = 1000

class MeanReversion(CustomFactor):
    """Compute ratio of latest monthly return to 12m average,
       normalized by std dev of monthly returns"""
    inputs = [Returns(window_length=MONTH)]
    window_length = YEAR

    def compute(self, today, assets, out, monthly_returns):
        df = pd.DataFrame(monthly_returns)
        out[:] = df.iloc[-1].sub(df.mean()).div(df.std())
```

```
def compute_factors():
    """Create factor pipeline incl. mean reversion,
        filtered by 30d Dollar Volume; capture factor ranks"""
    mean_reversion = MeanReversion()
    dollar_volume = AverageDollarVolume(window_length=30)
    return Pipeline(columns={'longs'  : mean_reversion.bottom(N_LONGS),
                             'shorts' : mean_reversion.top(N_SHORTS),
                             'ranking':
                             mean_reversion.rank(ascending=False)},
                    screen=dollar_volume.top(VOL_SCREEN))
```

The result would allow us to place long and short orders. We will see in the next chapter how to build a portfolio by choosing a rebalancing period and adjusting portfolio holdings as new signals arrive.

The `initialize()` method registers the `compute_factors()` pipeline, and the `before_trading_start()` method ensures the pipeline runs on a daily basis. The `record()` function adds the pipeline's `ranking` column as well as the current asset prices to the performance `DataFrame` returned by the `run_algorithm()` function:

```
def initialize(context):
    """Setup: register pipeline, schedule rebalancing,
        and set trading params"""
    attach_pipeline(compute_factors(), 'factor_pipeline')

def before_trading_start(context, data):
    """Run factor pipeline"""
    context.factor_data = pipeline_output('factor_pipeline')
    record(factor_data=context.factor_data.ranking)
    assets = context.factor_data.index
    record(prices=data.current(assets, 'price'))
```

Finally, define the start and end `Timestamp` objects in UTC terms, set a capital base and execute `run_algorithm()` with references to the key execution methods. The `performance` DataFrame contains nested data, for example, the `prices` column consists of a `pd.Series` for each cell. Hence, subsequent data access is easier when stored in the `pickle` format:

```
start, end = pd.Timestamp('2015-01-01', tz='UTC'), pd.Timestamp('2018-
            01-01', tz='UTC')
capital_base = 1e7

performance = run_algorithm(start=start,
                            end=end,
                            initialize=initialize,
                            before_trading_start=before_trading_start,
```

```
                        capital_base=capital_base)

performance.to_pickle('single_factor.pickle')
```

We will use the factor and pricing data stored in the `performance` DataFrame to evaluate the factor performance for various holding periods in the next section, but first, we'll take a look at how to create more complex signals by combining several alpha factors from a diverse set of data sources on the Quantopian platform.

Combining factors from diverse data sources

The Quantopian research environment is tailored to the rapid testing of predictive alpha factors. The process is very similar because it builds on `zipline`, but offers much richer access to data sources. The following code sample illustrates how to compute alpha factors not only from market data as previously but also from fundamental and alternative data. See the Notebook `multiple_factors_quantopian_research.ipynb` for details.

Quantopian provides several hundred MorningStar fundamental variables for free and also includes `stocktwits` signals as an example of an alternative data source. There are also custom universe definitions such as `QTradableStocksUS` that applies several filters to limit the backtest universe to stocks that were likely tradeable under realistic market conditions:

```
from quantopian.research import run_pipeline
from quantopian.pipeline import Pipeline
from quantopian.pipeline.data.builtin import USEquityPricing
from quantopian.pipeline.data.morningstar import income_statement,
    operation_ratios, balance_sheet
from quantopian.pipeline.data.psychsignal import stocktwits
from quantopian.pipeline.factors import CustomFactor,
    SimpleMovingAverage, Returns
from quantopian.pipeline.filters import QTradableStocksUS
```

We will use a custom `AggregateFundamentals` class to use the last reported fundamental data point. This aims to address the fact that fundamentals are reported quarterly, and Quantopian does not currently provide an easy way to aggregate historical data, say to obtain the sum of the last four quarters, on a rolling basis:

```
class AggregateFundamentals(CustomFactor):
    def compute(self, today, assets, out, inputs):
        out[:] = inputs[0]
```

We will again use the custom `MeanReversion` factor from the preceding code. We will also compute several other factors for the given universe definition using the `rank()` method's `mask` parameter:

```
def compute_factors():
    universe = QTradableStocksUS()

    profitability = (AggregateFundamentals(inputs=
                        [income_statement.gross_profit],
                                        window_length=YEAR) /
                    balance_sheet.total_assets.latest).rank(mask=universe)

    roic = operation_ratios.roic.latest.rank(mask=universe)
    ebitda_yield = (AggregateFundamentals(inputs=
                        [income_statement.ebitda],
                                        window_length=YEAR) /
                    USEquityPricing.close.latest).rank(mask=universe)
    mean_reversion = MeanReversion().rank(mask=universe)
    price_momentum = Returns(window_length=QTR).rank(mask=universe)
    sentiment = SimpleMovingAverage(inputs=
                            [stocktwits.bull_minus_bear],
                            window_length=5).rank(mask=universe)

    factor = profitability + roic + ebitda_yield + mean_reversion +
            price_momentum + sentiment

    return Pipeline(
            columns={'Profitability'      : profitability,
                    'ROIC'                : roic,
                    'EBITDA Yield'        : ebitda_yield,
                    "Mean Reversion (1M)": mean_reversion,
                    'Sentiment'           : sentiment,
                    "Price Momentum (3M)": price_momentum,
                    'Alpha Factor'        : factor})
```

This algorithm uses a naive method to combine the six individual factors by simply adding the ranks of assets for each of these factors. Instead of equal weights, we would like to take into account the relative importance and incremental information in predicting future returns. The ML algorithms of the next chapters will allow us to do exactly this, using the same backtesting framework.

Execution also relies on `run_algorithm()`, but the return `DataFrame` on the Quantopian platform only contains the factor values created by the `Pipeline`. This is convenient because this data format can be used as input for `alphalens`, the library for the evaluation of the predictive performance of alpha factors.

Separating signal and noise – how to use alphalens

Quantopian has open sourced the Python library, `alphalens`, for the performance analysis of predictive stock factors that integrates well with the backtesting library `zipline` and the portfolio performance and risk analysis library `pyfolio` that we will explore in the next chapter.

`alphalens` facilitates the analysis of the predictive power of alpha factors concerning the:

- Correlation of the signals with subsequent returns
- Profitability of an equal or factor-weighted portfolio based on a (subset of) the signals
- Turnover of factors to indicate the potential trading costs
- Factor-performance during specific events
- Breakdowns of the preceding by sector

The analysis can be conducted using tearsheets or individual computations and plots. The tearsheets are illustrated in the online repo to save some space.

Creating forward returns and factor quantiles

To utilize `alphalens`, we need to provide signals for a universe of assets like those returned by the ranks of the `MeanReversion` factor, and the forward returns earned by investing in an asset for a given holding period. See Notebook `03_performance_eval_alphalens.ipynb` for details.

We will recover the `prices` from the `single_factor.pickle` file as follows (`factor_data` accordingly):

```
performance = pd.read_pickle('single_factor.pickle')

prices = pd.concat([df.to_frame(d) for d, df in
performance.prices.items()],axis=1).T
prices.columns = [re.findall(r"\[(.+)\]", str(col))[0] for col in
                  prices.columns]
prices.index = prices.index.normalize()
prices.info()

<class 'pandas.core.frame.DataFrame'>
DatetimeIndex: 755 entries, 2015-01-02 to 2017-12-29
```

```
Columns: 1661 entries, A to ZTS
dtypes: float64(1661)
```

The GitHub repository's `alpha factor evaluation` Notebook has more detail on how to conduct the evaluation in a sector-specific way.

We can create the `alphalens` input data in the required format using the `get_clean_factor_and_forward_returns` utility function that also returns the signal quartiles and the forward returns for the given holding periods:

```
HOLDING_PERIODS = (5, 10, 21, 42)
QUANTILES = 5
alphalens_data = get_clean_factor_and_forward_returns(factor=factor_data,
                                                      prices=prices,
                                                      periods=HOLDING_PERIODS,
                                                      quantiles=QUANTILES)
```

```
Dropped 14.5% entries from factor data: 14.5% in forward returns
computation and 0.0% in binning phase (set max_loss=0 to see potentially
suppressed Exceptions). max_loss is 35.0%, not exceeded: OK!
```

The `alphalens_data` DataFrame contains the returns on an investment in the given asset on a given date for the indicated holding period, as well as the factor value, that is, the asset's `MeanReversion` ranking on that date, and the corresponding quantile value:

date	asset	5D	10D	21D	42D	factor	factor_quantile
01/02/15	A	0.07%	-5.70%	-2.32%	4.09%	2618	4
	AAL	-3.51%	-7.61%	-11.89%	-10.23%	1088	2
	AAP	1.10%	-5.40%	-0.94%	-3.81%	791	1
	AAPL	2.45%	-3.05%	8.52%	15.62%	2917	5
	ABBV	-0.17%	-2.05%	-6.43%	-13.70%	2952	5

The forward returns and the signal quantiles are the basis for evaluating the predictive power of the signal. Typically, a factor should deliver markedly different returns for distinct quantiles, such as negative returns for the bottom quintile of the factor values and positive returns for the top quantile.

Predictive performance by factor quantiles

As a first step, we would like to visualize the average period return by factor quantile. We can use the built-in function `mean_return_by_quantile` from the `performance` and `plot_quantile_returns_bar` from the `plotting` modules:

```
from alphalens.performance import mean_return_by_quantile
from alphalens.plotting import plot_quantile_returns_bar
mean_return_by_q, std_err = mean_return_by_quantile(alphalens_data)
plot_quantile_returns_bar(mean_return_by_q);
```

The result is a bar chart that breaks down the mean of the forward returns for the four different holding periods based on the quintile of the factor signal. As you can see, the bottom quintiles yielded markedly more negative results than the top quintiles, except for the longest holding period:

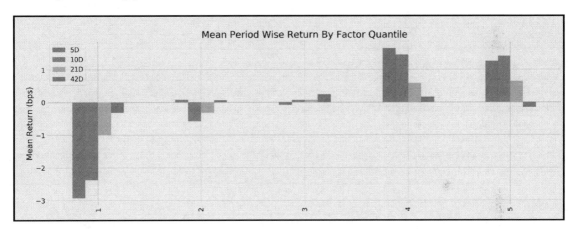

The 10D holding period provides slightly better results for the first and fourth quartiles. We would also like to see the performance over time of investments driven by each of the signal quintiles. We will calculate daily, as opposed to average returns for the 5D holding period, and `alphalens` will adjust the period returns to account for the mismatch between daily signals and a longer holding period (for details, see docs):

```
from alphalens.plotting import plot_cumulative_returns_by_quantile
mean_return_by_q_daily, std_err =
    mean_return_by_quantile(alphalens_data, by_date=True)
plot_cumulative_returns_by_quantile(mean_return_by_q_daily['5D'],
    period='5D');
```

The resulting line plot shows that, for most of this three-year period, the top two quintiles significantly outperformed the bottom two quintiles. However, as suggested by the previous plot, signals by the fourth quintile produced a better performance than those by the top quintile:

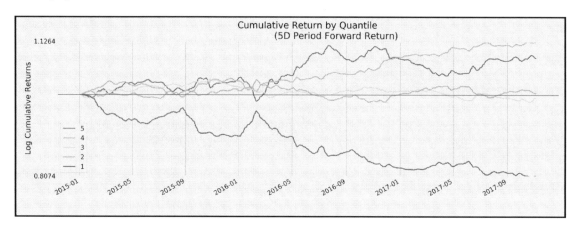

A factor that is useful for a trading strategy shows the preceding pattern where cumulative returns develop along clearly distinct paths because this allows for a long-short strategy with lower capital requirements and correspondingly lower exposure to the overall market.

However, we also need to take the dispersion of period returns into account rather than just the averages. To this end, we can rely on the built-in `plot_quantile_returns_violin`:

```
from alphalens.plotting import plot_quantile_returns_violin
plot_quantile_returns_violin(mean_return_by_q_daily);
```

This distributional plot highlights that the range of daily returns is fairly wide and, despite different means, the separation of the distributions is very limited so that, on any given day, the differences in performance between the different quintiles may be rather limited:

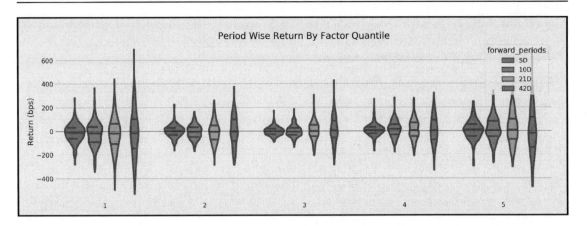

While we focus on the evaluation of a single alpha factor, we are simplifying things by ignoring practical issues related to trade execution that we will relax when we address proper backtesting in the next chapter. Some of these include:

- The transaction costs of trading
- Slippage, the difference between the price at decision and trade execution, for example, due to the market impact

The information coefficient

Most of this book is about the design of alpha factors using ML models. ML is about optimizing some predictive objective, and in this section, we will introduce the key metrics used to measure the performance of an alpha factor. We will define alpha as the average return in excess of a benchmark.

This leads to the **information ratio** (**IR**) that measures the average excess return per unit of risk taken by dividing alpha by the tracking risk. When the benchmark is the risk-free rate, the IR corresponds to the well-known Sharpe ratio, and we will highlight crucial statistical measurement issues that arise in the typical case when returns are not normally distributed. We will also explain the fundamental law of active management that breaks the IR down into a combination of forecasting skill and a strategy's ability to effectively leverage the forecasting skills.

The goal of alpha factors is the accurate directional prediction of future returns. Hence, a natural performance measure is the correlation between an alpha factor's predictions and the forward returns of the target assets.

It is better to use the non-parametric Spearman rank correlation coefficient that measures how well the relationship between two variables can be described using a monotonic function, as opposed to the Pearson correlation that measures the strength of a linear relationship.

We can obtain the information coefficient using `alphalens`, which relies on `scipy.stats.spearmanr` under the hood (see the repo for an example on how to use `scipy` directly to obtain p-values). The `factor_information_coefficient` function computes the period-wise correlation and `plot_ic_ts` creates a time-series plot with one-month moving average:

```
from alphalens.performance import factor_information_coefficient
from alphalens.plotting import plot_ic_ts
ic = factor_information_coefficient(alphalens_data)
plot_ic_ts(ic[['5D']])
```

This time series plot shows extended periods with significantly positive moving-average IC. An IC of 0.05 or even 0.1 allows for significant outperformance if there are sufficient opportunities to apply this forecasting skill, as the fundamental law of active management will illustrate:

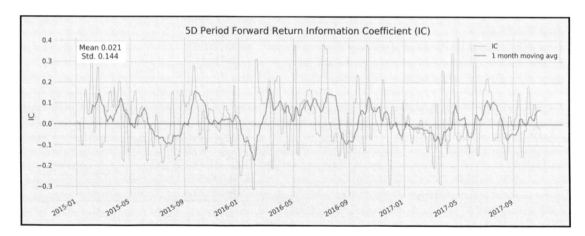

A plot of the annual mean IC highlights how the factor's performance was historically uneven:

```
ic = factor_information_coefficient(alphalens_data)
ic_by_year = ic.resample('A').mean()
ic_by_year.index = ic_by_year.index.year
ic_by_year.plot.bar(figsize=(14, 6))
```

This produces the following chart:

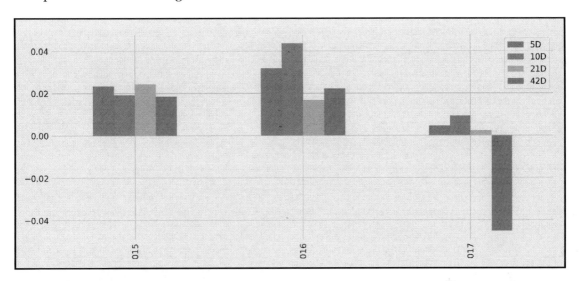

An information coefficient below 0.05 as in this case, is low but significant and can produce positive residual returns relative to a benchmark as we will see in the next section. The `create_summary_tear_sheet(alphalens_data)` creates IC summary statistics, where the risk-adjusted IC results from dividing the mean IC by the standard deviation of the IC, which is also subjected to a two-sided t-test with the null hypothesis $IC = 0$ using `scipy.stats.ttest_1samp`:

	5D	10D	21D	42D
IC Mean	0.01	0.02	0.01	0.00
IC Std.	0.14	0.13	0.12	0.12
Risk-Adjusted IC	0.10	0.13	0.10	0.01
t-stat(IC)	2.68	3.53	2.53	0.14
p-value(IC)	0.01	0.00	0.01	0.89
IC Skew	0.41	0.22	0.19	0.21
IC Kurtosis	0.18	-0.33	-0.42	-0.27

Factor turnover

Factor turnover measures how frequently the assets associated with a given quantile change, that is, how many trades are required to adjust a portfolio to the sequence of signals. More specifically, it measures the share of assets currently in a factor quantile that was not in that quantile in the last period. The following table is produced by this command:

```
create_turnover_tear_sheet(alphalens_data)
```

The share of assets that were to join a quintile-based portfolio is fairly high, suggesting that the trading costs pose a challenge to reaping the benefits from the predictive performance:

Mean Turnover	5D	10D	21D	42D
Quantile 1	59%	83%	83%	41%
Quantile 2	74%	80%	81%	65%
Quantile 3	76%	80%	81%	68%
Quantile 4	74%	81%	81%	64%
Quantile 5	57%	81%	81%	39%

An alternative view on factor turnover is the correlation of the asset rank due to the factor over various holding periods, also part of the tear sheet:

	5D	10D	21D	42D
Mean Factor Rank Autocorrelation	0.711	0.452	-0.031	-0.013

Generally, more stability is preferable to keep trading costs manageable.

Alpha factor resources

The research process requires designing and selecting alpha factors with respect to the predictive power of their signals. An algorithmic trading strategy will typically build on multiple alpha factors that send signals for each asset. These factors may be aggregated using an ML model to optimize how the various signals translate into decisions about the timing and sizing of individual positions, as we will see in subsequent chapters.

Alternative algorithmic trading libraries

Additional open-source Python libraries for algorithmic trading and data collection include (see links on GitHub):

- QuantConnect is a competitor to Quantopian
- WorldQuant offers online competition and recruits community contributors to a crowd-sourced hedge fund
- Alpha Trading Labs offers high-frequency focused testing infrastructure with a business model similar to Quantopian
- Python Algorithmic Trading Library (PyAlgoTrade) focuses on backtesting and offers support for paper-trading and live-trading. It allows you to evaluate an idea for a trading strategy with historical data and aims to do so with minimal effort.
- pybacktest is a vectorized backtesting framework that uses pandas and aims to be compact, simple and fast (the project is currently on hold)
- ultrafinance is an older project that combines real-time financial data collection, analyzing and backtesting of trading strategies
- Trading with Python offers courses and a collection of functions and classes for Quantitative trading
- Interactive Brokers offers a Python API for live trading on their platform

Summary

In this chapter, we covered the use of the `zipline` library for the event-driven simulation of a trading algorithm, both offline and on the Quantopian online platform. We have illustrated the design and evaluation of individual alpha factors to derive signals for an algorithmic trading strategy from market, fundamental, and alternative data, and demonstrated a naive way of combining multiple factors. We also introduced the `alphalens` library that permits the comprehensive evaluation of the predictive performance and trading turnover of signals.

The portfolio construction process, in turn, takes a broader perspective and aims at the optimal sizing of positions from a risk and return perspective. We will now turn to various strategies to balance risk and returns in a portfolio process. We will also look in more detail at the challenges of backtesting trading strategies on a limited set of historical data and how to address these challenges.

5
Strategy Evaluation

Alpha factors drive an algorithmic strategy that translates into trades that, in turn, produce a portfolio. The returns and risk of the resulting portfolio determine the success of the strategy. Testing a strategy requires simulating the portfolios generated by an algorithm to verify its performance under market conditions. Strategy evaluation includes backtesting against historical data to optimize the strategy's parameters, and forward-testing to validate the in-sample performance against new, out-of-sample data and avoid false discoveries from tailoring a strategy to specific past circumstances.

In a portfolio context, positive asset returns can offset negative price movements in a non-linear way so that the overall variation of portfolio returns is less than the weighted average of the variation of the portfolio positions unless their returns are perfectly and positively correlated. Harry Markowitz developed the theory behind modern portfolio management based on diversification in 1952, which gave rise to mean-variance optimization: for a given set of assets, portfolio weights can be optimized to reduce risk, measured as the standard deviation of returns for a given expected level of returns.

The **capital asset pricing model (CAPM)** introduced a risk premium as an equilibrium reward for holding an asset that compensates for the exposure to a single risk factor—the market—that cannot be diversified away. Risk management has evolved to become much more sophisticated as additional risk factors and more granular choices for exposure have emerged. The Kelly Rule is a popular approach to dynamic portfolio optimization, which is the choice of a sequence of positions over time; it has been famously adapted from its original application in gambling to the stock market by Edward Thorp in 1968.

As a result, there are several approaches to optimize portfolios that include the application of **machine learning (ML)** to learn hierarchical relationships among assets and treat their holdings as complements or substitutes with respect to the portfolio risk profile.

In this chapter, we will cover the following topics:

- How to build and test a portfolio based on alpha factors using `zipline`
- How to measure portfolio risk and return
- How to evaluate portfolio performance using `pyfolio`
- How to manage portfolio weights using mean-variance optimization and alternatives
- How to use machine learning to optimize asset allocation in a portfolio context

The code examples for this chapter are in the `05_strategy_evaluation_and_portfolio_management` directory of the companion GitHub repository.

How to build and test a portfolio with zipline

In the last chapter, we introduced `zipline` to simulate the computation of alpha factors from trailing cross-sectional market, fundamental, and alternative data. Now we will exploit the alpha factors to derive and act on buy and sell signals. We will postpone optimizing the portfolio weights until later in this chapter, and for now, just assign positions of equal value to each holding. The code for this section is in the `01_trading_zipline` subdirectory.

Scheduled trading and portfolio rebalancing

We will use the custom `MeanReversion` factor developed in the last chapter—see the implementation in `alpha_factor_zipline_with_trades.py`.

The `Pipeline` created by the `compute_factors()` method returns a table with a long and a short column for the 25 stocks with the largest negative and positive deviations of their last monthly return from its annual average, normalized by the standard deviation. It also limited the universe to the 500 stocks with the highest average trading volume over the last 30 trading days. `before_trading_start()` ensures the daily execution of the pipeline and the recording of the results, including the current prices.

The new `rebalance()` method submits trade orders to the `exec_trades()` method for the assets flagged for long and short positions by the pipeline with equal positive and negative weights. It also divests any current holdings that are no longer included in the factor signals:

```
def exec_trades(data, assets, target_percent):
    """Place orders for assets using target portfolio percentage"""
    for asset in assets:
        if data.can_trade(asset) and not get_open_orders(asset):
            order_target_percent(asset, target_percent)

def rebalance(context, data):
    """Compute long, short and obsolete holdings; place trade orders"""
    factor_data = context.factor_data
    assets = factor_data.index

    longs = assets[factor_data.longs]
    shorts = assets[factor_data.shorts]
    divest = context.portfolio.positions.keys() - longs.union(shorts)

    exec_trades(data, assets=divest, target_percent=0)
    exec_trades(data, assets=longs, target_percent=1 / N_LONGS)
    exec_trades(data, assets=shorts, target_percent=-1 / N_SHORTS)
```

The `rebalance()` method runs according to `date_rules` and `time_rules` set by the `schedule_function()` utility at the beginning of the week, right after `market_open` as stipulated by the built-in `US_EQUITIES` calendar (see docs for details on rules). You can also specify a trade commission both in relative terms and as a minimum amount. There is also an option to define slippage, which is the cost of an adverse change in price between trade decision and execution:

```
def initialize(context):
    """Setup: register pipeline, schedule rebalancing,
        and set trading params"""
    attach_pipeline(compute_factors(), 'factor_pipeline')
    schedule_function(rebalance,
                      date_rules.week_start(),
                      time_rules.market_open(),
                      calendar=calendars.US_EQUITIES)

    set_commission(us_equities=commission.PerShare(cost=0.00075,
min_trade_cost=.01))
    set_slippage(us_equities=slippage.VolumeShareSlippage(volume_limit=0.0025,
price_impact=0.01))
```

The algorithm continues to execute after calling the `run_algorithm()` function and returns the same backtest performance `DataFrame`. We will now turn to common measures of portfolio return and risk, and how to compute them using the `pyfolio` library.

How to measure performance with pyfolio

ML is about optimizing objective functions. In algorithmic trading, the objectives are the return and the risk of the overall investment portfolio, typically relative to a benchmark (which may be cash or the risk-free interest rate).

There are several metrics to evaluate these objectives. We will briefly review the most commonly-used metrics and how to compute them using the `pyfolio` library, which is also used by `zipline` and Quantopian. We will also review how to apply these metrics on Quantopian when testing an algorithmic trading strategy.

We'll use some simple notations: let R be the time series of one-period simple portfolio returns, $R=(r_1, ..., r_T)$, from dates 1 to T, and $R^f=(r^f_1, ..., r^f_T)$ be the matching time series of risk-free rates, so that $R^e=R-R^f=(r_1-r^f_1,..., r_T-r^f_T)$ is the excess return.

The Sharpe ratio

The ex-ante **Sharpe ratio (SR)** compares the portfolio's expected excess portfolio to the volatility of this excess return, measured by its standard deviation. It measures the compensation as the average excess return per unit of risk taken:

$$\mu \equiv E(R_t)$$
$$\sigma^2_{R^e} \equiv \text{Var}(R - R^f)$$
$$\text{SR} \equiv \frac{\mu - R_f}{\sigma_{R^e}}$$

Expected returns and volatilities are not observable, but can be estimated as follows using historical data:

$$\hat{\mu}_{R^e} = \frac{1}{T} \sum_{t=1}^{T} r_t^e$$

$$\hat{\sigma}_{R^e}^2 = \frac{1}{T} \sum_{t=1}^{T} (r_t^e - \hat{\mu}_{R^e})^2$$

$$\hat{SR} = \frac{\hat{\mu}_{R^e}}{\hat{\sigma}_{R_e}}$$

Unless the risk-free rate is volatile (as in emerging markets), the standard deviation of excess and raw returns will be similar. When the SR is used with a benchmark other than the risk-free rate, for example, the S&P 500, it is called the **information ratio**. In this case, it measures the excess return of the portfolio, also called **alpha**, relative to the tracking error, which is the deviation of the portfolio returns from the benchmark returns.

For **independently and identically-distributed (iid)** returns, the derivation of the distribution of the estimator of the SR for tests of statistical significance follows from the application of the Central Limit Theorem, according to large-sample statistical theory, to $\hat{\mu}$ and $\hat{\sigma}^2$.

However, financial returns often violate the iid assumptions. Andrew Lo has derived the necessary adjustments to the distribution and the time aggregation for returns that are stationary but autocorrelated returns. This is important because the time-series properties of investment strategies (for example, mean reversion, momentum, and other forms of serial correlation) can have a non-trivial impact on the SR estimator itself, especially when annualizing the SR from higher-frequency data (Lo 2002).

The fundamental law of active management

A high **Information Ratio (IR)** implies attractive out-performance relative to the additional risk taken. The Fundamental Law of Active Management breaks the IR down into the **information coefficient (IC)** as a measure of forecasting skill, and the ability to apply this skill through independent bets. It summarizes the importance to play both often (high breadth) and to play well (high IC):

$$IR = IC * \sqrt{breadth}$$

The IC measures the correlation between an alpha factor and the forward returns resulting from its signals and captures the accuracy of a manager's forecasting skills. The breadth of the strategy is measured by the independent number of bets an investor makes in a given time period, and the product of both values is proportional to the IR, also known as **appraisal risk** (Treynor and Black).

This framework has been extended to include the **transfer coefficient (TC)** to reflect portfolio constraints (for example, on short-selling) that may limit the information ratio below a level otherwise achievable given IC or strategy breadth. The TC proxies the efficiency with which the manager translates insights into portfolio bets (Clarke et al. 2002).

The fundamental law is important because it highlights the key drivers of outperformance: both accurate predictions and the ability to make independent forecasts and act on these forecasts matter. In practice, managers with a broad set of investment decisions can achieve significant risk-adjusted excess returns with information coefficients between 0.05 and 0.15 (if there is space possibly include simulation chart).

In practice, estimating the breadth of a strategy is difficult given the cross-sectional and time-series correlation among forecasts.

In and out-of-sample performance with pyfolio

Pyfolio facilitates the analysis of portfolio performance and risk in-sample and out-of-sample using many standard metrics. It produces tear sheets covering the analysis of returns, positions, and transactions, as well as event risk during periods of market stress using several built-in scenarios, and also includes Bayesian out-of-sample performance analysis.

It relies on portfolio returns and position data, and can also take into account the transaction costs and slippage losses of trading activity. The metrics are computed using the `empyrical` library that can also be used on a standalone basis.

The performance `DataFrame` produced by the `zipline` backtesting engine can be translated into the requisite `pyfolio` input.

Getting pyfolio input from alphalens

However, `pyfolio` also integrates with `alphalens` directly and permits the creation of `pyfolio` input data using `create_pyfolio_input`:

```
from alphalens.performance import create_pyfolio_input

qmin, qmax = factor_data.factor_quantile.min(),
            factor_data.factor_quantile.max()
input_data = create_pyfolio_input(alphalens_data,
                                  period='1D',
                                  capital=100000,
                                  long_short=False,
                                  equal_weight=False,
                                  quantiles=[1, 5],
                                  benchmark_period='1D')
returns, positions, benchmark = input_data
```

There are two options to specify how portfolio weights will be generated:

- `long_short`: If `False`, weights will correspond to factor values divided by their absolute value so that negative factor values generate short positions. If `True`, factor values are first demeaned so that long and short positions cancel each other out and the portfolio is market neutral.
- `equal_weight`: If `True`, and `long_short` is `True`, assets will be split into two equal-sized groups with the top/bottom half making up long/short positions.

Long-short portfolios can also be created for groups if `factor_data` includes, for example, sector info for each asset.

Getting pyfolio input from a zipline backtest

The result of a `zipline` backtest can be converted into the required `pyfolio` input using `extract_rets_pos_txn_from_zipline`:

```
returns, positions, transactions =
        extract_rets_pos_txn_from_zipline(backtest)
```

Walk-forward testing out-of-sample returns

Testing a trading strategy involves backtesting against historical data to fine-tune alpha factor parameters, as well as forward-testing against new market data to validate that the strategy performs well out of sample or if the parameters are too closely tailored to specific historical circumstances.

Pyfolio allows for the designation of an out-of-sample period to simulate walk-forward testing. There are numerous aspects to take into account when testing a strategy to obtain statistically reliable results, which we will address here.

The `plot_rolling_returns` function displays cumulative in and out-of-sample returns against a user-defined benchmark (we are using the S&P 500):

```
from pyfolio.plotting import plot_rolling_returns
plot_rolling_returns(returns=returns,
                     factor_returns=benchmark_rets,
                     live_start_date='2017-01-01',
                     cone_std=(1.0, 1.5, 2.0))
```

The plot includes a cone that shows expanding confidence intervals to indicate when out-of-sample returns appear unlikely given random-walk assumptions. Here, our strategy did not perform well against the benchmark during the simulated 2017 out-of-sample period:

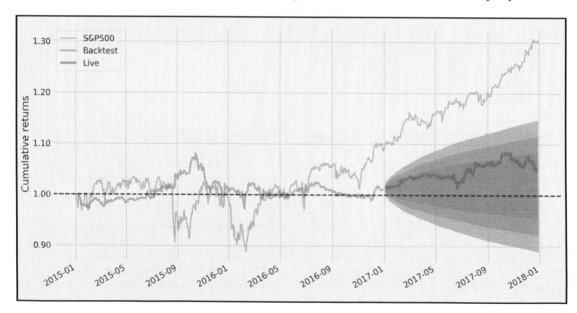

Summary performance statistics

`pyfolio` offers several analytic functions and plots. The `perf_stats` summary displays the annual and cumulative returns, volatility, skew, and kurtosis of returns and the SR. The following additional metrics (which can also be calculated individually) are most important:

- **Max drawdown**: Highest percentage loss from the previous peak
- **Calmar ratio**: Annual portfolio return relative to maximal drawdown
- **Omega ratio**: The probability-weighted ratio of gains versus losses for a return target, zero per default
- **Sortino ratio**: Excess return relative to downside standard deviation
- **Tail ratio**: Size of the right tail (gains, the absolute value of the 95th percentile) relative to the size of the left tail (losses, abs. value of the 5th percentile)
- **Daily value at risk (VaR)**: Loss corresponding to a return two standard deviations below the daily mean
- **Alpha**: Portfolio return unexplained by the benchmark return
- **Beta**: Exposure to the benchmark

```
from pyfolio.timeseries import perf_stats
perf_stats(returns=returns,
           factor_returns=benchmark_rets,
           positions=positions,
           transactions=transactions)
```

For the simulated long-short portfolio derived from the `MeanReversion` factor, we obtain the following performance statistics:

Metric	All	In-sample	Out-of-sample	Metric	All	In-sample	Out-of-sample
Annual return	1.80%	0.60%	4.20%	Skew	0.34	0.40	0.09
Cumulative returns	5.40%	1.10%	4.20%	Kurtosis	3.70	3.37	2.59
Annual volatility	5.80%	6.30%	4.60%	Tail ratio	0.91	0.88	1.03
Sharpe ratio	0.33	0.12	0.92	Daily value at risk	-0.7%	-0.8%	-0.6%
Calmar ratio	0.17	0.06	1.28	Gross leverage	0.38	0.37	0.42
Stability	0.49	0.04	0.75	Daily turnover	4.70%	4.40%	5.10%
Max drawdown	-10.10%	-10.10%	-3.30%	Alpha	0.01	0.00	0.04
Omega ratio	1.06	1.02	1.18	Beta	0.15	0.16	0.03
Sortino Ratio	0.48	0.18	1.37				

See the appendix for details on the calculation and interpretation of portfolio risk and return metrics.

Drawdown periods and factor exposure

The `plot_drawdown_periods(returns)` function plots the principal drawdown periods for the portfolio, and several other plotting functions show the rolling SR and rolling factor exposures to the market beta or the Fama French size, growth, and momentum factors:

```
fig, ax = plt.subplots(nrows=2, ncols=2, figsize=(16, 10))
axes = ax.flatten()

plot_drawdown_periods(returns=returns, ax=axes[0])
plot_rolling_beta(returns=returns, factor_returns=benchmark_rets,
                  ax=axes[1])
plot_drawdown_underwater(returns=returns, ax=axes[2])
plot_rolling_sharpe(returns=returns)
```

This plot, which highlights a subset of the visualization contained in the various tear sheets, illustrates how pyfolio allows us to drill down into the performance characteristics and exposure to fundamental drivers of risk and returns:

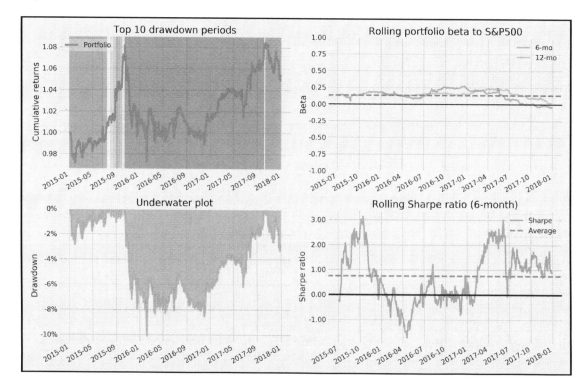

Modeling event risk

Pyfolio also includes timelines for various events that you can use to compare the performance of a portfolio to a benchmark during this period, for example, during the fall 2015 selloff following the Brexit vote:

```
interesting_times = extract_interesting_date_ranges(returns=returns)
interesting_times['Fall2015'].to_frame('pf') \
  .join(benchmark_rets) \
  .add(1).cumprod().sub(1) \
  .plot(lw=2, figsize=(14, 6), title='Post-Brexit Turmoil')
```

The resulting plot looks as follows:

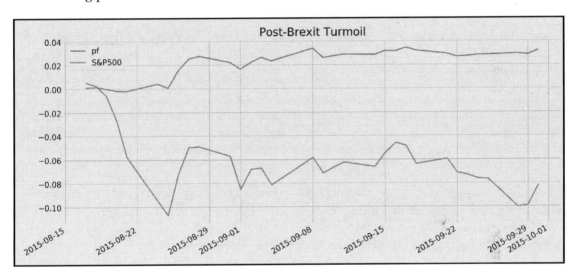

How to avoid the pitfalls of backtesting

Backtesting simulates an algorithmic strategy using historical data with the goal of identifying patterns that generalize to new market conditions. In addition to the generic challenges of predicting an uncertain future in changing markets, numerous factors make mistaking positive in-sample performance for the discovery of true patterns very likely. These factors include aspects of the data, the implementation of the strategy simulation, and flaws with the statistical tests and their interpretation. The risks of false discoveries multiply with the use of more computing power, bigger datasets, and more complex algorithms that facilitate the identification of apparent patterns in the noise.

We will list the most serious and common methodological mistakes and refer to the literature on multiple testing for further detail. We will also introduce the deflated SR that illustrates how to adjust metrics that result from repeated trials when using the same set of financial data for your analysis.

Data challenges

Challenges to the backtest validity due to data issues include look-ahead bias, survivorship bias, and outlier control.

Look-ahead bias

Tests of trading rules derived from past data will yield biased results when the sample data used to develop the rules contains information that was not, in fact, available or known at the point in time the data refers to.

A typical source of this bias is the failure to account for the common ex-post corrections of reported financials. Stock splits or reverse splits can also generate look-ahead bias. When computing the earnings yield, earnings-per-share data comes from company financials with low frequency, while market prices are available at least daily. Hence, both EPS and price data need to be adjusted for splits at the same time.

The solution lies in the careful analysis of the timestamps associated with all data that enters a backtest to ensure that only point-in-time data is used. High-quality data providers, such as Compustat, ensure that these criteria are met. When point-in-time data is not available, assumptions about the lag in reporting needs to be made.

Survivorship bias

Survivorship bias emerges when a backtest is conducted on data that only contains currently active securities and omits assets that have disappeared over time, for example, due to bankruptcy, delisting, or acquisition. Securities that are no longer part of the investment universe often did not perform well, and including these cases can positively skew the backtest result.

The solution, naturally, is to verify that datasets include all securities available over time as opposed to only those that are still available when running the test.

Outlier control

Data preparation before analysis typically includes treatment of outliers, example, by winsorizing, or clipping, extreme values. The challenge is to identify outliers that are truly not representative of the period under analysis, as opposed to extreme values that are an integral part of the market environment at that time. Many market models assume normally-distributed data when extreme values are observed more frequently, as suggested by fat-tailed distributions.

The solution involves careful analysis of outliers with respect to the probability of extreme values occurring and adjusting the strategy parameters to this reality.

Unrepresentative period

A backtest will not yield a representative result that generalizes to future periods if the time period used does not reflect the current environment well, lacks relevant market regime aspects, and does not include enough data points or captures extreme historical events that are unlikely to repeat.

The solution involves using sample periods that include important market phenomena, or generate synthetic data that reflect relevant market characteristics (see the *Resources* section for guidance on implementation).

Implementation issues

Practical issues related to the implementation of the historical simulation include failure to mark to market, i.e. accurately reflect underlying market prices and account for drawdowns, unrealistic assumptions about the availability, cost, or market impact of trades, or the timing of signals and trade execution.

Mark-to-market performance

This strategy may perform well over the course of the backtest but lead to unacceptable losses or volatility over time.

The solution involves plotting performance over time or calculating (rolling) risk metrics, such as **value at risk (VaR)** or the Sortino Ratio (see appendix for details).

Trading costs

This strategy may assume short sales that require a counter-party, hold less liquid assets that may move the market when traded or underestimate the costs that arise due to broker fees or slippage, which is the difference between the market price at the decision to trade and subsequent execution.

The solution includes a limitation to a highly liquid universe and realistic parameter assumptions for trading and slippage costs (as illustrated in the preceding `zipline` example). This also safeguards against the inclusion of unstable factor signals with a high decay and, hence, turnover.

Timing of trades

The simulation could make unrealistic assumptions about the timing of the evaluation of the alpha factor signals and the resulting trades. For instance, signals may be evaluated at close prices when the next trade is only available at the often-quite-different open prices. As a consequence, the backtest will be significantly biased when the close price is used to evaluate trading performance.

The solution involves careful orchestration of the sequence of signal arrival, trade execution, and performance evaluation.

Data-snooping and backtest-overfitting

The most prominent challenge to backtest validity, including to published results, relates to the discovery of spurious patterns due to multiple testing during the strategy-selection process. Selecting a strategy after testing different candidates on the same data will likely bias the choice because a positive outcome is more likely to be due to the stochastic nature of the performance measure itself. In other words, the strategy is overly tailored, or overfit, to the data at hand and produces deceptively positive results.

Hence, backtest performance is not informative unless the number of trials is reported to allow for an assessment of the risk of selection bias. This is rarely the case in practical or academic research, inviting doubts about the validity of many published claims.

The risk of overfitting a backtest to a particular dataset does not only arise from directly running numerous tests but includes strategies designed based on prior knowledge of what works and doesn't, that is, knowledge of different backtests run by others on the same data. As a result, backtest-overfitting is hard to avoid in practice.

Solutions include selecting tests to undertake based on investment or economic theory rather than broad data-mining efforts. It also implies testing in a variety of contexts and scenarios, including possibly on synthetic data.

The minimum backtest length and the deflated SR

Marcos Lopez de Prado (http://www.quantresearch.info/) has published extensively on the risks of backtesting, and how to detect or avoid it. This includes an online simulator of backtest-overfitting (http://datagrid.lbl.gov/backtest/).

Another result includes an estimate of the minimum length of the backtest that an investor should require given the number of trials attempted, to avoid selecting a strategy with a given in-sample SR during a given number of trials that has an expected out-of-sample SR of zero. This implies that, e.g., if only two years of daily backtest data is available no more than seven strategy variations should be tried, and if only five years of daily backtest data is available, no more than 45 strategy variations should be tried. See references for implementation details.

De Lopez Prado and Bailey (2014) also derive a deflated SR to compute the probability that the SR is statistically significant while controlling for the inflationary effect of multiple testing, non-normal returns, and shorter sample lengths (see the 03_multiple_testing subdirectory for the Python implementation of deflated_sharpe_ratio.py and references for the derivation of the related formulas).

Optimal stopping for backtests

In addition to limiting backtests to strategies that can be justified on theoretical grounds as opposed to as mere data-mining exercises, an important question is when to stop running additional tests.

Based on the solution to the *secretary problem* from optimal stopping theory, the recommendation is to decide according to the following rule of thumb: test a random sample of 1/e (roughly 37%) of reasonable strategies and record their performance. Then, continue tests until a strategy outperforms those tested before.

This rule applies to tests of several alternatives with the goal to choose a near-best as soon as possible while minimizing the risk of a false positive.

How to manage portfolio risk and return

Portfolio management aims to take positions in financial instruments that achieve the desired risk-return trade-off regarding a benchmark. In each period, a manager selects positions that optimize diversification to reduce risks while achieving a target return. Across periods, the positions will be rebalanced to account for changes in weights resulting from price movements to achieve or maintain a target risk profile.

Diversification permits us to reduce risks for a given expected return by exploiting how price movements interact with each other as one asset's gains can make up for another asset's losses. Harry Markowitz invented **Modern Portfolio Theory (MPT)** in 1952 and provided the mathematical tools to optimize diversification by choosing appropriate portfolio weights. Markowitz showed how portfolio risk, measured as the standard deviation of portfolio returns, depends on the covariance among the returns of all assets and their relative weights. This relationship implies the existence of an efficient frontier of portfolios that maximize portfolio returns given a maximal level of portfolio risk.

However, mean-variance frontiers are highly sensitive to the estimates of the input required for their calculation, such as expected returns, volatilities, and correlations. In practice, mean-variance portfolios that constrain these input to reduce sampling errors have performed much better. These constrained special cases include equal-weighted, minimum-variance, and risk-parity portfolios.

The Capital Asset Pricing Model (CAPM) is an asset valuation model that builds on the MPT risk-return relationship. It introduces the concept of a risk premium that an investor can expect in market equilibrium for holding a risky asset; the premium compensates for the time value of money and the exposure to overall market risk that cannot be eliminated through diversification (as opposed to the idiosyncratic risk of specific assets). The economic rationale for non-diversifiable risk is, for example, macro drivers of the business risks affecting equity returns or bond defaults. Hence, an asset's expected return, $E[r_i]$, is the sum of the risk-free interest rate, r_f, and a risk premium proportional to the asset's exposure to the expected excess return of the market portfolio, r_m, over the risk-free rate:

$$E[r_i] = \alpha_i + r_f + \beta_i \left(E[r_m] - r_f \right)$$

In theory, the market portfolio contains all investable assets and will be held by all rational investors in equilibrium. In practice, a broad value-weighted index approximates the market, for example, the S&P 500 for US equity investments. β_i measures the exposure to the excess returns of the market portfolio. If the CAPM is valid, the intercept component, α_i, should be zero. In reality, the CAPM assumptions are often not met, and alpha captures the returns left unexplained by exposure to the broad market.

Over time, research uncovered non-traditional sources of risk premiums, such as the momentum or the equity value effects that explained some of the original alpha. Economic rationales, such as behavioral biases of under or overreaction by investors to new information justify risk premiums for exposure to these alternative risk factors. They evolved into investment styles designed to capture these alternative betas that also became tradable in the form of specialized index funds. After isolating contributions from these alternative risk premiums, true alpha becomes limited to idiosyncratic asset returns and the manager's ability to time risk exposures.

The EMH has been refined over the past several decades to rectify many of the original shortcomings of the CAPM, including imperfect information and the costs associated with transactions, financing, and agency. Many behavioral biases have the same effect, and some frictions are modeled as behavioral biases.

ML plays an important role in deriving new alpha factors using supervised and unsupervised learning techniques based on the market, fundamental, and alternative data sources discussed in the previous chapters. The inputs to a machine learning model consist of both raw data and features engineered to capture informative signals. ML models are also used to combine individual predictive signals and deliver higher-aggregate predictive power.

Modern portfolio theory and practice have evolved significantly over the last several decades. We will introduce:

- Mean-variance optimization, and its shortcomings
- Alternatives such as minimum-risk and 1/n allocation
- Risk parity approaches
- Risk factor approaches

Mean-variance optimization

MPT solves for the optimal portfolio weights to minimize volatility for a given expected return, or maximize returns for a given level of volatility. The key requisite input are expected asset returns, standard deviations, and the covariance matrix.

How it works

Diversification works because the variance of portfolio returns depends on the covariance of the assets and can be reduced below the weighted average of the asset variances by including assets with less than perfect correlation. In particular, given a vector, ω, of portfolio weights and the covariance matrix, Σ, the portfolio variance, σ_{PF}, is defined as:

$$\sigma_{PF} = \omega^T \Sigma \omega$$

Markowitz showed that the problem of maximizing the expected portfolio return subject to a target risk has an equivalent dual representation of minimizing portfolio risk subject to a target expected return level, μ_{PF}. Hence, the optimization problem becomes:

$$\min_{\omega} \quad \sigma^2_{PF} = \omega^T \Sigma \omega$$
$$\text{s.t.} \quad \mu_{PF} = \omega^T \mu$$
$$\|\omega\| = 1$$

The efficient frontier in Python

We can calculate an efficient frontier using `scipy.optimize.minimize` and the historical estimates for asset returns, standard deviations, and the covariance matrix. The code can be found in the `efficient_frontier` subfolder of the repo for this chapter and implements the following sequence of steps:

1. The simulation generates random weights using the Dirichlet distribution, and computes the mean, standard deviation, and SR for each sample portfolio using the historical return data:

```
def simulate_portfolios(mean_ret, cov, rf_rate=rf_rate,
short=True):
    alpha = np.full(shape=n_assets, fill_value=.01)
    weights = dirichlet(alpha=alpha, size=NUM_PF)
    weights *= choice([-1, 1], size=weights.shape)

    returns = weights @ mean_ret.values + 1
    returns = returns ** periods_per_year - 1
    std = (weights @ monthly_returns.T).std(1)
    std *= np.sqrt(periods_per_year)
    sharpe = (returns - rf_rate) / std

    return pd.DataFrame({'Annualized Standard Deviation': std,
```

```
                         'Annualized Returns': returns,
                         'Sharpe Ratio': sharpe}), weights
```

2. Set up the quadratic optimization problem to solve for the minimum standard deviation for a given return or the maximum SR. To this end, define the functions that measure the key metrics:

```python
def portfolio_std(wt, rt=None, cov=None):
    """Annualized PF standard deviation"""
    return np.sqrt(wt @ cov @ wt * periods_per_year)

def portfolio_returns(wt, rt=None, cov=None):
    """Annualized PF returns"""
    return (wt @ rt + 1) ** periods_per_year - 1

def portfolio_performance(wt, rt, cov):
    """Annualized PF returns & standard deviation"""
    r = portfolio_returns(wt, rt=rt)
    sd = portfolio_std(wt, cov=cov)
    return r, sd
```

3. Define a target function that represents the negative SR for scipy's minimize function to optimize given the constraints that the weights are bounded by, [-1, 1], and sum to one in absolute terms:

```python
def neg_sharpe_ratio(weights, mean_ret, cov):
    r, sd = portfolio_performance(weights, mean_ret, cov)
    return -(r - rf_rate) / sd

weight_constraint = {'type': 'eq',
                     'fun': lambda x: np.sum(np.abs(x)) - 1}

def max_sharpe_ratio(mean_ret, cov, short=True):
    return minimize(fun=neg_sharpe_ratio,
                    x0=x0,
                    args=(mean_ret, cov),
                    method='SLSQP',
                    bounds=((-1 if short else 0, 1),) * n_assets,
                    constraints=weight_constraint,
                    options={'tol':1e-10, 'maxiter':1e4})
```

4. Compute the efficient frontier by iterating over a range of target returns and solving for the corresponding minimum variance portfolios. The optimization problem and the constraints on portfolio risk and return as a function of the weights can be formulated as follows:

```python
def neg_sharpe_ratio(weights, mean_ret, cov):
```

```
      r, sd = pf_performance(weights, mean_ret, cov)
      return -(r - RF_RATE) / sd

  def pf_volatility(w, r, c):
      return pf_performance(w, r, c)[1]

  def efficient_return(mean_ret, cov, target):
      args = (mean_ret, cov)
      def ret_(weights):
          return pf_ret(weights, mean_ret)

      constraints = [{'type': 'eq', 'fun': lambda x: ret_(x) -
                          target},
                      {'type': 'eq', 'fun': lambda x: np.sum(x) - 1}]
      bounds = ((0.0, 1.0),) * n_assets
      return minimize(pf_volatility,
                      x0=x0,
                      args=args, method='SLSQP',
                      bounds=bounds,
                      constraints=constraints)
```

5. The solution requires iterating over ranges of acceptable values to identify optimal risk-return combinations:

```
  def min_vol_target(mean_ret, cov, target, short=True):

      def ret_(wt):
          return portfolio_returns(wt, mean_ret)

      constraints = [{'type': 'eq', 'fun': lambda x: ret_(x) -
  target},
                      weight_constraint]

      bounds = ((-1 if short else 0, 1),) * n_assets
      return minimize(portfolio_std, x0=x0, args=(mean_ret, cov),
                      method='SLSQP', bounds=bounds,
                      constraints=constraints,
                      options={'tol': 1e-10, 'maxiter': 1e4})

  def efficient_frontier(mean_ret, cov, ret_range):
      return [min_vol_target(mean_ret, cov, ret) for ret in
  ret_range]
```

The simulation yields a subset of the feasible portfolios, and the efficient frontier identifies the optimal in-sample return-risk combinations that were achievable given historic data. The below figure shows the result including the minimum variance portfolio and the portfolio that maximizes the SR and several portfolios produce by alternative optimization strategies that we discuss in the following sections.

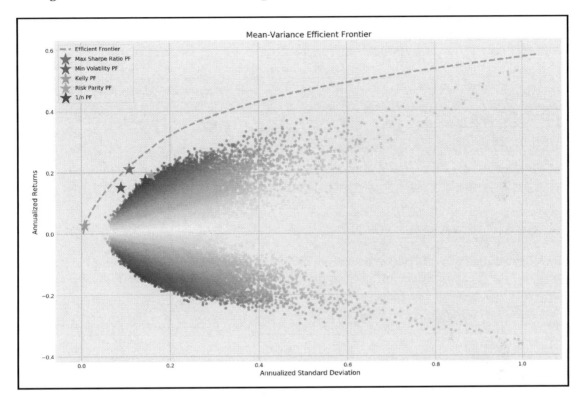

The portfolio optimization can be run at every evaluation step of the trading strategy to optimize the positions.

Challenges and shortcomings

The preceding mean-variance frontier example illustrates the in-sample, backward-looking optimization. In practice, portfolio optimization requires forward-looking input. Expected returns are notoriously difficult to estimate accurately.

The covariance matrix can be estimated somewhat more reliably, which has given rise to several alternative approaches. However, covariance matrices with correlated assets pose computational challenges since the optimization problem requires inverting the matrix. The high condition number induces numerical instability, which in turn gives rise to Markovitz curse: the more diversification is required (by correlated investment opportunities), the more unreliable the weights produced by the algorithm.

Many investors prefer to use portfolio-optimization techniques with less onerous input requirements. We now introduce several alternatives that aim to address these shortcomings, including more recent approaches based on machine learning.

Alternatives to mean-variance optimization

The challenges with accurate input for the mean-variance optimization problem have led to the adoption of several practical alternatives that constrain the mean, the variance, or both, or omit return estimates that are more challenging, such as the risk parity approach.

The 1/n portfolio

Simple portfolios provide useful benchmarks to gauge the added value of complex models that generate the risk of overfitting. The simplest strategy—an equally-weighted portfolio—has been shown to be one of the best performers.

Famously, de Miguel, Garlappi, and Uppal (2009) compared the out-of-sample performance of portfolios produced by various mean-variance optimizers, including robust Bayesian estimators, portfolio constraints, and optimal combinations of portfolios, to the simple 1/N rule. They found that the 1/N portfolio produced a higher Sharpe ratio than each asset class position, explained by the high cost of estimation errors that often outweighs the benefits of sophisticated optimization out-of-sample.

The 1/n portfolio is also included in the efficient frontier figure above.

The minimum-variance portfolio

Another alternative is the **global minimum variance (GMV)** portfolio, which prioritizes the minimization of risk. It is shown in the efficient frontier figure and can be calculated as follows by minimizing the portfolio standard deviation using the mean-variance framework:

```
def min_vol(mean_ret, cov, short=True):
    return minimize(fun=portfolio_std,
                    x0=x0,
                    args=(mean_ret, cov),
                    method='SLSQP',
                    bounds=bounds = ((-1 if short else 0, 1),) *
                        n_assets,
                    constraints=weight_constraint,
                    options={'tol': 1e-10, 'maxiter': 1e4})
```

The corresponding `min.` volatility portfolio lies on the efficient frontier as shown above.

Global Portfolio Optimization - The Black-Litterman approach

The Global Portfolio Optimization approach of Black and Litterman (1992) combines economic models with statistical learning and is popular because it generates estimates of expected returns that are plausible in many situations.

The technique departs from the assumption that the market is a mean-variance portfolio implied by the CAPM equilibrium model, and builds on the fact that the observed market capitalization can be considered as optimal weights assigned by the market. Market weights reflect market prices that, in turn, embody the market's expectations of future returns.

Hence, the approach can reverse-engineer the unobservable future expected returns from the assumption that the market is close enough to equilibrium, as defined by the CAPM, and allow investors to adjust these estimates to their own beliefs using a shrinkage estimator. The model can be interpreted as a Bayesian approach to portfolio optimization. We will introduce Bayesian methods in `Chapter 9`, *Bayesian Machine Learning*.

How to size your bets – the Kelly rule

The Kelly rule has a long history in gambling because it provides guidance on how much to stake on each of an (infinite) sequence of bets with varying (but favorable) odds to maximize terminal wealth. It was published as A New Interpretation of the Information Rate in 1956 by John Kelly who was a colleague of Claude Shannon's at Bell Labs. He was intrigued by bets placed on candidates at the new quiz show The $64,000 Question, where a viewer on the west coast used the three-hour delay to obtain insider information about the winners.

Kelly drew a connection to Shannon's information theory to solve for the bet that is optimal for long-term capital growth when the odds are favorable, but uncertainty remains. His rule maximizes logarithmic wealth as a function of the odds of success of each game, and includes implicit bankruptcy protection since log(0) is negative infinity so that a Kelly gambler would naturally avoid losing everything.

The optimal size of a bet

Kelly began by analyzing games with a binary win-lose outcome. The key variables are:

- **b**: The odds define the amount won for a $1 bet. Odds = 5/1 implies a $5 gain if the bet wins, plus recovery of the $1 capital.
- **p**: The probability defines the likelihood of a favorable outcome.
- **f**: The share of the current capital to bet.
- **V**: The value of the capital as a result of betting.

The Kelly rule aims to maximize the value's growth rate, G, of infinitely-repeated bets:

$$G = \lim_{N \to \infty} \frac{1}{N} \log \frac{V_N}{V_0}$$

When W and L are the numbers of wins and losses, then:

$$V_N = (1 + b*f)^W (1 - f)^L V_0 \qquad \Rightarrow$$
$$G = \lim_{N \to \infty} \left[\frac{W}{N} \log(1 + \text{odds} * \text{share}) + \frac{L}{N} \log(1 - f) \right] \qquad \Leftrightarrow$$
$$= p \log(1 + b*f) + (1 - p) \log(1 - f)$$

We can maximize the rate of growth *G* by maximizing *G* with respect to *f*, as illustrated using `sympy` as follows:

```
from sympy import symbols, solve, log, diff

share, odds, probability = symbols('share odds probability')
Value = probability * log(1 + odds * share) + (1 - probability) * log(1
          - share)
solve(diff(Value, share), share)

[(odds*probability + probability - 1)/odds]
```

We arrive at the optimal share of capital to bet:

$$\text{Kelly Criterion:} \quad f^* = \frac{b*p+p-1}{b}$$

Optimal investment – single asset

In a financial market context, both outcomes and alternatives are more complex, but the Kelly rule logic does still apply. It was made popular by Ed Thorp, who first applied it profitably to gambling (described in Beat the Dealer) and later started the successful hedge fund Princeton/Newport Partners.

With continuous outcomes, the growth rate of capital is defined by an integrate over the probability distribution of the different returns that can be optimized numerically:

$$E[G] = \int \log(1 * fr)P(r)dr \Leftrightarrow$$

$$\frac{d}{df}E[G] = \int_{-\infty}^{+\infty} \frac{r}{1 * fr}P(r)dr = 0$$

We can solve this expression for the optimal f* using the `scipy.optimize` module:

```
def norm_integral(f, m, st):
    val, er = quad(lambda s: np.log(1+f*s)*norm.pdf(s, m, st), m-3*st,
                   m+3*st)
    return -val


def norm_dev_integral(f, m, st):
    val, er = quad(lambda s: (s/(1+f*s))*norm.pdf(s, m, st), m-3*st,
                   m+3*st)
    return val
```

```
m = .058
s = .216
# Option 1: minimize the expectation integral
sol = minimize_scalar(norm_integral, args=(
                m, s), bounds=[0., 2.], method='bounded')
print('Optimal Kelly fraction: {:.4f}'.format(sol.x))
```

Optimal investment – multiple assets

We will use an example with various equities. E. Chan (2008) illustrates how to arrive at a multi-asset application of the Kelly Rule, and that the result is equivalent to the (potentially levered) maximum Sharpe ratio portfolio from the mean-variance optimization.

The computation involves the dot product of the precision matrix, which is the inverse of the covariance matrix, and the return matrix:

```
mean_returns = monthly_returns.mean()
cov_matrix = monthly_returns.cov()
precision_matrix = pd.DataFrame(inv(cov_matrix), index=stocks,
columns=stocks)
kelly_wt = precision_matrix.dot(mean_returns).values
```

The Kelly Portfolio is also shown in the efficient frontier diagram (after normalization so that the absolute weights sum to one). Many investors prefer to reduce the Kelly weights to reduce the strategy's volatility, and Half-Kelly has become particularly popular.

Risk parity

The fact that the previous 15 years have been characterized by two major crises in the global equity markets, a consistently upwardly-sloping yield curve, and a general decline in interest rates made risk parity look like a particularly compelling option. Many institutions carved out strategic allocations to risk parity to further diversify their portfolios.

A simple implementation of risk parity allocates assets according to the inverse of their variances, ignoring correlations and, in particular, return forecasts:

```
var = monthly_returns.var()
risk_parity_weights = var / var.sum()
```

The risk parity portfolio is also shown in the efficient frontier diagram at the beginning of this section.

Risk factor investment

An alternative framework for estimating input is to work down to the underlying determinants, or factors, that drive the risk and returns of assets. If we understand how the factors influence returns, and we understand the factors, we will be able to construct more robust portfolios.

The concept of factor investing looks beyond asset class labels to the underlying factor risks to maximize the benefits of diversification. Rather than distinguishing investment vehicles by labels such as hedge funds or private equity, factor investing aims to identify distinct risk-return profiles based on differences in exposure to fundamental risk factors. The naïve approach to mean-variance investing plugs (artificial) groupings as distinct asset classes into a mean-variance optimizer. Factor investing recognizes that such groupings share many of the same factor risks as traditional asset classes. Diversification benefits can be overstated, as investors discovered during the last crisis when correlations among risky asset classes increased due to exposure to the same underlying factor risks.

Hierarchical risk parity

Mean-variance optimization is very sensitive to the estimates of expected returns and the covariance of these returns. The covariance matrix inversion also becomes more challenging and less accurate when returns are highly correlated, as is often the case in practice. The result has been called the Markowitz curse: when diversification is more important because investments are correlated, conventional portfolio optimizers will likely produce an unstable solution. The benefits of diversification can be more than offset by mistaken estimates. As discussed, even naive, equally-weighted portfolios can beat mean-variance and risk-based optimization out of sample.

More robust approaches have incorporated additional constraints (Clarke et al., 2002), Bayesian priors (Black and Litterman, 1992), or used shrinkage estimators to make the precision matrix more numerically stable (Ledoit and Wolf [2003], available in scikit-learn (`http://scikit-learn.org/stable/modules/generated/sklearn.covariance.LedoitWolf.html`). **Hierarchical risk parity** (HRP), in contrast, leverages unsupervised machine learning to achieve superior out-of-sample portfolio allocations.

A recent innovation in portfolio optimization leverages graph theory and hierarchical clustering to construct a portfolio in three steps (Lopez de Prado, 2015):

1. Define a distance metric so that correlated assets are close to each other, and apply single-linkage clustering to identify hierarchical relationships

2. Use the hierarchical correlation structure to quasi-diagonalize the covariance matrix.

3. Apply top-down inverse-variance weighting using a recursive bisectional search to treat clustered assets as complements rather than substitutes in portfolio construction and to reduce the number of degrees of freedom.

A related method to construct **hierarchical clustering portfolios (HCP)** was presented by Raffinot (2016). Conceptually, complex systems such as financial markets tend to have a structure and are often organized in a hierarchical way, while the interaction among elements in the hierarchy shapes the dynamics of the system. Correlation matrices also lack the notion of hierarchy, which allows weights to vary freely and in potentially unintended ways.

Both HRP and HCP have been tested by JPM on various equity universes. The HRP, in particular, produced equal or superior risk-adjusted returns and Sharpe ratios compared to naive diversification, the maximum-diversified portfolios, or GMV portfolios.

We will present the Python implementation in `Chapter 12`, *Unsupervised Learning*.

Summary

In this chapter, we covered the important topic of portfolio management, which involves the combination of investment positions with the objective of managing risk-return trade-offs. We introduced `pyfolio` to compute and visualize key risk and return metrics and to compare the performance of various algorithms.

We saw how important accurate predictions are to optimize portfolio weights and maximize diversification benefits. We also explored how ML can facilitate more effective portfolio construction by learning hierarchical relationships from the asset-returns covariance matrix.

We will now move on to the second part of this book, which focuses on the use of ML models. These models will produce more accurate predictions by making more effective use of more diverse information to capture more complex patterns than the simpler alpha factors that were most prominent so far.

We will begin by training, testing, and tuning linear models for regression and classification using cross-validation to achieve robust out-of-sample performance. We will also embed these models within the framework of defining and backtesting algorithmic trading strategies, which we covered in the last two chapters.

6
The Machine Learning Process

In this chapter, we will start to illustrate how you can use a broad range of supervised and unsupervised **machine learning (ML)** models for algorithmic trading. We will explain each model's assumptions and use cases before we demonstrate relevant applications using various Python libraries. The categories of models will include:

- Linear models for the regression and classification of cross-section, time series, and panel data
- Generalized additive models, including non-linear tree-based models, such as **decision trees**
- Ensemble models, including random forest and gradient-boosting machines
- Unsupervised linear and nonlinear methods for dimensionality reduction and clustering
- Neural network models, including recurrent and convolutional architectures
- Reinforcement learning models

We will apply these models to the market, fundamental, and alternative data sources introduced in the first part of this book. We will further build on the material covered so far by showing you how to embed these models in an algorithmic trading strategy to generate or combine alpha factors or to optimize the portfolio-management process and evaluate their performance.

There are several aspects that many of these models and their uses have in common. This chapter covers these common aspects so that we can focus on model-specific usage in the following chapters. They include the overarching goal of learning a functional relationship from data by optimizing an objective or loss function. They also include the closely related methods of measuring model performance.

We distinguish between unsupervised and supervised learning and supervised regression and classification problems, and outline use cases for algorithmic trading. We contrast the use of supervised learning for statistical inference of relationships between input and output data with the use for the prediction of future outputs from future inputs. We also illustrate how prediction errors are due to the model's bias or variance, or because of a high noise-to-signal ratio in the data. Most importantly, we present methods to diagnose sources of errors and improve your model's performance.

In this chapter, we will cover the following topics:

- How supervised and unsupervised learning using data works
- How to apply the ML workflow
- How to formulate loss functions for regression and classification
- How to train and evaluate supervised learning models
- How the bias-variance trade-off impacts prediction errors
- How to diagnose and address prediction errors
- How to train a model using cross-validation to manage the bias-variance trade-off
- How to implement cross-validation using scikit-learn
- Why the nature of financial data requires different approaches to out-of-sample testing

If you are already quite familiar with ML, feel free to skip ahead and dive right into learning how to use linear models to produce and combine alpha factors for an algorithmic trading strategy.

Learning from data

There have been many definitions of ML, which all revolve around the automated detection of meaningful patterns in data. Two prominent examples include:

- AI pioneer **Arthur Samuelson** defined ML in 1959 as a subfield of computer science that gives computers the ability to learn without being explicitly programmed.
- **Toni Mitchell**, one of the current leaders in the field, pinned down a well-posed learning problem more specifically in 1998: a computer program learns from experience with respect to a task and a performance measure whether the performance of the task improves with experience.

Experience is presented to an algorithm in the form of training data. The principal difference to previous attempts at building machines that solve problems is that the rules that an algorithm uses to make decisions are learned from the data as opposed to being programmed or hard-coded—this was the case for expert systems prominent in the 1980s.

The key challenge of automated learning is to identify patterns in the training data that are meaningful when generalizing the model's learning to new data. There are a large number of potential patterns that a model could identify, while the training data only constitute a sample of the larger set of phenomena that the algorithm needs to perform the task in the future. The infinite number of functions that could generate the given outputs from the given input make the search process impossible to solve without restrictions on the eligible set of functions.

The types of patterns that an algorithm is capable of learning are limited by the size of its hypothesis space on the one hand and the amount of information contained in the sample data on the other. The size of the hypothesis space varies significantly between algorithms. On the one hand, this limitation enables a successful search and on the other hand, it implies an inductive bias as the algorithm generalizes from the training sample to new data.

Hence, the key challenge becomes a matter of how to choose a model with a hypothesis space large enough to contain a solution to the learning problem, yet small enough to ensure reliable generalization given the size of the training data. With more and more informative data, a model with a larger hypothesis space will be successful.

The **no-free-lunch theorem** states that there is no universal learning algorithm. Instead, a learner's hypothesis space has to be tailored to a specific task using prior knowledge about the task domain in order for the search of meaningful patterns to succeed. We will pay close attention to the assumptions that a model makes about data relationships for a specific task throughout this chapter, and emphasize the importance of matching these assumptions with empirical evidence gleaned from data exploration. The process required to master the task can be differentiated into supervised, unsupervised, and reinforcement learning.

Supervised learning

Supervised learning is the most commonly used type of ML. We will dedicate most of the chapters in this book to learning about the various applications of models in this category. The term *supervised* implies the presence of an outcome variable that guides the learning process—that is, it teaches the algorithm the correct solution to the task that is being learned. Supervised learning aims at generalizing a functional relationship between input and output data that is learned from individual samples and applying it to new data.

The output variable is also, depending on the field, interchangeably called the label, target, outcome, endogenous, or left-hand-side variable. We will use y_i for observations $i = 1, ...,$ N, or y in vector notation. Some tasks are represented by several outcomes, also called **multilabel problems**. The input data for a supervised learning problem is also known as features, exogenous, and right-hand-side variables, denoted by an x_i for a vector of features for observations $i = 1, ..., N$, or X in matrix notation.

The solution to a supervised learning problem is a function ($\hat{f}$) that represents what the model learned about the input-output relationship from the sample and approximates the true relationship, represented with $y \approx \hat{f}(X)$. This function can be used to infer statistical associations or potentially even causal relationships among variables of interest beyond the sample, or it can be used to predict outputs for new input data.

Both goals face an important trade-off: more complex models have more *moving parts* that are capable of representing more nuanced relationships, but they may also be more difficult to inspect. They are also likely to overfit and learn random noise particular to the training sample, as opposed to a systematic signal that represents a general pattern of the input-output relationship. Overly simple models, on the other hand, will miss signals and deliver biased results. This trade-off is known as the **bias-variance trade-off** in supervised learning, but conceptually this also applies to the other forms of ML where overly complex models may perform poorly beyond the training data.

Unsupervised learning

When solving an unsupervised learning problem, we only observe the features and have no measurements of the outcome. Instead of the prediction of future outcomes or the inference of relationships among variables, the task is to find structure in the data without any outcome information to guide the search process.

Often, unsupervised algorithms aim to learn a new representation of the input data that is useful for some other tasks. This includes coming up with labels that identify commonalities among observations, or a summarized description that captures relevant information while requiring data points or features. Unsupervised learning algorithms also differ from supervised learning algorithms in the assumptions they make about the nature of the structure they are aiming to discover.

Applications

There are several helpful uses of unsupervised learning that can be applied to algorithmic trading, including the following:

- Grouping together securities with similar risk and return characteristics (see hierarchical risk parity in this chapter (which looks at portfolio optimization))
- Finding a small number of risk factors driving the performance of a much larger number of securities
- Identifying trading and price patterns that differ systematically and may pose higher risks
- Identifying latent topics in a body of documents (for example, earnings call transcripts) that comprise the most important aspects of those documents

At a high level, these applications rely on methods to identify clusters and methods to reduce the dimensionality of the data.

Cluster algorithms

Cluster algorithms use a measure of similarity to identify observations or data attributes that contain similar information. They summarize a dataset by assigning a large number of data points to a smaller number of clusters so that the cluster members are more closely related to each other than to members of other clusters.

Cluster algorithms primarily differ with respect to the type of clusters that they will produce, which implies different assumptions about the data generation process, listed as follows:

- **K-means clustering**: Data points belong to one of the k clusters of equal size that take an elliptical form
- **Gaussian mixture models**: Data points have been generated by any of the various multivariate normal distributions

- **Density-based clusters**: Clusters are of an arbitrary shape and are defined only by the existence of a minimum number of nearby data points
- **Hierarchical clusters**: Data points belong to various supersets of groups that are formed by successively merging smaller clusters

Dimensionality reduction

Dimensionality reduction produces new data that captures the most important information contained in the source data. Rather than grouping existing data into clusters, these algorithms transform existing data into a new dataset that uses significantly fewer features or observations to represent the original information.

Algorithms differ with respect to the nature of the new dataset they will produce, as shown in the following list:

- **Principal component analysis (PCA)**: Finds the linear transformation that captures most of the variance in the existing dataset
- **Manifold learning**: Identifies a nonlinear transformation that produces a lower-dimensional representation of the data
- **Autoencoders**: Uses neural networks to compress data non-linearly with minimal loss of information

We will dive deeper into linear, non-linear, and neural-network-based unsupervised learning models in several of the following chapters, including important applications of **natural language processing** (**NLP**) in the form of topic modeling and Word2vec feature extraction.

Reinforcement learning

Reinforcement learning is the third type of ML. It aims to choose the action that yields the highest reward, given a set of input data that describes a context or environment. It is both dynamic and interactive: the stream of positive and negative rewards impacts the algorithm's learning, and actions taken now may influence both the environment and future rewards.

The trade-off between the exploitation of a course of action that has been learned to yield a certain reward and the exploration of new actions that may increase the reward in the future gives rise to a trial-and-error approach. Reinforcement learning optimizes the agent's learning using dynamical systems theory and, in particular, the optimal control of Markov decision processes with incomplete information.

Reinforcement learning differs from supervised learning, where the available training data lays out both the context and the correct decision for the algorithm. It is tailored to interactive settings where the outcomes only become available over time and learning has to proceed in an *online* or continuous fashion as the agent acquires new experience. However, some of the most notable progress in **Artificial Intelligence (AI)** involves reinforcement that uses deep learning to approximate functional relationships between actions, environments, and future rewards. It also differs from unsupervised learning because feedback of the consequences will be available, albeit with a delay.

Reinforcement learning is particularly suitable for algorithmic trading because the concept of a return-maximizing agent in an uncertain, dynamic environment has much in common with an investor or a trading strategy that interacts with financial markets. This approach has been successfully applied to game-playing agents, most prominently to the game of Go, but also to complex video games. It is also used in robotics—for example, self-driving cars—or to personalize services such as website offerings based on user interaction. We will introduce reinforcement learning approaches to building an algorithmic trading strategy in Chapter 21, *Reinforcement Learning*.

The machine learning workflow

Developing a ML solution for an algorithmic trading strategy requires a systematic approach to maximize the chances of success while economizing on resources. It is also very important to make the process transparent and replicable in order to facilitate collaboration, maintenance, and later refinements.

The following chart outlines the key steps from problem definition to the deployment of a predictive solution:

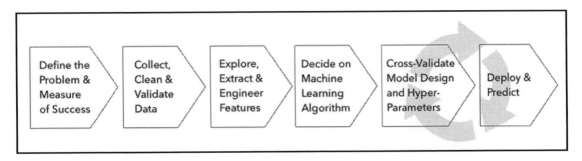

The process is iterative throughout the sequence, and the effort required at different stages will vary according to the project, but this process should generally include the following steps:

1. Frame the problem, identify a target metric, and define success
2. Source, clean, and validate the data
3. Understand your data and generate informative features
4. Pick one or more machine learning algorithms suitable for your data
5. Train, test, and tune your models
6. Use your model to solve the original problem

We will walk through these steps in the following sections using a simple example to illustrate some of the key points.

Basic walkthrough – k-nearest neighbors

The `machine_learning_workflow.ipynb` notebook in this chapter's folder of the book's GitHub repository contains several examples that illustrate the machine learning workflow using a dataset of house prices.

We will use the fairly straightforward **k-nearest neighbors** (**KNN**) algorithm that allows us to tackle both regression and classification problems.

In its default `sklearn` implementation, it identifies the `k` nearest data points (based on the Euclidean distance) to make a prediction. It predicts the most frequent class among the neighbors or the average outcome in the classification or regression case, respectively.

Frame the problem – goals and metrics

The starting point for any machine learning exercise is the ultimate use case it aims to address. Sometimes, this goal will be statistical inference in order to identify an association between variables or even a causal relationship. Most frequently, however, the goal will be the direct prediction of an outcome to yield a trading signal.

Both inference and prediction use metrics to evaluate how well a model achieves its objective. We will focus on common objective functions and the corresponding error metrics for predictive models that can be distinguished by the variable type of the output: continuous output variables imply a regression problem, categorical variables imply classification, and the special case of ordered categorical variables implies ranking problems.

The problem may be the efficient combination of several alpha factors and could be framed as a regression problem that aims to predict returns, a binary classification problem that aims to predict the direction of future price movements, or a multiclass problem that aims to assign stocks to various performance classes. In the following section, we will introduce these objectives and look at how to measure and interpret related error metrics.

Prediction versus inference

The functional relationship produced by a supervised learning algorithm can be used for inference—that is, to gain insights into how the outcomes are generated—or for prediction—that is, to generate accurate output estimates (represented $\hat{y}$ by) for unknown or future inputs (represented by X).

For algorithmic trading, inference can be used to estimate the causal or statistical dependence of the returns of an asset on a risk factor, whereas prediction can be used to forecast the risk factor. Combining the two can yield a prediction of the asset price, which in turn can be translated into a trading signal.

Statistical inference is about drawing conclusions from sample data about the parameters of the underlying probability distribution or the population. Potential conclusions include hypothesis tests about the characteristics of the distribution of an individual variable, or the existence or strength of numerical relationships among variables. They also include point or interval estimates of statistical metrics.

Inference depends on the assumptions about the process that generates the data in the first place. We will review these assumptions and the tools that are used for inference with linear models where they are well established. More complex models make fewer assumptions about the structural relationship between input and output, and instead approach the task of function approximation more openly while treating the data-generating process as a black box. These models, including decision trees, ensemble models, and neural networks, are focused on and often outperform when used for prediction tasks. However, random forests have recently gained a framework for inference that we will introduce later.

Causal inference

Causal inference aims to identify relationships so that certain input values imply certain outputs—for example, a certain constellation of macro variables causing the price of a given asset to move in a certain way, assuming all other variables remain constant.

Statistical inference about relationships among two or more variables produces measures of correlation that can only be interpreted as a causal relationship when several other conditions are met—for example, when alternative explanations or reverse causality has been ruled out. Meeting these conditions requires an experimental setting where all relevant variables of interest can be fully controlled to isolate causal relationships. Alternatively, quasi-experimental settings expose units of observations to changes in inputs in a randomized way to rule out that other observable or unobservable features are responsible for the observed effects of the change in the environment.

These conditions are rarely met so inferential conclusions need to be treated with care. The same applies to the performance of predictive models that also rely on the statistical association between features and outputs, which may change with other factors that are not part of the model.

The non-parametric nature of the KNN model does not lend itself well to inference, so we'll postpone this step in the workflow until we encounter linear models in the next chapter.

Regression problems

Regression problems aim to predict a continuous variable. The **root-mean-square error** (**RMSE**) is the most popular loss function and error metric, not least because it is differentiable. The loss is symmetric, but larger errors weigh more in the calculation. Using the square root has the advantage of measuring the error in the units of the target variable. The same metric in combination with the **RMSE log of the error** (**RMSLE**) is appropriate when the target is subject to exponential growth because of its asymmetric penalty that weights negative errors less than positive errors. You can also log-transform the target first and then use the RMSE, as we do in the example later in this section.

The **mean absolute errors** (**MAE**) and **median absolute errors** (**MedAE**) are symmetric but do not weigh larger errors more. The MedAE is robust to outliers.

The explained variance score computes the proportion of the target variance that the model accounts for and varies between 0 and 1. The R^2 score or coefficient of determination yields the same outcome the mean of the residuals is 0, but can differ otherwise. In particular, it can be negative when calculated on out-of-sample data (or for a linear regression without intercept).

The following table defines the formulas used for calculation and the corresponding `sklearn` function that can be imported from the `metrics` module. The `scoring` parameter is used in combination with automated train-test functions (such as `cross_val_score` and `GridSearchCV`) that we will introduce later in this section, and which are illustrated in the accompanying notebook:

Name	Formula	sklearn	Scoring parameter
Mean squared error	$\frac{1}{N}\sum_{i=1}^{N}(y_i - \hat{y}_i)^2$	`mean_squared_error`	`neg_mean_squared_error`
Mean squared log error	$\frac{1}{N}\sum_{i=1}^{N}(\ln(1+y_i)-\ln(1+\hat{y}_i))^2$	`mean_squared_log_error`	`neg_mean_squared_log_error`
Mean absolute error	$\frac{1}{N}\sum_{i=1}^{N}|y_i - \hat{y}_i|$	`mean_absolute_error`	`neg_mean_absolute_error`
Median absolute error	$\mathrm{median}\,(|y_1 - \hat{y}_1|,\ldots,|y_n - \hat{y}_n|)$	`median_absolute_error`	`neg_median_absolute_error`
Explained variance	$1 - \dfrac{\mathrm{var}(y - \hat{y})}{\mathrm{var}(y)}$	`explained_variance_score`	`explained_variance`
R^2 score	$1 - \dfrac{\sum_{i=1}^{N}(y_i - \hat{y}_i)^2}{\sum_{i=1}^{N}(y_i - \bar{y})^2}$	`r2_score`	`r2`

The following screenshot shows the various error metrics for the house price regression demonstrated in the notebook:

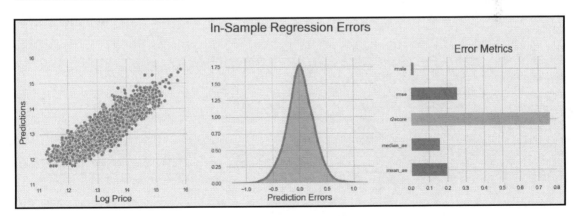

The `sklearn` function also supports multilabel evaluation—that is, assigning multiple outcome values to a single observation; see the documentation referenced on GitHub for more details (`https://github.com/PacktPublishing/Hands-On-Machine-Learning-for-Algorithmic-Trading/tree/master/Chapter06`).

Classification problems

Classification problems have categorical outcome variables. Most predictors will output a score to indicate whether an observation belongs to a certain class. In the second step, these scores are then translated into actual predictions.

In the binary case, where we will label the classes positive and negative, the score typically varies between zero or is normalized accordingly. Once the scores are converted into 0-1 predictions, there can be four outcomes, because each of the two existing classes can be either correctly or incorrectly predicted. With more than two classes, there can be more cases if you differentiate between the several potential mistakes.

All error metrics are computed from the breakdown of predictions across the four fields of the 2 x 2 confusion matrix that associates actual and predicted classes. The metrics listed in the table shown in the following diagram, such as accuracy, evaluate a model for a given threshold:

	Actual (Truth)					
	Positive	**Negative**	Accuracy	$=$	$\frac{\text{\# Correct Predictions}}{\text{\# Cases}} =$	$\frac{TP + TN}{TP + FP + TN + FN}$
Prediction **Positive**	True Positive (TP)	False Positive (FP)	True Positive Rate (Sensitivity, Recall)	$=$	$\frac{\text{\# Correct Positive Predictions}}{\text{\# Positive Cases}} =$	$\frac{TP}{TP + FN}$
			False Negative Rate (Miss Rate)	$=$	1 - True Positive Rate	
Negative	False Negative (FN)	True Negative (TN)	True Negative Rate (Specificity)	$=$	$\frac{\text{\# Correct Negative Predictions}}{\text{\# Negative Cases}} =$	$\frac{TN}{TN + FP}$
			False Positive Rate (Fall-Out)	$=$	1 - True Negative Rate	

A classifier does not necessarily need to output calibrated probabilities, but should rather produce scores that are relative to each other in distinguishing positive from negative cases. Hence, the threshold is a decision variable that can and should be optimized, taking into account the costs and benefits of correct and incorrect predictions. A lower threshold implies more positive predictions, with a potentially rising false positive rate, and for a higher threshold, the opposite is likely to be true.

Receiver operating characteristics and the area under the curve

The **receiver operating characteristics (ROC)** curve allows us to visualize, organize, and select classifiers based on their performance. It computes all the combinations of **true positive rates (TPR)** and **false positive rates (FPR)** that result from producing predictions using any of the predicted scores as a threshold. It then plots these pairs on a square, the side of which has a measurement of one in length.

A classifier that makes random predictions (taking into account class imbalance) will on average yield TPR and FPR that are equal so that the combinations will lie on the diagonal, which becomes the benchmark case. Since an underperforming classifier would benefit from relabeling the predictions, this benchmark also becomes the minimum.

The **area under the curve (AUC)** is defined as the area under the ROC plot that varies between 0.5 and the maximum of 1. It is a summary measure of how well the classifier's scores are able to rank data points with respect to their class membership. More specifically, the AUC of a classifier has the important statistical property of representing the probability that the classifier will rank a randomly chosen positive instance higher than a randomly chosen negative instance, which is equivalent to the Wilcoxon ranking test. In addition, the AUC has the benefit of not being sensitive to class imbalances.

Precision-recall curves

When predictions for one of the classes are of particular interest, precision and recall curves visualize the trade-off between these error metrics for different thresholds. Both measures evaluate the quality of predictions for a particular class. The following list shows how they are applied to the positive class:

- **Recall** measures the share of actual positive class members that a classifier predicts as positive for a given threshold. It originates in information retrieval and measures the share of relevant documents successfully identified by a search algorithm.
- **Precision**, in contrast, measures the share of positive predictions that are correct.

Recall typically increases with a lower threshold, but precision may decrease. Precision-recall curves visualize the attainable combinations and allow for the optimization of the threshold given the costs and benefits of missing a lot of relevant cases or producing lower-quality predictions.

The F1 score is a harmonic mean of precision and recall for a given threshold and can be used to numerically optimize the threshold while taking into account the relative weights that these two metrics should assume.

The following chart illustrates the ROC curve and corresponding AUC alongside the precision-recall curve and the F1 score that, using equal weights for precision and recall, yields an optimal threshold of 0.37. The chart is taken from the accompanying notebook where you can find the code for the KNN classifier that operates on binarized housing prices:

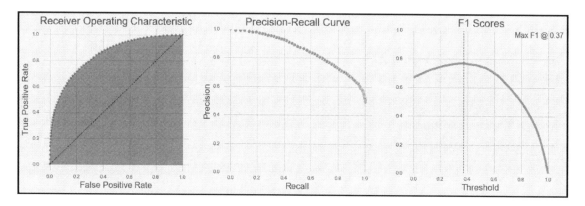

Collecting and preparing the data

We already addressed important aspects of the sourcing of market, fundamental, and alternative data, and will continue to work with various examples of these sources as we illustrate the application of the various models.

In addition to market and fundamental data that we will access through the Quantopian platform, we will also acquire and transform text data as we explore natural language processing and image data when we look at image processing and recognition. Besides obtaining, cleaning, and validating the data to relate it to trading data typically available in a time-series format, it is important to store it in a format that allows for fast access to enable quick exploration and iteration. We have recommended the HDF and parquet formats. For larger data volumes, Apache Spark represents the best solution.

Explore, extract, and engineer features

Understanding the distribution of individual variables and the relationships among outcomes and features is the basis for picking a suitable algorithm. This typically starts with visualizations such as scatter plots, as illustrated in the companion notebook (and shown in the following image), but also includes numerical evaluations ranging from linear metrics, such as the correlation, to nonlinear statistics, such as the Spearman rank correlation coefficient that we encountered when we introduced the information coefficient. It also includes information-theoretic measures, such as mutual information, as illustrated in the next subsection:

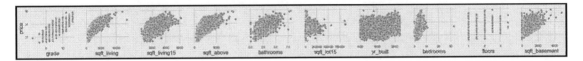

Scatter plots

A systematic exploratory analysis is also the basis of what is often the single most important ingredient of a successful predictive model: the engineering of features that extract information contained in the data, but which are not necessarily accessible to the algorithm in their raw form. Feature engineering benefits from domain expertise, the application of statistics and information theory, and creativity.

It relies on an ingenious choice of data transformations that effectively tease out the systematic relationship between input and output data. There are many choices that include outlier detection and treatment, functional transformations, and the combination of several variables, including unsupervised learning. We will illustrate examples throughout but will emphasize that this feature is best learned through experience. Kaggle is a great place to learn from other data scientists who share their experiences with the Kaggle community.

Using information theory to evaluate features

The **mutual information (MI)** between a feature and the outcome is a measure of the mutual dependence between the two variables. It extends the notion of correlation to nonlinear relationships. More specifically, it quantifies the information obtained about one random variable through the other random variable.

The concept of MI is closely related to the fundamental notion of entropy of a random variable. Entropy quantifies the amount of information contained in a random variable. Formally, the mutual information—$I(X, Y)$—of two random variables, X and Y, is defined as the following:

$$I(X,Y) = \int_Y \int_X p(x,y) \log\left(\frac{p(x,y)}{p(x)p(y)}\right)$$

The `sklearn` function implements `feature_selection.mutual_info_regression` that computes the mutual information between all features and a continuous outcome to select the features that are most likely to contain predictive information. There is also a classification version (see the documentation for more details). The notebook `mutual_information.ipynb` notebook contains an application to the financial data we created in `Chapter 4`, *Alpha Factor Research*.

Selecting an ML algorithm

The remainder of this book will introduce several model families, ranging from linear models, which make fairly strong assumptions about the nature of the functional relationship between input and output variables, to deep neural networks, which make very few assumptions. As mentioned in the introductory section, fewer assumptions will require more data with significant information about the relationship so that the learning process can be successful.

We will outline the key assumptions and how to test them where applicable as we introduce these models.

Design and tune the model

The ML process includes steps to diagnose and manage model complexity based on estimates of the model's generalization error. An unbiased estimate requires a statistically sound and efficient procedure, as well as error metrics that align with the output variable type, which also determines whether we are dealing with a regression, classification, or ranking problem.

The bias-variance trade-off

The errors that an ML model makes when predicting outcomes for new input data can be broken down into reducible and irreducible parts. The irreducible part is due to random variation (noise) in the data that is not measured, such as relevant but missing variables or natural variation. The reducible part of the generalization error, in turn, can be broken down into bias and variance. Both are due to differences between the true functional relationship and the assumptions made by the machine learning algorithm, as detailed in the following list:

- **Error due to bias**: The hypothesis is too simple to capture the complexity of the true functional relationship. As a result, whenever the model attempts to learn the true function, it makes systematic mistakes and, on average, the predictions will be similarly biased. This is also called **underfitting**.
- **Error due to variance**: The algorithm is overly complex in view of the true relationship. Instead of capturing the true relationship, it overfits to the data and extracts patterns from the noise. As a result, it learns different functional relationships from each sample, and out-of-sample predictions will vary widely.

Underfitting versus overfitting

The following diagram illustrates overfitting by approximating a cosine function using increasingly complex polynomials and measuring the in-sample error. More specifically, we draw 10 random samples with some added noise ($n = 30$) to learn a polynomial of varying complexity (see the code in the accompanying notebook). Each time, the model predicts new data points and we capture the mean-squared error for these predictions, as well as the standard deviation of these errors.

The left-hand panel in the following diagram shows a polynomial of degree 1; a straight line clearly underfits the true function. However, the estimated line will not differ dramatically from one sample drawn from the true function to the next. The middle panel shows that a degree 5 polynomial approximates the true relationship reasonably well on the [0, 1] interval. On the other hand, a polynomial of degree 15 fits the small sample almost perfectly, but provides a poor estimate of the true relationship: it overfits to the random variation in the sample data points, and the learned function will vary strongly with each sample drawn:

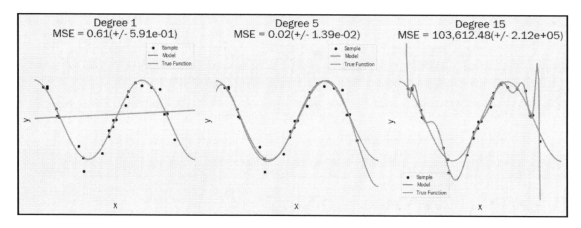

Managing the trade-off

Let's further illustrate the impact of overfitting versus underfitting by trying to learn a Taylor series approximation of the cosine function of ninth degree with some added noise. In the following diagram, we draw random samples of the true function and fit polynomials that underfit, overfit, and provide an approximately correct degree of flexibility. We then predict out-of-sample and measure the RMSE.

The high bias but low variance of a polynomial of degree 3 compares to the low bias but exceedingly high variance of the various prediction errors visible in the first panel. The left-hand panel shows the distribution of the errors that result from subtracting the true function values. The underfit case of a straight line produces a poor in-sample fit and is significantly off target out of sample. The overfit model shows the best fit in-sample with the smallest dispersion of errors, but the price is a large variance out-of-sample. The appropriate model that matches the functional form of the true model performs the best by far out-of-sample.

The right-hand panel of the following screenshot shows the actual predictions rather than the errors to demonstrate what the different types of fit look like in practice:

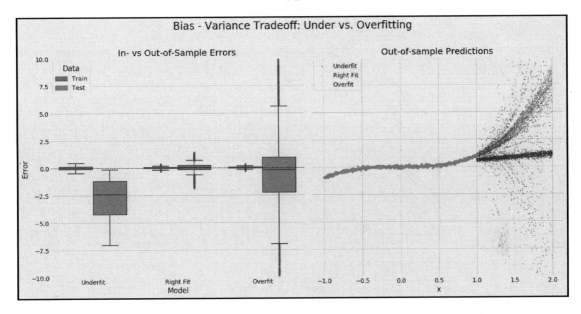

Learning curves

A learning curve plots the evolution of train and test errors against the size of the dataset used to learn the functional relationship. It is a useful tool to diagnose the bias-variance trade-off for a given model because the errors will behave differently. A model with a high bias will have a high but similar training error, both in-sample and out-of-sample, whereas an overfit model will have a very low training error.

The declining out-of-sample error illustrates that overfit models may benefit from additional data or tools to limit the model's complexity, such as regularization, whereas underfit models need to use either more features or otherwise increase the complexity of the model, as shown in the following screenshot:

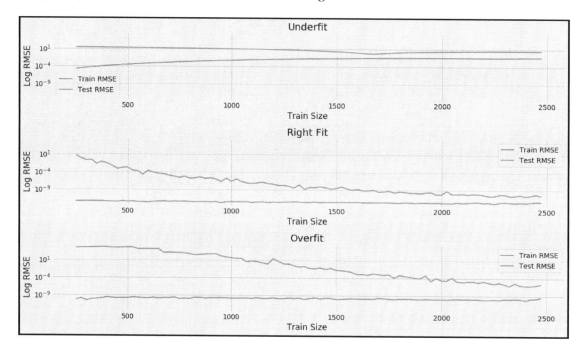

How to use cross-validation for model selection

When several candidate models (that is, algorithms) are available for your use case, the act of choosing one of them is called the **model selection** problem. Model selection aims to identify the model that will produce the lowest prediction error given new data.

An unbiased estimate of this generalization error requires a test on data that was not part of model training. Hence, we only use part of the available data to train the model and set aside another part of the data to test the model. In order to obtain an unbiased estimate of the prediction error, absolutely no information about the test set may leak into the training set, as shown in the following diagram:

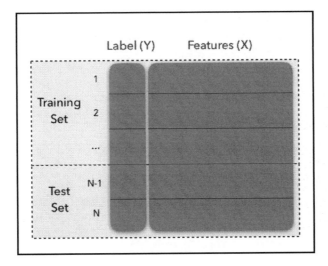

There are several methods that can be used to split the available data, which differ in terms of the amount of data used for training, the variance of the error estimates, the computational intensity, and whether structural aspects of the data are taken into account when splitting the data.

How to implement cross-validation in Python

We will illustrate various options for splitting data into training and test sets by showing how the indices of a mock dataset with ten observations are assigned to the train and test set (see `cross_validation.py` for details), as shown in following code:

```
data = list(range(1, 11))
[1, 2, 3, 4, 5, 6, 7, 8, 9, 10]
```

Basic train-test split

For a single split of your data into a training and a test set, use `sklearn.model_selection.train_test_split`, where the `shuffle` parameter, by default ensures the randomized selection of observations, which in turn can be replicated by setting `random_state`. There is also a `stratify` parameter that, for a classification problem, ensures that the train and test sets will contain approximately the same shares of each class, as shown in the following code:

```
train_test_split(data, train_size=.8)
[[8, 7, 4, 10, 1, 3, 5, 2], [6, 9]]
```

In this case, we train a model using all data except row numbers 6 and 9, which will be used to generate predictions and measure the errors given on the know labels. This method is useful for quick evaluation but is sensitive to the split, and the standard error of the test error estimate will be higher.

Cross-validation

Cross-validation (CV) is a popular strategy for model selection. The main idea behind CV is to split the data one or several times so that each split is used once as a validation set and the remainder as a training set: part of the data (the training sample) is used to train the algorithm, and the remaining part (the validation sample) is used for estimating the risk of the algorithm. Then, CV selects the algorithm with the smallest estimated risk.

While the data-splitting heuristic is very general, a key assumption of CV is that the data is **independently and identically distributed (IID)**. In the following sections, we will see that, for time series data, this is often not the case and requires a different approach.

Using a hold-out test set

When selecting hyperparameters based on their validation score, be aware that this validation score is biased because of multiple tests, and is no longer a good estimate of the generalization error. For an unbiased estimate of the error rate, we have to estimate the score from a fresh dataset, as shown in the following diagram:

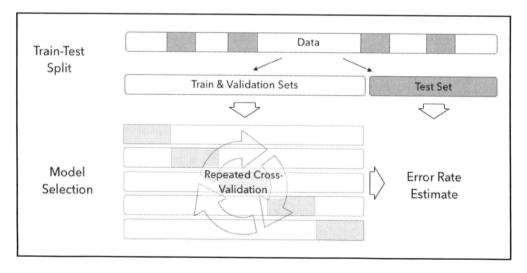

For this reason, we use a three-way split of the data, as illustrated in the preceding diagram: one part is used in cross-validation and is repeatedly split into a training and validation set. The remainder is set aside as a hold-out set that is only used once cross-validation is complete to generate an unbiased test error estimate. We will illustrate this method as we start building ML models in the next chapter.

KFold iterator

The `sklearn.model_selection.KFold` iterator produces several disjunct splits and assigns each of these splits once to the validation set, as shown in the following code:

```
kf = KFold(n_splits=5)
for train, validate in kf.split(data):
    print(train, validate)

[2 3 4 5 6 7 8 9] [0 1]
[0 1 4 5 6 7 8 9] [2 3]
[0 1 2 3 6 7 8 9] [4 5]
[0 1 2 3 4 5 8 9] [6 7]
[0 1 2 3 4 5 6 7] [8 9]
```

In addition to the number of splits, most CV objects take a `shuffle` argument that ensures randomization. To render results reproducible, set the `random_state`, as follows:

```
kf = KFold(n_splits=5, shuffle=True, random_state=42)
for train, validate in kf.split(data):
    print(train, validate)

[0 2 3 4 5 6 7 9] [1 8]
[1 2 3 4 6 7 8 9] [0 5]
[0 1 3 4 5 6 8 9] [2 7]
[0 1 2 3 5 6 7 8] [4 9]
[0 1 2 4 5 7 8 9] [3 6]
```

Leave-one-out CV

The original CV implementation used a leave-one-out method that used each observation once as the validation set, as shown in the following code:

```
loo = LeaveOneOut()
for train, validate in loo.split(data):
    print(train, validate)

[1 2 3 4 5 6 7 8 9] [0]
[0 2 3 4 5 6 7 8 9] [1]
. . .
```

```
[0 1 2 3 4 5 6 7 9] [8]
[0 1 2 3 4 5 6 7 8] [9]
```

This maximizes the number of models that are trained, which increases computational costs. While the validation sets do not overlap, the overlap of training sets is maximized, driving up the correlation of models and their prediction errors. As a result, the variance of the prediction error is higher for a model with a larger number of folds.

Leave-P-Out CV

A similar version to leave-one-out CV is leave-P-out CV, which generates all possible combinations of p data rows, as shown in the following code:

```
lpo = LeavePOut(p=2)
for train, validate in lpo.split(data):
    print(train, validate)

[2 3 4 5 6 7 8 9] [0 1]
[1 3 4 5 6 7 8 9] [0 2]
...
[0 1 2 3 4 5 6 8] [7 9]
[0 1 2 3 4 5 6 7] [8 9]
```

ShuffleSplit

The `sklearn.model_selection.ShuffleSplit` object creates independent splits with potentially overlapping validation sets, as shown in the following code:

```
ss = ShuffleSplit(n_splits=3, test_size=2, random_state=42)
for train, validate in ss.split(data):
    print(train, validate)
[4 9 1 6 7 3 0 5] [2 8]
[1 2 9 8 0 6 7 4] [3 5]
[8 4 5 1 0 6 9 7] [2 3]
```

Parameter tuning with scikit-learn

Model selection typically involves repeated cross-validation of the out-of-sample performance of models using different algorithms (such as linear regression and random forest) or different configurations. Different configurations may involve changes to hyperparameters or the inclusion or exclusion of different variables.

The `yellowbricks` library extends the `sklearn` API to generate diagnostic visualization tools to facilitate the model-selection process. These tools can be used to investigate relationships among features, analyze classification or regression errors, monitor cluster algorithm performance, inspect the characteristics of text data, and help with model selection. We will demonstrate validation and learning curves that provide valuable information during the parameter-tuning phase—see the `machine_learning_workflow.ipynb` notebook for implementation details.

Validation curves with yellowbricks

Validation curves (see the left-hand panel in the following graph) visualize the impact of a single hyperparameter on a model's cross-validation performance. This is useful to determine whether the model underfits or overfits the given dataset.

In our example of the **KNeighborsRegressor** that only has a single hyperparameter, we can clearly see that the model underfits for values of *k* above 20, where the validation error drops as we reduce the number of neighbors, thereby making our model more complex, because it makes predictions for more distinct groups of neighbors or areas in the feature space. For values below 20, the model begins to overfit as training and validation errors diverge and average out-of-sample performance quickly deteriorates, as shown in the following graph:

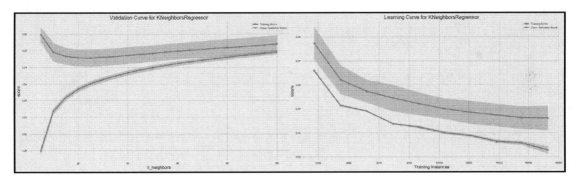

Learning curves

The learning curve (see the right-hand panel of the preceding chart for our house price regression example) helps determine whether a model's cross-validation performance would benefit from additional data and whether prediction errors are more driven by bias or by variance.

If training and cross-validation performance converges, then more data is unlikely to improve the performance. At this point, it is important to evaluate whether the model performance meets expectations, determined by a human benchmark. If this is not the case, then you should modify the model's hyperparameter settings to better capture the relationship between the features and the outcome, or choose a different algorithm with a higher capacity to capture complexity.

In addition, the variation of train and test errors shown by the shaded confidence intervals provide clues about the bias and variance sources of the prediction error. Variability around the cross-validation error is evidence of variance, whereas variability for the training set suggests bias, depending on the size of the training error.

In our example, the cross-validation performance has continued to drop, but the incremental improvements have shrunk and the errors have plateaued, so there are unlikely to be many benefits from a larger training set. On the other hand, the data is showing substantial variance given the range of validation errors compared to that shown for the training errors.

Parameter tuning using GridSearchCV and pipeline

Since hyperparameter tuning is a key ingredient of the machine learning workflow, there are tools to automate this process. The `sklearn` library includes a `GridSearchCV` interface that cross-validates all combinations of parameters in parallel, captures the result, and automatically trains the model using the parameter setting that performed best during cross-validation on the full dataset.

In practice, the training and validation sets often require some processing prior to cross-validation. Scikit-learn offers the `Pipeline` to also automate any requisite feature-processing steps in the automated hyperparameter tuning facilitated by `GridSearchCV`.

You can look at the implementation examples in the included `machine_learning_workflow.ipynb` notebook to see these tools in action.

Challenges with cross-validation in finance

A key assumption for the cross-validation methods discussed so far is the **independent and identical (iid)** distribution of the samples available for training.

For financial data, this is often not the case. On the contrary, financial data is neither independently nor identically distributed because of serial correlation and time-varying standard deviation, also known as **heteroskedasticity** (see the next two chapters for more details). The TimeSeriesSplit in the sklearn.model_selection module aims to address the linear order of time-series data.

Time series cross-validation with sklearn

The time series nature of the data implies that cross-validation produces a situation where data from the future will be used to predict data from the past. This is unrealistic at best and data snooping at worst, to the extent that future data reflects past events.

To address time dependency, the sklearn.model_selection.TimeSeriesSplit object implements a walk-forward test with an expanding training set, where subsequent training sets are supersets of past training sets, as shown in the following code:

```
tscv = TimeSeriesSplit(n_splits=5)
for train, validate in tscv.split(data):
    print(train, validate)

[0 1 2 3 4] [5]
[0 1 2 3 4 5] [6]
[0 1 2 3 4 5 6] [7]
[0 1 2 3 4 5 6 7] [8]
[0 1 2 3 4 5 6 7 8] [9]
```

You can use the max_train_size parameter to implement walk-forward cross-validation, where the size of the training set remains constant over time, similar to how zipline tests a trading algorithm. Scikit-learn facilitates the design of custom cross-validation methods using subclassing, which we will implement in the following chapters.

Purging, embargoing, and combinatorial CV

For financial data, labels are often derived from overlapping data points as returns are computed from prices in multiple periods. In the context of trading strategies, the results of a model's prediction, which may imply taking a position in an asset, may only be known later, when this decision is evaluated—for example, when a position is closed out.

The resulting risks include the leaking of information from the test into the training set, likely leading to an artificially inflated performance that needs to be addressed by ensuring that all data is point-in-time—that is, truly available and known at the time it is used as the input for a model. Several methods have been proposed by Marcos Lopez de Prado in *Advances in Financial Machine Learning* to address these challenges of financial data for cross-validation, as shown in the following list:

- **Purging**: Eliminate training data points where the evaluation occurs after the prediction of a point-in-time data point in the validation set to avoid look-ahead bias.
- **Embargoing**: Further eliminate training samples that follow a test period.
- **Combinatorial cross-validation**: Walk-forward CV severely limits the historical paths that can be tested. Instead, given T observations, compute all possible train/test splits for $N<T$ groups that each maintain their order, and purge and embargo potentially overlapping groups. Then, train the model on all combinations of $N-k$ groups while testing the model on the remaining k groups. The result is a much larger number of possible historical paths.

Prado's *Advances in Financial Machine Learning* contains sample code to implement these approaches; the code is also available via the new library, `timeseriescv`.

Summary

In this chapter, we introduced the challenge of learning from data and looked at supervised, unsupervised, and reinforcement models as the principal forms of learning that we will study in this book to build algorithmic trading strategies. We discussed the need for supervised learning algorithms to make assumptions about the functional relationships that they attempt to learn in order to limit the search space while incurring an inductive bias that may lead to excessive generalization errors.

We presented key aspects of the ML workflow, introduced the most common error metrics for regression and classification models, explained the bias-variance trade-off, and illustrated the various tools for managing the model selection process using cross-validation.

In the following chapter, we will dive into linear models for regression and classification to develop our first algorithmic trading strategies that use ML.

7

Linear Models

The family of linear models represents one of the most useful hypothesis classes. Many learning algorithms that are widely applied in algorithmic trading rely on linear predictors because they can be efficiently trained in many cases, they are relatively robust to noisy financial data, and they have strong links to the theory of finance. Linear predictors are also intuitive, easy to interpret, and often fit the data reasonably well or at least provide a good baseline.

Linear regression has been known for over 200 years when Legendre and Gauss applied it to astronomy and began to analyze its statistical properties. Numerous extensions have since adapted the linear regression model and the baseline **ordinary least squares** (**OLS**) method to learn its parameters:

- **Generalized linear models** (**GLM**) expand the scope of applications by allowing for response variables that imply an error distribution other than the normal distribution. GLM include the probit or logistic models for **categorical response variables** that appear in classification problems.
- More **robust estimation methods** enable statistical inference where the data violates baseline assumptions due to, for example, correlation over time or across observations. This is often the case with panel data that contains repeated observations on the same units such as historical returns on a universe of assets.
- **Shrinkage methods** aim to improve the predictive performance of linear models. They use a complexity penalty that biases the coefficients learned by the model with the goal of reducing the model's variance and improving out-of-sample predictive performance.

In practice, linear models are applied to regression and classification problems with the goals of inference and prediction. Numerous asset pricing models that have been developed by academic and industry researchers leverage linear regression. Applications include the identification of significant factors that drive asset returns, for example, as a basis for risk management, as well as the prediction of returns over various time horizons. Classification problems, on the other hand, include directional price forecasts.

In this chapter, we will cover the following topics:

- How linear regression works and which assumptions it makes
- How to train and diagnose linear regression models
- How to use linear regression to predict future returns
- How use regularization to improve the predictive performance
- How logistic regression works
- How to convert a regression into a classification problem

For code examples, additional resources, and references, see the directory for this chapter in the online GitHub repository.

Linear regression for inference and prediction

As the name suggests, linear regression models assume that the output is the result of a linear combination of the inputs. The model also assumes a random error that allows for each observation to deviate from the expected linear relationship. The reasons that the model does not perfectly describe the relationship between inputs and output in a deterministic way include, for example, missing variables, measurement, or data collection issues.

If we want to draw statistical conclusions about the true (but not observed) linear relationship in the population based on the regression parameters estimated from the sample, we need to add assumptions about the statistical nature of these errors. The baseline regression model makes the strong assumption that the distribution of the errors is identical across errors and that errors are independent of each other, that is, knowing one error does not help to forecast the next error. The assumption of **independent and identically distributed (iid)** errors implies that their covariance matrix is the identity matrix multiplied by a constant representing the error variance.

These assumptions guarantee that the OLS method delivers estimates that are not only unbiased but also efficient, that is, they have the lowest sampling error learning algorithms. However, these assumptions are rarely met in practice. In finance, we often encounter panel data with repeated observations on a given cross-section. The attempt to estimate the systematic exposure of a universe of assets to a set of risk factors over time typically surfaces correlation in the time or cross-sectional dimension, or both. Hence, alternative learning algorithms have emerged that assume more error covariance matrices that differ from multiples of the identity matrix.

On the other hand, methods that learn biased parameters for a linear model may yield estimates with a lower variance and, hence, improve the predictive performance. **Shrinkage methods** reduce the model complexity by applying regularization that adds a penalty term to the linear objective function. The penalty is positively related to the absolute size of the coefficients so that these are shrunk relative to the baseline case. Larger coefficients imply a more complex model that reacts more strongly to variations in the inputs. Properly calibrated, the penalty can limit the growth of the model's coefficients beyond what an optimal bias-variance trade-off would suggest.

We will introduce the baseline cross-section and panel techniques for linear models and important enhancements that produce accurate estimates when key assumptions are violated. We will then illustrate these methods by estimating factor models that are ubiquitous in the development of algorithmic trading strategies. Lastly, we will focus on regularization methods.

The multiple linear regression model

We will introduce the model's specification and objective function, methods to learn its parameters, statistical assumptions that allow for inference and diagnostics of these assumptions, as well as extensions to adapt the model to situations where these assumptions fail.

How to formulate the model

The multiple regression model defines a linear functional relationship between one continuous outcome variable and p input variables that can be of any type but may require preprocessing. Multivariate regression, in contrast, refers to the regression of multiple outputs on multiple input variables.

In the population, the linear regression model has the following form for a single instance of the output y, an input vector $\mathbf{x}^T = (x_1, \ldots, x_p)$, and the error ε:

$$y = f(\mathbf{x}) + \epsilon = \beta_0 + \beta_1 x_1 \ldots + \beta_p x_p + \epsilon = \beta_0 + \sum_{j=1}^{p} \beta_j x_j + \epsilon$$

The interpretation of the coefficients is straightforward: the value of a coefficient β_i is the partial, average effect of the variable x_i on the output, holding all other variables constant.

The model can also be written more compactly in matrix form. In this case, y is a vector of N output observations, X is the design matrix with N rows of observations on the p variables plus a column of 1s for the intercept, and β is the vector containing the $P = p+1$ coefficients $\beta_0, \ldots, \beta_p$:

$$\underset{(N \times 1)}{y} = \underset{(N \times P)(P \times 1)}{X \quad \beta} + \underset{(N \times 1)}{\epsilon}$$

The model is linear in its $p+1$ parameters but can model non-linear relationships by choosing or transforming variables accordingly, for example by including a polynomial basis expansion or logarithmic terms. It can also use categorical variables with dummy encoding, and interactions between variables by creating new inputs of the form $x_i \cdot x_j$.

To complete the formulation of the model from a statistical point of view so that we can test a hypothesis about the parameters, we need to make specific assumptions about the error term. We'll do this after first introducing the alternative methods to learn the parameters.

How to train the model

There are several methods to learn the model parameters β from the data: **ordinary least squares (OLS)**, **maximum likelihood estimation (MLE)**, and **stochastic gradient descent (SGD)**.

Least squares

The least squares method is the original method to learn the parameters of the hyperplane that best approximates the output from the input data. As the name suggests, the best approximation minimizes the sum of the squared distances between the output value and the hyperplane represented by the model.

The difference between the model's prediction and the actual outcome for a given data point is the residual (whereas the deviation of the true model from the true output in the population is called **error**). Hence, in formal terms, the least squares estimation method chooses the coefficient vector β to minimize the **residual sum of squares (RSS)**:

$$RSS(\beta) = \sum_{i=1}^{N} \epsilon_i^2 = \sum_{i=1}^{N}(y_i - f(x_i))^2 = \sum_{i=1}^{N}\left(y_i - \beta_0 - \sum_{j=1}^{p} x_{ij}\beta_j\right)^2 = (y - X\beta)^T(y - X\beta)$$

Hence, the least-squares coefficients β^{LS} are computed as:

$$\underset{\beta^{LS}}{\text{argmin}} = \text{RSS} = (\boldsymbol{y} - \boldsymbol{X}\beta)^T (\boldsymbol{y} - \boldsymbol{X}\beta)$$

The optimal parameter vector that minimizes RSS results from setting the derivatives of the preceding expression with respect to β to zero. This produces a unique solution, assuming X has full column rank, that is, the input variables are not linearly dependent, as follows:

$$\hat{\beta} = (\boldsymbol{X}^T X)^{-1} \boldsymbol{X}^T \boldsymbol{y}$$

When y and X have been de-meaned by subtracting their respective means, β represents the ratio of the covariance between the inputs and the outputs $\boldsymbol{X}^T\boldsymbol{y}$ and the output variance $(\boldsymbol{X}^T X)^{-1}$. There is also a geometric interpretation: the coefficients that minimize RSS ensure that the vector of residuals $\boldsymbol{y} - \hat{\boldsymbol{y}}$ is orthogonal to the subspace of $\mathbb{R}^N$ spanned by the columns of X, and the estimates $\hat{\boldsymbol{y}}$ are orthogonal projections into that subspace.

Maximum likelihood estimation

MLE is an important general method to estimate the parameters of a statistical model. It relies on the likelihood function that computes how likely it is to observe the sample of output values for a given set of both input data as a function of the model parameters. The likelihood differs from probabilities in that it is not normalized to range from 0 to 1.

We can set up the likelihood function for the linear regression example by assuming a distribution for the error term, such as the standard normal distribution:

$$\epsilon_i \sim N(0, 1) \quad \forall\, i = 1, \ldots, n.$$

This allows us to compute the conditional probability of observing a given output y_i given the corresponding input vector x_i and the parameters, $p(y_i|\boldsymbol{x}_i, \beta)$:

$$p(y_i|\boldsymbol{x}_i, \beta) = \frac{1}{\sigma\sqrt{2\pi}} e^{-\frac{\epsilon_i^2}{2\sigma}} = \frac{1}{\sigma\sqrt{2\pi}} e^{-\frac{(y_i - \boldsymbol{x}_i\beta)^2}{2\sigma}}$$

Assuming the output values are conditionally independent given the inputs, the likelihood of the sample is proportional to the product of the conditional probabilities of the individual output data points. Since it is easier to work with sums than with products, we apply the logarithm to obtain the log-likelihood function:

$$\log \mathcal{L}(\boldsymbol{y}, \boldsymbol{x}, \boldsymbol{\beta}) = \sum_{i=i}^{n} \log \frac{1}{\sigma\sqrt{2\pi}} e^{-\frac{(y_i - x_i \beta)^2}{2\sigma}}$$

The goal of MLE is to maximize the probability of the output sample that has in fact been observed by choosing model parameters, taking the observed inputs as given. Hence, the MLE parameter estimate results from maximizing the (log) likelihood function:

$$\beta_{\text{MLE}} = \underset{\beta}{\text{argmin}}\, \mathcal{L}$$

Due to the assumption of normal distribution, maximizing the log-likelihood function produces the same parameter solution as least squares because the only expression that depends on the parameters is squared residual in the exponent. For other distributional assumptions and models, MLE will produce different results, and in many cases, least squares is not applicable, as we will see later for logistic regression.

Gradient descent

Gradient descent is a general-purpose optimization algorithm that will find stationary points of smooth functions. The solution will be a global optimum if the objective function is convex. Variations of gradient descent are widely used in the training of complex neural networks, but also to compute solutions for MLE problems.

The algorithm uses the gradient of the objective function that contains its partial derivatives with respect to the parameters. These derivatives indicate how much the objective changes for infinitesimal steps in the direction of the corresponding parameters. It turns out that the maximal change of the function value results from a step in the direction of the gradient itself.

Hence, when minimizing a function that describes, for example, the cost of a prediction error, the algorithm computes the gradient for the current parameter values using the training data and modifies each parameter according to the negative value of its corresponding gradient component. As a result, the objective function will assume a lower value and move the parameters move closer to the solution. The optimization stops when the gradient becomes small, and the parameter values change very little.

The size of these steps is the learning rate, which is a critical parameter that may require tuning; many implementations include the option for this learning rate to increase with the number of iterations gradually. Depending on the size of the data, the algorithm may iterate many times over the entire dataset. Each such iteration is called an **epoch.** The number of epochs and the tolerance used to stop further iterations are hyperparameters you can tune.

Stochastic gradient descent randomly selects a data point and computes the gradient for this data point as opposed to an average over a larger sample to achieve a speedup. There are also batch versions that use a certain number of data points for each step.

The Gauss—Markov theorem

To assess the statistical of the model and conduct inference, we need to make assumptions about the residuals, that is, the properties of the unexplained part of the input. The **Gauss—Markov theorem (GMT)** defines the assumptions required for OLS to produce unbiased estimates of the model parameters β, and when these estimates have the lowest standard error among all linear models for cross-sectional data.

The baseline multiple regression model makes the following GMT assumptions:

1. In the population, **linearity** holds, $y = \beta_0 + \beta_1 x_1 \ldots + \beta_k x_k + \epsilon$ where β_i are unknown but constant and ϵ is a random error
2. The data for the input variables $x_1, \ldots, x_k$ are a **random sample** from the population
3. No perfect **collinearity**—there are no exact linear relationships among the input variables
4. The **error has a conditional mean of zero** given any of the inputs: $E[\epsilon | x_1, \ldots, x_k] = 0$
5. **Homoskedasticity**, the error term ϵ has constant variance given the inputs: $E[\epsilon | x_1, \ldots, x_k] = \sigma^2$

The fourth assumption implies that no missing variable exists that is correlated with any of the input variables. Under the first four assumptions, the OLS method delivers **unbiased** estimates: including an irrelevant variable does not bias the intercept and slope estimates, but omitting a relevant variable will bias the OLS estimates. OLS is then also **consistent**: as the sample size increases, the estimates converge to the true value as the standard errors become arbitrary. The converse is unfortunately also true: if the conditional expectation of the error is not zero because the model misses a relevant variable or the functional form is wrong (that is, quadratic or log terms are missing), then all parameter estimates are biased. If the error is correlated with any of the input variables then OLS is also not consistent, that is, adding more data will not remove the bias.

If we add the fifth assumptions, then OLS also produces the best linear, unbiased estimates (BLUE), where best means that the estimates have the lowest standard error among all linear estimators. Hence, if the five assumptions hold and statistical inference is the goal, then the OLS estimates is the way to go. If the goal, however, is to predict, then we will see that other estimators exist that trade off some bias for a lower variance to achieve superior predictive performance in many settings.

Now that we have introduced the basic OLS assumptions, we can take a look at inference in small and large samples.

How to conduct statistical inference

Inference in the linear regression context aims to draw conclusions about the true relationship in the population from the sample data. This includes tests of hypothesis about the significance of the overall relationship or the values of particular coefficients, as well as estimates of confidence intervals.

The key ingredient for statistical inference is a test statistic with a known distribution. We can use it to assume that the null hypothesis is true and compute the probability of observing the value for this statistic in the sample, familiar as the p-value. If the p-value drops below a significance threshold (typically five percent) then we reject the hypothesis because it makes the actual sample value very unlikely. At the same time, we accept that the p-value reflects the probability that we are wrong in rejecting what is, in fact, a correct hypothesis.

In addition to the five GMT assumptions, the classical linear model assumes **normality**—the population error is normally distributed and independent of the input variables. This assumption implies that the output variable is normally distributed, conditional on the input variables. This strong assumption permits the derivation of the exact distribution of the coefficients, which in turn implies exact distributions of the test statistics required for similarly exact hypotheses tests in small samples. This assumption often fails—asset returns, for instance, are not normally distributed—but, fortunately, the methods used under normality are also approximately valid.

We have the following distributional characteristics and test statistics, approximately under GMT assumptions 1–5, and exactly when normality holds:

- The parameter estimates follow a multivariate normal distribution:
  $\hat{\beta} \sim N(\beta, (\boldsymbol{X}^T \boldsymbol{X})^{-1} \sigma)$.

- Under GMT 1–5, the parameter estimates are already unbiased and we can get an unbiased estimate of σ, the constant error variance, using

  $$\hat{\sigma} = \frac{1}{N-p-1} \sum_{i=i}^{N} (y_i - \hat{y}_i)^2$$.

- The t statistic for a hypothesis tests about an individual coefficient β_j is

  $t_j = \frac{\hat{\beta}_j}{\hat{\sigma}\sqrt{v_j}} \sim t_{N-p-1}$ and follows a t distribution with *N-p-1* degrees of freedom where v_j is the j's element of the diagonal of $(\boldsymbol{X}^T \boldsymbol{X})^{-1}$.

- The *t* distribution converges to the normal distribution and since the 97.5 quantile of the normal distribution is 1.96, a useful rule of thumb for a 95% confidence interval around a parameter estimate is $\hat{\beta} \pm 2 \cdot \text{se}(\hat{\beta})$. An interval that includes zero implies that we can't reject the null hypothesis that the true parameter is zero and, hence, irrelevant for the model.

- The *F* statistic allows for tests of restrictions on several parameters, including whether the entire regression is significant. It measures the change (reduction) in the RSS that results from additional variables.

- Finally, the **Lagrange Multiplier (LM)** test is an alternative to the *F* test to restrict multiple restrictions.

How to diagnose and remedy problems

Diagnostics validate the model assumptions and prevent wrong conclusions when interpreting the result and conducting statistical inference. They include measures of goodness of fit and various tests of the assumptions about the error term, including how closely the residuals match a normal distribution. Furthermore, diagnostics test whether the residual variance is indeed constant or exhibits heteroskedasticity, and if the errors are conditionally uncorrelated or exhibit serial correlation, that is, if knowing one error helps to predict consecutive errors.

In addition to the tests outlined as follows, it is always important to visually inspect the residuals to detect whether there are systematic patterns because these indicate that the model is missing one or more factors that drive the outcome.

Goodness of fit

Goodness-of-fit measures assess how well a model explains the variation in the outcome. They help to assess the quality of model specification, for instance, to select among different model designs. They differ in how they evaluate the fit. The measures discussed here provide in-sample information; we will use out-of-sample testing and cross-validation when we focus on predictive models in the next section.

Prominent goodness-of-fit measures include the (adjusted) R^2 that should be maximized and is based on the least-squares estimate:

- R^2 measures the share of the variation in the outcome data explained by the model and is computed as $R^2 = 1 - \frac{\text{RSS}}{\text{TSS}}$, where TSS is the sum of squared deviations of the outcome from its mean. It also corresponds to the squared correlation coefficient between the actual outcome values and those estimated (fitted) by the model. The goals is to maximize R^2 but it never decreases as the model adds more variables and, hence, encourages overfitting.

- The adjusted R^2 penalizes R^2 for adding more variables; each additional variable needs to reduce RSS significantly to produce better goodness of fit.

Alternatively, the Akaike (AIC) and the **Bayesian Information Criterion (BIC)** are to be minimized and are based on the maximum-likelihood estimate:

- $\text{AIC} = -2\log(\mathcal{L}^*) + 2k$, where $\mathcal{L}^*$ is the value of the maximized likelihood function, k is the number of parameters
- $\text{BIC} = -2\log(\mathcal{L}^*) + \log(N)k$ where N is the sample size

Both metrics penalize for complexity, with BIC imposing a higher penalty so that it might underfit whereas AIC might overfit in relative terms. Conceptually, AIC aims at finding the model that best describes an unknown data-generating process, whereas BIC tries to find the best model among the set of candidates. In practice, both criteria can be used jointly to guide model selection when the goal is in-sample fit; otherwise, cross-validation and selection based on estimates of generalization error are preferable.

Heteroskedasticity

GMT assumption 5 requires the residual covariance to take the shape $\Sigma = \sigma^2 I$, that is, a diagonal matrix with entries equal to the constant variance of the error term. Heteroskedasticity occurs when the residual variance is not constant but differs across observations. If the residual variance is positively correlated with an input variable, that is, when errors are larger for input values that are far from their mean, then OLS standard error estimates will be too low, and, consequently, the t-statistic will be inflated leading to false discoveries of relationships where none actually exist.

Diagnostics starts with a visual inspection of the residuals. Systematic patterns in the (supposedly random) residuals suggest statistical tests of the null hypothesis that errors are homoscedastic against various alternatives. These tests include the Breusch—Pagan and White tests.

There are several ways to correct OLS estimates for heteroskedasticity:

- Robust standard errors (sometimes called white standard errors) take heteroskedasticity into account when computing the error variance using a so-called **sandwich estimator**.
- Clustered standard errors assume that there are distinct groups in your data that are homoscedastic but the error variance differs between groups. These groups could be different asset classes or equities from different industries.

Several alternatives to OLS estimate the error covariance matrix using different assumptions when $\Sigma \neq \sigma^2 I$. The following are available in `statsmodels`:

- **Weighted least squares (WLS)**: For heteroskedastic errors where the covariance matrix has only diagonal entries as for OLS, but now the entries are allowed to vary
- Feasible **generalized least squares (GLSAR)**, for autocorrelated errors that follow an autoregressive AR (p) process (see the chapter on linear time series models)
- **Generalized least squares (GLS)** for arbitrary covariance matrix structure; yields efficient and unbiased estimates in the presence of heteroskedasticity or serial correlation

Serial correlation

Serial correlation means that consecutive residuals produced by linear regression are correlated, which violates the fourth GMT assumption. Positive serial correlation implies that the standard errors are underestimated and the t-statistics will be inflated, leading to false discoveries if ignored. However, there are procedures to correct for serial correlation when calculating standard errors.

The Durbin—Watson statistic diagnoses serial correlation. It tests the hypothesis that the OLS residuals are not autocorrelated against the alternative that they follow an autoregressive process (that we will explore in the next chapter). The test statistic ranges from 0 to 4, and values near 2 indicate non-autocorrelation, lower values suggest positive, and higher values indicate negative autocorrelation. The exact threshold values depend on the number of parameters and observations and need to be looked up in tables.

Multicollinearity

Multicollinearity occurs when two or more independent variables are highly correlated. This poses several challenges:

- It is difficult to determine which factors influence the dependent variable
- The individual p values can be misleading—a p-value can be high even if the variable is important
- The confidence intervals for the regression coefficients will be excessive, possibly even including zero, making it impossible to determine the effect of an independent variable on the outcome

There is no formal or theory-based solution that corrects for multicollinearity. Instead, try to remove one or more of the correlated input variables, or increase the sample size.

How to run linear regression in practice

The accompanying notebook `linear_regression_intro.ipynb` illustrates a simple and then a multiple linear regression, the latter using both OLS and gradient descent. For the multiple regression, we generate two random input variables x_1 and x_2 that range from -50 to +50, and an outcome variable calculated as a linear combination of the inputs plus random Gaussian noise to meet the normality assumption GMT 6:

$$y = 50 + x_1 + 3x_2 + \epsilon, \qquad \epsilon \sim N(0, 50)$$

OLS with statsmodels

We use `statsmodels` to estimate a multiple regression model that accurately reflects the data generating process as follows:

```
from statsmodels.api import
X_ols = add_constant(X)
model = OLS(y, X_ols).fit()
model.summary()
```

This yields the following **OLS Regression Results** summary:

```
                            OLS Regression Results
===============================================================================
Dep. Variable:                      Y   R-squared:                       0.779
Model:                            OLS   Adj. R-squared:                  0.778
Method:                 Least Squares   F-statistic:                     1095.
Date:                Mon, 03 Sep 2018   Prob (F-statistic):          1.85e-204
Time:                        17:38:41   Log-Likelihood:                -3332.6
No. Observations:                 625   AIC:                             6671.
Df Residuals:                     622   BIC:                             6685.
Df Model:                           2
Covariance Type:            nonrobust
===============================================================================
                 coef    std err          t      P>|t|      [0.025      0.975]
-------------------------------------------------------------------------------
const         50.9371      2.007     25.376      0.000      46.995      54.879
X_1            1.0813      0.067     16.185      0.000       0.950       1.212
X_2            2.9328      0.067     43.900      0.000       2.802       3.064
===============================================================================
Omnibus:                        0.267   Durbin-Watson:                   2.140
Prob(Omnibus):                  0.875   Jarque-Bera (JB):                0.196
Skew:                           0.040   Prob(JB):                        0.907
Kurtosis:                       3.032   Cond. No.                         30.0
===============================================================================

Warnings:
[1] Standard Errors assume that the covariance matrix of the errors is correctly specified.
```

Summary of OLS Regression Results

The upper part of the summary displays the dataset characteristics, namely the estimation method, the number of observations and parameters, and indicates that standard error estimates do not account for heteroskedasticity. The middle panel shows the coefficient values that closely reflect the artificial data generating process. We can confirm that the estimates displayed in the middle of the summary result can be obtained using the OLS formula derived previously:

```
beta = np.linalg.inv(X_ols.T.dot(X_ols)).dot(X_ols.T.dot(y))
pd.Series(beta, index=X_ols.columns)

const    50.94
X_1       1.08
X_2       2.93
```

The following diagram illustrates the hyperplane fitted by the model to the randomly generated data points:

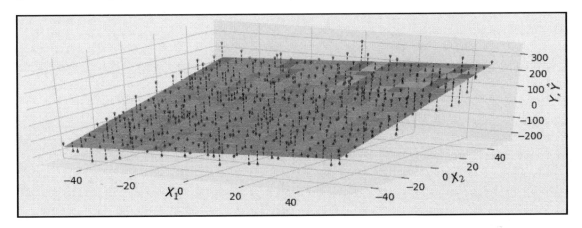

Hyperplane

The upper right part of the panel displays the goodness-of-fit measures just discussed, alongside the F-test that rejects the hypothesis that all coefficients are zero and irrelevant. Similarly, the t-statistics indicate that intercept and both slope coefficients are, unsurprisingly, highly significant.

The bottom part of the summary contains the residual diagnostics. The left panel displays skew and kurtosis that are used to test the normality hypothesis. Both the Omnibus and the Jarque—Bera test fails to reject the null hypothesis that the residuals are normally distributed. The Durbin—Watson statistic tests for serial correlation in the residuals and has a value near 2 which, given 2 parameters and 625 observations, fails to reject the hypothesis of no serial correlation.

Lastly, the condition number provides evidence about multicollinearity: it is the ratio of the square roots of the largest and the smallest eigenvalue of the design matrix that contains the input data. A value above 30 suggests that the regression may have significant multicollinearity.

statsmodels includes additional diagnostic tests that are linked in the notebook.

Stochastic gradient descent with sklearn

The `sklearn` library includes an `SGDRegressor` model in its `linear_models` module. To learn the parameters for the same model using this method, we need to first standardize the data because the gradient is sensitive to the scale. We use `StandardScaler()` for this purpose that computes the mean and the standard deviation for each input variable during the fit step, and then subtracts the mean and divides by the standard deviation during the transform step that we can conveniently conduct in a single `fit_transform()` command:

```
scaler = StandardScaler()
X_ = scaler.fit_transform(X)
```

Then we instantiate the `SGDRegressor` using the default values except for a `random_state` setting to facilitate replication:

```
sgd = SGDRegressor(loss='squared_loss', fit_intercept=True,
                   shuffle=True, random_state=42,   # shuffle training data
for better gradient estimates
                   learning_rate='invscaling',      # reduce learning rate
over time
                   eta0=0.01, power_t=0.25)         # parameters for
learning rate path
```

Now we can fit the `sgd` model, create the in-sample predictions for both the OLS and the `sgd` models, and compute the root mean squared error for each:

```
sgd.fit(X=X_, y=y)
resids = pd.DataFrame({'sgd': y - sgd.predict(X_),
                       'ols': y - model.predict(sm.add_constant(X))})
resids.pow(2).sum().div(len(y)).pow(.5)

ols    50.06
sgd    50.06
```

As expected, both models yield the same result. We will now take on a more ambitious project using linear regression to estimate a multi-factor asset pricing model.

How to build a linear factor model

Algorithmic trading strategies use **linear factor models** to quantify the relationship between the return of an asset and the sources of risk that represent the main drivers of these returns. Each factor risk carries a premium, and the total asset return can be expected to correspond to a weighted average of these risk premia.

There are several practical applications of factor models across the portfolio management process from construction and asset selection to risk management and performance evaluation. The importance of factor models continues to grow as common risk factors are now tradeable:

- A summary of the returns of many assets by a much smaller number of factors reduces the amount of data required to estimate the covariance matrix when optimizing a portfolio
- An estimate of the exposure of an asset or a portfolio to these factors allows for the management of the resultant risk, for instance by entering suitable hedges when risk factors are themselves traded
- A factor model also permits the assessment of the incremental signal content of new alpha factors
- A factor model can also help assess whether a manager's performance relative to a benchmark is indeed due to skill in selecting assets and timing the market, or if instead, the performance can be explained by portfolio tilts towards known return drivers that can today be replicated as low-cost, passively managed funds without incurring active management fees

The following examples apply to equities, but risk factors have been identified for all asset classes (see references in the GitHub repository).

From the CAPM to the Fama—French five-factor model

Risk factors have been a key ingredient to quantitative models since the **Capital Asset Pricing Model (CAPM)** explained the expected returns of all N assets $r_i, \quad i = 1, \ldots, N$ using their respective exposure β_i to a single factor, the expected excess return of the overall market over the risk-free rate r_f. The model takes the following linear form:

$$E[r_i] = \alpha_i + r_f + \beta_i(E[r_m] - r_f)$$

This differs from classic fundamental analysis a la Dodd and Graham where returns depend on firm characteristics. The rationale is that, in the aggregate, investors cannot eliminate this so-called systematic risk through diversification. Hence, in equilibrium, they require compensation for holding an asset commensurate with its systematic risk. The model implies that, given efficient markets where prices immediately reflect all public information, there should be no superior risk-adjusted returns, that is, the value of α should be zero.

Empirical tests of the model use linear regression and have consistently failed, prompting a debate whether the efficient markets or the single factor aspect of the joint hypothesis is to blame. It turns out that both premises are probably wrong:

- Joseph Stiglitz earned the 2001 Nobel Prize in economics in part for showing that markets are generally not perfectly efficient: if markets are efficient, there is no value in collecting data because this information is already reflected in prices. However, if there is no incentive to gather information, it is hard to see how it should be already reflected in prices.
- On the other hand, theoretical and empirical improvements on the CAPM suggest that additional factors help explain some of the anomalies that consisted in superior risk-adjusted returns that do not depend on overall market exposure, such as higher returns for smaller firms.

Stephen Ross proposed the **Arbitrage Pricing Theory (APT)** in 1976 as an alternative that allows for several risk factors while eschewing market efficiency. In contrast to the CAPM, it assumes that opportunities for superior returns due to mispricing may exist but will quickly be arbitraged away. The theory does not specify the factors, but research by the author suggests that the most important are changes in inflation and industrial production, as well as changes in risk premia or the term structure of interest rates.

Kenneth French and Eugene Fama (who won the 2013 Nobel Prize) identified additional risk factors that depend on firm characteristics and are widely used today. In 1993, the Fama—French three-factor model added the relative size and value of firms to the single CAPM source of risk. In 2015, the five-factor model further expanded the set to include firm profitability and level of investment that had been shown to be significant in the intervening years. In addition, many factor models include a price momentum factor.

The Fama—French risk factors are computed as the return difference on diversified portfolios with high or low values according to metrics that reflect a given risk factor. These returns are obtained by sorting stocks according to these metrics and then going long stocks above a certain percentile while shorting stocks below a certain percentile. The metrics associated with the risk factors are defined as follows:

- **Size: Market Equity (ME)**
- **Value: Book Value of Equity (BE)** divided by ME
- **Operating Profitability (OP)**: Revenue minus cost of goods sold/assets
- **Investment**: Investment/assets

There are also unsupervised learning techniques for a data-driven discovery of risk factors using factors and principal component analysis that we will explore in `Chapter 12, Unsupervised Learning`.

Obtaining the risk factors

Fama and French make updated risk factor and research portfolio data available through their website, and you can use the `pandas_datareader` library to obtain the data. For this application, refer to the `fama_macbeth.ipynb` notebook for additional detail.

In particular, we will be using the five Fama—French factors that result from sorting stocks first into three size groups and then into two for each of the remaining three firm-specific factors. Hence, the factors involve three sets of value-weighted portfolios formed as 3 x 2 sorts on size and book-to-market, size and operating profitability, and size and investment. The risk factor values computed as the average returns of the **portfolios (PF)** as outlined in the following table:

Concept	Label	Name	Risk factor calculation
Size	SMB	Small minus big	Nine small stock PF minus nine large stock PF
Value	HML	High minus low	Two value PF minus two growth (with low BE/ME value) PF
Profitability	RMW	Robust minus weak	Two robust OP PF minus two weak OP PF
Investment	CMA	Conservative minus aggressive	Two conservative investment portfolios minus two aggressive investment portfolios
Market	Rm-Rf	Excess return on the market	Value-weight return of all firms incorporated in and listed on major US exchanges with good data minus the one-month Treasury bill rate

We will use returns at a monthly frequency that we obtain for the period 2010 – 2017 as follows:

```
import pandas_datareader.data as web
ff_factor = 'F-F_Research_Data_5_Factors_2x3'
ff_factor_data = web.DataReader(ff_factor, 'famafrench', start='2010',
end='2017-12')[0]
ff_factor_data.info()

PeriodIndex: 96 entries, 2010-01 to 2017-12
Freq: M
Data columns (total 6 columns):
Mkt-RF 96 non-null float64
SMB 96 non-null float64
HML 96 non-null float64
RMW 96 non-null float64
CMA 96 non-null float64
```

```
RF 96 non-null float64
```

Fama and French also make available numerous portfolios that we can illustrate the estimation of the factor exposures, as well as the value of the risk premia available in the market for a given time period. We will use a panel of the 17 industry portfolios at a monthly frequency. We will subtract the risk-free rate from the returns because the factor model works with excess returns:

```
ff_portfolio = '17_Industry_Portfolios'
ff_portfolio_data = web.DataReader(ff_portfolio, 'famafrench',
start='2010', end='2017-12')[0]
ff_portfolio_data = ff_portfolio_data.sub(ff_factor_data.RF, axis=0)
ff_factor_data = ff_factor_data.drop('RF', axis=1)
ff_portfolio_data.info()

PeriodIndex: 96 entries, 2010-01 to 2017-12
Freq: M
Data columns (total 17 columns):
Food      96 non-null float64
Mines     96 non-null float64
Oil       96 non-null float64
...
Rtail     96 non-null float64
Finan     96 non-null float64
Other     96 non-null float64
```

We will now build a linear factor model based on this panel data using a method that addresses the failure of some basic linear regression assumptions.

Fama—Macbeth regression

Given data on risk factors and portfolio returns, it is useful to estimate the portfolio's exposure, that is, how much the risk factors drive portfolio returns, as well as how much the exposure to a given factor is worth, that is, the what market's risk factor premium is. The risk premium then permits to estimate the return for any portfolio provided the factor exposure is known or can be assumed.

More formally, we will have $i=1, ..., N$ asset or portfolio returns over $t=1, ..., T$ periods and each asset's excess period return will be denoted r_{it}. The goals is to test whether the $j=1, ..., M$ factors F_{jt} explain the excess returns and the risk premium associated with each factor. In our case, we have $N=17$ portfolios and $M=5$ factors, each with $=96$ periods of data.

Factor models are estimated for many stocks in a given period. Inference problems will likely arise in such cross-sectional regressions because the fundamental assumptions of classical linear regression may not hold. Potential violations include measurement errors, covariation of residuals due to heteroskedasticity and serial correlation, and multicollinearity.

To address the inference problem caused by the correlation of the residuals, Fama and MacBeth proposed a two-step methodology for a cross-sectional regression of returns on factors. The two-stage Fama—Macbeth regression is designed to estimate the premium rewarded for the exposure to a particular risk factor by the market. The two stages consist of:

- **First stage**: N time-series regression, one for each asset or portfolio, of its excess returns on the factors to estimate the factor loadings. In matrix form, for each asset:

$$\underset{T \times 1}{r_i} = \underset{T \times (m+1)}{F} \underset{(m+1) \times 1}{\beta_i} + \underset{T \times 1}{\epsilon_i}$$

- **Second stage**: T cross-sectional regression, one for each time period, to estimate the risk premium. In matrix form, we obtain a vector $\hat{\lambda}_t$ of risk premia for each period:

$$\underset{N \times (M+1)}{r_t} = \underset{N \times (M+1)}{\hat{\beta}} \underset{(M+1) \times 1}{\lambda_t}$$

Now we can compute the factor risk premia as the time average and get t-statistic to assess their individual significance, using the assumption that the risk premia estimates are independent over time: $t = \dfrac{\lambda_j}{\sigma(\lambda_j)/\sqrt{(T)}}$.

If we had a very large and representative data sample on traded risk factors we could use the sample mean as a risk premium estimate. However, we typically do not have a sufficiently long history to and the margin of error around the sample mean could be quite large. The Fama—Macbeth methodology leverages the covariance of the factors with other assets to determine the factor premia. The second moment of asset returns is easier to estimate than the first moment, and obtaining more granular data improves estimation considerably, which is not true of mean estimation.

We can implement the first stage to obtain the 17 factor loading estimates as follows:

```
betas = []
for industry in ff_portfolio_data:
    step1 = OLS(endog=ff_portfolio_data[industry],
                exog=add_constant(ff_factor_data)).fit()
    betas.append(step1.params.drop('const'))

betas = pd.DataFrame(betas,
                     columns=ff_factor_data.columns,
                     index=ff_portfolio_data.columns)
betas.info()
Index: 17 entries, Food  to Other
Data columns (total 5 columns):
Mkt-RF    17 non-null float64
SMB       17 non-null float64
HML       17 non-null float64
RMW       17 non-null float64
CMA       17 non-null float64
```

For the second stage, we run 96 regressions of the period returns for the cross section of portfolios on the factor loadings:

```
lambdas = []
for period in ff_portfolio_data.index:
    step2 = OLS(endog=ff_portfolio_data.loc[period, betas.index],
                exog=betas).fit()
    lambdas.append(step2.params)

lambdas = pd.DataFrame(lambdas,
                       index=ff_portfolio_data.index,
                       columns=betas.columns.tolist())
lambdas.info()
PeriodIndex: 96 entries, 2010-01 to 2017-12
Freq: M
Data columns (total 5 columns):
Mkt-RF    96 non-null float64
SMB       96 non-null float64
HML       96 non-null float64
RMW       96 non-null float64
CMA       96 non-null float64
```

Finally, we compute the average for the 96 periods to obtain our factor risk premium estimates:

```
lambdas.mean()
Mkt-RF     1.201304
SMB        0.190127
HML       -1.306792
RMW       -0.570817
CMA       -0.522821
```

The `linear_models` library extends `statsmodels` with various models for panel data and also implements the two-stage Fama—MacBeth procedure:

```
model = LinearFactorModel(portfolios=ff_portfolio_data,
                          factors=ff_factor_data)
res = model.fit()
```

This provides us with the same result:

```
                     LinearFactorModel Estimation Summary
================================================================================
No. Test Portfolios:              17   R-squared:                      0.6943
No. Factors:                       6   J-statistic:                    19.155
No. Observations:                 95   P-value                         0.0584
Date:                Wed, Oct 31 2018   Distribution:                 chi2(11)
Time:                       15:15:52
Cov. Estimator:                robust

                          Risk Premia Estimates
==============================================================================
           Parameter   Std. Err.    T-stat    P-value    Lower CI   Upper CI
------------------------------------------------------------------------------
Mkt-RF        1.2446      0.3928     3.1689     0.0015      0.4748     2.0144
SMB           0.0074      0.7055     0.0105     0.9917     -1.3753     1.3901
HML          -0.6970      0.5334    -1.3067     0.1913     -1.7424     0.3484
RMW          -0.2558      0.6888    -0.3713     0.7104     -1.6057     1.0942
CMA          -0.3086      0.4737    -0.6515     0.5147     -1.2371     0.6198
RF           -0.0133      0.0132    -1.0092     0.3129     -0.0393     0.0126
==============================================================================

Covariance estimator:
HeteroskedasticCovariance
See full_summary for complete results
```

LinearFactorModel Estimation Summary

The accompanying notebook illustrates the use of categorical variables by using industry dummies when estimating risk premia for a larger panel of individual stocks.

Shrinkage methods: regularization for linear regression

The least squares methods to train a linear regression model will produce the best, linear, and unbiased coefficient estimates when the Gauss—Markov assumptions are met. Variations like GLS fare similarly well even when OLS assumptions about the error covariance matrix are violated. However, there are estimators that produce biased coefficients to reduce the variance to achieve a lower generalization error overall.

When a linear regression model contains many correlated variables, their coefficients will be poorly determined because the effect of a large positive coefficient on the RSS can be canceled by a similarly large negative coefficient on a correlated variable. Hence, the model will have a tendency for high variance due to this wiggle room of the coefficients that increases the risk that the model overfits to the sample.

How to hedge against overfitting

One popular technique to control overfitting is that of **regularization**, which involves the addition of a penalty term to the error function to discourage the coefficients from reaching large values. In other words, size constraints on the coefficients can alleviate the resultant potentially negative impact on out-of-sample predictions. We will encounter regularization methods for all models since overfitting is such a pervasive problem.

In this section, we will introduce shrinkage methods that address two motivations to improve on the approaches to linear models discussed so far:

- **Prediction accuracy**: The low bias but high variance of least squares estimates suggests that the generalization error could be reduced by shrinking or setting some coefficients to zero, thereby trading off a slightly higher bias for a reduction in the variance of the model.
- **Interpretation**: A large number of predictors may complicate the interpretation or communication of the big picture of the results. It may be preferable to sacrifice some detail to limit the model to a smaller subset of parameters with the strongest effects.

Shrinkage models restrict the regression coefficients by imposing a penalty on their size. These models achieve this goal by adding a term to the objective function so that the coefficients of a shrinkage model minimize the RSS plus a penalty that is positively related to the (absolute) size of the coefficients. The added penalty turns finding the linear regression coefficients into a constrained minimization problem that, in general, takes the following Lagrangian form:

$$\hat{\beta}^S = \underset{\beta^S}{\text{argmin}} \sum_{i=1}^{N} \left[(y_i - \beta_0 - \sum_{j=1}^{p} \beta_j x_j)^2 + \lambda S(\beta) \right] = \underset{\beta^S}{\text{argmin}} \; y - X\beta - \lambda S(\beta)$$

The regularization parameter λ determines the size of the penalty effect, that is, the strength of the regularization. As soon as λ is positive, the coefficients will differ from the unconstrained least squared parameters, which implies a biased estimate. The hyperparameter λ should be adaptively chosen using cross-validation to minimize an estimate of expected prediction error.

Shrinkage models differ by how they calculate the penalty, that is, the functional form of S. The most common versions are the ridge regression that uses the sum of the squared coefficients, whereas the lasso model bases the penalty on the sum of the absolute values of the coefficients.

How ridge regression works

The ridge regression shrinks the regression coefficients by adding a penalty to the objective function that equals the sum of the squared coefficients, which in turn corresponds to the L^2 norm of the coefficient vector:

$$S(\beta) = \sum_{i=1}^{p} \beta_i^2 = \|\beta\|^2$$

Hence, the ridge coefficients are defined as:

$$\hat{\beta}^{\text{Ridge}} = \underset{\beta^{\text{Ridge}}}{\text{argmin}} \sum_{i=1}^{N} \left[(y_i - \beta_0 - \sum_{j=1}^{p} \beta_j x_j)^2 + \lambda \sum_{j=1}^{p} \beta_j^2 \right] = \underset{\beta^{\text{Ridge}}}{\text{argmin}} \; (y - X\beta)^T (y - X\beta) + \lambda \beta^T \beta$$

The intercept β_0 has been excluded from the penalty to make the procedure independent of the origin chosen for the output variable—otherwise, adding a constant to all output values would change all slope parameters as opposed to a parallel shift.

It is important to standardize the inputs by subtracting from each input the corresponding mean and dividing the result by the input's standard deviation because the ridge solution is sensitive to the scale of the inputs. There is also a closed solution for the ridge estimator that resembles the OLS case:

$$\hat{\beta}^{\text{Ridge}} = (X^T X + \lambda I)^{-1} X^T y$$

The solution adds the scaled identity matrix λI to $X^T X$ before inversion, which guarantees that the problem is non-singular, even if $X^T X$ does not have full rank. This was one of the motivations for using this estimator when it was originally introduced.

The ridge penalty results in proportional shrinkage of all parameters. In the case of **orthonormal inputs**, the ridge estimates are just a scaled version of the least squares estimates, that is:

$$\hat{\beta}^{\text{Ridge}} = \frac{\hat{\beta}^{\text{LS}}}{1 + \lambda}$$

Using the **singular value decomposition (SVD)** of the input matrix X, we can gain insight into how the shrinkage affects inputs in the more common case where they are not orthonormal. The SVD of a centered matrix represents the principal components of a matrix (refer to `Chapter 11`, *Gradient Boosting Machines*, on unsupervised learning) that capture uncorrelated directions in the column space of the data in descending order of variance.

Ridge regression shrinks coefficients on input variables that are associated with directions in the data that have less variance more than input variables that correlate with directions that exhibit more variance. Hence, the implicit assumption of ridge regression is that the directions in the data that vary the most will be most influential or most reliable when predicting the output.

How lasso regression works

The lasso, known as basis pursuit in signal processing, also shrinks the coefficients by adding a penalty to the sum of squares of the residuals, but the lasso penalty has a slightly different effect. The lasso penalty is the sum of the absolute values of the coefficient vector, which corresponds to its L^1 norm. Hence, the lasso estimate is defined by:

$$\hat{\beta}^{\text{Lasso}} = \underset{\beta^{\text{Lasso}}}{\operatorname{argmin}} \sum_{i=1}^{N} \left[(y_i - \beta_0 - \sum_{j=1}^{p} \beta_j x_j)^2 + \lambda \sum_{j=1}^{p} |\beta_j| \right] = \underset{\beta^{\text{Ridge}}}{\operatorname{argmin}} (\boldsymbol{y} - \boldsymbol{X\beta})^T (\boldsymbol{y} - \boldsymbol{X\beta}) + \lambda |\boldsymbol{\beta}|$$

Similarly to ridge regression, the inputs need to be standardized. The lasso penalty makes the solution nonlinear, and there is no closed-form expression for the coefficients as in ridge regression. Instead, the lasso solution is a quadratic programming problem and there are available efficient algorithms that compute the entire path of coefficients that result for different values of λ with the same computational cost as for ridge regression.

The lasso penalty had the effect of gradually reducing some coefficients to zero as the regularization increases. For this reason, the lasso can be used for the continuous selection of a subset of features.

How to use linear regression to predict returns

The notebook `linear_regression.ipynb` contains examples for the prediction of stock prices using OLS with `statsmodels` and `sklearn`, as well as ridge and lasso models. It is designed to run as a notebook on the Quantopian research platform and relies on the `factor_library` introduced in Chapter 4, *Alpha Factors Research*.

Prepare the data

We need to select a universe of equities and a time horizon, build and transform alpha factors that we will use as features, calculate forward returns that we aim to predict, and potentially clean our data.

Universe creation and time horizon

We will use equity data for the years 2014 and 2015 from a custom `Q100US` universe that uses built-in filters, factors, and classifiers to select the 100 stocks with the highest average dollar volume of the last 200 trading days filtered by additional default criteria (see Quantopian docs linked on GitHub for detail). The universe dynamically updates based on the filter criteria so that, while there are 100 stocks at any given point, there may be more than 100 distinct equities in the sample:

```
def Q100US():
    return filters.make_us_equity_universe(
        target_size=100,
        rankby=factors.AverageDollarVolume(window_length=200),
        mask=filters.default_us_equity_universe_mask(),
        groupby=classifiers.fundamentals.Sector(),
        max_group_weight=0.3,
        smoothing_func=lambda f: f.downsample('month_start'),
    )
```

Target return computation

We will test predictions for various `lookahead` periods to identify the best holding periods that generate the best predictability, measured by the information coefficient. More specifically, we compute returns for 1, 5, 10, and 20 days using the built-in `Returns` function, resulting in over 50,000 observations for the universe of 100 stocks over two years (that include approximately 252 trading days each):

```
lookahead = [1, 5, 10, 20]
returns = run_pipeline(Pipeline({'Returns{}D'.format(i):
Returns(inputs=[USEquityPricing.close],
                                window_length=i+1, mask=UNIVERSE)
for i in lookahead},
                        screen=UNIVERSE),
            start_date=START,
            end_date=END)
return_cols = ['Returns{}D'.format(i) for i in lookahead]
returns.info()

MultiIndex: 50362 entries, (2014-01-02 00:00:00+00:00, Equity(24 [AAPL]))
to (2015-12-31 00:00:00+00:00, Equity(47208 [GPRO]))
Data columns (total 4 columns):
Returns10D     50362 non-null float64
Returns1D      50362 non-null float64
Returns20D     50360 non-null float64
Returns5D      50362 non-null float64
```

Alpha factor selection and transformation

We will use over 50 features that cover a broad range of factors based on market, fundamental, and alternative data. The notebook also includes custom transformations to convert fundamental data that is typically available in quarterly reporting frequency to rolling annual totals or averages to avoid excessive season fluctuations.

Once the factors have been computed through the various pipelines outlined in Chapter 4, *Alpha Factors Research,* we combine them using pd.concat(), assign index names, and create a categorical variable that identifies the asset for each data point:

```
data = pd.concat([returns, value_factors, momentum_factors,
                  quality_factors, payout_factors, growth_factors,
                  efficiency_factors, risk_factors], axis=1).sortlevel()
data.index.names = ['date', 'asset']
data['stock'] = data.index.get_level_values('asset').map(lambda x:
x.asset_name)
```

Data cleaning – missing data

In a next step, we remove rows and columns that lack more than 20 percent of the observations, resulting in a loss of six percent of the observations and three columns:

```
rows_before, cols_before = data.shape
data = (data
        .dropna(axis=1, thresh=int(len(data) * .8))
        .dropna(thresh=int(len(data.columns) * .8)))
data = data.fillna(data.median())
rows_after, cols_after = data.shape
print('{:,d} rows and {:,d} columns dropped'.format(rows_before -
rows_after, cols_before - cols_after))
2,985 rows and 3 columns dropped
```

At this point, we have 51 features and the categorical identifier of the stock:

```
data.sort_index(1).info()

MultiIndex: 47377 entries, (2014-01-02, Equity(24 [AAPL])) to (2015-12-
                          31, Equity(47208 [GPRO]))
Data columns (total 52 columns):
AssetToEquityRatio           47377 non-null float64
AssetTurnover                47377 non-null float64
CFO To Assets                47377 non-null float64
...
WorkingCapitalToAssets       47377 non-null float64
WorkingCapitalToSales        47377 non-null float64
```

```
stock                           47377 non-null object
dtypes: float64(51), object(1)
```

Data exploration

For linear regression models, it is important to explore the correlation among the features to identify multicollinearity issues, and to check the correlation between the features and the target. The notebook contains a seaborn clustermap that shows the hierarchical structure of the feature correlation matrix. It identifies a small number of highly correlated clusters.

Dummy encoding of categorical variables

We need to convert the categorical `stock` variable into a numeric format so that the linear regression can process it. For this purpose, we use dummy encoding that creates individual columns for each category level and flags the presence of this level in the original categorical column with an entry of 1, and 0 otherwise. The pandas function `get_dummies()` automates dummy encoding. It detects and properly converts columns of type objects as illustrated next. If you need dummy variables for columns containing integers, for instance, you can identify them using the keyword `columns`:

```
df = pd.DataFrame({'categories': ['A','B', 'C']})

    categories
0            A
1            B
2            C


pd.get_dummies(df)

     categories_A   categories_B   categories_C
0               1              0              0
1               0              1              0
2               0              0              1
```

When converting all categories to dummy variables and estimating the model with an intercept (as you typically would), you inadvertently create multicollinearity: the matrix now contains redundant information and no longer has full rank, that is, becomes singular. It is simple to avoid this by removing one of the new indicator columns. The coefficient on the missing category level will now be captured by the intercept (which is always 1 when every other category dummy is 0). Use the `drop_first` keyword to correct the dummy variables accordingly:

```
pd.get_dummies(df, drop_first=True)

     categories_B   categories_C
0               0              0
1               1              0
2               0              1
```

Applied to our combined features and returns, we obtain 181 columns because there are more than 100 stocks as the universe definition automatically updates the stock selection:

```
X = pd.get_dummies(data.drop(return_cols, axis=1), drop_first=True)
X.info()

MultiIndex: 47377 entries, (2014-01-02 00:00:00+00:00, Equity(24 [AAPL]))
to (2015-12-31 00:00:00+00:00, Equity(47208 [GPRO]))
Columns: 181 entries, DividendYield to stock_YELP INC
dtypes: float64(182)
memory usage: 66.1+ MB
```

Creating forward returns

The goal is to predict returns over a given holding period. Hence, we need to align the features with return values with the corresponding return data point 1, 5, 10, or 20 days into the future for each equity. We achieve this by combining the pandas `.groupby()` method with the `.shift()` method as follows:

```
y = data.loc[:, return_cols]
shifted_y = []
for col in y.columns:
    t = int(re.search(r'\d+', col).group(0))
    shifted_y.append(y.groupby(level='asset')['Returns{}D'.format(t)].shift(-
t).to_frame(col))
y = pd.concat(shifted_y, axis=1)
y.info()

MultiIndex: 47377 entries, (2014-01-02, Equity(24 [AAPL])) to (2015-12-31,
Equity(47208 [GPRO]))
```

```
Data columns (total 4 columns):
Returns1D     47242 non-null float64
Returns5D     46706 non-null float64
Returns10D    46036 non-null float64
Returns20D    44696 non-null float64
dtypes: float64(4)
```

There are now different numbers of observations for each return series as the forward shift has created missing values at the tail end for each equity.

Linear OLS regression using statsmodels

We can estimate a linear regression model using OLS with statsmodels as demonstrated previously. We select a forward return, for example for a 10-day holding period, remove outliers below the 2.5% and above the 97.5% percentiles, and fit the model accordingly:

```
target = 'Returns10D'
model_data = pd.concat([y[[target]], X], axis=1).dropna()
model_data =
model_data[model_data[target].between(model_data[target].quantile(.025),
model_data[target].quantile(.975))]

model = OLS(endog=model_data[target], exog=model_data.drop(target, axis=1))
trained_model = model.fit()
trained_model.summary()
```

Diagnostic statistics

The summary is available in the notebook to save some space due to the large number of variables. The diagnostic statistics show that, given the high p-value on the Jarque—Bera statistic, the hypothesis that the residuals are normally distributed cannot be rejected.

However, the Durbin—Watson statistic is low at 1.5 so we can reject the null hypothesis of no autocorrelation comfortably at the 5% level. Hence, the standard errors are likely positively correlated. If our goal were to understand which factors are significantly associated with forward returns, we would need to rerun the regression using robust standard errors (a parameter in statsmodels .fit() method), or use a different method altogether such as a panel model that allows for more complex error covariance.

Linear OLS regression using sklearn

Since sklearn is tailored towards prediction, we will evaluate the linear regression model based on its predictive performance using cross-validation.

Custom time series cross-validation

Our data consists of grouped time series data that requires a custom cross-validation function to provide the train and test indices that ensure that the test data immediately follows the training data for each equity and we do not inadvertently create a look-ahead bias or leakage.

We can achieve this using the following function that returns a `generator` yielding pairs of train and test dates. The set of train dates that ensure a minimum length of the training periods. The number of pairs depends on the parameter `nfolds`. The distinct test periods do not overlap and are located at the end of the period available in the data. After a test period is used, it becomes part of the training data that grow in size accordingly:

```python
def time_series_split(d=model_data, nfolds=5, min_train=21):
    """Generate train/test dates for nfolds
    with at least min_train train obs
    """
    train_dates = d[:min_train].tolist()
    n = int(len(dates)/(nfolds + 1)) + 1
    test_folds = [d[i:i + n] for i in range(min_train, len(d), n)]
    for test_dates in test_folds:
        if len(train_dates) > min_train:
            yield train_dates, test_dates
        train_dates.extend(test_dates)
```

Select features and target

We need to select the appropriate return series (we will again use a 10-day holding period) and remove outliers. We will also convert returns to log returns as follows:

```python
target = 'Returns10D'
outliers = .01
model_data = pd.concat([y[[target]], X],
axis=1).dropna().reset_index('asset', drop=True)
model_data =
model_data[model_data[target].between(*model_data[target].quantile([outlier
s, 1-outliers]).values)]

model_data[target] = np.log1p(model_data[target])
```

```
features = model_data.drop(target, axis=1).columns
dates = model_data.index.unique()

DatetimeIndex: 45114 entries, 2014-01-02 to 2015-12-16
Columns: 183 entries, Returns10D to stock_YELP INC
dtypes: float64(183)
```

Cross-validating the model

We will use 250 folds to generally predict about 2 days of forward returns following the historical training data that will gradually increase in length. Each iteration obtains the appropriate training and test dates from our custom cross-validation function, selects the corresponding features and targets, and then trains and predicts accordingly. We capture the root mean squared error as well as the Spearman rank correlation between actual and predicted values:

```
nfolds = 250
lr = LinearRegression()

test_results, result_idx, preds = [], [], pd.DataFrame()
for train_dates, test_dates in time_series_split(dates, nfolds=nfolds):
    X_train = model_data.loc[idx[train_dates], features]
    y_train = model_data.loc[idx[train_dates], target]
    lr.fit(X=X_train, y=y_train)

    X_test = model_data.loc[idx[test_dates], features]
    y_test = model_data.loc[idx[test_dates], target]
    y_pred = lr.predict(X_test)

    rmse = np.sqrt(mean_squared_error(y_pred=y_pred, y_true=y_test))
    ic, pval = spearmanr(y_pred, y_test)

    test_results.append([rmse, ic, pval])
    preds =
preds.append(y_test.to_frame('actuals').assign(predicted=y_pred))
    result_idx.append(train_dates[-1])
```

Test results – information coefficient and RMSE

We have captured the test predictions from the 250 folds and can compute both the overall and a 21-day rolling average:

```
fig, axes = plt.subplots(nrows=2)
rolling_result = test_result.rolling(21).mean()
rolling_result[['ic', 'pval']].plot(ax=axes[0], title='Information
Coefficient')
axes[0].axhline(test_result.ic.mean(), lw=1, ls='--', color='k')
rolling_result[['rmse']].plot(ax=axes[1], title='Root Mean Squared Error')
axes[1].axhline(test_result.rmse.mean(), lw=1, ls='--', color='k')
```

We obtain the following chart that highlights the negative correlation of IC and RMSE and their respective values:

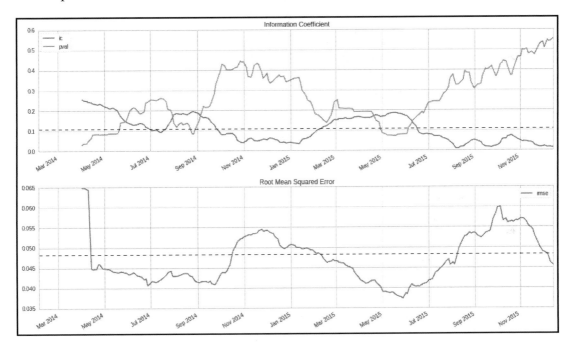

Chart highlighting the negative correlation of IC and RMSE

For the entire period, we see that the Information Coefficient measured by the rank correlation of actual and predicted returns is weakly positive and statistically significant:

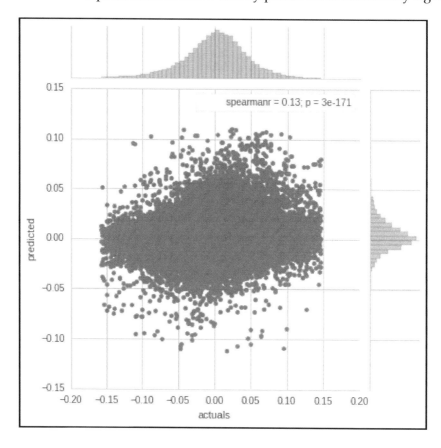

Ridge regression using sklearn

For the ridge regression, we need to tune the regularization parameter with the keyword `alpha` that corresponds to the λ we used previously. We will try 21 values from 10^{-5} to 10^{5} in logarithmic steps.

The scale sensitivity of the ridge penalty requires us to standardize the inputs using the StandardScaler. Note that we always learn the mean and the standard deviation from the training set using the .fit_transform() method and then apply these learned parameters to the test set using the .transform() method.

Tuning the regularization parameters using cross-validation

We then proceed to cross-validate the hyperparameter values again using 250 folds as follows:

```
nfolds = 250
alphas = np.logspace(-5, 5, 21)
scaler = StandardScaler()

ridge_result, ridge_coeffs = pd.DataFrame(), pd.DataFrame()
for i, alpha in enumerate(alphas):
    coeffs, test_results = [], []
    lr_ridge = Ridge(alpha=alpha)
    for train_dates, test_dates in time_series_split(dates, nfolds=nfolds):
        X_train = model_data.loc[idx[train_dates], features]
        y_train = model_data.loc[idx[train_dates], target]
        lr_ridge.fit(X=scaler.fit_transform(X_train), y=y_train)
        coeffs.append(lr_ridge.coef_)

        X_test = model_data.loc[idx[test_dates], features]
        y_test = model_data.loc[idx[test_dates], target]
        y_pred = lr_ridge.predict(scaler.transform(X_test))

        rmse = np.sqrt(mean_squared_error(y_pred=y_pred, y_true=y_test))
        ic, pval = spearmanr(y_pred, y_test)

        test_results.append([train_dates[-1], rmse, ic, pval, alpha])
    test_results = pd.DataFrame(test_results, columns=['date', 'rmse',
'ic', 'pval', 'alpha'])
    ridge_result = ridge_result.append(test_results)
    ridge_coeffs[alpha] = np.mean(coeffs, axis=0)
```

Cross-validation results and ridge coefficient paths

We can now plot the information coefficient obtained for each hyperparameter value and also visualize how the coefficient values evolve as the regularization increases. The results show that we get the highest IC value for a value of $\lambda=10$. For this level of regularization, the right-hand panel reveals that the coefficients have been already significantly shrunk compared to the (almost) unconstrained model with $\lambda=10^{-5}$:

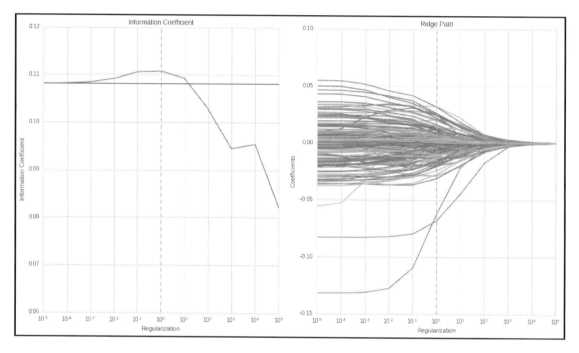

Cross-validation results and ridge coefficient paths

Top 10 coefficients

The standardization of the coefficients allows us to draw conclusions about their relative importance by comparing their absolute magnitude. The 10 most relevant coefficients are:

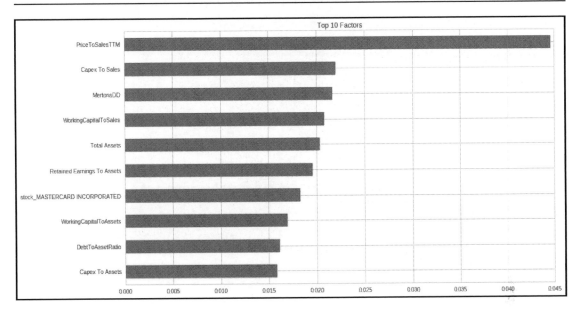

Top 10 coefficients

Lasso regression using sklearn

The lasso implementation looks very similar to the ridge model we just ran. The main difference is that lasso needs to arrive at a solution using iterative coordinate descent whereas ridge can rely on a closed-form solution:

```
nfolds = 250
alphas = np.logspace(-8, -2, 13)
scaler = StandardScaler()

lasso_results, lasso_coeffs = pd.DataFrame(), pd.DataFrame()
for i, alpha in enumerate(alphas):
    coeffs, test_results = [], []
    lr_lasso = Lasso(alpha=alpha)
    for i, (train_dates, test_dates) in enumerate(time_series_split(dates,
nfolds=nfolds)):
        X_train = model_data.loc[idx[train_dates], features]
        y_train = model_data.loc[idx[train_dates], target]
        lr_lasso.fit(X=scaler.fit_transform(X_train), y=y_train)

        X_test = model_data.loc[idx[test_dates], features]
        y_test = model_data.loc[idx[test_dates], target]
        y_pred = lr_lasso.predict(scaler.transform(X_test))
```

```
        rmse = np.sqrt(mean_squared_error(y_pred=y_pred, y_true=y_test))
        ic, pval = spearmanr(y_pred, y_test)

        coeffs.append(lr_lasso.coef_)
        test_results.append([train_dates[-1], rmse, ic, pval, alpha])
    test_results = pd.DataFrame(test_results, columns=['date', 'rmse',
'ic', 'pval', 'alpha'])
    lasso_results = lasso_results.append(test_results)
    lasso_coeffs[alpha] = np.mean(coeffs, axis=0)
```

Cross-validated information coefficient and Lasso Path

As before, we can plot the average information coefficient for all test sets used during cross-validation. We see again that regularization improves the IC over the unconstrained model, delivering the best out-of-sample result at a level of $\lambda=10^{-5}$. The optimal regularization value is quite different from ridge regression because the penalty consists of the sum of the absolute, not the squared values of the relatively small coefficient values. We can also see that for this regularization level, the coefficients have been similarly shrunk, as in the ridge regression case:

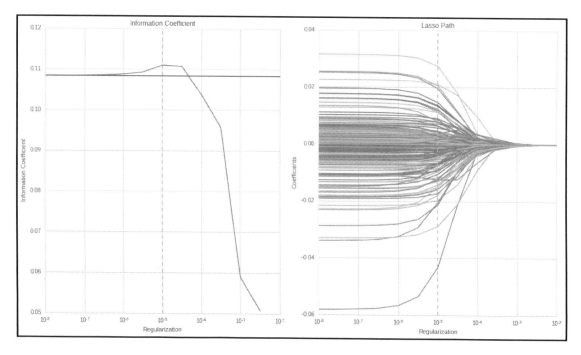

Cross-validated information coefficient and Lasso Path

In sum, ridge and lasso will produce similar results. Ridge often computes faster, but lasso also yields continuous features subset selection by gradually reducing coefficients to zero, hence eliminating features.

Linear classification

The linear regression model discussed so far assumes a quantitative response variable. In this section, we will focus on approaches to modeling qualitative output variables for inference and prediction, a process that is known as **classification** and that occurs even more frequently than regression in practice.

Predicting a qualitative response for a data point is called **classifying** that observation because it involves assigning the observation to a category, or class. In practice, classification methods often predict probabilities for each of the categories of a qualitative variable and then use this probability to decide on the proper classification.

We could approach the classification problem ignoring the fact that the output variable assumes discrete values, and apply the linear regression model to try to predict a categorical output using multiple input variables. However, it is easy to construct examples where this method performs very poorly. Furthermore, it doesn't make intuitive sense for the model to produce values larger than 1 or smaller than 0 when we know that $y \in [0, 1]$.

There are many different classification techniques, or classifiers, that are available to predict a qualitative response. In this section, we will introduce the widely used logistic regression which is closely related to linear regression. We will address more complex methods in the following chapters, on generalized additive models that include decision trees and random forests, as well as gradient boosting machines and neural networks.

The logistic regression model

The logistic regression model arises from the desire to model the probabilities of the output classes given a function that is linear in x, just like the linear regression model, while at the same time ensuring that they sum to one and remain in the [0, 1] as we would expect from probabilities.

In this section, we introduce the objective and functional form of the logistic regression model and describe the training method. We then illustrate how to use logistic regression for statistical inference with macro data using statsmodels, and how to predict price movements using the regularized logistic regression implemented by sklearn.

Objective function

For illustration, we'll use the output variable y that takes on the value 1 if a stock return is positive over a given time horizon d, and 0 otherwise:

$$y_t = \begin{cases} 1 & r_{t+d} > 0 \\ 0 & \text{otherwise} \end{cases}$$

We could easily extend y to three categories, where 0 and 2 reflect negative and positive price moves beyond a certain threshold, and 1 otherwise. Rather than modeling the output variable y, however, logistic regression models the probability that y belongs to either of the categories given a vector of alpha factors or features x_t. In other words, the logistic regression models the probability that the stock price goes up, conditional on the values of the variables included in the model:

$$p(x_t) = Pr(y_t = 1 | x_t)$$

The logistic function

To prevent the model from producing values outside the [0, 1] interval, we must model $p(x)$ using a function that only gives outputs between 0 and 1 over the entire domain of x. The logistic function meets this requirement and always produces an S-shaped curve (see notebook examples), and so, regardless of the value of X, we will obtain a sensible prediction:

$$p(x) = \frac{e^{\beta_0 + \sum_{i=1}^{p} \beta_i x_i}}{1 + e^{\beta_0 + \sum_{i=1}^{p} \beta_i x_i}} = \frac{e^{x\beta}}{1 + e^{x\beta}}$$

Here, the vector x includes a 1 for the intercept captured by the first component of β, β_0. We can transform this expression to isolate the part that looks like a linear regression to arrive at:

$$\underbrace{\frac{p(x)}{1 - p(x)}}_{\text{odds}} = e^{\beta_0 + \sum_{i=1}^{p} \beta_i} \iff \underbrace{\log\left(\frac{p(x)}{1 - p(x)}\right)}_{\text{logit}} = \beta_0 + \sum_{i=1}^{p} \beta_i$$

The quantity *p(x)/[1−p(x)]* is called the **odds**, an alternative way to express probabilities that may be familiar from gambling, and can take on any value odds between 0 and ∞, where low values also imply low probabilities and high values imply high probabilities.

The logit is also called log-odds (since it is the logarithm of the odds). Hence, the logistic regression represents a logit that is linear in *x* and looks a lot like the preceding linear regression.

Maximum likelihood estimation

The coefficient vector β must be estimated using the available training data. Although we could use (non-linear) least squares to fit the logistic regression model, the more general method of maximum likelihood is preferred, since it has better statistical properties. As we have just discussed, the basic intuition behind using maximum likelihood to fit a logistic regression model is to seek estimates for β such that the predicted probability $\hat{p}(x)$

corresponds as closely as possible to the actual outcome. In other words, we try to find $\hat{\beta}$ such that these estimates yield a number close to 1 for all cases where the stock price went up, and a number close to 0 otherwise. More formally, we are seeking to maximize the likelihood function:

$$\max_{\beta} \mathcal{L}(\beta) = \prod_{i:y_i=1} p(x_i) \prod_{i':y_{i'}=0} (1 - p(x_{i'}))$$

It is easier to work with sums than with products, so let's take logs on both sides to get the log-likelihood function and the corresponding definition of the logistic regression coefficients:

$$\beta^{\mathrm{ML}} = \mathrm{argmax} \log \mathcal{L}(\beta) = \sum_{i=1}^{N} (y_i \log p(x_i, \beta) + (1 - y_i \log(1 - p(x_i, \beta)))$$

Maximizing this equation by setting the derivatives of $\mathcal{L}$ with respect to β to zero yields p+1 so-called score equations that are nonlinear in the parameters that can be solved using iterative numerical methods for the concave log-likelihood function.

How to conduct inference with statsmodels

We will illustrate how to use logistic regression with `statsmodels` based on a simple built-in dataset containing quarterly US macro data from 1959 – 2009 (see the notebook `logistic_regression_macro_data.ipynb` for detail).

The variables and their transformations are listed in the following table:

Variable	Description	Transformation
realgdp	Real gross domestic product	Annual Growth Rate
realcons	Real personal consumption expenditures	Annual Growth Rate
realinv	Real gross private domestic investment	Annual Growth Rate
realgovt	Real federal expenditures and gross investment	Annual Growth Rate
realdpi	Real private disposable income	Annual Growth Rate
m1	M1 nominal money stock	Annual Growth Rate
tbilrate	Monthly 3 treasury bill rate	Level
unemp	Seasonally adjusted unemployment rate (%)	Level
infl	Inflation rate	Level
realint	Real interest rate	Level

To obtain a binary target variable, we compute the 20-quarter rolling average of the annual growth rate of quarterly real GDP. We then assign 1 if current growth exceeds the moving average and 0 otherwise. Finally, we shift the indicator variables to align next quarter's outcome with the current quarter.

We use an intercept and convert the quarter values to dummy variables and train the logistic regression model as follows:

```
import statsmodels.api as sm

data = pd.get_dummies(data.drop(drop_cols, axis=1), columns=['quarter'],
drop_first=True).dropna()
model = sm.Logit(data.target, sm.add_constant(data.drop('target', axis=1)))
result = model.fit()
result.summary()
```

This produces the following summary for our model with 198 observations and 13 variables, including intercept:

```
                    Logit Regression Results
==========================================================================
Dep. Variable:            target   No. Observations:                 198
Model:                     Logit   Df Residuals:                     185
Method:                      MLE   Df Model:                          12
Date:            Mon, 10 Sep 2018   Pseudo R-squ.:                 0.5022
Time:                   20:27:53   Log-Likelihood:               -67.907
converged:                  True   LL-Null:                      -136.42
                                   LLR p-value:                 2.375e-23
==========================================================================
                 coef    std err         z     P>|z|    [0.025    0.975]
--------------------------------------------------------------------------
const         -8.5881      1.908    -4.502     0.000   -12.327    -4.849
realcons     130.1446     26.633     4.887     0.000    77.945   182.344
realinv       18.8414      4.053     4.648     0.000    10.897    26.786
realgovt     -19.0318      6.010    -3.166     0.002   -30.812    -7.252
realdpi      -52.2473     19.912    -2.624     0.009   -91.275   -13.220
m1            -1.3462      6.177    -0.218     0.827   -13.453    10.761
tbilrate      60.8607     44.350     1.372     0.170   -26.063   147.784
unemp          0.9487      0.249     3.818     0.000     0.462     1.436
infl         -60.9647     44.362    -1.374     0.169  -147.913    25.984
realint      -61.0453     44.359    -1.376     0.169  -147.987    25.896
quarter_2      0.1128      0.618     0.182     0.855    -1.099     1.325
quarter_3     -0.1991      0.609    -0.327     0.744    -1.393     0.995
quarter_4      0.0007      0.608     0.001     0.999    -1.191     1.192
==========================================================================
```

Logit Regression results

The summary indicates that the model has been trained using maximum likelihood and provides the maximized value of the log-likelihood function at -67.9.

The LL-Null value of -136.42 is the result of the maximized log-likelihood function when only an intercept is included. It forms the basis for the pseudo-R^2 statistic and the Log-**Likelihood Ratio (LLR)** test.

The pseudo-R^2 statistic is a substitute for the familiar R^2 available under least squares. It is computed based on the ratio of the maximized log-likelihood function for the null model m_0 and the full model m_1 as follows:

$$\rho^2 = 1 - \frac{\log \mathcal{L}(m_1^*)}{\log \mathcal{L}(m_0^*)}$$

The values vary from 0 (when the model does not improve the likelihood) to 1 where the model fits perfectly and the log-likelihood is maximized at 0. Consequently, higher values indicate a better fit.

The LLR test generally compares a more restricted model and is computed as:

$$\text{LLR} = -2\log(\mathcal{L}(m_0^*)/\mathcal{L}(m_1^*)) = 2(\log\mathcal{L}(m_1^*) - \log\mathcal{L}(m_0^*))$$

The null hypothesis is that the restricted model performs better but the low p-value suggests that we can reject this hypothesis and prefer the full model over the null model. This is similar to the F-test for linear regression (where we can also use the LLR test when we estimate the model using MLE).

The z-statistic plays the same role as the t-statistic in the linear regression output and is equally computed as the ratio of the coefficient estimate and its standard error. The p-values also indicate the probability of observing the test statistic assuming the null hypothesis $H_0 : \beta = 0$ that the population coefficient is zero. We can reject this hypothesis for the `intercept`, `realcons`, `realinv`, `realgovt`, `realdpi`, and `unemp`.

How to use logistic regression for prediction

The lasso L_1 penalty and the ridge L_2 penalty can both be used with logistic regression. They have the same shrinkage effect as we have just discussed, and the lasso can again be used for variable selection with any linear regression model.

Just as with linear regression, it is important to standardize the input variables as the regularized models are scale sensitive. The regularization hyperparameter also requires tuning using cross-validation as in the linear regression case.

How to predict price movements using sklearn

We continue the price prediction example but now we binarize the outcome variable so that it takes on the value 1 whenever the 10-day return is positive and 0 otherwise; see the notebook `logistic_regression.ipynb` in the sub directory `stock_price_prediction`:

```
target = 'Returns10D'
label = (y[target] > 0).astype(int).to_frame(target)
```

With this new categorical outcome variable, we can now train a logistic regression using the default L_2 regularization. For logistic regression, the regularization is formulated inversely to linear regression: higher values for λ imply less regularization and vice versa. We evaluate 11 parameter values using cross validation as follows:

```
nfolds = 250
Cs = np.logspace(-5, 5, 11)
scaler = StandardScaler()

logistic_results, logistic_coeffs = pd.DataFrame(), pd.DataFrame()
for C in Cs:
    coeffs = []
    log_reg = LogisticRegression(C=C)
    for i, (train_dates, test_dates) in enumerate(time_series_split(dates,
nfolds=nfolds)):
        X_train = model_data.loc[idx[train_dates], features]
        y_train = model_data.loc[idx[train_dates], target]
        log_reg.fit(X=scaler.fit_transform(X_train), y=y_train)

        X_test = model_data.loc[idx[test_dates], features]
        y_test = model_data.loc[idx[test_dates], target]
        y_pred = log_reg.predict_proba(scaler.transform(X_test))[:, 1]

        coeffs.append(log_reg.coef_.squeeze())
        logistic_results = (logistic_results
                            .append(y_test
                                    .to_frame('actuals')
                                    .assign(predicted=y_pred, C=C)))
    logistic_coeffs[C] = np.mean(coeffs, axis=0)
```

We then use the `roc_auc_score` discussed in the previous chapter to compare the predictive accuracy across the various regularization parameters:

```
auc_by_C = logistic_results.groupby('C').apply(lambda x:
roc_auc_score(y_true=x.actuals.astype(int),
y_score=x.predicted))
```

We can again plot the AUC result for the range of hyperparameter values alongside the coefficient path that shows the improvements in predictive accuracy as the coefficients are a bit shrunk at the optimal regularization value 10^2:

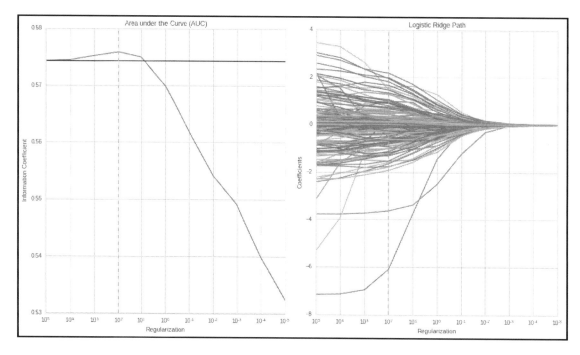

AUC and Logistic Ridge path

Summary

In this chapter, we introduced the first machine learning models using the important baseline case of linear models for regression and classification. We explored the formulation of the objective functions for both tasks, learned about various training methods, and learned how to use the model for both inference and prediction.

We applied these new machine learning techniques to estimate linear factor models that are very useful to manage risks, assess new alpha factors, and attribute performance. We also applied linear regression and classification to accomplish the first predictive task of predicting stock returns in absolute and directional terms.

In the next chapter, we will look at the important topic of linear time series models that are designed to capture serial correlation patterns in the univariate and multivariate case. We will also learn about new trading strategies as we explore pairs trading based on the concept of cointegration that captures dynamic correlation among two stock price series.

8

Time Series Models

In the last chapter, we focused on linear models tailored to cross-sectional data where the input data belongs to the same time period as the output they aim to explain or predict. In this chapter, we will focus on time series data where observations differ by period, which also creates a natural ordering. Our goal will be to identify historical patterns in data and leverage these patterns to predict how the time series will behave in the future.

We already encountered panel data with both a cross-sectional and a time series dimension in the last chapter and learned how the Fama-Macbeth regression estimates the value of taking certain factor risks over time and across assets. However, the relationship between returns across time is typically fairly low, so this procedure could largely ignore the time dimension. The models in this chapter focus on time series models where past values contain predictive signals about future developments. Time series models can also predict features that are then used in cross-sectional models.

More specifically, in this chapter, we focus on models that extract signals from previously observed data to predict future values for the same time series. The time dimension of trading makes the application of time series models to market, fundamental, and alternative data very popular. Time series data will become even more prevalent as an ever broader array of connected devices collects regular measurements that may contain predictive signals. Key applications include the prediction of asset returns, correlations or covariances, or volatility.

We focus on linear time series models in this chapter as a baseline for non-linear models like recurrent or convolutional neural networks that we apply to time series data in part 4 of this book. We being by introducing tools to diagnose time series characteristics, including stationarity, and extract features that capture potential patterns. Then we introduce univariate and multivariate time series models and apply them to forecast macro data and volatility patterns. We conclude with the concept of cointegration and how to apply it to develop a pairs trading strategy.

In particular, we will cover the following topics:

- How to use time series analysis to diagnose diagnostic statistics that inform the modeling process
- How to estimate and diagnose autoregressive and moving-average time series models
- How to build Autoregressive Conditional Heteroskedasticity (ARCH) models to predict volatility
- How to build vector autoregressive models
- How to use cointegration for a pairs trading strategy

Analytical tools for diagnostics and feature extraction

Time series data is a sequence of values separated by discrete time intervals that are typically even-spaced (except for missing values). A time series is often modeled as a stochastic process consisting of a collection of random variables, $y(t_1)$, ..., $y(t_T)$, with one variable for each point in time, t_i, i=1, ..., T. A univariate time series consists of a single value, y, at each point in time, whereas a multivariate time series consists of several observations that can be represented by a vector.

The number of periods, $\Delta t = t_i - t_j$, between distinct points in time, t_i, t_j, is called lag, with T-1 lags for each time series. Just as relationships between different variables at a given point in time is key for cross-sectional models, relationships between data points separated by a given lag are fundamental to analyzing and exploiting patterns in time series. For cross-sectional models, we distinguished between input and output variables, or target and predictors, with the labels y and x, respectively. In a time series context, the lagged values of the outcome play the role of the input or x values in the cross-section context.

A time series is called white noise if it is a sequence of independent and identically-distributed random variables, ε_t, with finite mean and variance. In particular, the series is called a Gaussian white noise if the random variables are normally distributed with a mean of zero and a constant variance of σ.

A time series is linear if it can be written as a weighted sum of past disturbances, ε_t, that are also called innovations, and are here assumed to represent white noise, and the mean of the series, μ:

$$y_t = \mu + \sum_{i=0}^{\infty} a_i \epsilon_{t-i}, \quad a_0 = 1, \epsilon \sim \text{i.i.d.}$$

A key goal of time series analysis is to understand the dynamic behavior driven by the coefficients, a_i. The analysis of time series offers methods tailored to this type of data with the goal of extracting useful patterns that, in turn, help us to build predictive models. We will introduce the most important tools for this purpose, including the decomposition into key systematic elements, the analysis of autocorrelation, and rolling window statistics such as moving averages. Linear time series models often make certain assumptions about the data, such as stationarity, and we will also introduce both the concept, diagnostic tools, and typical transformations to achieve stationarity.

For most of the examples in this chapter, we work with data provided by the Federal Reserve that you can access using the `pandas datareader` that we introduced in Chapter 2, *Market and Fundamental Data*. The code examples for this section are available in the notebook `tsa_and_arima` notebook.

How to decompose time series patterns

Time series data typically contains a mix of various patterns that can be decomposed into several components, each representing an underlying pattern category. In particular, time series often consist of the systematic components trend, seasonality and cycles, and unsystematic noise. These components can be combined in an additive, linear model, in particular when fluctuations do not depend on the level of the series, or in a non-linear, multiplicative model.

These components can be split up automatically. `statsmodels` includes a simple method to split the time series into a trend, seasonal, and residual component using moving averages. We can apply it to monthly data on industrial manufacturing production with both a strong trend and seasonality component, as follows:

```
import statsmodels.tsa.api as tsa
industrial_production = web.DataReader('IPGMFN', 'fred', '1988',
'2017-12').squeeze()
components = tsa.seasonal_decompose(industrial_production,
model='additive')
```

```
ts = (industrial_production.to_frame('Original')
      .assign(Trend=components.trend)
      .assign(Seasonality=components.seasonal)
      .assign(Residual=components.resid))
ts.plot(subplots=True, figsize=(14, 8));
```

The resulting charts show the additive components. The residual component would be the focus of additional modeling, assuming that the trend and seasonality components are more deterministic and amenable to simple extrapolation:

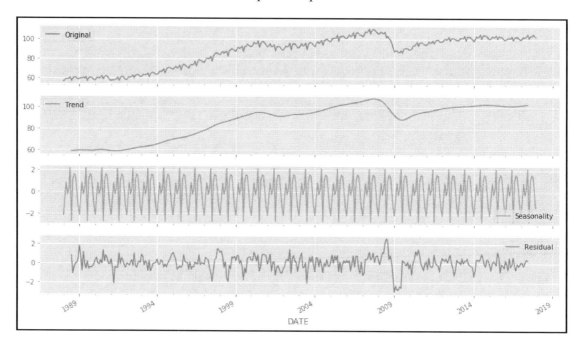

There are more sophisticated, model-based approaches that are included in the references available on GitHub.

How to compute rolling window statistics

Given the sequential ordering of time series data, it is natural to compute familiar descriptive statistics for periods of a given length to detect stability or changes in behavior and obtain a smoothed representation that captures systematic aspects while filtering out the noise.

Rolling window statistics serve this process: they produce a new time series where each data point represents a summary statistic computed for a certain period of the original data. Moving averages are the most familiar example. The original data points can enter the computation with equal weights, or using weights to, for example, emphasize more recent data points. Exponential moving averages recursively compute weights that shrink or decay, for data points further away from the present. The new data points are typically a summary of all preceding data points, but they can also be computed from a surrounding window.

The pandas library includes very flexible functionality to define various window types, including rolling, exponentially weighted and expanding windows. In a second step, you can apply computations to each data captured by a window. These computations include built-in standard computations for individual series, such as the mean or the sum, the correlation or covariance for several series, as well as user-defined functions. The moving average and exponential smoothing examples in the following section make use of these tools.

Moving averages and exponential smoothing

Early forecasting models included moving-average models with exponential weights called exponential smoothing models. We will encounter moving averages again as key building blocks for linear time series.

Forecasts that rely on exponential smoothing methods use weighted averages of past observations, where the weights decay exponentially as the observations get older. Hence, a more recent observation receives a higher associated weight. These methods are popular for time series that do not have very complicated or abrupt patterns.

Exponential smoothing is a popular technique based on weighted averages of past observations, with the weights decaying exponentially as the observations get older. In other words, the more recent the observation, the higher the associated weight. This framework generates reliable forecasts quickly and for a wide range of time series, which is a great advantage and of major importance to applications in industry.

How to measure autocorrelation

Autocorrelation (also called serial correlation) adapts the concept of correlation to the time series context: just as the correlation coefficient measures the strength of a linear relationship between two variables, the autocorrelation coefficient, ρ_k, measures the extent of a linear relationship between time series values separated by a given lag, k:

$$\rho_k = \frac{\sum_{t=k+1}^{T} (y_t - \bar{y})(y_{t-k} - \bar{y})}{\sum_{t=1}^{T} (y_t - \bar{y})^2}$$

Hence, we can calculate one autocorrelation coefficient for each of the T-1 lags in a time series; T is the length of the series. The autocorrelation function (ACF) computes the correlation coefficients as a function of the lag.

The autocorrelation for a lag larger than 1 (that is, between observations more than one time step apart) reflects both the direct correlation between these observations and the indirect influence of the intervening data points. The partial autocorrelation removes this influence and only measures the linear dependence between data points at the given lag distance. The **partial autocorrelation function (PACF)** provides all the correlations that result once the effects of a correlation at shorter lags have been removed.

There are algorithms that estimate the partial autocorrelation from the sample autocorrelation based on the exact theoretical relationship between the PACF and the ACF.

A correlogram is simply a plot of the ACF or PACF for sequential lags, k=0,1,...,n. It allows us to inspect the correlation structure across lags at one glance. The main usage of correlograms is to detect any autocorrelation after the removal of the effects of deterministic trend or seasonality. Both the ACF and the PACF are key diagnostic tools for the design of linear time series models and we will review examples of ACF and PACF plots in the following section on time series transformations.

How to diagnose and achieve stationarity

The statistical properties, such as the mean, variance, or autocorrelation, of a stationary time series are independent of the period, that is, they don't change over time. Hence, stationarity implies that a time series does not have a trend or seasonal effects and that descriptive statistics, such as the mean or the standard deviation, when computed for different rolling windows, are constant or do not change much over time. It reverts to its mean, and the deviations have constant amplitude, while short-term movements always look the same in the statistical sense.

More formally, strict stationarity requires the joint distribution of any subset of time series observations to be independent of time with respect to all moments. So, in addition to the mean and variance, higher moments such as skew and kurtosis, also need to be constant, irrespective of the lag between different observations. In most applications, we limit stationarity to first and second moments so that the time series is covariance stationary with constant mean, variance, and autocorrelation.

Note that we specifically allow for dependence between observations at different lags, just like we want the input data for linear regression to be correlated with the outcome. Stationarity implies that these relationships are stable, which facilitates prediction as the model can focus on learning systematic patterns that take place within stable statistical properties. It is important because classical statistical models assume that the time series input data is stationary.

The following sections introduce diagnostics that help detect when data is not stationary, and transformations that help meet these assumptions.

Time series transformations

To satisfy the stationarity assumption of linear time series models, we need to transform the original time series, often in several steps. Common transformations include the application of the (natural) logarithm to convert an exponential growth pattern into a linear trend and stabilize the variance. Deflation implies dividing a time series by another series that causes trending behavior, for example dividing a nominal series by a price index to convert it into a real measure.

A series is trend-stationary if it reverts to a stable long-run linear trend. It can often be made stationary by fitting a trend line using linear regression and using the residuals, or by including the time index as an independent variable in a regression or AR(I)MA model (see the following section on univariate time series models), possibly combined with logging or deflating.

In many cases, de-trending is not sufficient to make the series stationary. Instead, we need to transform the original data into a series of period-to-period and/or season-to-season differences. In other words, we use the result of subtracting neighboring data points or values at seasonal lags from each other. Note that when such differencing is applied to a log-transformed series, the results represent instantaneous growth rates or returns in a financial context.

If a univariate series becomes stationary after differencing d times, it is said to be integrated of the order of d, or simply integrated if d=1. This behavior is due to so-called unit roots.

How to diagnose and address unit roots

Unit roots pose a particular problem for determining the transformation that will render a time series stationary. Time series are often modeled as stochastic processes of the following autoregressive form that we will explore in more detail as a building block for ARIMA models:

$$y_t = a_1 y_{t-1} + a_2 y_{t-2} + \ldots + a_p y_{t-p} + \epsilon_t$$

Where the current value is a weighted sum of past values plus a random disturbance. Such a process has a characteristic equation of the following form:

$$m^p - m^{p-1} a_1 - m^{p-2} a_2 - \ldots - a_p = 0$$

If one of the roots of this equation equals 1, then the process is said to have a unit root. It will be non-stationary but does not necessarily need to have a trend. If the remaining roots of the characteristic equation are less than 1 in absolute terms, the first difference of the process will be stationary, and the process is integrated (of order 1) or I(1). With additional roots larger than 1 in absolute terms, the order of integration is higher and additional differencing will be required.

In practice, time series of interest rates or asset prices are often not stationary, for example, because there does not exist a price level to which the series reverts. The most prominent example of a non-stationary series is the random walk for a time series of price, p_t, for a given starting price, p_0 (for example, a stock's IPO price) and a white-noise disturbance, ϵ, that satisfies the following:

$$p_t = p_{t-1} + \epsilon_t = \sum_{s=0}^{t} \epsilon_s + p_0$$

Repeated substitution shows that the current value, p_t, is the sum of all prior disturbances or innovations, ϵ, and the initial price, p_0. If the equation includes a constant term, then the random walk is said to have drift. Hence, the random walk is an autoregressive stochastic process of the following form:

$$y_t = a_1 y_{t-1} + \epsilon_t, \quad a_1 = 1$$

With the characteristic equation, $m - a_1 = 0$, that has a unit root and is both non-stationary and integrated of order 1. On the one hand, given the i.i.d. nature of ε, the variance of the time series equals σ^2, which is not second-order stationary and implies that, in principle, the series could, over time, assume any variable. On the other hand, taking the first difference, $\Delta p_t = p_t - p_{t-1}$, leaves $\Delta p_t = \varepsilon$, which is stationary, given the statistical assumption about ε.

The defining characteristic of a unit-root non-stationary series is long memory: since current values are the sum of past disturbances, large innovations persist for much longer than for a mean-reverting, stationary series.

In addition to using the difference between neighboring data points to remove a constant pattern of change, it can be used to apply seasonal differencing to remove patterns of seasonal change. This involves taking the difference of values at a lag distance that represents the length of a seasonal pattern, which is four quarters, or 12 months, apart to remove both seasonality and linear trend.

Identifying the correct transformation, and in particular, the appropriate number and lags for differencing is not always clear-cut. Some rules have been suggested, summarized as follows:

- **Positive autocorrelations up to 10+ lags**: Probably needs higher-order differencing.
- **Lag-1 autocorrelation close to zero or negative, or generally small and patternless**: No need for higher-order differencing.
- **Lag-1 autocorrelation < -0.5**: Series may be over-differenced.
- Slightly over- or under-differencing can be corrected with AR or MA terms.
- Optimal differencing often produces the lowest standard deviation, but not always.
- A model without differencing assumes that the original series is stationary, including mean-reverting. It normally includes a constant term to allow for a non-zero mean.
- A model with one order of differencing assumes that the original series has a constant average trend and should include a constant term.
- A model with two orders of differencing assumes that the original series has a time-varying trend and should not include a constant.

Some authors recommend fractional differencing as a more flexible approach to rendering an integrated series stationary and may be able to keep more information or signal than simple or seasonal differences at discrete intervals (see references on GitHub).

Unit root tests

Statistical unit root tests are a common way to determine objectively whether (additional) differencing is necessary. These are statistical hypothesis tests of stationarity that are designed to determine whether differencing is required.

The augmented Dickey-Fuller (ADF) test evaluates the null hypothesis that a time series sample has unit root against the alternative of stationarity. It regresses the differenced time series on a time trend, the first lag, and all lagged differences, and computes a test statistic from the value of the coefficient on the lagged time series value. `statsmodels` makes it easy to implement (see companion notebook).

Formally, the ADF test for a time series, y_t, runs the linear regression:

$$\Delta y_t = \alpha + \beta t + \gamma y_{t-1} + \delta_1 \Delta y_{t-1} + \ldots + \delta_{p-1} \Delta y_{t-p+1} + \epsilon_t$$

Where α is a constant, β is a coefficient on a time trend, and p refers to the number of lags used in the model. The $\alpha=\beta=0$ constraint implies a random walk, whereas only $\beta=0$ implies a random walk with drift. The lag order is usually decided using the AIC and BIC information criteria introduced in `Chapter 7`, *Linear Models*.

The ADF test statistics uses the sample coefficient, γ, that, under the null hypothesis of unit-root non-stationarity equals zero, and is negative otherwise. It intends to demonstrate that, for an integrated series, the lagged series value should not provide useful information in predicting the first difference above and beyond lagged differences.

How to apply time series transformations

The following chart shows time series for the NASDAQ stock index and industrial production for the 30 years through 2017 in original form, as well as the transformed versions after applying the logarithm and subsequently applying first and seasonal differences (at lag 12), respectively. The charts also display the ADF p-value, which allows us to reject the hypothesis of unit-root non-stationarity after all transformations in both cases:

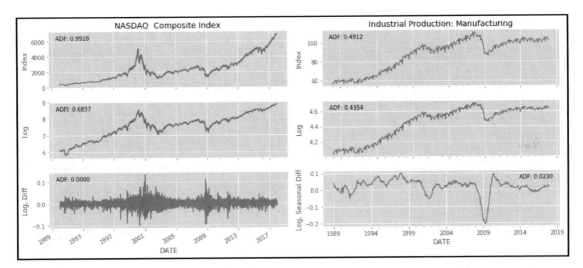

We can further analyze the relevant time series characteristics for the transformed series using a Q-Q plot that compares the quantiles of the distribution of the time series observation to the quantiles of the normal distribution and the correlograms based on the ACF and PACF.

For the NASDAQ plot, we notice that while there is no trend, the variance is not constant but rather shows clustered spikes around periods of market turmoil in the late 1980s, 2001, and 2008. The Q-Q plot highlights the fat tails of the distribution with extreme values more frequent than the normal distribution would suggest. The ACF and the PACF show similar patterns with autocorrelation at several lags appearing significant:

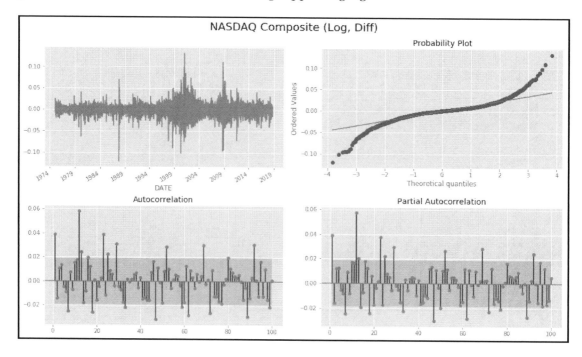

For the monthly time series on industrial manufacturing production, we notice a large negative outlier following the 2008 crisis as well as the corresponding skew in the Q-Q plot. The autocorrelation is much higher than for the NASDAQ returns and declines smoothly. The PACF shows distinct positive autocorrelation patterns at lag 1 and 13, and significant negative coefficients at lags 3 and 4:

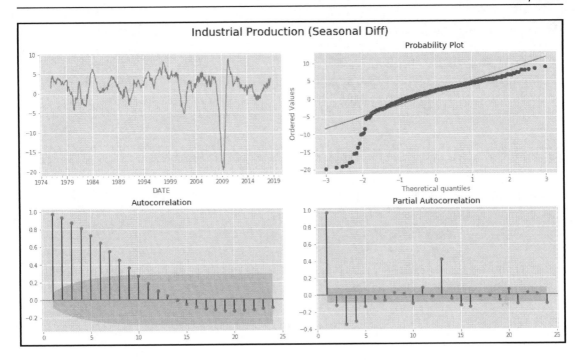

Univariate time series models

Multiple linear-regression models expressed the variable of interest as a linear combination of predictors or input variables. Univariate time series models relate the value of the time series at the point in time of interest to a linear combination of lagged values of the series and possibly past disturbance terms.

While exponential smoothing models are based on a description of the trend and seasonality in the data, ARIMA models aim to describe the autocorrelations in the data. ARIMA(p, d, q) models require stationarity and leverage two building blocks:

- **Autoregressive (AR)** terms consisting of p-lagged values of the time series
- **Moving average (MA)** terms that contain q-lagged disturbances

The I stands for integrated because the model can account for unit-root non-stationarity by differentiating the series d times. The term autoregression underlines that ARIMA models imply a regression of the time series on its own values.

We will introduce the ARIMA building blocks, simple autoregressive (AR) and moving average (MA) models, and explain how to combine them in autoregressive moving-average (ARMA) models that may account for series integration as ARIMA models or include exogenous variables as AR(I)MAX models. Furthermore, we will illustrate how to include seasonal AR and MA terms to extend the toolbox to also include SARMAX models.

How to build autoregressive models

An AR model of order p aims to capture the linear dependence between time series values at different lags and can be written as follows:

$$\text{AR}(p): \quad y_t = \phi_0 + \phi_1 y_{t-1} + \phi_2 y_{t-2} + \ldots + \phi_p y_{t-p} + \epsilon_t, \quad \epsilon \sim \text{i.i.d.}$$

This closely resembles a multiple linear regression on lagged values of y_t. This model has the following characteristic equation:

$$1 - \phi_1 x - \phi_2 x^2 - \ldots - \phi_p x^p = 0$$

The inverses of the solution to this equation in x are the characteristic roots, and the AR(p) process is stationary if these roots are all less than 1 in absolute terms, and unstable otherwise. For a stationary series, multi-step forecasts will converge to the mean of the series.

We can estimate the model parameters with the familiar least squares method using the p+1, ..., T observations to ensure there is data for each lagged term and the outcome.

How to identify the number of lags

In practice, the challenge consists in deciding on the appropriate order p of lagged terms. The time series analysis tools for serial correlation play a key role. The ACF estimates the autocorrelation between observations at different lags, which in turn results from both direct and indirect linear dependence.

Hence, for an AR model of order k, the ACF will show a significant serial correlation up to lag k and, due to the inertia caused by the indirect effects of the linear relationship, will extend to subsequent lags and eventually trail off as the effect was weakened. On the other hand, the PACF only measures the direct linear relationship between observations a given lag apart so that it will not reflect correlation for lags beyond *k*.

How to diagnose model fit

If the model captures the linear dependence across lags, then the residuals should resemble white noise.

In addition to inspecting the ACF to verify the absence of significant autocorrelation coefficients, the Ljung-Box Q statistic allows us to test the hypothesis that the residual series follows white noise. The null hypothesis is that all m serial correlation coefficients are zero against the alternative that some coefficients are not. The test statistic is computed from the sample autocorrelation coefficients, ρ_k, for different lags, k, and follows an X^2 distribution:

$$Q(m) = T(T+2) \sum_{l=1}^{m} \frac{\rho_l^2}{T-l}$$

As we will see, `statsmodels` provides information about the significance of coefficients for different lags, and insignificant coefficients should be removed. If the Q statistic rejects the null hypothesis of no autocorrelation, you should consider additional AR terms.

How to build moving average models

An MA model of order q uses q past disturbances rather than lagged values of the time series in a regression-like model, as follows:

$$MA(q): \quad y_t = c + \epsilon_t + \theta_1 \epsilon_{t-1} + \theta_2 \epsilon_{t-2} + \ldots + \theta_q \epsilon_{t-q}, \quad \epsilon \sim \text{i.i.d.}$$

Since we do not observe the white-noise disturbance values, ϵ_t, MA(q) is not a regression model like the ones we have seen so far. Rather than using least squares, MA(q) models are estimated using **maximum likelihood** (**MLE**), alternatively initializing or estimating the disturbances at the beginning of the series and then recursively and iteratively computing the remainder.

The MA(q) model gets its name from representing each value of y_t as a weighted moving average of the past q innovations. In other words, current estimates represent a correction relative to past errors made by the model. The use of moving averages in MA(q) models differs from that of exponential smoothing or the estimation of seasonal time series components because an MA(q) model aims to forecast future values as opposed to de-noising or estimating the trend cycle of past values.

MA(q) processes are always stationary because they are the weighted sum of white noise variables that are themselves stationary.

How to identify the number of lags

A time series generated by an MA(q) process is driven by the residuals from the q prior-model predictions. Hence, the ACF for the MA(q) process will show significant coefficients for values up to the lag, q, and then decline sharply because this is how the series values are assumed to have been generated.

The relationship between AR and MA models

An AR(p) model can be expressed as an MA(∞) process using repeated substitution. When imposing constraints on the size of its coefficients, an MA(q) process, it becomes invertible and can be expressed as an AR(∞) process.

How to build ARIMA models and extensions

Autoregressive integrated moving-average ARIMA(p, d, q) models combine AR(p) and MA(q) processes to leverage the complementarity of these building blocks and simplify model development by using a more compact form and reducing the number of parameters, in turn reducing the risk of overfitting.

The models also take care of eliminating unit-root nonstationarity by using the dth difference of the time series values. An ARIMA(p, 1, q) model is the same as using an ARMA(p, q) model with the first differences of the series. Using y' to denote the original series after non-seasonal differencing d times, the ARIMA(p, d, q) model is simply:

$$\text{ARIMA}(p, d, q): \quad y_t = \text{AR}(p) + \text{MA}(q) = \phi_0 + \phi_1 y_{t-1} + \ldots + \phi_p y_{t-p} + \epsilon_t + \theta_1 \epsilon_{t-1} + \ldots + \theta_q \epsilon_{t-q}, \quad \epsilon \sim \text{i.i.d.}$$

ARIMA models are also estimated using Maximum Likelihood. Depending on the implementation, higher-order models may generally subsume lower-order models. For example, `statsmodels` includes all lower-order p and q terms and does not permit removing coefficients for lags below the highest value. In this case, higher-order models will always fit better. Be careful not to overfit your model to the data by using too many terms.

How to identify the number of AR and MA terms

Since AR(p) and MA(q) terms interact, the information provided by the ACF and PACF is no longer reliable and can only be used as a starting point.

Traditionally, the AIC and BIC information criteria have been used to rely on in-sample fit when selecting the model design. Alternatively, we can rely on out-of-sample tests to cross-validate multiple parameter choices.

The following summary provides some generic guidance to choose the model order in the case of considering AR and MA models in isolation:

- The lag beyond which the PACF cuts off is the indicated number of AR terms. If the PACF of the differenced series cuts off sharply and/or the lag-1 autocorrelation is positive, add one or more AR terms.
- The lag beyond which the ACF cuts off is the indicated number of MA terms. If the ACF of the differenced series displays a sharp cutoff and/or the lag-1 autocorrelation is negative, consider adding an MA term to the model.
- AR and MA terms may cancel out each other's effects, so always try to reduce the number of AR and MA terms by 1 if your model contains both to avoid overfitting, especially if the more complex model requires more than 10 iterations to converge.
- If the AR coefficients sum to nearly 1 and suggest a unit root in the AR part of the model, eliminate 1 AR term and difference the model once (more).
- If the MA coefficients sum to nearly 1 and suggest a unit root in the MA part of the model, eliminate 1 MA term and reduce the order of differencing by 1.
- Unstable long-term forecasts suggest there may be a unit root in the AR or MA part of the model.

Adding features – ARMAX

An ARMAX model adds input variables or covariate on the right-hand side of the ARMA time series model (assuming the series is stationary so we can skip differencing):

$$\text{ARIMA}(p, d, q): \quad y_t = \beta x_t + \text{AR}(p) + \text{MA}(q) = \beta x_t + \phi_0 + \phi_1 y_{t-1} + \ldots + \phi_p y_{t-p} + \epsilon_t + \theta_1 \epsilon_{t-1} + \ldots + \theta_q \epsilon_{t-q}, \quad \epsilon \sim \text{i.i.d.}$$

This resembles a linear regression model but is quite difficult to interpret because the effect of β on y_t is not the effect of an increase in x_t by one unit as in linear regression. Instead, the presence of lagged values of y_t on the right-hand side of the equation implies that the coefficient can only be interpreted given the lagged values of the response variable, which is hardly intuitive.

Adding seasonal differencing – SARIMAX

For time series with seasonal effects, we can include AR and MA terms that capture the seasonality's periodicity. For instance, when using monthly data and the seasonal effect length is one year, the seasonal AR and MA terms would reflect this particular lag length.

The ARIMAX(p, d, q) model then becomes a SARIMAX(p, d, q) x (P, D, Q)$_s$ model, which is a bit more complicated to write out, but the references on GitHub, including the statsmodels documentation, provide this information in detail.

We will now build a seasonal ARMA model using macro-data to illustrate the implementation.

How to forecast macro fundamentals

We will build a SARIMAX model for monthly data on an industrial production time series for the 1988-2017 period. As illustrated in the first section on analytical tools, the data has been log-transformed, and we are using seasonal (lag-12) differences. We estimate the model for a range of both ordinary and conventional AR and MA parameters using a rolling window of 10 years of training data, and evaluate the RMSE of the 1-step-ahead forecast, as shown in the following simplified code (see GitHub for details):

```
for p1 in range(4):            # AR order
    for q1 in range(4):        # MA order
        for p2 in range(3):        # seasonal AR order
            for q2 in range(3):    # seasonal MA order
                y_pred = []
                for i, T in enumerate(range(train_size, len(data))):
                    train_set = data.iloc[T - train_size:T]
                    model = tsa.SARIMAX(endog=train_set,            # model
specification
                                        order=(p1, 0, q1),
                                        seasonal_order=(p2, 0, q2,
12)).fit()

                    preds.iloc[i, 1] = model.forecast(steps=1)[0]     # 1-
step ahead forecast

                mse = mean_squared_error(preds.y_true, preds.y_pred)
                test_results[(p1, q1, p2, q2)] = [np.sqrt(mse),
preds.y_true.sub(preds.y_pred).std(),
                                                  np.mean(aic)]
```

We also collect the AIC and BIC criteria that show a very high rank correlation coefficient of 0.94, with BIC favoring models with slightly fewer parameters than AIC. The best five models by RMSE are:

p1	q1	p2	q2	RMSE	AIC	BIC
2	3	1	0	0.009323	−772.247023	−752.734581
3	2	1	0	0.009467	−768.844028	−749.331586
2	2	1	0	0.009540	−770.904835	−754.179884
	3	0	0	0.009773	−760.248885	−743.523935
	2	0	0	0.009986	−758.775827	−744.838368

We re-estimate a SARIMA(2, 0 ,3) x (1, 0, 0) model, as follows:

```
best_model = tsa.SARIMAX(endog=industrial_production_log_diff, order=(2, 0, 3),
                    seasonal_order=(1, 0, 0, 12)).fit()
print(best_model.summary())
```

We obtain the following summary:

```
                          Statespace Model Results
==============================================================================
Dep. Variable:                              IPGMFN   No. Observations:                  348
Model:             SARIMAX(2, 0, 3)x(1, 0, 0, 12)   Log Likelihood              1139.719
Date:                            Sat, 22 Sep 2018   AIC                        -2265.438
Time:                                    17:48:17   BIC                        -2238.472
Sample:                                01-01-1989   HQIC                       -2254.702
                                     - 12-01-2017
Covariance Type:                               opg
==============================================================================
                 coef    std err          z      P>|z|      [0.025      0.975]
------------------------------------------------------------------------------
ar.L1          1.4934      0.104     14.351      0.000       1.289       1.697
ar.L2         -0.5159      0.102     -5.083      0.000      -0.715      -0.317
ma.L1         -0.5499      0.114     -4.813      0.000      -0.774      -0.326
ma.L2          0.2872      0.062      4.662      0.000       0.166       0.408
ma.L3          0.1815      0.070      2.589      0.010       0.044       0.319
ar.S.L12      -0.4486      0.047     -9.533      0.000      -0.541      -0.356
sigma2      8.141e-05   5.65e-06     14.399      0.000    7.03e-05    9.25e-05
==============================================================================
Ljung-Box (Q):                       61.58   Jarque-Bera (JB):              9.97
Prob(Q):                              0.02   Prob(JB):                      0.01
Heteroskedasticity (H):               1.07   Skew:                         -0.20
Prob(H) (two-sided):                  0.71   Kurtosis:                      3.73
==============================================================================

Warnings:
[1] Covariance matrix calculated using the outer product of gradients (complex-step).
```

The coefficients are significant, and the Q statistic rejects the hypothesis of further autocorrelation. The correlogram similarly indicates that we have successfully eliminated the series' autocorrelation:

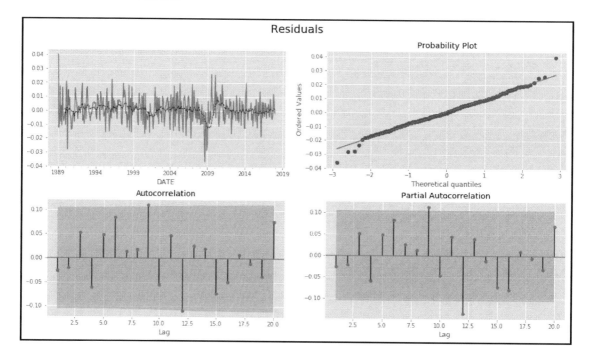

How to use time series models to forecast volatility

A particularly important area of application for univariate time series models is the prediction of volatility. The volatility of financial time series is usually not constant over time but changes, with bouts of volatility clustering together. Changes in variance create challenges for time series forecasting using the classical ARIMA models. To address this challenge, we will now model volatility so that we can predict changes in variance.

Heteroskedasticity is the technical term for changes in a variable's variance.
The **autoregressive conditional heteroskedasticity (ARCH)** model expresses
the variance of the error term as a function of the errors in previous periods. More
specifically, it assumes that the error variance follows an AR(p) model.

The **generalized autoregressive conditional heteroskedasticity (GARCH)** model broadens
the scope to ARMA models. Time series forecasting often combines ARIMA models for the
expected mean and ARCH/GARCH models for the expected variance of a time series. The
2003 Nobel Prize in Economics was awarded to Robert Engle and Clive Granger for
developing this class of models. The former also runs the Volatility Lab at New York
University's Stern School (see GitHub references) with numerous online examples and tools
concerning the models we will discuss and their numerous extensions.

The autoregressive conditional heteroskedasticity (ARCH) model

The ARCH(p) model is simply an AR(p) model applied to the variance of the residuals of a
time series model that makes this variance at time t conditional on lagged observations of
the variance. More specifically, the error terms, ε_t, are residuals of a linear model, such as
ARIMA, on the original time series and are split into a time-dependent standard deviation,
σ_t, and a disturbance, z_t, as follows:

$$\text{ARCH}(p): \quad \text{var}(x_t) = \sigma_t^2 = \omega + \alpha_1 \epsilon_{t-1}^2 + \ldots + \alpha_p \epsilon_{t-p}^2, \quad \epsilon_t = \sigma_t z_t, \quad z_t \sim \text{i.i.d.}$$

An ARCH(p) model can be estimated using OLS. Engle proposed a method to identify the
appropriate ARCH order using the Lagrange multiplier test that corresponds to the F-test
of the hypothesis that all coefficients in linear regression are zero (see `Chapter 7`, *Linear
Models*).

One strength of the model is that it produces volatility, estimates positive excess
kurtosis—that is, fat tails relative to the normal distribution—which in turn is in line with
empirical observations about returns. Weaknesses include that the model assumes the same
effect for positive and negative volatility shocks because it depends on the square of the
previous shocks, whereas asset prices are known to respond differently to positive and
negative shocks. The ARCH model also does not offer new insight into the source of
variations of a financial time series because it just mechanically describes the conditional
variance. Finally, ARCH models are likely to overpredict the volatility because they
respond slowly to large, isolated shocks to the return series.

For a properly-specified ARCH model, the standardized residuals (divided by the model estimate for the period of standard deviation) should resemble white noise and can be subjected to a Ljung-Box Q test.

Generalizing ARCH – the GARCH model

The ARCH model is relatively simple but often requires many parameters to capture the volatility patterns of an asset-return series. The **generalized ARCH (GARCH)** model applies to a log-return series, r_t, with disturbances, $\varepsilon_t = r_t - \mu$, that follow a GARCH(p, q) model if:

$$\epsilon_t = \sigma_t z_t, \quad \sigma_t^2 = \omega + \sum_{i=1}^{p} \alpha_i \epsilon_{t-i}^2 + \sum_{j=1}^{q} \beta_i \sigma_{t-j}^2, \quad z_t \sim \text{i.i.d.}$$

The GARCH(p, q) model assumes an ARMA(p, q) model for the variance of the error term, ε_t.

Similar to ARCH models, the tail distribution of a GARCH(1,1) process is heavier than that of a normal distribution. The model encounters the same weaknesses as the ARCH model. For instance, it responds equally to positive and negative shocks.

Selecting the lag order

To configure the lag order for ARCH and GARCH models, use the squared residuals of the time series trained to predict the mean of the original series. The residuals are zero-centered so that their squares are also the variance. Then inspect the ACF and PACF plots of the squared residuals to identify autocorrelation patterns in the variance of the time series.

How to build a volatility-forecasting model

The development of a volatility model for an asset-return series consists of four steps:

1. Build an ARMA time series model for the financial time series based on the serial dependence revealed by the ACF and PACF.
2. Test the residuals of the model for ARCH/GARCH effects, again relying on the ACF and PACF for the series of the squared residual.
3. Specify a volatility model if serial correlation effects are significant, and jointly estimate the mean and volatility equations.
4. Check the fitted model carefully and refine it if necessary.

 When applying volatility forecasting to return series, the serial dependence may be limited so that a constant mean may be used instead of an ARMA model.

The `arch` library provides several options to estimate volatility-forecasting models. It offers several options to model the expected mean, including a constant mean, the AR(p) model discussed in the section on univariate time series models above as well as more recent heterogeneous autoregressive processes (HAR) that use daily (1 day), weekly (5 days), and monthly (22 days) lags to capture the trading frequencies of short-, medium-, and long-term investors.

The mean models can be jointly defined and estimated with several conditional heteroskedasticity models that include, in addition to ARCH and GARCH, the **exponential GARCH (EGARCH)** model, which allows for asymmetric effects between positive and negative returns and the **heterogeneous ARCH (HARCH)** model, which complements the HAR mean model.

We will use daily NASDAQ returns from 1998-2017 to demonstrate the usage of a GARCH model (see the notebook `arch_garch_models` for details):

```
nasdaq = web.DataReader('NASDAQCOM', 'fred', '1998',
'2017-12-31').squeeze()
nasdaq_returns = np.log(nasdaq).diff().dropna().mul(100) # rescale to
facilitate optimization
```

The rescaled daily return series exhibits only limited autocorrelation, but the squared deviations from the mean do have substantial memory reflected in the slowly-decaying ACF and the PACF high for the first two and cutting off only after the first six lags:

```
plot_correlogram(nasdaq_returns.sub(nasdaq_returns.mean()).pow(2),
lags=120, title='NASDAQ Daily Volatility')
```

The function `plot_correlogram` produces the following output:

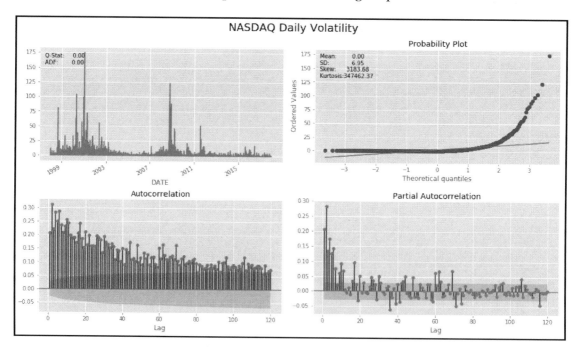

Hence, we can estimate a GARCH model to capture the linear relationship of past volatilities. We will use rolling 10-year windows to estimate a GARCH(p, q) model with p and q ranging from 1-4 to generate 1-step out-of-sample forecasts. We then compare the RMSE of the predicted volatility relative to the actual squared deviation of the return from its mean to identify the most predictive model. We are using winsorized data to limit the impact of extreme return values reflected in the very high positive skew of the volatility:

```
trainsize = 10 * 252   # 10 years
data = nasdaq_returns.clip(lower=nasdaq_returns.quantile(.05),
                           upper=nasdaq_returns.quantile(.95))
T = len(nasdaq_returns)
test_results = {}
for p in range(1, 5):
    for q in range(1, 5):
        print(f'{p} | {q}')
        result = []
        for s, t in enumerate(range(trainsize, T-1)):
            train_set = data.iloc[s: t]
            test_set = data.iloc[t+1]   # 1-step ahead forecast
            model = arch_model(y=train_set, p=p, q=q).fit(disp='off')
            forecast = model.forecast(horizon=1)
            mu = forecast.mean.iloc[-1, 0]
            var = forecast.variance.iloc[-1, 0]
            result.append([(test_set-mu)**2, var])
        df = pd.DataFrame(result, columns=['y_true', 'y_pred'])
        test_results[(p, q)] = np.sqrt(mean_squared_error(df.y_true,
df.y_pred))
```

The GARCH(2, 2) model achieves the lowest RMSE (same value as GARCH(4, 2) but with fewer parameters), so we go ahead and estimate this model to inspect the summary:

```
am = ConstantMean(nasdaq_returns.clip(lower=nasdaq_returns.quantile(.05),
                                      upper=nasdaq_returns.quantile(.95)))
am.volatility = GARCH(2, 0, 2)
am.distribution = Normal()
model = am.fit(update_freq=5)
print(model.summary())
```

The output shows the maximized log-likelihood as well as the AIC and BIC criteria that are commonly minimized when selecting models based on in-sample performance (see Chapter 7, *Linear Models*). It also displays the result for the mean model, which in this case is just a constant estimate, as well as the GARCH parameters for the constant omega, the AR parameters, α, and the MA parameters, β, all of which are statistically significant:

```
                 Constant Mean - GARCH Model Results
================================================================================
Dep. Variable:             NASDAQCOM   R-squared:                        -0.001
Mean Model:            Constant Mean   Adj. R-squared:                   -0.001
Vol Model:                     GARCH   Log-Likelihood:                  -7484.02
Distribution:                 Normal   AIC:                              14980.0
Method:          Maximum Likelihood   BIC:                              15019.0
                                       No. Observations:                    4852
Date:              Sun, Sep 23 2018    Df Residuals:                        4846
Time:                      15:43:41    Df Model:                               6
                                 Mean Model
================================================================================
                 coef    std err          t      P>|t|      95.0% Conf. Int.
--------------------------------------------------------------------------------
mu             0.0521  1.491e-02      3.491  4.804e-04  [2.284e-02,8.130e-02]
                              Volatility Model
================================================================================
                 coef    std err          t      P>|t|      95.0% Conf. Int.
--------------------------------------------------------------------------------
omega          0.0196  8.287e-03      2.365  1.804e-02  [3.354e-03,3.584e-02]
alpha[1]       0.0247  1.470e-02      1.678  9.340e-02  [-4.148e-03,5.346e-02]
alpha[2]       0.0627  2.196e-02      2.853  4.324e-03     [1.962e-02,  0.106]
beta[1]        0.5648      0.181      3.120  1.806e-03     [  0.210,   0.920]
beta[2]        0.3337      0.180      1.853  6.393e-02  [-1.932e-02,   0.687]
================================================================================

Covariance estimator: robust
```

Let's now explore models for multiple time series and the concept of cointegration, which will enable a new trading strategy.

Multivariate time series models

Multivariate time series models are designed to capture the dynamic of multiple time series simultaneously and leverage dependencies across these series for more reliable predictions.

Systems of equations

Univariate time series models like the ARMA approach, we just discussed are limited to statistical relationships between a target variable and its lagged values or lagged disturbances and exogenous series in the ARMAX case. In contrast, multivariate time series models also allow for lagged values of other time series to affect the target. This effect applies to all series, resulting in complex interactions, as illustrated in the following diagram:

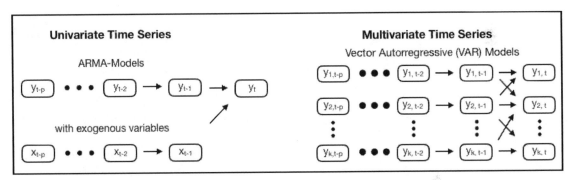

In addition to potentially better forecasting, multivariate time series are also used to gain insights into cross-series dependencies. For example, in economics, multivariate time series are used to understand how policy changes to one variable, for example, an interest rate, may affect other variables over different horizons. The impulse-response function produced by the multivariate model we will look at serves this purpose and allows us to simulate how one variable responds to a sudden change in other variables. The concept of Granger causality analyzes whether one variable is useful in forecasting another (in the least squares sense). Furthermore, multivariate time series models allow for a decomposition of the prediction error variance to analyze how other series contribute.

The vector autoregressive (VAR) model

We will see how the vector autoregressive VAR(p) model extends the AR(p) model to k series by creating a system of k equations where each contains p lagged values of all k series. In the simplest case, a VAR(1) model for *k=2* takes the following form:

$$y_{1,t} = c_1 + a_{1,1}y_{1,t-1} + a_{1,2}y_{2,t-1} + \epsilon_{1,t}$$
$$y_{2,t} = c_2 + a_{2,1}y_{1,t-1} + a_{2,2}y_{2,t-1} + \epsilon_{1,t}$$

This model can be expressed somewhat more concisely in matrix form:

$$\begin{bmatrix} y_{1,t} \\ y_{2,t} \end{bmatrix} = \begin{bmatrix} c_1 \\ c_2 \end{bmatrix} + \begin{bmatrix} a_{1,1} & a_{1,2} \\ a_{2,1} & a_{2,2} \end{bmatrix} \begin{bmatrix} y_{1,t-1} \\ y_{2,t-1} \end{bmatrix} + \begin{bmatrix} \epsilon_{1,t} \\ \epsilon_{2,t} \end{bmatrix}$$

The coefficients on the own lags provide information about the dynamics of the series itself, whereas the cross-variable coefficients offer some insight into the interactions across the series. This notation extends to the k series and order p, as follows:

$$\underset{k \times 1}{y_t} = \underset{k \times 1}{c} + \underset{k \times k}{A_1}\underset{k \times 1}{y_{t-1}} + \ldots + \underset{k \times k}{A_p}\underset{k \times 1}{y_{t-p}} + \underset{k \times 1}{\epsilon_t}$$

VAR(p) models also require stationarity, so that the initial steps from univariate time series modeling carry over. First, explore the series and determine the necessary transformations, then apply the Augmented Dickey-Fuller test to verify that the stationarity criterion is met for each series and apply further transformations otherwise. It can be estimated with OLS conditional on initial information or with maximum likelihood, which is equivalent for normally-distributed errors but not otherwise.

If some or all of the k series are unit-root non-stationary, they may be co-integrated. This extension of the unit root concept to multiple time series means that a linear combination of two or more series is stationary and, hence, mean-reverting. The VAR model is not equipped to handle this case without differencing, instead use the Vector Error Correction model (VECM, see references on GitHub). We will further explore cointegration because, if present and assumed to persist, it can be leveraged for a pairs-trading strategy.

The determination of the lag order also takes its cues from the ACF and PACF for each series but is constrained by the fact that the same lag order applies to all series. After model estimation, residual diagnostics also call for a result resembling white noise, and model selection can use in-sample information criteria or, preferably, out-of-sample predictive performance to cross-validate alternative model designs if the ultimate goal is to use the model for prediction.

As mentioned in the univariate case, predictions of the original time series require us to reverse the transformations applied to make a series stationary before training the model.

How to use the VAR model for macro fundamentals forecasts

We will extend the univariate example of a single time series of monthly data on industrial production and add a monthly time series on consumer sentiment, both provided by the Federal Reserve's data service. We will use the familiar `pandas-datareader` library to retrieve data from 1970 through 2017:

```
df = web.DataReader(['UMCSENT', 'IPGMFN'], 'fred', '1970',
'2017-12').dropna()
df.columns = ['sentiment', 'ip']
```

Log-transforming the industrial production series and seasonal differencing using lag 12 of both series yields stationary results:

```
df_transformed = pd.DataFrame({'ip': np.log(df.ip).diff(12),
                               'sentiment': df.sentiment.diff(12)}).dropna()

test_unit_root(df_transformed) # see notebook for details and additional
plots


          p-value
ip         0.0003
sentiment  0.0000
```

This leaves us with the following series:

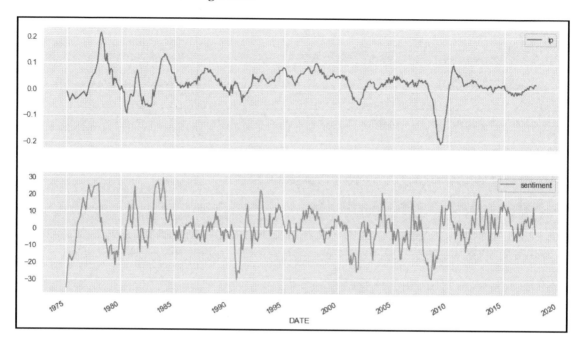

To limit the size of the output, we will just estimate a VAR(1) model using the statsmodels VARMAX implementation (which allows for optional exogenous variables) with a constant trend using the first 480 observations:

```
model = VARMAX(df_transformed.iloc[:480], order=(1,1),
trend='c').fit(maxiter=1000)
```

This results in the following summary:

```
                         Statespace Model Results
================================================================================
Dep. Variable:      ['ip', 'sentiment']   No. Observations:              480
Model:                    VARMA(1,1)      Log Likelihood             -68.938
                          + intercept     AIC                        163.875
Date:             Sun, 23 Sep 2018        BIC                        218.134
Time:                     17:53:02        HQIC                       185.203
Sample:                          0
                             - 480
Covariance Type:               opg
================================================================================
Ljung-Box (Q):            129.82, 165.15  Jarque-Bera (JB):      140.59, 16.05
Prob(Q):                      0.00, 0.00  Prob(JB):                  0.00, 0.00
Heteroskedasticity (H):       0.47, 1.10  Skew:                      0.19, 0.21
Prob(H) (two-sided):          0.00, 0.55  Kurtosis:                  5.62, 3.79
                          Results for equation ip
================================================================================
                 coef     std err         z     P>|z|     [0.025     0.975]
--------------------------------------------------------------------------------
const          0.0016       0.001     2.531     0.011      0.000      0.003
L1.ip          0.9276       0.010    95.539     0.000      0.909      0.947
L1.sentiment   0.0006    5.92e-05    10.283     0.000      0.000      0.001
L1.e(ip)       0.0095       0.037     0.259     0.796     -0.062      0.081
L1.e(sentiment) -0.0001      0.000    -0.836     0.403     -0.000      0.000
                       Results for equation sentiment
================================================================================
                 coef     std err         z     P>|z|     [0.025     0.975]
--------------------------------------------------------------------------------
const          0.3773       0.272     1.388     0.165     -0.155      0.910
L1.ip        -14.5753       5.375    -2.712     0.007    -25.109     -4.041
L1.sentiment   0.8795       0.023    37.840     0.000      0.834      0.925
L1.e(ip)      40.2063      18.695     2.151     0.032      3.565     76.847
L1.e(sentiment) 0.0411      0.051     0.800     0.424     -0.060      0.142
                         Error covariance matrix
================================================================================
                      coef    std err         z     P>|z|    [0.025     0.975]
--------------------------------------------------------------------------------
sqrt.var.ip         0.0128      0.000    41.131     0.000     0.012      0.013
sqrt.cov.ip.sentiment 0.0309    0.229     0.135     0.893    -0.418      0.480
sqrt.var.sentiment  5.2713      0.147    35.759     0.000     4.982      5.560
================================================================================

Warnings:
[1] Covariance matrix calculated using the outer product of gradients (complex-step).
```

The output contains the coefficients for both time series equations, as outlined in the preceding VAR(1) illustration. statsmodels provides diagnostic plots to check whether the residuals meet the white noise assumptions, which are not exactly met in this simple case:

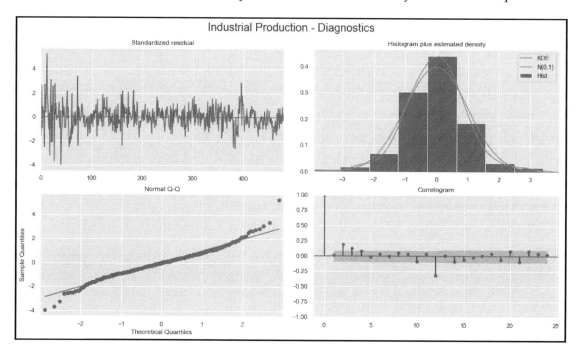

Out-of-sample predictions can be generated as follows:

```
preds = model.predict(start=480, end=len(df_transformed)-1)
```

A visualization of actual and predicted values shows how the prediction lags the actual values and does not capture non-linear out-of-sample patterns well:

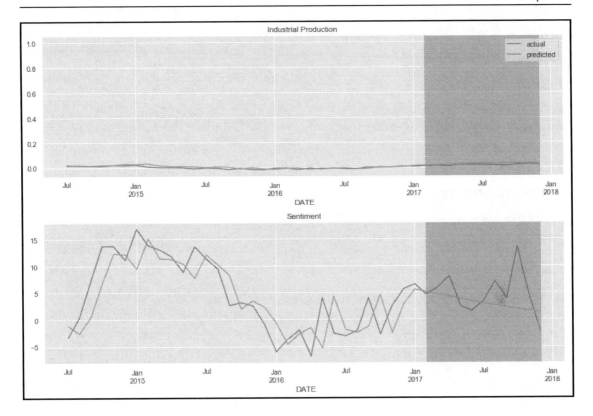

Cointegration – time series with a common trend

The concept of an integrated multivariate series is complicated by the fact that all the component series of the process may be individually integrated but the process is not jointly integrated in the sense that one or more linear combinations of the series exist that produce a new stationary series.

In other words, a combination of two co-integrated series has a stable mean to which this linear combination reverts. A multivariate series with this characteristic is said to be co-integrated. This also applies when the individual series are integrated of a higher order and the linear combination reduces the overall order of integration.

cointegration is different from correlation: two series can be highly correlated but need not be co-integrated. For example, if two growing series are constant multiples of each other, their correlation will be high but any linear combination will also grow rather than revert to the mean.

The VAR analysis can still be applied to integrated processes using the error-correction form of a VAR model that uses the first differences of the individual series plus an error correction term in levels.

Testing for cointegration

There are two major approaches to testing for cointegration:

- The Engle–Granger two-step method
- The Johansen procedure

The Engle–Granger method involves regressing one series on another, and then applying an ADF unit-root test to the regression residual. If the null hypothesis can be rejected so that we assume the residuals are stationary, then the series are co-integrated. A key benefit of this approach is that the regression coefficient represents the multiplier that renders the combination stationary, that is, mean-reverting. We will return to this aspect when leveraging cointegration for a pairs-trading strategy. On the other hand, this approach is limited to identifying cointegration for pairs of series as opposed to larger groups of series.

The Johansen procedure, in contrast, tests the restrictions imposed by cointegration on a **vector autoregression** (**VAR**) model as discussed in the previous section. More specifically, after subtracting the target vector from both sides of the generic VAR(p) preceding equation, we obtain the **error correction model** (**ECM**) formulation:

$$\Delta y_t = c + \Pi y_{t-1} + \Gamma_1 \Delta y_{t-1} + \ldots + \Gamma_p \Delta y_{t-p} + \epsilon_t$$

The resulting modified VAR(p) equation has only one vector term in levels, that is, not expressed as difference using the operator, Δ. The nature of cointegration depends on the properties of the coefficient matrix, Π, of this term, in particular on its rank. While this equation appears structurally similar to the ADF test setup, there are now several potential constellations of common trends and orders of integration because there are multiple series involved. For details, see the references listed on GitHub, including with respect to practical challenges regarding the scaling of individual series.

How to use cointegration for a pairs-trading strategy

Pairs-trading relies on a stationary, mean-reverting relationship between two asset prices. In other words, the ratio or difference between the two prices, also called the spread, may over time diverge but should ultimately return to the same level. Given such a pair, the strategy consists of going long (that is, purchasing) the under-performing asset because it would require a period of outperformance to close the gap. At the same time, one would short the asset that has moved away from the price anchor in the positive direction to fund the purchase.

cointegration represents precisely this type of stable relationship between two price series anchored by a common mean. Assuming cointegration persists, convergence must ultimately ensue, either by the underperforming stock rising or the outperforming stock coming down. The strategy would be profitable regardless, which has the added advantage of being hedged against general market movements either way.

However, the spread will constantly change, sometimes widening and sometimes narrowing, or remain unchanged as both assets move in unison. The challenge of pairs-trading consists of maintaining a hedged position by adjusting the relative holdings as the spread changes.

In practice, given a universe of assets, a pairs-trading strategy will search for co-integrated pairs by running a statistical test on each pair. The key challenge here is to account for multiple testing biases, as outlined in `Chapter 6`, *Machine Learning Workflow*. The `statsmodels` library implements both the Engle-Granger cointegration test and the Johansen test.

In order to estimate the spread, run a linear regression to get the coefficient for the linear combination of two integrated asset price series that produce a stationary combined series. As mentioned, using linear regression to estimate the coefficient is known as the Engle-Granger test of cointegration.

Summary

In this chapter, we explored linear time series models for the univariate case of individual series as well as multivariate models for several interacting series. We encountered applications that predict macro fundamentals, models that forecast asset or portfolio volatility with widespread use in risk management, as well as multivariate VAR models that capture the dynamics of multiple macro series, as well as the concept of cointegration, which underpins the popular pair-trading strategy.

Similar to the previous chapter, we saw how linear models add a lot of structure to the model, that is, they make strong assumptions that potentially require transformations and extensive testing to verify that these assumptions are met. If they are, model-training and - interpretation is straightforward, and the models provide a good baseline case that more complex models may be able to improve on, as we will see in the following chapters.

Bayesian Machine Learning

9

In this chapter, we will introduce Bayesian approaches to machine learning, and how their different perspectives on uncertainty add value when developing and evaluating algorithmic trading strategies.

Bayesian statistics allow us to quantify the uncertainty about future events and refine our estimates in a principled way as new information arrives. This dynamic approach adapts well to the evolving nature of financial markets. It is particularly useful when there is less relevant data and we require methods that systematically integrate prior knowledge or assumptions.

We will see that Bayesian approaches to machine learning allow for richer insights into the uncertainty around statistical metrics, parameter estimates, and predictions. The applications range from more granular risk management to dynamic updates of predictive models that incorporate changes in the market environment. The Black-Litterman approach to asset allocation (see Chapter 5, *Strategy Evaluation*, can be interpreted as a Bayesian model. It computes the expected return as an average of the market equilibrium and the investor's views, weighted by each asset's volatility, cross-asset correlations, and the confidence in each forecast.

More specifically, in this chapter, we will cover the following topics:

- How Bayesian statistics apply to machine learning
- How to use probabilistic programming with PyMC3
- How to define and train machine learning models
- How to run state-of-the-art sampling methods to conduct approximate inference
- How to apply Bayesian machine learning to compute dynamic Sharpe ratios, build Bayesian classifiers, and estimate stochastic volatility

 References, links to additional material, and the code examples for this chapter are in the corresponding directory of the GitHub repository. Please follow the installation instructions provided in Chapter 1, *Machine Learning for Trading*.

How Bayesian machine learning works

Classical statistics is also called frequentist because it interprets probability as the relative frequency of an event over the long run, that is, after observing a large number of trials. In the context of probabilities, an event is a combination of one or more elementary outcomes of an experiment, such as any of six equal results in rolls of two dice or an asset price dropping by 10% or more on a given day.

Bayesian statistics, in contrast, views probability as a measure of the confidence or belief in the occurrence of an event. The Bayesian perspective of probability leaves more room for subjective views and, consequently, differences in opinions than the frequentist interpretation. This difference is most striking for events that do not happen often enough to arrive at an objective measure of long-term frequency.

Put differently, frequentist statistics assume that data is a random sample from a population and aims to identify the fixed parameters that generated the data. Bayesian statistics, in turn, take the data as given and considers the parameters to be random variables with a distribution that can be inferred from data. As a result, frequentist approaches require at least as many data points as there are parameters to be estimated. Bayesian approaches, on the other hand, are compatible with smaller datasets and are well-suited for online learning, one sample at a time.

The Bayesian view is very useful for many real-world events that are rare or unique, at least in important respects. Examples include the outcome of the next election or the question of whether the markets will crash within three months. In each case, there is both relevant historical data as well as unique circumstances that unfold as the event approaches.

First, we will introduce Bayes' theorem, which crystallizes the concept of updating beliefs by combining prior assumptions with new empirical evidence and comparing the resulting parameter estimates with their frequentist counterparts. We will then demonstrate two approaches to Bayesian statistical inference that produce insights into the posterior distribution of the latent, that is, unobserved parameters, such as their expected values, under different circumstances:

1. Conjugate priors facilitate the updating process by providing a closed-form solution, but exact, analytical methods are not always available.
2. Approximate inference simulates the distribution that results from combining assumptions and data and uses samples from this distribution to compute statistical insights.

How to update assumptions from empirical evidence

The theorem that Reverend Thomas Bayes came up with over 250 years ago uses fundamental probability theory to prescribe how probabilities or beliefs should change as relevant new information arrives. The following quote by – John Maynard Keynes captures the Bayesian mindset:

> *"When the facts change, I change my mind. What do you do, sir?"*

It relies on the conditional and total probability and the chain rule; see the references on GitHub for reviews of these concepts.

The belief concerns a single or vector of parameters θ (also called hypotheses). Each parameter can be discrete or continuous. θ could be a one-dimensional statistic like the (discrete) mode of a categorical variable or a (continuous) mean, or a higher dimensional set of values like a covariance matrix or the weights of a deep neural network.

A key difference of frequentist statistics is that Bayesian assumptions are expressed as probability distributions rather than parameter values. Consequently, while frequentist inference focuses on point estimates, Bayesian inference yields probability distributions.

Bayes' Theorem updates the beliefs about the parameters of interest by computing the posterior probability distribution from the following inputs, as shown in the following diagram:

- The **prior** distribution indicates how likely we consider each possible hypothesis.
- The **likelihood function** outputs the probability of observing a dataset given certain values for the θ parameters.

- The **evidence** measures how likely the observed data is given all possible hypotheses. Hence, it is the same for all parameter values and serves to normalize the numerator:

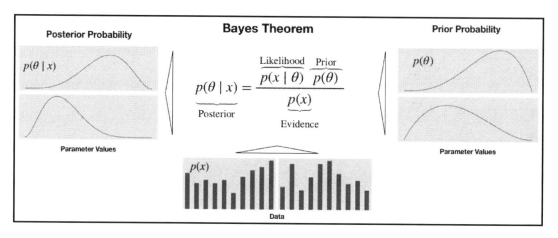

Bayes Theorem

The posterior is the product of prior and likelihood, divided by the evidence, and reflects the updated probability distribution of the hypotheses, taking into account both prior assumptions and the data. Viewed differently, the product of the prior and the likelihood results from applying the chain rule to factorize the joint distribution of data and parameters.

With higher-dimensional, continuous variables, the formulation becomes more complex and involves (multiple) integrals. An alternative formulation uses odds to express the posterior odds as the product of the prior odds times the likelihood ratio (see the references for more details).

Exact inference: Maximum a Posteriori estimation

Practical applications of Bayes' rule to exactly compute posterior probabilities are quite limited because the computation of the evidence term in the denominator is quite challenging. The evidence reflects the probability of the observed data over all possible parameter values. It is also called the marginal likelihood because it requires *marginalizing out* the parameters' distribution by adding or integrating over their distribution. This is generally only possible in simple cases with a small number of discrete parameters that assume very few values.

Maximum a posteriori probability (MAP) estimation leverages that the evidence is a constant factor that scales the posterior to meet the requirements for a probability distribution. Since the evidence does not depend on θ, the posterior distribution is proportional to the product of the likelihood and the prior. Hence, MAP estimation chooses the value of θ that maximizes the posterior given the observed data and the prior belief, that is, the mode of the posterior.

The MAP approach contrasts with the **maximum likelihood estimation (MLE)** of parameters, which define a probability distribution. MLE picks the parameter value θ that maximizes the likelihood function for the observed training data.

A look at the definitions highlights that MAP differs from MLE by including the prior distribution. In other words, unless the prior is a constant, the MAP estimate θ will differ from its MLE counterpart:

$$\theta_{MLE} = arg\max_{\theta} P(X|\theta)$$

$$\theta_{MAP} = arg\max_{\theta} P(X|\theta)P(\theta)$$

The MLE solution tends to reflect the frequentist notion that probability estimates should reflect observed ratios. On the other hand, the impact of the prior on the MAP estimate often corresponds to adding data that reflects the prior assumptions to the MLE. For example, a strong prior that a coin is biased can be incorporated in the MLE context by adding skewed trial data.

Prior distributions are a critical ingredient for Bayesian models. We will now introduce some convenient choices that facilitate analytical inference.

How to select priors

The prior should reflect knowledge of the distribution of the parameters because it influences the MAP estimate. If a prior is not known with certainty, we need to make a choice, often from several reasonable options. In general, it is good practice to justify the prior and check for robustness by testing whether alternatives lead to the same conclusion.

There are several types of priors:

- **Objective** priors maximize the impact of the data on the posterior. If the parameter distribution is unknown, we can select an uninformative prior like a uniform distribution, also called a flat prior, over a relevant range of parameter values.

- In contrast, **subjective** priors aim to incorporate information that's external to the model into the estimate.
- An **empirical** prior combines Bayesian and frequentist methods and uses historical data to eliminate subjectivity, such as by estimating various moments to fit a standard distribution.

In the context of a machine learning model, the prior can be viewed as a regularizer because it limits the values that the posterior can assume. Parameters that have zero prior probability, for example, are not part of the posterior distribution. Generally, more good data allows for stronger conclusions and reduces the influence of the prior.

How to keep inference simple – conjugate priors

A prior distribution is conjugate with respect to the likelihood when the resulting posterior is of the same type of distribution as the prior, except for different parameters. When both the prior and the likelihood are normally distributed, then the posterior is also normally distributed.

The conjugacy of the prior and likelihood implies a closed-form solution for the posterior that facilitates the update process and avoids the need to use numerical methods to approximate the posterior. Moreover, the resulting posterior can be used as prior for the next update step.

Let's illustrate this process using a binary classification example for stock price movements.

How to dynamically estimate the probabilities of asset price moves

When the data consists of binary Bernoulli random variables with a certain success probability for a positive outcome, the number of successes in repeated trials follows a Binomial distribution. The conjugate prior is the Beta distribution with support over the interval [0, 1] and two shape parameters to model arbitrary prior distributions over the success probability. Hence, the posterior distribution is also a Beta distribution that we can derive by directly updating the parameters.

We will collect samples of different sizes of binarized daily S&P 500 returns, where the positive outcome is a price increase. Starting from an uninformative prior that allocates equal probability to each possible success probability in the interval [0, 1], we compute the posterior for different evidence samples.

The following code sample shows that the update consists of simply adding the observed numbers of success and failure to the parameters of the prior distribution to obtain the posterior:

```
n_days = [0, 1, 3, 5, 10, 25, 50, 100, 500]
outcomes = sp500_binary.sample(n_days[-1])
p = np.linspace(0, 1, 100)

# uniform (uninformative) prior
a = b = 1
for i, days in enumerate(n_days):
    up = outcomes.iloc[:days].sum()
    down = days - up
    update = stats.beta.pdf(p, a + up , b + down)
```

The resulting posterior distributions are plotted in the following graphs. They illustrate the evolution from a uniform prior that views all success probabilities as equally likely to an increasingly peaked distribution.

After 500 samples, the probability is concentrated near the actual probability of a positive move at 54.7% from 2010 to 2017. It also shows the small differences between MLE and MAP estimates, where the latter tends to be pulled slightly toward the expected value of the uniform prior, as shown in the following diagram:

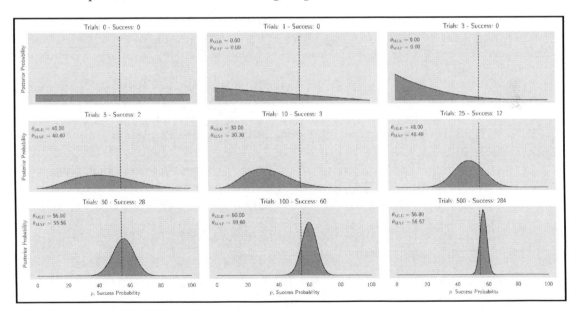

Posterior probabilities

In practice, the use of conjugate priors is limited to low-dimensional cases. In addition, the simplified MAP approach avoids computing the evidence term, but has several shortcomings even when it is available; it does not return a distribution so that we can derive a measure of uncertainty, or use it as a prior. Hence, we need to resort to approximates rather than exact inference using numerical methods and stochastic simulation, which we will introduce next.

Approximate inference: stochastic versus deterministic approaches

For most models of practical relevance, it will not be possible to derive the exact posterior distribution analytically and compute the expected values for the latent parameters. The model may have too many parameters, or the posterior distribution may be too complex for an analytical solution. For continuous variables, the integrals may not have closed-form solutions, while the dimensionality of the space and the complexity of the integrand may prohibit numerical integration. For discrete variables, the marginalizations involve summing over all possible configurations of the hidden variables, and though this is always possible in principle, we often find in practice that there may be exponentially many hidden states so that exact calculation is prohibitively expensive.

Although for some applications the posterior distribution over unobserved parameters will be of interest, more often than not it is primarily required to evaluate expectations, for example, to make predictions. In such situations, we can rely on approximate inference:

- **Stochastic** techniques based on **Markov Chain Monte Carlo (MCMC)** sampling have popularized the use of Bayesian methods across many domains. They generally have the ability to converge to the exact result. In practice, sampling methods can be computationally demanding and are often limited to small-scale problems.
- **Deterministic** methods, known as variational inference or variational Bayes, are based on analytical approximations to the posterior distribution and can scale well to large applications. They make simplified assumptions, for example, that the posterior factorizes in a particular way or it has a specific parametric form such as a Gaussian. Hence, they do not generate exact results and can be used as complements to sampling methods.

Sampling-based stochastic inference

Sampling is about drawing samples, $X=(x_1, ..., x_n)$, from a given distribution, $p(x)$. Assuming the samples are independent, the law of large numbers ensures that for a growing number of samples, the fraction of a given instance, x_i, in the sample (for the discrete case) corresponds to its probability, $p(x=x_i)$. In the continuous case, the analogous reasoning applies to a given region of the sample space. Hence, averages over samples can be used as unbiased estimators of the expected values of parameters of the distribution.

A practical challenge consists in ensuring independent sampling because the distribution is unknown. Dependent samples may still be unbiased, but tend to increase the variance of the estimate so that more samples will be needed for an equally precise estimate as for independent samples.

Sampling from a multivariate distribution is computationally demanding as the number of states increases exponentially with the number of dimensions. Numerous algorithms facilitate the process (see references for an overview). Now, we will introduce a few popular variations of MCMC-based methods.

Markov chain Monte Carlo sampling

A Markov chain is a dynamic stochastic model that describes a random walk over a set of states, connected by transition probabilities. The Markov property stipulates that the process has no memory, and the next step only depends on the current state. In other words, it's conditional on the present, past, and future being independent, that is, information about past states does not help to predict the future beyond what we know from the present.

Monte Carlo methods rely on repeated random sampling to approximate results that may be deterministic, but that does not permit an analytic, exact solution. It was developed during the Manhattan Project to estimate energy at the atomic level and received its enduring code name to ensure secrecy.

Many algorithms apply the Monte Carlo method to a Markov Chain, and generally proceed as follows:

1. Start at the current position.
2. Draw a new position from a proposal distribution.

3. Evaluate the probability of the new position in light of data and prior distributions:
    1. If sufficiently likely, move to the new position
    2. Otherwise, remain at the current position
4. Repeat from step 1.
5. After a given number of iterations, return all accepted positions.

MCMC aims to identify and explore interesting regions of the posterior that concentrate on significant probability density. The memoryless process is said to converge when it consistently moves through nearby high probability states of the posterior where the acceptance rate increases. A key challenge is to balance the need for random exploration of the sample space with the risk of reducing the acceptance rate.

The initial steps of this process are likely to be more reflective of the starting position than the posterior and are typically discarded as **burn-in** samples. A key MCMC property is that the process should forget about its initial position after a certain (but unknown) number of iterations.

The remaining samples are called the trace of the process. Assuming convergence, the relative frequency of samples approximates the posterior and can be used to compute expected values based on the law of large numbers.

As indicated previously, the precision of the estimate depends on the serial correlation of the samples collected by the random walk, each of which, by design, depends only on the previous state. Higher correlation limits the effective exploration of the posterior and needs to be subjected to diagnostic tests.

General techniques to design such a Markov chain include Gibbs sampling, the Metropolis-Hastings algorithm, and more recent Hamiltonian MCMC methods that tend to perform better.

Gibbs sampling

Gibbs sampling simplifies multivariate sampling to a sequence of one-dimensional draws. From a starting point, it iteratively holds $n-1$ variables constant while sampling the nth variable. It incorporates this sample and repeats.

The algorithm is very simple and easy to implement but produces highly correlated samples that slow down convergence. Its sequential nature also prevents parallelization.

Metropolis-Hastings sampling

The Metropolis-Hastings algorithm randomly proposes new locations based on its current state to effectively explore the sample space and reduce the correlation of samples relative to Gibbs sampling. To ensure that it samples from the posterior, it evaluates the proposal using the product of prior and likelihood, which is proportional to the posterior. It accepts with a probability that depends on the result, which is relative to the corresponding value for the current sample.

A key benefit of the proposal evaluation method is that it works with a proportional evaluation rather than an exact evaluation of the posterior. However, it can take a long time to converge because the random movements that are not related to the posterior can reduce the acceptance rate so that a large number of steps produces only a small number of (potentially correlated) samples. The acceptance rate can be tuned by reducing the variance of the proposal distribution, but the resulting smaller steps imply less exploration.

Hamiltonian Monte Carlo – going NUTS

Hamiltonian Monte Carlo (HMC) is a hybrid method that leverages the first-order derivative information of the gradient of the likelihood to propose new states for exploration and overcome some of the challenges of MCMC. In addition, it incorporates momentum to efficiently jump around the posterior. As a result, it converges faster to a high-dimensional target distribution than simpler random-walk Metropolis or Gibbs sampling.

The No-U-Turn sampler is a self-tuning HMC extension that adaptively regulates the size and number of moves around the posterior before selecting a proposal. It works well on high-dimensional and complex posterior distributions and allows many complex models to be fit without specialized knowledge about the fitting algorithm itself. As we will see in the next section, it is the default sampler in PyMC3.

Variational Inference

Variational Inference (VI) is a machine learning method that approximates probability densities through optimization. In the Bayesian context, it approximates the posterior distribution as follows:

1. Select a parametrized family of probability distributions
2. Find the member of this family closest to the target, as measured by Kullback-Leibler divergence

Compared to MCMC, Variational Bayes tends to converge faster and scales to large data better. While MCMC approximates the posterior with samples from the chain that will eventually converge arbitrarily close to the target, variational algorithms approximate the posterior with the result of the optimization, which is not guaranteed to coincide with the target.

Variational Inference is better suited for large datasets and to quickly explore many models. In contrast, MCMC will deliver more accurate results on smaller datasets or when time and computational resources pose fewer constraints.

Automatic Differentiation Variational Inference (ADVI)

The downside of Variational Inference is the need for model-specific derivations and the implementation of a tailored optimization routine that has slowed down widespread adoption.

The recent **Automatic Differentiation Variational Inference (ADVI)** algorithm automates this process so that the user only specifies the model, expressed as a program, and ADVI automatically generates a corresponding variational algorithm (see references on GitHub for implementation details).

We will see that PyMC3 supports various Variational Inference techniques, including ADVI.

Probabilistic programming with PyMC3

Probabilistic programming provides a language to describe and fit probability distributions so that we can design, encode, and automatically estimate and evaluate complex models. It aims to abstract away some of the computational and analytical complexity to allow us to focus on the conceptually more straightforward and intuitive aspects of Bayesian reasoning and inference.

The field has become quite dynamic since new languages emerged. Uber open sourced Pyro (based on PyTorch) and Google recently added a probability module to TensorFlow (see the resources linked on GitHub).

As a result, the practical relevance and use of Bayesian methods in machine learning will likely increase to generate insights into uncertainty and for use cases that require transparent rather than black-box models in particular.

In this section, we will introduce the popular PyMC3 library, which implements advanced MCMC sampling and Variational Inference for machine learning models using Python. Together with Stan, named after Stanislaw Ulam, who invented the Monte Carlo method, and developed by Andrew Gelman at Columbia University since 2012, it is the most popular probabilistic programming language.

Bayesian machine learning with Theano

PyMC3 was released in January 2017 to add Hamiltonian MC methods to the Metropolis-Hastings sampler that's used in PyMC2 (released in 2012). PyMC3 uses Theano as its computational backend for dynamic C compilation and automatic differentiation. Theano is a matrix-focused and GPU-enabled optimization library that was developed at Yoshua Bengio's Montreal Institute for Learning Algorithms (MILA) and inspired TensorFlow. MILA recently ceased to further develop Theano due to the success of newer deep learning libraries (see Chapter 16 *Deep Learning* for details). PyMC4, which is planned for 2019, will use TensorFlow instead, with presumably limited impact on the API.

The PyMC3 workflow

PyMC3 aims for intuitive and readable, yet powerful syntax that reflects how statisticians describe models. The modeling process generally follows these five steps:

1. Encode a probability model by defining the following:
    1. The prior distributions that quantify knowledge and uncertainty about latent variables
    2. The likelihood function that conditions the parameters on observed data
2. Analyze the posterior using one of the options described in the previous section:
    1. Obtain a point estimate using MAP inference
    2. Sample from the posterior using MCMC methods
3. Approximate the posterior using variational Bayes.
4. Check your model using various diagnostic tools.
5. Generate predictions.

The resulting model can be used for inference to gain detailed insights into parameter values as well as to predict outcomes for new data points.

We will illustrate this workflow using simple logistic regression (see the notebook bayesian_logistic_regression). Subsequently, we will use PyMC3 to compute and compare Bayesian Sharpe ratios, estimate dynamic pairs trading ratios, and implement Bayesian linear time series models.

Model definition – Bayesian logistic regression

As discussed in Chapter 6, *Machine Learning Workflow*, logistic regression estimates a linear relationship between a set of features and a binary outcome, which is mediated by a sigmoid function to ensure that the model produces probabilities. The frequentist approach resulted in point estimates for the parameters that measure the influence of each feature on the probability that a data point belongs to the positive class, with confidence intervals based on assumptions about the parameter distribution.

In contrast, Bayesian logistic regression estimates the posterior distribution over the parameters itself. The posterior allows for more robust estimates of what is called a Bayesian credible interval for each parameter, with the benefit of more transparency about the model's uncertainty.

A probabilistic program consists of observed and unobserved random variables (RVs). As we have discussed, we define the observed RVs via likelihood distributions and unobserved RVs via prior distributions. PyMC3 includes numerous probability distributions for this purpose.

We will use a simple dataset that classifies 30,000 individuals by income using a threshold of $50K per year. This dataset will contain information on age, sex, hours worked, and years of education. Hence, we are modeling the probability that an individual earns more than $50K using these features.

The PyMC3 library makes it very straightforward to perform approximate Bayesian inference for logistic regression. Logistic regression models the probability that individual i earns a high income based on k features, as outlined on the left-hand side of the following diagram:

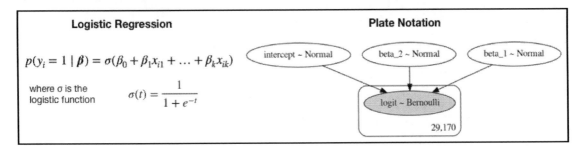

We will use the context manager `with` to define a `manual_logistic_model` that we can refer to later as a probabilistic model:

1. The random variables for the unobserved parameters for intercept and two features are expressed using uninformative priors that assume normal distributions with a mean of 0 and a standard deviation of 100.
2. The likelihood combines the parameters with the data according to the specification of the logistic regression.
3. The outcome is modeled as a Bernoulli RV with success probability given by the likelihood:

```
with pm.Model() as manual_logistic_model:
    # coefficients as rvs with uninformative priors
    intercept = pm.Normal('intercept', 0, sd=100)
    b1 = pm.Normal('beta_1', 0, sd=100)
    b2 = pm.Normal('beta_2', 0, sd=100)

    # Likelihood transforms rvs into probabilities p(y=1)
    # according to logistic regression model.
    likelihood = pm.invlogit(intercept + b1 * data.hours + b2 * data.educ)

    # Outcome as Bernoulli rv with success probability
    # given by sigmoid function conditioned on actual data
    pm.Bernoulli(name='logit', p=likelihood, observed=data.income)
```

Visualization and plate notation

The `pm.model_to_graphviz(manual_logistic_model)` command produces the plate notation displayed in the preceding diagram on the right. It shows the unobserved parameters as light and the observed elements as dark circles. The rectangle indicates the number of repetitions of the observed model element implied by the data included in the model definition.

The Generalized Linear Models module

PyMC3 includes numerous common models so that we can usually leave the manual specification for custom applications. The following code defines the same logistic regression as a member of the **Generalized Linear Models (GLM)** family using the formula format inspired by the statistical language R that's ported to Python by the `patsy` library:

```
with pm.Model() as logistic_model:
    pm.glm.GLM.from_formula('income ~ hours + educ',
                            data,
                            family=pm.glm.families.Binomial())
```

MAP inference

We obtain point MAP estimates for the three parameters using the just defined model's `.find_MAP()` method:

```
with logistic_model:
    map_estimate = pm.find_MAP()
print_map(map_estimate)
Intercept    -6.561862
hours         0.040681
educ          0.350390
```

PyMC3 solves the optimization problem of finding the posterior point with the highest density using the quasi-Newton **Broyden-Fletcher-Goldfarb-Shanno (BFGS)** algorithm, but offers several alternatives, which are provided by the sciPy library. The result is virtually identical to the corresponding statsmodels estimate (see the notebook for more information).

Approximate inference – MCMC

We will use a slightly more complicated model to illustrate Markov chain Monte Carlo inference:

```
formula = 'income ~ sex + age+ I(age ** 2) + hours + educ'
```

Patsy's function, `I()`, allows us to use regular Python expressions to create new variables on the fly. Here, we square `age` to capture the non-linear relationship that more experience adds less income later in life.

Note that variables measured on very different scales can slow down the sampling process. Hence, we first apply sklearn's `scale()` function to standardize the `age`, `hours`, and `educ` variables.

Once we have defined our model with the new formula, we are ready to perform inference to approximate the posterior distribution. MCMC sampling algorithms are available through the `pm.sample()` function.

By default, PyMC3 automatically selects the most efficient sampler and initializes the sampling process for efficient convergence. For a continuous model, PyMC3 chooses the NUTS sampler that we discussed in the previous section. It also runs variational inference via ADVI to find good starting parameters for the sampler. One among several alternatives is to use the MAP estimate.

To see what convergence looks like, we first draw only 100 samples after tuning the sampler for 1000 iterations. This will be discarded afterwards. The sampling process can be parallelized for multiple chains using the `cores` argument (except when using GPU):

```
with logistic_model:
    trace = pm.sample(draws=100, tune=1000,
                      init='adapt_diag', # alternative initialization
                      chains=4, cores=2,
                      random_seed=42)
```

The resulting trace contains the sampled values for each random variable. We can continue sampling by providing the trace of a prior run as input (see the notebook for more information).

Credible intervals

We can compute the credible intervals—the Bayesian counterpart of confidence intervals—as percentiles of the trace. The resulting boundaries reflect confidence about the range of the parameter value for a given probability threshold, as opposed to the number of times the parameter will be within this range for a large number of trials. The notebook illustrates computation and visualization.

Approximate inference – variational Bayes

The interface for variational inference is very similar to the MCMC implementation. We just use the `fit()` function instead of the `sample()` function, with the option to include an early stopping `CheckParametersConvergence` callback if the distribution-fitting process converged up to a given tolerance:

```
with logistic_model:
    callback = CheckParametersConvergence(diff='absolute')
    approx = pm.fit(n=100000,
                    callbacks=[callback])
```

We can draw samples from the approximated distribution to obtain a trace object like we did previously for the MCMC sampler:

```
trace_advi = approx.sample(10000)
```

Inspection of the trace summary shows that the results are slightly less accurate.

Model diagnostics

Bayesian model diagnostics includes validating that the sampling process has converged and consistently samples from high probability areas of the posterior, and confirming that the model represents the data well.

Convergence

We can visualize the samples over time and their distributions to check the quality of the results. The following charts show the posterior distributions after an initial 100 and an additional 100,000 samples, respectively, and illustrate how convergence implies that multiple chains identify the same distribution. The `pm.trace_plot()` function shows the evolution of the samples as well (see the notebook for more information):

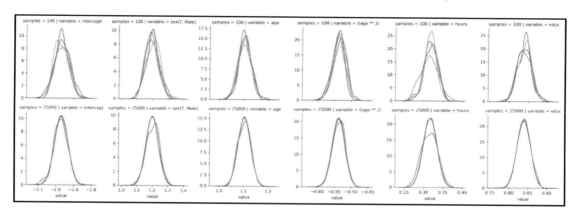

Posterior distributions

PyMC3 produces various summary statistics for a sampler. These are available as individual functions in the stats module, or by providing a trace to the `pm.summary()` function:

	statsmodels	mean	sd	hpd_2.5	hpd_97.5	n_eff	Rhat
Intercept	-1.97	-1.97	0.04	-2.04	-1.89	69,492.17	1.00

sex[T. Male]	1.20	1.20	0.04	1.12	1.28	72,374.10	1.00
age	1.10	1.10	0.03	1.05	1.15	68,446.73	1.00
I(age ** 2)	-0.54	-0.54	0.02	-0.58	-0.50	66,539.66	1.00
hours	0.32	0.32	0.02	0.28	0.35	93,008.86	1.00
educ	0.84	0.84	0.02	0.80	0.87	98,125.26	1.00

The preceding tables includes the (separately computed) statsmodels `logit` coefficients in the first column to show that, in this simple case, both models agree because the sample mean is very close to the coefficients.

The remaining columns contain the **highest posterior density (HPD)** estimate for the minimum width credible interval, the Bayesian version of a confidence interval, which here is computed at the 95% level. The `n_eff` statistic summarizes the number of effective (not rejected) samples resulting from the ~100K draws.

R-hat, also known as the Gelman-Rubin statistic, checks convergence by comparing the variance between chains to the variance within each chain. If the sampler converged, these variances should be identical, that is, the chains should look similar. Hence, the statistic should be near 1. The `pm.forest_plot()` function also summarizes this statistic for the multiple chains (see the notebook for more information).

For high-dimensional models with many variables, it becomes cumbersome to inspect numerous traces. When using NUTS, the energy plot helps to assess problems of convergence. It summarizes how efficiently the random process explores the posterior. The plot shows the energy and the energy transition matrix, which should be well-matched, as in the following example (see references for conceptual detail):

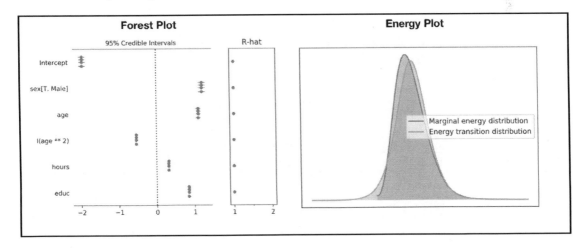

Posterior Predictive Checks

Posterior Predictive Checks (PPCs) are very useful for examining how well a model fits the data. They do so by generating data from the model using parameters from draws from the posterior. We use the `pm.sample_ppc` function for this purpose and obtain *n* samples for each observation (the GLM module automatically names the outcome `'y'`):

```
ppc = pm.sample_ppc(trace_NUTS, samples=500, model=logistic_model)
ppc['y'].shape
(500, 29170)
```

We can evaluate the in-sample fit using the auc score, for example, to compare different models:

```
roc_auc_score(y_score=np.mean(ppc['y'], axis=0),
              y_true=data.income)
0.8294958565103577
```

Prediction

Predictions use Theano's shared variables to replace the training data with test data before running posterior predictive checks. To facilitate visualization, we create a variable with a single predictor hours, create the train and test datasets, and convert the former to a shared variable. Note that we need to use numPy arrays and provide a list of column labels (see the notebook for details):

```
X_shared = theano.shared(X_train.values
with pm.Model() as logistic_model_pred:
    pm.glm.GLM(x=X_shared, labels=labels,
               y=y_train, family=pm.glm.families.Binomial())
```

We then run the sampler as before, and apply the `pm.sample_ppc` function to the resulting trace after replacing the train with test data:

```
X_shared.set_value(X_test)
ppc = pm.sample_ppc(pred_trace, model=logistic_model_pred,
                    samples=100)
```

The AUC score for this model with a single feature is 0.65. The following plot shows the actual outcomes and uncertainty surrounding the predictions for each sampled predictor value:

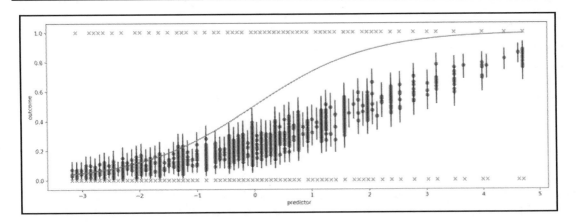

We will now illustrate how to apply Bayesian analysis to trading-related use cases.

Practical applications

There are numerous applications to Bayesian machine learning methods to investment. The transparency that probabilistic estimates create are naturally useful for risk management and performance evaluation. We will illustrate the computation and comparison of a metric like the Sharpe ratio. The GitHub repository also includes two notebooks referenced below that present the use of Bayesian ML for modeling linear time series and stochastic volatility.

These notebooks have been adapted from tutorials created at Quantopian where Thomas Wiecki leads data science and has significantly contributed to popularizing the use of Bayesian methods. The references also include a tutorial on using Bayesian ML to estimate pairs trading hedging ratios.

Bayesian Sharpe ratio and performance comparison

In this section, we will illustrate how to define the Sharpe ratio as a probability model and compare the resulting posterior distributions for different return series. The Bayesian estimation for two groups provides complete distributions of credible values for the effect size, group means and their difference, standard deviations and their difference, and the normality of the data.

Key use cases include the analysis of differences between alternative strategies, or between a strategy's in-sample return in relation to its out-of-sample return (see the `bayesian_sharpe_ratio` notebook for details). The Bayesian Sharpe ratio is also part of pyfolio's Bayesian tearsheet.

Model definition

To model the Sharpe ratio as a probabilistic model, we need the priors about the distribution of returns and the parameters that govern this distribution. The student t distribution exhibits fat tails that are relative to the normal distribution for low **degrees of freedom (df)**, and is a reasonable choice to capture this aspect of returns.

Hence, we need to model the three parameters of this distribution, namely the mean and standard deviation of returns, and the degrees of freedom. We'll assume normal and uniform distributions for the mean and the standard deviation, respectively, and an exponential distribution for the df with a sufficiently low expected value to ensure fat tails. Returns are based on these probabilistic inputs, and the annualized Sharpe ratio results from the standard computation, ignoring a risk-free rate (using daily returns):

```
mean_prior = data.stock.mean()
std_prior = data.stock.std()
std_low = std_prior / 1000
std_high = std_prior * 1000

with pm.Model() as sharpe_model:
    mean = pm.Normal('mean', mu=mean_prior, sd=std_prior)
    std = pm.Uniform('std', lower=std_low, upper=std_high)
    nu = pm.Exponential('nu_minus_two', 1 / 29, testval=4) + 2.
    returns = pm.StudentT('returns', nu=nu, mu=mean, sd=std,
observed=data.stock)

    sharpe = returns.distribution.mean / returns.distribution.variance **
.5 * np.sqrt(252)
    pm.Deterministic('sharpe', sharpe)
```

The notebook contains details on sampling and evaluating the Sharpe ratio for a single stock.

Performance comparison

To compare the performance of two return series, we model each group's Sharpe ratio separately and compute the effect size as the difference between the volatility-adjusted returns. Visualizing the traces reveals granular performance insights into the distributions of each metric, as illustrated by the following chart:

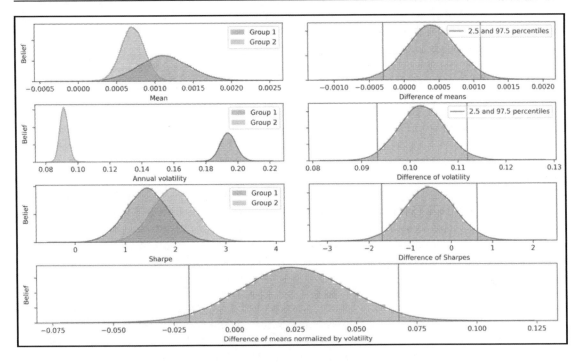

Bayesian Linear Regression for Pairs Trading

In the last chapter, we introduced pairs trading as a popular algorithmic trading strategy that relies on the cointegration of two or more assets. Given such assets, we need to estimate the hedging ratio to decide on the relative magnitude of long and short positions. A basic approach uses linear regression.

The `linear_regression` notebook illustrates how Bayesian linear regression tracks changes in the relationship between two assets over time.

Bayesian time series models

PyMC3 includes AR(p) models that allow us to gain similar insights into the parameter uncertainty, as for the previous models. The `bayesian_time_series` notebook illustrates a time series model for one or more lags.

Stochastic volatility models

As discussed in the last chapter, asset prices have time-varying volatility. In some periods, returns are highly variable, while in others, they are very stable. Stochastic volatility models model this with a latent volatility variable, which is modeled as a stochastic process. The No-U-Turn sampler was introduced using such a model, and the `stochastic_volatility` notebook illustrates this use case.

Summary

In this chapter, we explored Bayesian approaches to machine learning. We saw that they have several advantages, including the ability to encode prior knowledge or opinions, deeper insights into the uncertainty surrounding model estimates and predictions, and the suitability for online learning, where each training sample incrementally impacts the model's prediction.

We learned to apply the Bayesian workflow from model specification to estimation, diagnostics, and prediction using PyMC3 and explored several relevant applications. We will encounter more Bayesian models in Chapter 14, *Topic Modeling* and in Chapter 19 on unsupervised deep learning where we will introduce variational autoencoders.

The next two chapter introduce tree-based, non-linear ensemble models, namely random forests and gradient boosting machines.

10

Decision Trees and Random Forests

In this chapter, we will learn about two new classes of machine learning models: decision trees and random forests. We will see how decision trees learn rules from data that encodes non-linear relationships between the input and the output variables. We will illustrate how to train a decision tree and use it for prediction for regression and classification problems, visualize and interpret the rules learned by the model, and tune the model's hyperparameters to optimize the bias-variance tradeoff and prevent overfitting. Decision trees are not only important standalone models but are also frequently used as components in other models.

In the second part of this chapter, we will introduce ensemble models that combine multiple individual models to produce a single aggregate prediction with lower prediction-error variance. We will illustrate bootstrap aggregation, often called bagging, as one of several methods to randomize the construction of individual models and reduce the correlation of the prediction errors made by an ensemble's components.

Boosting is a very powerful alternative method that merits its own chapter to address a range of recent developments. We will illustrate how bagging effectively reduces the variance, and learn how to configure, train, and tune random forests. We will see how random forests as an ensemble of a large number of decision trees, can dramatically reduce prediction errors, at the expense of some loss in interpretation.

In short, in this chapter, we will cover the following:

- How to use decision trees for regression and classification
- How to gain insights from decision trees and visualize the decision rules learned from the data
- Why ensemble models tend to deliver superior results
- How bootstrap aggregation addresses the overfitting challenges of decision trees
- How to train, tune, and interpret random forests

Decision trees

Decision trees are a machine learning algorithm that predicts the value of a target variable based on decision rules learned from training data. The algorithm can be applied to both regression and classification problems by changing the objective function that governs how the tree learns the decision rules.

We will discuss how decision trees use rules to make predictions, how to train them to predict (continuous) returns as well as (categorical) directions of price movements, and how to interpret, visualize, and tune them effectively.

How trees learn and apply decision rules

The linear models we studied in Chapters 7, *Linear Models* and Chapter 8, *Time Series Models*, learn a set of parameters to predict the outcome using a linear combination of the input variables, possibly after transformation by an S-shaped link function in the case of logistic regression.

Decision trees take a different approach: they learn and sequentially apply a set of rules that split data points into subsets and then make one prediction for each subset. The predictions are based on the outcome values for the subset of training samples that result from the application of a given sequence of rules. As we will see in more detail further, classification trees predict a probability estimated from the relative class frequencies or the value of the majority class directly, whereas regression models compute prediction from the mean of the outcome values for the available data points.

Each of these rules relies on one particular feature and uses a threshold to split the samples into two groups with values either below or above the threshold with respect to this feature. A binary tree naturally represents the logic of the model: the root is the starting point for all samples, nodes represent the application of the decision rules, and the data moves along the edges as it is split into smaller subsets until arriving at a leaf node where the model makes a prediction.

For a linear model, the parameter values allow for an interpretation of the impact of the input variables on the output and the model's prediction. In contrast, for a decision tree, the path from the root to the leaves creates transparency about how the features and their values lead to specific decisions by the model.

The following figure highlights how the model learns a rule. During training, the algorithm scans the features and, for each feature, seeks to find a cutoff that splits the data to minimize the loss that results from predictions made using the subsets that would result from the split, weighted by the number of samples in each subset:

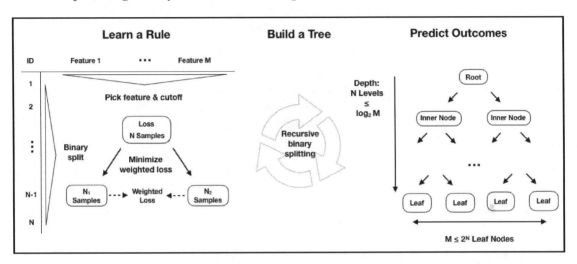

To build an entire tree during training, the learning algorithm repeats this process of dividing the feature space, that is, the set of possible values for the p input variables, X_1, X_2, ..., X_p, into mutually-exclusive and collectively-exhaustive regions, each represented by a leaf node. Unfortunately, the algorithm will not be able to evaluate every possible partition of the feature space given the explosive number of possible combinations of sequences of features and thresholds. Tree-based learning takes a top-down, greedy approach, known as recursive binary splitting to overcome this computational limitation.

This process is recursive because it uses subsets of data resulting from prior splits. It is top-down because it begins at the root node of the tree, where all observations still belong to a single region and then successively creates two new branches of the tree by adding one more split to the predictor space. It is greedy because the algorithm picks the best rule in the form of a feature-threshold combination based on the immediate impact on the objective function rather than looking ahead and evaluating the loss several steps ahead. We will return to the splitting logic in the more specific context of regression and classification trees because this represents the major difference.

The number of training samples continues to shrink as recursive splits add new nodes to the tree. If rules split the samples evenly, resulting in a perfectly balanced tree with an equal number of children for every node, then there would be 2^n nodes at level n, each containing a corresponding fraction of the total number of observations. In practice, this is unlikely, so the number of samples along some branches may diminish rapidly, and trees tend to grow to different levels of depth along different paths.

To arrive at a prediction for a new observation, the model uses the rules that it inferred during training to decide which leaf node the data point should be assigned to, and then uses the mean (for regression) or the mode (for classification) of the training observations in the corresponding region of the feature space. A smaller number of training samples in a given region of the feature space, that is, in a given leaf node, reduces the confidence in the prediction and may reflect overfitting.

Recursive splitting would continue until each leaf node contains only a single sample and the training error has been reduced to zero. We will introduce several criteria to limit splits and prevent this natural tendency of decision trees to produce extreme overfitting.

How to use decision trees in practice

In this section, we illustrate how to use tree-based models to gain insight and make predictions. To demonstrate regression trees we predict returns, and for the classification case, we return to the example of positive and negative asset price moves. The code examples for this section are in the notebook `decision_trees` unless stated otherwise.

How to prepare the data

We use a simplified version of the data set constructed in Chapter 4, *Alpha Factor Research*. It consists of daily stock prices provided by Quandl for the 2010-2017 period and various engineered features. The details can be found in the `data_prep` notebook in the GitHub repo for this chapter. The decision tree models in this chapter are not equipped to handle missing or categorical variables, so we will apply dummy encoding to the latter after dropping any of the former.

How to code a custom cross-validation class

We also construct a custom cross-validation class tailored to the format of the data just created, which has pandas MultiIndex with two levels, one for the ticker and one for the data:

```
class OneStepTimeSeriesSplit:
    """Generates tuples of train_idx, test_idx pairs
    Assumes the index contains a level labeled 'date'"""

    def __init__(self, n_splits=3, test_period_length=1, shuffle=False):
        self.n_splits = n_splits
        self.test_period_length = test_period_length
        self.shuffle = shuffle
        self.test_end = n_splits * test_period_length

    @staticmethod
    def chunks(l, chunk_size):
        for i in range(0, len(l), chunk_size):
            yield l[i:i + chunk_size]

    def split(self, X, y=None, groups=None):
        unique_dates = (X.index
                        .get_level_values('date')
                        .unique()
                        .sort_values(ascending=False)[:self.test_end])

        dates = X.reset_index()[['date']]
        for test_date in self.chunks(unique_dates,
    self.test_period_length):
            train_idx = dates[dates.date < min(test_date)].index
            test_idx = dates[dates.date.isin(test_date)].index
            if self.shuffle:
                np.random.shuffle(list(train_idx))
            yield train_idx, test_idx
```

`OneStepTimeSeriesSplit` ensures a split of training and validation sets that avoids a lookahead bias by training models using only data up to period *T-1* for each stock when validating using data for month *T*. We will only use one-step-ahead forecasts.

How to build a regression tree

Regression trees make predictions based on the mean outcome value for the training samples assigned to a given node and typically rely on the mean-squared error to select optimal rules during recursive binary splitting.

Given a training set, the algorithm iterates over the predictors, X_1, X_2, ..., X_p, and possible cutpoints, s_1, s_1, ..., s_N, to find an optimal combination. The optimal rule splits the feature space into two regions, $\{X \mid X_i < s_j\}$ and $\{X \mid X_i > s_j\}$, with values for the X_i feature either below or above the s_j threshold so that predictions based on the training subsets maximize the reduction of the squared residuals relative to the current node.

Let's start with a simplified example to facilitate visualization and only use two months of lagged returns to predict the following month, in the vein of an AR(2) model from the last chapter:

$$r_t = f(r_{t-1}, r_{t-2})$$

Using `sklearn`, configuring and training a regression tree is very straightforward:

```
from sklearn.tree import DecisionTreeRegressor

# configure regression tree
regression_tree = DecisionTreeRegressor(criterion='mse',  # default
                                        max_depth=4,       # up to 4 splits
                                        random_state=42)
# Create training data
y = data.returns
X = data.drop('returns', axis=1)
X2 = X.loc[:, ['t-1', 't-2']]

# fit model
regression_tree.fit(X=X2, y=y)

# fit OLS model
ols_model = sm.OLS(endog=y, exog=sm.add_constant(X2)).fit()
```

The OLS summary and a visualization of the first two levels of the decision tree reveal the striking differences between the model. The OLS model provides three parameters for the intercepts and the two features in line with the linear assumption this model makes about the f function.

In contrast, the regression tree chart displays, for each node of the first two levels, the feature and threshold used to split the data (note that features can be used repeatedly), as well as the current value of the **mean-squared error** (**MSE**), the number of samples, and predicted value based on these training samples:

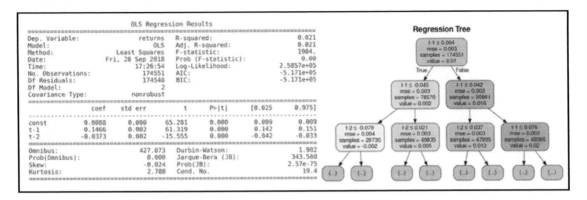

The regression tree chart

The tree chart also highlights the uneven distribution of samples across the nodes as the numbers vary between 28,000 and 49,000 samples after only two splits.

To further illustrate the different assumptions about the functional form of the relationships between the input variables and the output, we can visualize current return predictions as a function of the feature space, that is, as a function of the range of values for the lagged returns. The following figure shows the current period return as a function of returns one and two periods ago for linear regression and the regression tree:

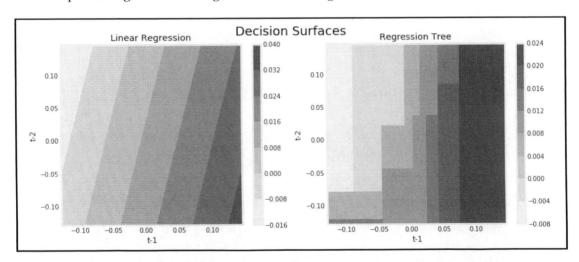

The linear-regression model result on the right side underlines the linearity of the relationship between lagged and current returns, whereas the regression tree chart on the left illustrates the non-linear relationship encoded in the recursive partitioning of the feature space.

How to build a classification tree

A classification tree works just like the regression version, except that categorical nature of the outcome requires a different approach to making predictions and measuring the loss. While a regression tree predicts the response for an observation assigned to a leaf node using the mean outcome of the associated training samples, a classification tree instead uses the mode, that is, the most common class among the training samples in the relevant region. A classification tree can also generate probabilistic predictions based on relative class frequencies.

How to optimize for node purity

When growing a classification tree, we also use recursive binary splitting but, instead of evaluating the quality of a decision rule using the reduction of the mean-squared error, we can use the classification error rate, which is simply the fraction of the training samples in a given (leave) node that do not belong to the most common class.

However, the alternative measures, Gini Index or Cross-Entropy, are preferred because they are more sensitive to node purity than the classification error rate. Node purity refers to the extent of the preponderance of a single class in a node. A node that only contains samples with outcomes belonging to a single class is pure and imply successful classification for this particular region of the feature space. They are calculated as follows for a classification outcome taking on K values, $0,1,...,K-1$, for a given node, m, that represents a region, R_m, of the feature space and where p_{mk} is the proportion of outcomes of the k class in the m node:

$$\text{Gini Impurity} = \sum_k p_{mk}(1 - p_{mk})$$

$$\text{Cross-Entropy} = -\sum_k p_{mk} log(p_{mk})$$

Both the Gini Impurity and the Cross-Entropy measure take on smaller values when the class proportions approach zero or one, that is, when the child nodes become pure as a result of the split and are highest when the class proportions are even or 0.5 in the binary case. The chart at the end of this section visualizes the values assumed by these two measures and the misclassification error rates across the [0, 1] interval of proportions.

How to train a classification tree

We will now train, visualize, and evaluate a classification tree with up to 5 consecutive splits using 80% of the samples for training to predict the remaining 20%. We are taking a shortcut here to simplify the illustration and use the built-in `train_test_split`, which does not protect against lookahead bias, as our custom iterator. The tree configuration implies up to $2^5=32$ leaf nodes that, on average in the balanced case, would contain over 4,300 of the training samples. Take a look at the following code:

```
# randomize train-test split
X_train, X_test, y_train, y_test = train_test_split(X, y_binary,
test_size=0.2, random_state=42)

# configure & train tree learner
classifier = DecisionTreeClassifier(criterion='gini',
                                    max_depth=5,
                                    random_state=42)
classifier.fit(X=X_train, y=y_train)

# Output:
DecisionTreeClassifier(class_weight=None, criterion='gini', max_depth=5,
            max_features=None, max_leaf_nodes=None,
            min_impurity_decrease=0.0, min_impurity_split=None,
            min_samples_leaf=1, min_samples_split=2,
            min_weight_fraction_leaf=0.0, presort=False, random_state=42,
            splitter='best')
```

The output after training the model displays all the `DecisionTreeClassifier` parameters that we will address in more detail in the next section when we discuss parameter-tuning.

How to visualize a decision tree

You can visualize the tree using the `graphviz` library (see GitHub for installation instructions) because `sklearn` can output a description of the tree using the `.dot` language used by that library. You can configure the output to include feature and class labels and limit the number of levels to keep the chart readable, as follows:

```
dot_data = export_graphviz(classifier,
                           out_file=None, # opt. save to file and convert
to png
                           feature_names=X.columns,
                           class_names=['Down', 'Up'],
                           max_depth=3,
                           filled=True,
```

```
                              rounded=True,
                              special_characters=True)
```

```
graphviz.Source(dot_data)
```

The result shows that the model uses a variety of different features and indicates the split rules for both continuous and categorical (dummy) variables. The chart displays, under the label **value**, the number of samples from each class and, under the label **class**, the most common class (there were more up months during the sample period):

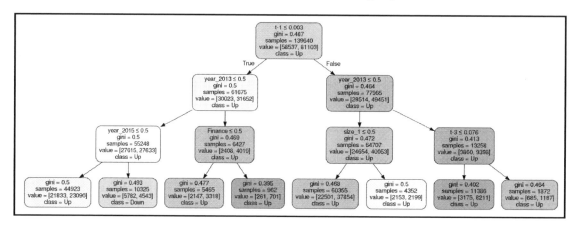

How to evaluate decision tree predictions

To evaluate the predictive accuracy of our first classification tree, we will use our test set to generate predicted class probabilities, as follows:

```
y_score = classifier.predict_proba(X=X_test)[:, 1] # only keep
probabilities for pos. class
```

The .predict_proba() method produces one probability for each class. In the binary class, these probabilities are complementary and sum to 1, so we only need the value for the positive class. To evaluate the generalization error, we will use the area under the curve based on the receiver-operating characteristic that we introduced in Chapter 6, *The Machine Learning Process*. The result indicates a significant improvement above and beyond the baseline value of 0.5 for a random prediction:

```
roc_auc_score(y_score=y_score, y_true=y_test)
0.5941
```

Feature importance

Decision trees can not only be visualized to inspect the decision path for a given feature, but also provide a summary measure of the contribution of each feature to the model fit to the training data.

The feature importance captures how much the splits produced by the feature helped to optimize the model's metric used to evaluate the split quality, which in our case is the Gini Impurity index. A feature's importance is computed as the (normalized) total reduction of this metric and takes into account the number of samples affected by a split. Hence, features used earlier in the tree where the nodes tend to contain more samples typically are considered of higher importance.

The following chart shows the feature importance for the top 15 features:

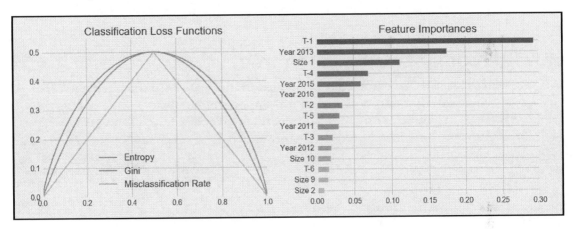

Overfitting and regularization

Decision trees have a strong tendency to overfit, especially when a dataset has a large number of features relative to the number of samples. As discussed in previous chapters, overfitting increases the prediction error because the model does not only learn the signal contained in the training data, but also the noise.

There are several ways to address the risk of overfitting:

- **Dimensionality reduction** (Chapter 12, *Unsupervised Learning*) improves the feature-to-sample ratio by representing the existing features with fewer, more informative, and less noisy features.

- **Ensemble models**, such as random forests, combine multiple trees while randomizing the tree construction, as we will see in the second part of this chapter.
- Decision trees provide several **regularization** hyperparameters to limit the growth of a tree and the associated complexity. While every split increases the number of nodes, it also reduces the number of samples available per node to support a prediction. For each additional level, twice the number of samples is needed to populate the new nodes with the same sample density.
- **Tree-pruning** is an additional tool to reduce the complexity of a tree by eliminating nodes or entire parts of a tree that add little value but increase the model's variance. Cost-complexity-pruning, for instance, starts with a large tree and recursively reduces its size by replacing nodes with leaves, essentially running the tree construction in reverse. The various steps produce a sequence of trees that can then be compared using cross-validation to select the ideal size.

How to regularize a decision tree

The following table lists key parameters available for this purpose in the sklearn decision tree implementation. After introducing the most important parameters, we will illustrate how to use cross-validation to optimize the hyperparameter settings with respect to the bias-variance tradeoff and lower prediction errors:

Parameter	Default	Options	Description
max_depth	None	int	Maximum number of levels: split nodes until reaching max_depth or all leaves are pure or contain fewer than min_samples_split samples.
max_features	None	None: all features; int float: fraction auto, sqrt: sqrt(n_features) log2: log2(n_features)	Number of features to consider for a split.
max_leaf_nodes	None	None: unlimited number of leaf nodes int	Split nodes until creating this many leaves.
min_impurity_decrease	0	float	Split node if impurity decreases by at least this value.
min_samples_leaf	1	int; float (as a percentage of N)	Minimum number of samples to be at a leaf node. A split will only be considered if there are at least min_samples_leaf training samples in each of the left and right branches. May smoothen the model, especially for regression.
min_samples_split	2	int; float (percent of N)	The minimum number of samples required to split an internal node:
min_weight_fraction_leaf	0		The minimum weighted fraction of the sum total of all sample weights needed at a leaf node. Samples have equal weight unless sample_weight provided in fit method.

The max_depth parameter imposes a hard limit on the number of consecutive splits and represents the most straightforward way to cap the growth of a tree.

The `min_samples_split` and `min_samples_leaf` parameters are alternative, data-driven ways to limit the growth of a tree. Rather than imposing a hard limit on the number of consecutive splits, these parameters control the minimum number of samples required to further split the data. The latter guarantees a certain number of samples per leaf, while the former can create very small leaves if a split results in a very uneven distribution. Small parameter values facilitate overfitting, while a high number may prevent the tree from learning the signal in the data. The default values are often quite low, and you should use cross-validation to explore a range of potential values. You can also use a float to indicate a percentage as opposed to an absolute number.

The sklearn documentation contains additional details about how to use the various parameters for different use cases; see GitHub references.

Decision tree pruning

Recursive binary-splitting will likely produce good predictions on the training set but tends to overfit the data and produce poor generalization performance because it leads to overly complex trees, reflected in a large number of leaf nodes or partitioning of the feature space. Fewer splits and leaf nodes imply an overall smaller tree and often lead to better predictive performance as well as interpretability.

One approach to limit the number of leaf nodes is to avoid further splits unless they yield significant improvements of the objective metric. The downside of this strategy, however, is that sometimes splits that result in small improvements enable more valuable splits later on as the composition of the samples keeps changing.

Tree-pruning, in contrast, starts by growing a very large tree before removing or pruning nodes to reduce the large tree to a less complex and overfit subtree. Cost-complexity-pruning generates a sequence of subtrees by adding a penalty for adding leaf nodes to the tree model and a regularization parameter, similar to the lasso and ridge linear-regression models, that modulates the impact of the penalty. Applied to the large tree, an increasing penalty will automatically produce a sequence of subtrees. Cross-validation of the regularization parameter can be used to identify the optimal, pruned subtree.

This method is not yet available in sklearn; see references on GitHub for further details and ways to manually implement pruning.

How to tune the hyperparameters

Decision trees offer an array of hyperparameters to control and tune the training result. Cross-validation is the most important tool to obtain an unbiased estimate of the generalization error, which in turn permits an informed choice among the various configuration options. sklearn offers several tools to facilitate the process of cross-validating numerous parameter settings, namely the GridSearchCV convenience class that we will illustrate in the next section. Learning curves also allow for diagnostics that evaluate potential benefits of collecting additional data to reduce the generalization error.

GridsearchCV for decision trees

sklearn provides a method to define ranges of values for multiple hyperparameters. It automates the process of cross-validating the various combinations of these parameter values to identify the optimal configuration. Let's walk through the process of automatically tuning your model.

The first step is to instantiate a model object and define a dictionary where the keywords name the hyperparameters, and the values list the parameter settings to be tested:

```
clf = DecisionTreeClassifier(random_state=42)
param_grid = {'max_depth': range(10, 20),
              'min_samples_leaf': [250, 500, 750],
              'max_features': ['sqrt', 'auto']
              }
```

Then, instantiate the GridSearchCV object, providing the estimator object and parameter grid, as well as a scoring method and cross-validation choice to the initialization method. We'll use an object of our custom OneStepTimeSeriesSplit class, initialized to use ten folds for the cv parameter, and set the scoring to the roc_auc metric. We can parallelize the search using the n_jobs parameter and automatically obtain a trained model that uses the optimal hyperparameters by setting refit=True.

With all settings in place, we can fit GridSearchCV just like any other model:

```
gridsearch_clf = GridSearchCV(estimator=clf,
                              param_grid=param_grid,
                              scoring='roc_auc',
                              n_jobs=-1,
                              cv=cv,  # custom OneStepTimeSeriesSplit
                              refit=True,
                              return_train_score=True)

gridsearch_clf.fit(X=X, y=y_binary)
```

The training process produces some new attributes for our `GridSearchCV` object, most importantly the information about the optimal settings and the best cross-validation score (now using the proper setup that avoids lookahead bias).

Setting `max_depth` to 13, `min_samples_leaf` to 500, and randomly selecting only a number corresponding to the square root of the total number of features when deciding on a split, produces the best results, with an AUC of 0.5855:

```
gridsearch_clf.best_params_
{'max_depth': 13, 'max_features': 'sqrt', 'min_samples_leaf': 500}

gridsearch_clf.best_score_
0.5855
```

The automation is quite convenient, but we also would like to inspect how the performance evolves for different parameter values. Upon completion of this process, the `GridSearchCV` object makes available detailed cross-validation results to gain more insights.

How to inspect the tree structure

The notebook also illustrates how to run cross-validation more manually to obtain custom tree attributes, such as the total number of nodes or leaf nodes associated with certain hyperparameter settings. The following function accesses the internal `.tree_` attribute to retrieve information about the total node count, and how many of these nodes are leaf nodes:

```
def get_leaves_count(tree):
    t = tree.tree_
    n = t.node_count
    leaves = len([i for i in range(t.node_count) if t.children_left[i]==
-1])
    return leaves
```

We can combine this information with the train and test scores to gain detailed knowledge about the model behavior throughout the cross-validation process, as follows:

```
train_scores, val_scores, leaves = {}, {}, {}
for max_depth in range(1, 26):
    print(max_depth, end=' ', flush=True)
    clf = DecisionTreeClassifier(criterion='gini',
                                 max_depth=max_depth,
                                 min_samples_leaf=500,
                                 max_features='auto',
                                 random_state=42)
```

```
    train_scores[max_depth], val_scores[max_depth], leaves[max_depth] = [],
[], []
    for train_idx, test_idx in cv.split(X):
        X_train, y_train,  = X.iloc[train_idx], y_binary.iloc[train_idx]
        X_test, y_test = X.iloc[test_idx], y_binary.iloc[test_idx]
        clf.fit(X=X_train, y=y_train)

        train_pred = clf.predict_proba(X=X_train)[:, 1]
        train_score = roc_auc_score(y_score=train_pred, y_true=y_train)
        train_scores[max_depth].append(train_score)

        test_pred = clf.predict_proba(X=X_test)[:, 1]
        val_score = roc_auc_score(y_score=test_pred, y_true=y_test)
        val_scores[max_depth].append(val_score)
        leaves[max_depth].append(get_leaves_count(clf))
```

The result is shown on the left panel of the following chart. It highlights the in- and out-of-sample performance across the range of `max_depth` settings, alongside a confidence interval around the error metrics. It also shows the number of leaf nodes on the right-hand log scale and indicates the best-performing setting at 13 consecutive splits, as indicated by the vertical black line.

Learning curves

A learning curve is a useful tool that displays how the validation and training score evolve as the number of training samples evolves.

The purpose of the learning curve is to find out whether and how much the model would benefit from using more data during training. It is also useful to diagnose whether the model's generalization error is more likely driven by bias or variance.

If, for example, both the validation score and the training score converge to a similarly low value despite an increasing training set size, the error is more likely due to bias, and additional training data is unlikely to help.

Take a look at the following visualization:

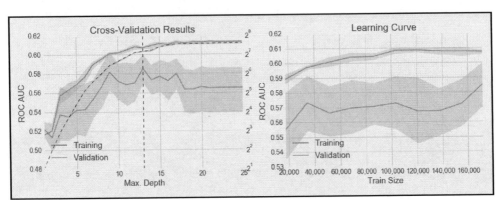

Strengths and weaknesses of decision trees

Regression and classification trees take a very different approach to prediction when compared to the linear models we have explored so far. How do you decide which model is more suitable to the problem at hand? Consider the following:

- If the relationship between the outcome and the features is approximately linear (or can be transformed accordingly), then linear regression will likely outperform a more complex method, such as a decision tree that does not exploit this linear structure.
- If the relationship appears highly non-linear and more complex, decision trees will likely outperform the classical models.

Several advantages have made decision trees very popular:

- They are fairly straightforward to understand and to interpret, not least because they can be easily visualized and are thus more accessible to a non-technical audience. Decision trees are also referred to as white-box models given the high degree of transparency about how they arrive at a prediction. Black-box models, such as ensembles and neural networks may deliver better prediction accuracy but the decision logic is often much more challenging to understand and interpret.
- Decision trees require less data preparation than models that make stronger assumptions about the data or are more sensitive to outliers and require data standardization (such as regularized regression).

- Some decision tree implementations handle categorical input, do not require the creation of dummy variables (improving memory efficiency), and can work with missing values, as we will see in `Chapter 11`, *Gradient Boosting Machines*, but this is not the case for sklearn.
- Prediction is fast because it is logarithmic in the number of leaf nodes (unless the tree becomes extremely unbalanced).
- It is possible to validate the model using statistical tests and account for its reliability (see GitHub references).

Decision trees also have several key disadvantages:

- Decision trees have a built-in tendency to overfit to the training set and produce a high generalization error. Key steps to address this weakness are pruning (not yet supported by sklearn) as well as regularization using the various early-stopping criteria outlined in the previous section.
- Closely related is the high variance of decision trees that results from their ability to closely adapt to a training set so that minor variations in the data can produce wide swings in the structure of the decision trees and, consequently, the predictions the model generates. The key mechanism to address the high variance of decision trees is the use of an ensemble of randomized decision trees that have low bias and produce uncorrelated prediction errors.
- The greedy approach to decision-tree learning optimizes based on local criteria, that is, to reduce the prediction error at the current node and does not guarantee a globally optimal outcome. Again, ensembles consisting of randomized trees help to mitigate this problem.
- Decision trees are also sensitive to unbalanced class weights and may produce biased trees. One option is to oversample the underrepresented or under-sample the more frequent class. It is typically better, though, to use class weights and directly adjust the objective function.

Random forests

Decision trees are not only useful for their transparency and interpretability but are also fundamental building blocks for much more powerful ensemble models that combine many individual trees with strategies to randomly vary their design to address the overfitting and high variance problems discussed in the preceding section.

Ensemble models

Ensemble learning involves combining several machine learning models into a single new model that aims to make better predictions than any individual model. More specifically, an ensemble integrates the predictions of several base estimators trained using one or more given learning algorithms to reduce the generalization error that these models may produce on their own.

For ensemble learning to achieve this goal, the individual models must be:

- **Accurate:** They outperform a naive baseline (such as the sample mean or class proportions)
- **Independent:** Their predictions are generated differently to produce different errors

Ensemble methods are among the most successful machine learning algorithms, in particular for standard numerical data. Large ensembles are very successful in machine learning competitions and may consist of many distinct individual models that have been combined by hand or using another machine learning algorithm.

There are several disadvantages to combining predictions made by different models. These include reduced interpretability, and higher complexity and cost of training, prediction, and model maintenance. As a result, in practice (outside of competitions), the small gains in accuracy from large-scale ensembling may not be worth the added costs.

There are two groups of ensemble methods that are typically distinguished depending on how they optimize the constituent models and then integrate the results for a single ensemble prediction:

- **Averaging methods** train several base estimators independently and then average their predictions. If the base models are not biased and make different prediction errors that are not highly correlated, then the combined prediction may have lower variance and can be more reliable. This resembles the construction of a portfolio from assets with uncorrelated returns to reduce the volatility without sacrificing the return.

- **Boosting methods**, in contrast, train base estimators sequentially with the specific goal to reduce the bias of the combined estimator. The motivation is to combine several weak models into a powerful ensemble.

We will focus on automatic averaging methods in the remainder of this chapter, and boosting methods in Chapter 11, *Gradient Boosting Machines*.

How bagging lowers model variance

We saw that decision trees are likely to make poor predictions due to high variance, which implies that the tree structure is quite sensitive to the composition of the training sample. We have also seen that a model with low variance, such as linear regression, produces similar estimates despite different training samples as long as there are sufficient samples given the number of features.

For a given a set of independent observations, each with a variance of σ^2, the standard error of the sample mean is given by σ/n. In other words, averaging over a larger set of observations reduces the variance. A natural way to reduce the variance of a model and its generalization error would thus be to collect many training sets from the population, train a different model on each dataset, and average the resulting predictions.

In practice, we do not typically have the luxury of many different training sets. This is where bagging, short for bootstrap aggregation, comes in. Bagging is a general-purpose method to reduce the variance of a machine learning model, which is particularly useful and popular when applied to decision trees.

Bagging refers to the aggregation of bootstrap samples, which are random samples with replacement. Such a random sample has the same number of observations as the original dataset but may contain duplicates due to replacement.

Bagging increases predictive accuracy but decreases model interpretability because it's no longer possible to visualize the tree to understand the importance of each feature. As an ensemble algorithm, bagging methods train a given number of base estimators on these bootstrapped samples and then aggregate their predictions into a final ensemble prediction.

Bagging reduces the variance of the base estimators by randomizing how, for example, each tree is grown and then averages the predictions to reduce their generalization error. It is often a straightforward approach to improve on a given model without the need to change the underlying algorithm. It works best with complex models that have low bias and high variance, such as deep decision trees, because its goal is to limit overfitting. Boosting methods, in contrast, work best with weak models, such as shallow decision trees.

There are several bagging methods that differ by the random sampling process they apply to the training set:

- Pasting draws random samples from the training data without replacement, whereas bagging samples with replacement
- Random subspaces randomly sample from the features (that is, the columns) without replacement
- Random patches train base estimators by randomly sampling both observations and features

Bagged decision trees

To apply bagging to decision trees, we create bootstrap samples from our training data by repeatedly sampling with replacement, then train one decision tree on each of these samples, and create an ensemble prediction by averaging over the predictions of the different trees.

Bagged decision trees are usually grown large, that is, have many levels and leaf nodes and are not pruned so that each tree has low bias but high variance. The effect of averaging their predictions then aims to reduce their variance. Bagging has been shown to substantially improve predictive performance by constructing ensembles that combine hundreds or even thousands of trees trained on bootstrap samples.

To illustrate the effect of bagging on the variance of a regression tree, we can use the `BaggingRegressor` meta-estimator provided by `sklearn`. It trains a user-defined base estimator based on parameters that specify the sampling strategy:

- `max_samples` and `max_features` control the size of the subsets drawn from the rows and the columns, respectively
- `bootstrap` and `bootstrap_features` determine whether each of these samples is drawn with or without replacement

The following example uses an exponential function to generate training samples for a single `DecisionTreeRegressor` and a `BaggingRegressor` ensemble that consists of ten trees, each grown ten levels deep. Both models are trained on the random samples and predict outcomes for the actual function with added noise.

Since we know the true function, we can decompose the mean-squared error into bias, variance, and noise, and compare the relative size of these components for both models according to the following breakdown:

$$E\left[y_0 - \hat{f}\left(x_0\right)\right]^2 = \text{Var}(\hat{f}\left(x_0\right)) + \left[\text{Bias}(\hat{f}\left(x_0\right))\right]^2 + \text{Var}(\epsilon)$$

For 100 repeated random training and test samples of 250 and 500 observations each, we find that the variance of the predictions of the individual decision tree is almost twice as high as that for the small ensemble of 10 bagged trees based on bootstrapped samples:

```
noise = .5  # noise relative to std(y)
noise = y.std() * noise_to_signal

X_test = choice(x, size=test_size, replace=False)

max_depth = 10
n_estimators=10

tree = DecisionTreeRegressor(max_depth=max_depth)
bagged_tree = BaggingRegressor(base_estimator=tree,
n_estimators=n_estimators)
learners = {'Decision Tree': tree, 'Bagging Regressor': bagged_tree}

predictions = {k: pd.DataFrame() for k, v in learners.items()}
for i in range(reps):
    X_train = choice(x, train_size)
    y_train = f(X_train) + normal(scale=noise, size=train_size)
    for label, learner in learners.items():
        learner.fit(X=X_train.reshape(-1, 1), y=y_train)
        preds = pd.DataFrame({i: learner.predict(X_test.reshape(-1, 1))},
index=X_test)
        predictions[label] = pd.concat([predictions[label], preds], axis=1)
```

For each model, the following plot shows the mean prediction and a band of two standard deviations around the mean for both models in the upper panel, and the bias-variance-noise breakdown based on the values for the true function in the bottom panel:

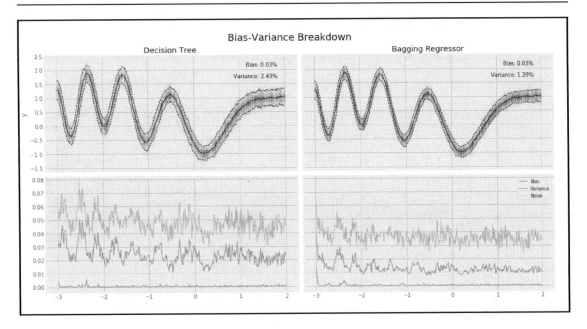

See the notebook `random_forest` for implementation details.

How to build a random forest

The random forest algorithm expands on the randomization introduced by the bootstrap samples generated by bagging to reduce variance further and improve predictive performance.

In addition to training each ensemble member on bootstrapped training data, random forests also randomly sample from the features used in the model (without replacement). Depending on the implementation, the random samples can be drawn for each tree or each split. As a result, the algorithm faces different options when learning new rules, either at the level of a tree or for each split.

The sizes of the feature samples differ for regression and classification trees:

- For **classification**, the sample size is typically the square root of the number of features.
- For **regression**, it can be anywhere from one-third to all features and should be selected based on cross-validation.

The following diagram illustrates how random forests randomize the training of individual trees and then aggregate their predictions into an ensemble prediction:

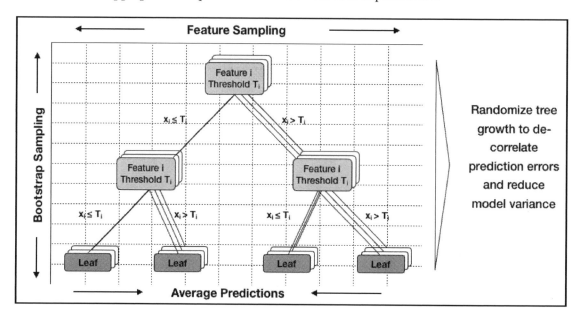

The goal of randomizing the features in addition to the training observations is to further de-correlate the prediction errors of the individual trees. All features are not created equal, and a small number of highly relevant features will be selected much more frequently and earlier in the tree-construction process, making decision trees more alike across the ensemble. However, the less the generalization errors of individual trees correlate, the more the overall variance will be reduced.

How to train and tune a random forest

The key configuration parameters include the various hyperparameters for the individual decision trees introduced in the section *How to tune the hyperparameters*. The following tables lists additional options for the two `RandomForest` classes:

Keyword	Default	Description
bootstrap	True	Bootstrap samples during training.
n_estimators	10	Number of trees in the forest.
oob_score	False	Uses out-of-bag samples to estimate the R^2 on unseen data.

The `bootstrap` parameter activates in the preceding bagging algorithm outline, which in turn enables the computation of the out-of-bag score (`oob_score`) that estimates the generalization accuracy using samples not included in the bootstrap sample used to train a given tree (see next section for detail).

The `n_estimators` parameter defines the number of trees to be grown as part of the forest. Larger forests perform better, but also take more time to build. It is important to monitor the cross-validation error as a function of the number of base learners to identify when the marginal reduction of the prediction error declines and the cost of additional training begins to outweigh the benefits.

The `max_features` parameter controls the size of the randomly selected feature subsets available when learning a new decision rule and split a node. A lower value reduces the correlation of the trees and, thus, the ensemble's variance, but may also increase the bias. Good starting values are `n_features` (the number of training features) for regression problems and `sqrt(n_features)` for classification problems, but will depend on the relationships among features and should be optimized using cross-validation.

Random forests are designed to contain deep fully-grown trees, which can be created using `max_depth=None` and `min_samples_split=2`. However, these values are not necessarily optimal, especially for high-dimensional data with many samples and, consequently, potentially very deep trees that can become very computationally-, and memory-, intensive.

The `RandomForest` class provided by `sklearn` support parallel training and prediction by setting the `n_jobs` parameter to the `k` number of jobs to run on different cores. The –1 value uses all available cores. The overhead of interprocess communication may limit the speedup from being linear so that *k* jobs may take more than *1/k* the time of a single job. Nonetheless, the speedup is often quite significant for large forests or deep individual trees that may take a meaningful amount of time to train when the data is large, and split evaluation becomes costly.

As always, the best parameter configuration should be identified using cross-validation. The following steps illustrate the process:

1. We will use `GridSearchCV` to identify an optimal set of parameters for an ensemble of classification trees:

```
rf_clf = RandomForestClassifier(n_estimators=10,
                                criterion='gini',
                                max_depth=None,
                                min_samples_split=2,
                                min_samples_leaf=1,
```

```
                                    min_weight_fraction_leaf=0.0,
                                    max_features='auto',
                                    max_leaf_nodes=None,
                                    min_impurity_decrease=0.0,
                                    min_impurity_split=None,
                                    bootstrap=True, oob_score=False,
                                    n_jobs=-1, random_state=42)
```

2. We will use 10-fold custom cross-validation and populate the parameter grid with values for the key configuration settings:

```
cv = OneStepTimeSeriesSplit(n_splits=10)
clf = RandomForestClassifier(random_state=42, n_jobs=-1)
param_grid = {'n_estimators': [200, 400],
              'max_depth': [10, 15, 20],
              'min_samples_leaf': [50, 100]}
```

3. Configure `GridSearchCV` using the preceding input:

```
gridsearch_clf = GridSearchCV(estimator=clf,
                              param_grid=param_grid,
                              scoring='roc_auc',
                              n_jobs=-1,
                              cv=cv,
                              refit=True,
                              return_train_score=True,
                              verbose=1)
```

4. Train the multiple ensemble models defined by the parameter grid:

```
gridsearch_clf.fit(X=X, y=y_binary)
```

5. Obtain the best parameters as follows:

```
gridsearch_clf.bestparams
{'max_depth': 15,
 'min_samples_leaf': 100,
 'n_estimators': 400}
```

6. The best score is a small but significant improvement over the single-tree baseline:

```
gridsearch_clf.bestscore_
0.6013
```

Feature importance for random forests

A random forest ensemble may contain hundreds of individual trees, but it is still possible to obtain an overall summary measure of feature importance from bagged models.

For a given feature, the importance score is the total reduction in the objective function's value, which results from splits based on this feature, averaged over all trees. Since the objective function takes into account how many features are affected by a split, this measure is implicitly a weighted average so that features used near the top of a tree will get higher scores due to the larger number of observations contained in the much smaller number of available nodes. By averaging over many trees grown in a randomized fashion, the feature importance estimate loses some variance and becomes more accurate.

The computation differs for classification and regression trees based on the different objectives used to learn the decision rules and is measured in terms of the mean square error for regression trees and the Gini index or entropy for classification trees.

`sklearn` further normalizes the feature-importance measure so that it sums up to 1. Feature importance thus computed is also used for feature selection as an alternative to the mutual information measures we saw in `Chapter 6`, *The Machine Learning Process* (see `SelectFromModel` in the `sklearn.feature_selection` module).

In our example, the importance values for the top-20 features are as shown here:

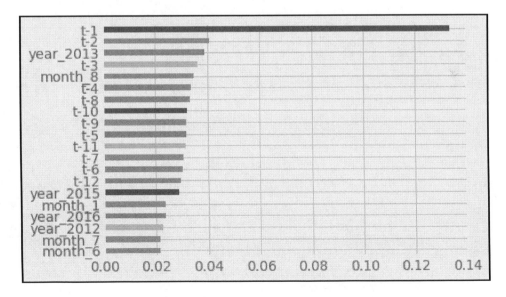

Feature-importance values

Out-of-bag testing

Random forests offer the benefit of built-in cross-validation because individual trees are trained on bootstrapped versions of the training data. As a result, each tree uses on average only two-thirds of the available observations. To see why, consider that a bootstrap sample has the same size, *n*, as the original sample, and each observation has the same probability, *1/n*, to be drawn. Hence, the probability of not entering a bootstrap sample at all is *(1-1/n)ⁿ*, which converges (quickly) to *1/e*, or roughly one-third.

This remaining one-third of the observations that are not included in the training set used to grow a bagged tree is called **out-of-bag** (**OOB**) observations and can serve as a validation set. Just as with cross-validation, we predict the response for an OOB sample for each tree built without this observation, and then average the predicted responses (if regression is the goal) or take a majority vote or predicted probability (if classification is the goal) for a single ensemble prediction for each OOB sample. These predictions produce an unbiased estimate of the generalization error, conveniently computed during training.

The resulting OOB error is a valid estimate of the generalization error for this observation because the prediction is produced using decision rules learned in the absence of this observation. Once the random forest is sufficiently large, the OOB error closely approximates the leave-one-out cross-validation error. The OOB approach to estimate the test error is very efficient for large datasets where cross-validation can be computationally costly.

Pros and cons of random forests

Bagged ensemble models have both advantages and disadvantages. The advantages of random forests include:

- The predictive performance can compete with the best supervised learning algorithms
- They provide a reliable feature importance estimate
- They offer efficient estimates of the test error without incurring the cost of repeated model training associated with cross-validation

On the other hand, random forests also have a few disadvantages:

- An ensemble model is inherently less interpretable than an individual decision tree
- Training a large number of deep trees can have high computational costs (but can be parallelized) and use a lot of memory
- Predictions are slower, which may create challenges for applications that require low latency

Summary

In this chapter, we learned about a new class of models capable of capturing a non-linear relationship, in contrast to the classical linear models we had explored so far. We saw how decision trees learn rules to partition the feature space into regions that yield predictions and thus segment the input data into specific regions.

Decision trees are very useful because they provide unique insights into the relationships between features and target variables, and we saw how to visualize the sequence of decision rules encoded in the tree structure.

Unfortunately, a decision tree is prone to overfitting. We learned that ensemble models and the bootstrap aggregation method manages to overcome some of the shortcomings of decision trees and render them useful, as components of much more powerful composite models.

In the next chapter, we will explore another ensemble model, which has come to be considered one of the most important machine learning algorithms.

11

Gradient Boosting Machines

In the previous chapter, we learned about how random forests improve the predictions made by individual decision trees by combining them into an ensemble that reduces the high variance of individual trees. Random forests use bagging, which is short for bootstrap aggregation, to introduce random elements into the process of growing individual trees.

More specifically, bagging draws samples from the data with replacement so that each tree is trained on a different but equal-sized random subset of the data (with some observations repeating). Random forests also randomly select a subset of the features so that both the rows and the columns of the data that are used to train each tree are random versions of the original data. The ensemble then generates predictions by averaging over the outputs of the individual trees.

Individual trees are usually grown deep to ensure low bias while relying on the randomized training process to produce different, uncorrelated prediction errors that have a lower variance when aggregated than individual tree predictions. In other words, the randomized training aims to decorrelate or diversify the errors made by the individual trees so that the ensemble is much less susceptible to overfitting, has lower variance, and generalizes better to new data.

In this chapter, we will explore boosting, an alternative **machine learning (ML)** algorithm for ensembles of decision trees that often produces even better results. The key difference is that boosting modifies the data that is used to train each tree based on the cumulative errors made by the model before adding the new tree. In contrast to random forests which train many trees independently from each other using different versions of the training set, boosting proceeds sequentially using reweighted versions of the data. State-of-the-art boosting implementations also adopt the randomization strategies of random forests.

In this chapter, we will see how boosting has evolved into one of the most successful ML algorithms over the last three decades. At the time of writing, it has come to dominate machine learning competitions for structured data (as opposed to high-dimensional images or speech, for example, where the relationship between the input and output is more complex, and deep learning excels at). More specifically, in this chapter we will cover the following topics:

- How boosting works, and how it compares to bagging
- How boosting has evolved from adaptive to gradient boosting
- How to use and tune AdaBoost and gradient boosting models with sklearn
- How state-of-the-art GBM implementations dramatically speed up computation
- How to prevent overfitting of gradient boosting models
- How to build, tune, and evaluate gradient boosting models on large datasets using `xgboost`, `lightgbm`, and `catboost`
- How to interpret and gain insights from gradient boosting models

Adaptive boosting

Like bagging, boosting is an ensemble learning algorithm that combines base learners (typically decision trees) into an ensemble. Boosting was initially developed for classification problems, but can also be used for regression, and has been called one of the most potent learning ideas introduced in the last 20 years (as described in *Elements of Statistical Learning* by Trevor Hastie, et al.; see GitHub for links to references). Like bagging, it is a general method or metamethod that can be applied to many statistical learning models.

The motivation for the development of boosting was to find a method to combine the outputs of many *weak* models (a predictor is called weak when it performs just slightly better than random guessing) into a more powerful, that is, boosted joint prediction. In general, boosting learns an additive hypothesis, H_M, of a form similar to linear regression. However, now each of the $m= 1,..., M$ elements of the summation is a weak base learner, called h_t that itself requires training. The following formula summarizes the approach:

$$H_M(x) = \sum_{m=1}^{M} \underbrace{h_t(x)}_{\text{weak learner}}$$

As discussed in the last chapter, bagging trains base learners on different random samples of the training data. Boosting, in contrast, proceeds sequentially by training the base learners on data that is repeatedly modified to reflect the cumulative learning results. The goal is to ensure that the next base learner compensates for the shortcomings of the current ensemble. We will see in this chapter that boosting algorithms differ in how they define shortcomings. The ensemble makes predictions using a weighted average of the predictions of the weak models.

The first boosting algorithm that came with a mathematical proof that it enhances the performance of weak learners was developed by Robert Schapire and Yoav Freund around 1990. In 1997, a practical solution for classification problems emerged in the form of the **adaptive boosting (AdaBoost)** algorithm, which won the Göedel Prize in 2003. About another five years later, this algorithm was extended to arbitrary objective functions when Leo Breiman (who invented random forests) connected the approach to gradient descent, and Jerome Friedman came up with gradient boosting in 1999. Numerous optimized implementations, such as XGBoost, LightGBM, and CatBoost, have emerged in recent years and firmly established gradient boosting as the go-to solution for structured data.

In the following sections, we will briefly introduce AdaBoost and then focus on the gradient boosting model, as well as several state-of-the-art implementations of this very powerful and flexible algorithm.

The AdaBoost algorithm

AdaBoost was the first boosting algorithm to iteratively adapt to the cumulative learning progress when fitting an additional ensemble member. In particular, AdaBoost changed the weights on the training data to reflect the cumulative errors of the current ensemble on the training set before fitting a new weak learner. AdaBoost was the most accurate classification algorithm at the time, and Leo Breiman referred to it as the best off-the-shelf classifier in the world at the 1996 NIPS conference.

The algorithm had a very significant impact on ML because it provided theoretical performance guarantees. These guarantees only require sufficient data and a weak learner that reliably predicts just better than a random guess. As a result of this adaptive method that learns in stages, the development of an accurate ML model no longer required accurate performance over the entire feature space. Instead, the design of a model could focus on finding weak learners that just outperformed a coin flip.

AdaBoost is a significant departure from bagging, which builds ensembles on very deep trees to reduce bias. AdaBoost, in contrast, grows shallow trees as weak learners, often producing superior accuracy with stumps—that is, trees formed by a single split. The algorithm starts with an equal-weighted training set and then successively alters the sample distribution. After each iteration, AdaBoost increases the weights of incorrectly classified observations and reduces the weights of correctly predicted samples so that subsequent weak learners focus more on particularly difficult cases. Once trained, the new decision tree is incorporated into the ensemble with a weight that reflects its contribution to reducing the training error.

The AdaBoost algorithm for an ensemble of base learners, $h_m(x)$, $m=1, ..., M$, that predict discrete classes, $y \in [-1, 1]$, and N training observations can be summarized as follows:

1. Initialize sample weights $w_i=1/N$ for observations $i=1, ..., N$.
2. For each base classifier h_m, $m=1, ..., M$, do the following:
    1. Fit $h_m(x)$ to the training data, weighted by w_i.
    2. Compute the base learner's weighted error rate ε_m on the training set.
    3. Compute the base learner's ensemble weight α_m as a function of its error rate, as shown in the following formula:

$$\alpha_m = \log\left(\frac{1 - \epsilon_m}{\epsilon_m}\right)$$

    4. Update the weights for misclassified samples according to $w_i * exp(\alpha_m)$.
3. Predict the positive class when the weighted sum of the ensemble members is positive, and negative otherwise, as shown in the following formula:

$$H(x) = \text{sign}\left(\sum_{m=1}^{M} \underbrace{\alpha_m h_m(x)}_{\text{weighted weak learner}}\right)$$

AdaBoost has many practical advantages, including ease of implementation and fast computation, and it can be combined with any method for identifying weak learners. Apart from the size of the ensemble, there are no hyperparameters that require tuning. AdaBoost is also useful for identifying outliers because the samples that receive the highest weights are those that are consistently misclassified and inherently ambiguous, which is also typical for outliers.

On the other hand, the performance of AdaBoost on a given dataset depends on the ability of the weak learner to adequately capture the relationship between features and outcome. As the theory suggests, boosting will not perform well when there is insufficient data, or when the complexity of the ensemble members is not a good match for the complexity of the data. It can also be susceptible to noise in the data.

AdaBoost with sklearn

As part of its ensemble module, sklearn provides an AdaBoostClassifier implementation that supports two or more classes. The code examples for this section are in the notebook gbm_baseline that compares the performance of various algorithms with a dummy classifier that always predicts the most frequent class.

We need to first define a base_estimator as a template for all ensemble members and then configure the ensemble itself. We'll use the default DecisionTreeClassifier with max_depth=1—that is, a stump with a single split. The complexity of the base_estimator is a key tuning parameter because it depends on the nature of the data. As demonstrated in the previous chapter, changes to max_depth should be combined with appropriate regularization constraints using adjustments to, for example, min_samples_split, as shown in the following code:

```
base_estimator = DecisionTreeClassifier(criterion='gini',
                                        splitter='best',
                                        max_depth=1,
                                        min_samples_split=2,
                                        min_samples_leaf=20,
                                        min_weight_fraction_leaf=0.0,
                                        max_features=None,
                                        random_state=None,
                                        max_leaf_nodes=None,
                                        min_impurity_decrease=0.0,
                                        min_impurity_split=None)
```

In the second step, we'll design the ensemble. The n_estimators parameter controls the number of weak learners and the learning_rate determines the contribution of each weak learner, as shown in the following code. By default, weak learners are decision tree stumps:

```
ada_clf = AdaBoostClassifier(base_estimator=base_estimator,
                             n_estimators=200,
                             learning_rate=1.0,
                             algorithm='SAMME.R',
                             random_state=42)
```

The main tuning parameters that are responsible for good results are n_estimators and the base estimator complexity because the depth of the tree controls the extent of the interaction among the features.

We will cross-validate the AdaBoost ensemble using a custom 12-fold rolling time-series split to predict 1 month ahead for the last 12 months in the sample, using all available prior data for training, as shown in the following code:

```
cv = OneStepTimeSeriesSplit(n_splits=12, test_period_length=1,
shuffle=True)
def run_cv(clf, X=X_dummies, y=y, metrics=metrics, cv=cv, fit_params=None):
    return cross_validate(estimator=clf,
                          X=X,
                          y=y,
                          scoring=list(metrics.keys()),
                          cv=cv,
                          return_train_score=True,
                          n_jobs=-1,                    # use all cores
                          verbose=1,
                          fit_params=fit_params)
```

The result shows a weighted test accuracy of 0.62, a test **AUC** of **0.6665**, and a negative log loss of **-0.6923**, as well as a test **F1** score of **0.5876**, as shown in the following screenshot:

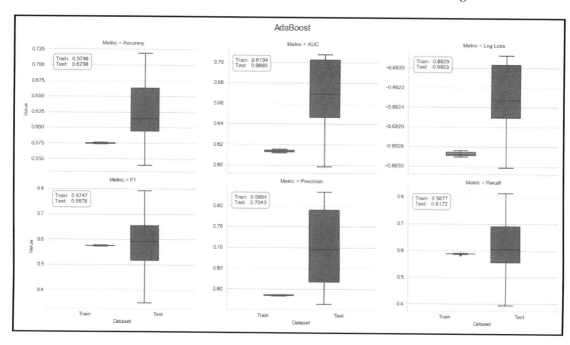

See the companion notebook for additional details on the code to cross-validate and process the results.

Gradient boosting machines

AdaBoost can also be interpreted as a stagewise forward approach to minimizing an exponential loss function for a binary $y \in [-1, 1]$ at each iteration m to identify a new base learner h_m with the corresponding weight α_m to be added to the ensemble, as shown in the following formula:

$$\underset{\alpha,h}{\operatorname{argmin}} \sum_{i=1}^{N} \exp\left(\underbrace{-y_i \left(f_{m-1}(x_i) \right.}_{\text{current ensemble}} + \underbrace{\left. \alpha_m h_m(x_i) \right)}_{\text{new member}} \right)$$

This interpretation of the AdaBoost algorithm was only discovered several years after its publication. It views AdaBoost as a coordinate-based gradient descent algorithm that minimizes a particular loss function, namely exponential loss.

Gradient boosting leverages this insight and applies the boosting method to a much wider range of loss functions. The method enables the design of machine learning algorithms to solve any regression, classification, or ranking problem as long as it can be formulated using a loss function that is differentiable and thus has a gradient. The flexibility to customize this general method to many specific prediction tasks is essential to boosting's popularity.

The main idea behind the resulting **Gradient Boosting Machines** (GBM) algorithm is the training of the base learners to learn the negative gradient of the current loss function of the ensemble. As a result, each addition to the ensemble directly contributes to reducing the overall training error given the errors made by prior ensemble members. Since each new member represents a new function of the data, gradient boosting is also said to optimize over the functions h_m in an additive fashion.

In short, the algorithm successively fits weak learners h_m, such as decision trees, to the negative gradient of the loss function that is evaluated for the current ensemble, as shown in the following formula:

$$H_m(x) = \underbrace{H_{m-1}(x)}_{\text{current ensemble}} + \underbrace{\gamma_m h_m(x)}_{\text{new member}} = H_{m-1}(x) + \underset{\gamma,h}{\operatorname{argmin}} \sum_{i=1}^{n} \underbrace{L(y_i, H_{m-1}(x_i) + h(x))}_{\text{loss function}}$$

In other words, at a given iteration *m*, the algorithm computes the gradient of the current loss for each observation and then fits a regression tree to these pseudo-residuals. In a second step, it identifies an optimal constant prediction for each terminal node that minimizes the incremental loss that results from adding this new learner to the ensemble.

This differs from standalone decision trees and random forests, where the prediction depends on the outcome values of the training samples present in the relevant terminal or leaf node: their average, in the case of regression, or the frequency of the positive class for binary classification. The focus on the gradient of the loss function also implies that gradient boosting uses regression trees to learn both regression and classification rules since the gradient is always a continuous function.

The final ensemble model makes predictions based on the weighted sum of the predictions of the individual decision trees, each of which has been trained to minimize the ensemble loss given the prior prediction for a given set of feature values, as shown in the following diagram:

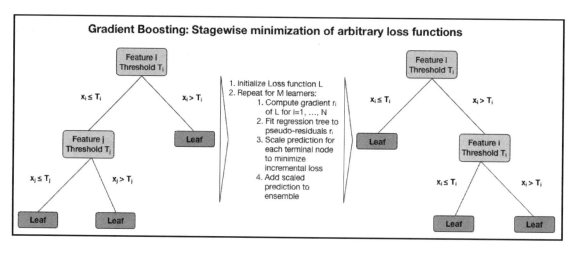

Gradient boosting trees have demonstrated state-of-the-art performance on many classification, regression, and ranking benchmarks. They are probably the most popular ensemble learning algorithm both as a standalone predictor in a diverse set of machine learning competitions, as well as in real-world production pipelines, for example, to predict click-through rates for online ads.

The success of gradient boosting is based on its ability to learn complex functional relationships in an incremental fashion. The flexibility of this algorithm requires the careful management of the risk of overfitting by tuning hyperparameters that constrain the model's inherent tendency to learn noise as opposed to the signal in the training data.

We will introduce the key mechanisms to control the complexity of a gradient boosting tree model, and then illustrate model tuning using the sklearn implementation.

How to train and tune GBM models

The two key drivers of gradient boosting performance are the size of the ensemble and the complexity of its constituent decision trees.

The control of complexity for decision trees aims to avoid learning highly specific rules that typically imply a very small number of samples in leaf nodes. We covered the most effective constraints used to limit the ability of a decision tree to overfit to the training data in the previous chapter. They include requiring:

- A minimum number of samples to either split a node or accept it as a terminal node, or
- A minimum improvement in node quality as measured by the purity or entropy or mean square error, in the case of regression.

In addition to directly controlling the size of the ensemble, there are various regularization techniques, such as shrinkage, that we encountered in the context of the Ridge and Lasso linear regression models in `Chapter 7`, *Linear Models*. Furthermore, the randomization techniques used in the context of random forests are also commonly applied to gradient boosting machines.

Ensemble size and early stopping

Each boosting iteration aims to reduce the training loss so that for a large ensemble, the training error can potentially become very small, increasing the risk of overfitting and poor performance on unseen data. Cross-validation is the best approach to find the optimal ensemble size that minimizes the generalization error because it depends on the application and the available data.

Since the ensemble size needs to be specified before training, it is useful to monitor the performance on the validation set and abort the training process when, for a given number of iterations, the validation error no longer decreases. This technique is called early stopping and frequently used for models that require a large number of iterations and are prone to overfitting, including deep neural networks.

Keep in mind that using early stopping with the same validation set for a large number of trials will also lead to overfitting, just to the particular validation set rather than the training set. It is best to avoid running a large number of experiments when developing a trading strategy as the risk of false discoveries increases significantly. In any case, keep a hold-out set to obtain an unbiased estimate of the generalization error.

Shrinkage and learning rate

Shrinkage techniques apply a penalty for increased model complexity to the model's loss function. For boosting ensembles, shrinkage can be applied by scaling the contribution of each new ensemble member down by a factor between 0 and 1. This factor is called the learning rate of the boosting ensemble. Reducing the learning rate increases shrinkage because it lowers the contribution of each new decision tree to the ensemble.

The learning rate has the opposite effect of the ensemble size, which tends to increase for lower learning rates. Lower learning rates coupled with larger ensembles have been found to reduce the test error, in particular for regression and probability estimation. Large numbers of iterations are computationally more expensive but often feasible with fast state-of-the-art implementations as long as the individual trees remain shallow. Depending on the implementation, you can also use adaptive learning rates that adjust to the number of iterations, typically lowering the impact of trees added later in the process. We will see some examples later in this chapter.

Subsampling and stochastic gradient boosting

As discussed in detail in the previous chapter, bootstrap averaging (bagging) improves the performance of an otherwise noisy classifier.

Stochastic gradient boosting uses sampling without replacement at each iteration to grow the next tree on a subset of the training samples. The benefit is both lower computational effort and often better accuracy, but subsampling should be combined with shrinkage.

As you can see, the number of hyperparameters keeps increasing, driving up the number of potential combinations, which in turn increases the risk of false positives when choosing the best model from a large number of parameter trials on a limited amount of training data. The best approach is to proceed sequentially and select parameter values individually or using combinations of subsets of low cardinality.

How to use gradient boosting with sklearn

The ensemble module of sklearn contains an implementation of gradient boosting trees for regression and classification, both binary and multiclass. The following `GradientBoostingClassifier` initialization code illustrates the key tuning parameters that we previously introduced, in addition to those that we are familiar with from looking at standalone decision tree models. The notebook `gbm_tuning_with_sklearn` contains the code examples for this section.

The available loss functions include the exponential loss that leads to the AdaBoost algorithm and the deviance that corresponds to the logistic regression for probabilistic outputs. The `friedman_mse` node quality measure is a variation on the mean squared error that includes an improvement score (see GitHub references for links to original papers), as shown in the following code:

```
gb_clf = GradientBoostingClassifier(loss='deviance',              #
deviance = logistic reg; exponential: AdaBoost
                              learning_rate=0.1,              #
shrinks the contribution of each tree
                              n_estimators=100,               #
number of boosting stages
                              subsample=1.0,                  #
fraction of samples used t fit base learners
                              criterion='friedman_mse',       #
measures the quality of a split
                              min_samples_split=2,
                              min_samples_leaf=1,
                              min_weight_fraction_leaf=0.0,   # min.
fraction of sum of weights
                              max_depth=3,                    # opt
value depends on interaction
                              min_impurity_decrease=0.0,
                              min_impurity_split=None,
                              max_features=None,
                              max_leaf_nodes=None,
                              warm_start=False,
                              presort='auto',
                              validation_fraction=0.1,
                              tol=0.0001)
```

Similar to `AdaBoostClassifier`, this model cannot handle missing values. We'll again use 12-fold cross-validation to obtain errors for classifying the directional return for rolling 1 month holding periods, as shown in the following code:

```
gb_cv_result = run_cv(gb_clf, y=y_clean, X=X_dummies_clean)
gb_result = stack_results(gb_cv_result)
```

We will parse and plot the result to find a slight improvement—using default parameter values—over the `AdaBoostClassifier`, as shown in the following screenshot:

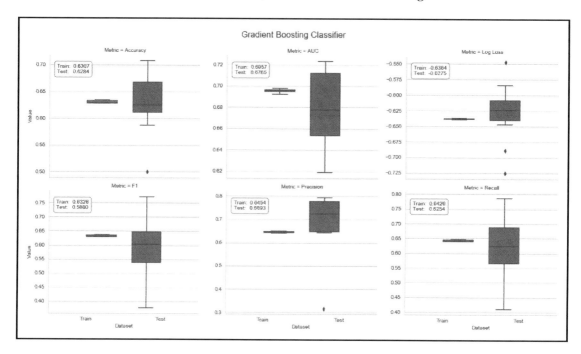

How to tune parameters with GridSearchCV

The `GridSearchCV` class in the `model_selection` module facilitates the systematic evaluation of all combinations of the hyperparameter values that we would like to test. In the following code, we will illustrate this functionality for seven tuning parameters that when defined will result in a total of 2^4 x 3^2 x 4 = 576 different model configurations:

```
cv = OneStepTimeSeriesSplit(n_splits=12)

param_grid = dict(
        n_estimators=[100, 300],
        learning_rate=[.01, .1, .2],
```

```
            max_depth=list(range(3, 13, 3)),
            subsample=[.8, 1],
            min_samples_split=[10, 50],
            min_impurity_decrease=[0, .01],
            max_features=['sqrt', .8, 1]
)
```

The .fit() method executes the cross-validation using the custom
OneStepTimeSeriesSplit and the roc_auc score to evaluate the 12-folds. Sklearn lets us
persist the result as it would for any other model using the joblib pickle implementation,
as shown in the following code:

```
gs = GridSearchCV(gb_clf,
                  param_grid,
                  cv=cv,
                  scoring='roc_auc',
                  verbose=3,
                  n_jobs=-1,
                  return_train_score=True)
gs.fit(X=X, y=y)

# persist result using joblib for more efficient storage of large numpy
arrays
joblib.dump(gs, 'gbm_gridsearch.joblib')
```

The GridSearchCV object has several additional attributes after completion that we can
access after loading the pickled result to learn which hyperparameter combination
performed best and its average cross-validation AUC score, which results in a modest
improvement over the default values. This is shown in the following code:

```
pd.Series(gridsearch_result.best_params_)
learning_rate                 0.01
max_depth                     9.00
max_features                  1.00
min_impurity_decrease         0.01
min_samples_split            10.00
n_estimators                300.00
subsample                     0.80

gridsearch_result.best_score_
0.6853
```

Parameter impact on test scores

The GridSearchCV result stores the average cross-validation scores so that we can analyze
how different hyperparameter settings affect the outcome.

The six `seaborn` swarm plots in the left-hand panel of the below chart show the distribution of AUC test scores for all parameter values. In this case, the highest AUC test scores required a low `learning_rate` and a large value for `max_features`. Some parameter settings, such as a low `learning_rate`, produce a wide range of outcomes that depend on the complementary settings of other parameters. Other parameters are compatible with high scores for all settings use in the experiment:

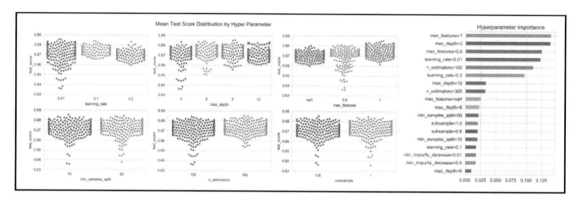

We will now explore how hyperparameter settings jointly affect the mean cross-validation score. To gain insight into how parameter settings interact, we can train a `DecisionTreeRegressor` with the mean test score as the outcome and the parameter settings, encoded as categorical variables in one-hot or dummy format (see the notebook for details). The tree structure highlights that using all features (`max_features_1`), a low `learning_rate`, and a `max_depth` over three led to the best results, as shown in the following diagram:

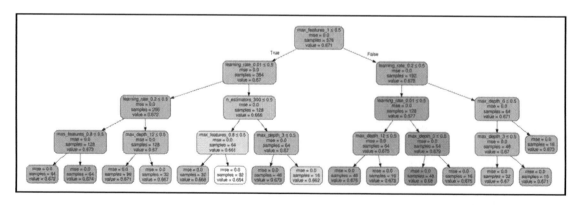

The bar chart in the right-hand panel of the first chart in this section displays the influence of the hyperparameter settings in producing different outcomes, measured by their feature importance for a decision tree that is grown to its maximum depth. Naturally, the features that appear near the top of the tree also accumulate the highest importance scores.

How to test on the holdout set

Finally, we would like to evaluate the best model's performance on the holdout set that we excluded from the `GridSearchCV` exercise. It contains the last six months of the sample period (through February 2018; see the notebook for details). We obtain a generalization performance estimate based on the AUC score of `0.6622` using the following code:

```
best_model = gridsearch_result.best_estimator_
preds= best_model.predict(test_feature_data)
roc_auc_score(y_true=test_target, y_score=preds)
0.6622
```

The downside of the sklearn gradient boosting implementation is the limited speed of computation which makes it difficult to try out different hyperparameter settings quickly. In the next section, we will see that several optimized implementations have emerged over the last few years that significantly reduce the time required to train even large-scale models, and have greatly contributed to a broader scope for applications of this highly effective algorithm.

Fast scalable GBM implementations

Over the last few years, several new gradient boosting implementations have used various innovations that accelerate training, improve resource efficiency, and allow the algorithm to scale to very large datasets. The new implementations and their sources are as follows:

- XGBoost (extreme gradient boosting), started in 2014 by Tianqi Chen at the University of Washington
- LightGBM, first released in January 2017, by Microsoft
- CatBoost, first released in April 2017 by Yandex

These innovations address specific challenges of training a gradient boosting model (see this chapter's README on GitHub for detailed references). The XGBoost implementation was the first new implementation to gain popularity: among the 29 winning solutions published by Kaggle in 2015, 17 solutions used XGBoost. Eight of these solely relied on XGBoost, while the others combined XGBoost with neural networks.

We will first introduce the key innovations that have emerged over time and subsequently converged (so that most features are available for all implementations) before illustrating their implementation.

How algorithmic innovations drive performance

Random forests can be trained in parallel by growing individual trees on independent bootstrap samples. In contrast, the sequential approach of gradient boosting slows down training, which in turn complicates experimentation with a large number of hyperparameters that need to be adapted to the nature of the task and the dataset.

To expand the ensemble by a tree, the training algorithm incrementally minimizes the prediction error with respect to the negative gradient of the ensemble's loss function, similar to a conventional gradient descent optimizer. Hence, the computational cost during training is proportional to the time it takes to evaluate the impact of potential split points for each feature on the decision tree's fit to the current gradient.

Second-order loss function approximation

The most important algorithmic innovations lower the cost of evaluating the loss function by using approximations that rely on second-order derivatives, resembling Newton's method to find stationary points. As a result, scoring potential splits during greedy tree expansion is faster relative to using the full loss function.

As mentioned previously, a gradient boosting model is trained in an incremental manner with the goal of minimizing the combination of the prediction error and the regularization penalty for the ensemble H_M. Denoting the prediction of the outcome y_i by the ensemble after step m as $\hat{y}_i^{(m)}$, l as a differentiable convex loss function that measures the difference between the outcome and the prediction, and Ω as a penalty that increases with the complexity of the ensemble H_M, the incremental hypothesis h_m aims to minimize the following objective:

$$\mathcal{L}^{(m)} = \sum_{i=1}^{n} \underbrace{l(y_i, \hat{y}_i^{(m)})}_{\text{Loss at step m}} + \sum_{i=1}^{t} \underbrace{\Omega(H_m)}_{\text{Regularization}}$$

$$= \sum_{i=1}^{n} l(y_i, \hat{y}_i^{(m-1)} + \underbrace{h_m(x_i)}_{\text{additional tree}}) + \Omega(h_m)$$

The regularization penalty helps to avoid overfitting by favoring the selection of a model that uses simple and predictive regression trees. In the case of XGBoost, for example, the penalty for a regression tree h depends on the number of leaves per tree T, the regression tree scores for each terminal node w, and the hyperparameters γ and λ. This is summarized in the following formula:

$$\Omega(h) = \gamma T + \frac{1}{2}\lambda\|w\|^2$$

Therefore, at each step, the algorithm greedily adds the hypothesis h_m that most improves the regularized objective. The second-order approximation of a loss function, based on a Taylor expansion, speeds up the evaluation of the objective, as summarized in the following formula:

$$\mathcal{L}^{(m)} \simeq \sum_{i=1}^{n}\left[g_i f_m(x_i) + \frac{1}{2}h_i f_m^2(x_i)\right] + \Omega(h_m)$$

Here, g_i is the first-order gradient of the loss function before adding the new learner for a given feature value, and h_i is the corresponding second-order gradient (or Hessian) value, as shown in the following formulas:

$$g_i = \partial_{\hat{y}_i^{(m-1)}} l\left(y_i, \hat{y}_i^{(m-1)}\right)$$
$$h_i = \partial_{\hat{y}_i^{(m-1)}}^2 l\left(y_i, \hat{y}_i^{(m-1)}\right)$$

The XGBoost algorithm was the first open-source algorithm to leverage this approximation of the loss function to compute the optimal leave scores for a given tree structure and the corresponding value of the loss function. The score consists of the ratio of the sums of the gradient and Hessian for the samples in a terminal node. It uses this value to score the information gain that would result from a split, similar to the node impurity measures we saw in the previous chapter, but applicable to arbitrary loss functions (see the references on GitHub for the detailed derivation).

Simplified split-finding algorithms

The gradient boosting implementation by sklearn finds the optimal split that enumerates all options for continuous features. This precise greedy algorithm is computationally very demanding because it must first sort the data by feature values before scoring the potentially very large number of split options and making a decision. This approach faces challenges when the data does not fit in memory or when training in a distributed setting on multiple machines.

An approximate split-finding algorithm reduces the number of split points by assigning feature values to a user-determined set of bins, which can also greatly reduce the memory requirements during training because only a single split needs to be stored for each bin. XGBoost introduced a quantile sketch algorithm that was also able to divide weighted training samples into percentile bins to achieve a uniform distribution. XGBoost also introduced the ability to handle sparse data caused by missing values, frequent zero-gradient statistics, and one-hot encoding, and can also learn an optimal default direction for a given split. As a result, the algorithm only needs to evaluate non-missing values.

In contrast, LightGBM uses **gradient-based one-side sampling (GOSS)** to exclude a significant proportion of samples with small gradients, and only uses the remainder to estimate the information gain and select a split value accordingly. Samples with larger gradients require more training and tend to contribute more to the information gain. LightGBM also uses exclusive feature bundling to combine features that are mutually exclusive, in that they rarely take nonzero values simultaneously, to reduce the number of features. As a result, LightGBM was the fastest implementation when released.

Depth-wise versus leaf-wise growth

LightGBM differs from XGBoost and CatBoost in how it prioritizes which nodes to split. LightGBM decides on splits leaf-wise, i.e., it splits the leaf node that maximizes the information gain, even when this leads to unbalanced trees. In contrast, XGBoost and CatBoost expand all nodes depth-wise and first split all nodes at a given depth before adding more levels. The two approaches expand nodes in a different order and will produce different results except for complete trees. The following diagram illustrates the two approaches:

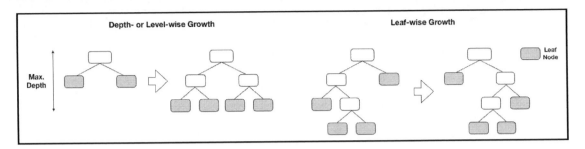

LightGBM's leaf-wise splits tend to increase model complexity and may speed up convergence, but also increase the risk of overfitting. A tree grown depth-wise with n levels has up to 2^n terminal nodes, whereas a leaf-wise tree with 2^n leaves can have significantly more levels and contain correspondingly fewer samples in some leaves. Hence, tuning LightGBM's num_leaves setting requires extra caution, and the library allows us to control max_depth at the same time to avoid undue node imbalance. More recent versions of LightGBM also offer depth-wise tree growth.

GPU-based training

All new implementations support training and prediction on one or more GPUs to achieve significant speedups. They are compatible with current CUDA-enabled GPUs. Installation requirements vary and are evolving quickly. The XGBoost and CatBoost implementations work for several current versions, but LightGBM may require local compilation (see GitHub for links to the relevant documentation).

The speedups depend on the library and the type of the data, and range from low, single-digit multiples to factors of several dozen. Activation of the GPU only requires the change of a task parameter and no other hyperparameter modifications.

DART – dropout for trees

In 2015, Rashmi and Gilad-Bachrach proposed a new model to train gradient boosting trees that aimed to address a problem they labeled over-specialization: trees added during later iterations tend only to affect the prediction of a few instances while making a minor contribution regarding the remaining instances. However, the model's out-of-sample performance can suffer, and it may become over-sensitive to the contributions of a small number of trees added earlier in the process.

The new algorithms employ dropouts which have been successfully used for learning more accurate deep neural networks where dropouts mute a random fraction of the neural connections during the learning process. As a result, nodes in higher layers cannot rely on a few connections to pass the information needed for the prediction. This method has made a significant contribution to the success of deep neural networks for many tasks and has also been used with other learning techniques, such as logistic regression, to mute a random share of the features. Random forests and stochastic gradient boosting also drop out a random subset of features.

DART operates at the level of trees and mutes complete trees as opposed to individual features. The goal is for trees in the ensemble generated using DART to contribute more evenly towards the final prediction. In some cases, this has been shown to produce more accurate predictions for ranking, regression, and classification tasks. The approach was first implemented in LightGBM and is also available for XGBoost.

Treatment of categorical features

The CatBoost and LightGBM implementations handle categorical variables directly without the need for dummy encoding.

The CatBoost implementation (which is named for its treatment of categorical features) includes several options to handle such features, in addition to automatic one-hot encoding, and assigns either the categories of individual features or combinations of categories for several features to numerical values. In other words, CatBoost can create new categorical features from combinations of existing features. The numerical values associated with the category levels of individual features or combinations of features depend on their relationship with the outcome value. In the classification case, this is related to the probability of observing the positive class, computed cumulatively over the sample, based on a prior, and with a smoothing factor. See the documentation for more detailed numerical examples.

The LightGBM implementation groups the levels of the categorical features to maximize homogeneity (or minimize variance) within groups with respect to the outcome values.

The XGBoost implementation does not handle categorical features directly and requires one-hot (or dummy) encoding.

Additional features and optimizations

XGBoost optimized computation in several respects to enable multithreading by keeping data in memory in compressed column blocks, where each column is sorted by the corresponding feature value. XGBoost computes this input data layout once before training and reuses it throughout to amortize the additional up-front cost. The search for split statistics over columns becomes a linear scan when using quantiles that can be done in parallel with easy support for column subsampling.

The subsequently released LightGBM and CatBoost libraries built on these innovations, and LightGBM further accelerated training through optimized threading and reduced memory usage. Because of their open source nature, libraries have tended to converge over time.

XGBoost also supports monotonicity constraints. These constraints ensure that the values for a given feature are only positively or negatively related to the outcome over its entire range. They are useful to incorporate external assumptions about the model that are known to be true.

How to use XGBoost, LightGBM, and CatBoost

XGBoost, LightGBM, and CatBoost offer interfaces for multiple languages, including Python, and have both a sklearn interface that is compatible with other sklearn features, such as GridSearchCV and their own methods to train and predict gradient boosting models. The gbm_baseline.ipynb notebook illustrates the use of the sklearn interface for each implementation. The library methods are often better documented and are also easy to use, so we'll use them to illustrate the use of these models.

The process entails the creation of library-specific data formats, the tuning of various hyperparameters, and the evaluation of results that we will describe in the following sections. The accompanying notebook contains the gbm_tuning.py, gbm_utils.py and, gbm_params.py files that jointly provide the following functionalities and have produced the corresponding results.

How to create binary data formats

All libraries have their own data format to precompute feature statistics to accelerate the search for split points, as described previously. These can also be persisted to accelerate the start of subsequent training.

The following code constructs binary train and validation datasets for each model to be used with the `OneStepTimeSeriesSplit`:

```python
cat_cols = ['year', 'month', 'age', 'msize', 'sector']
data = {}
for fold, (train_idx, test_idx) in enumerate(kfold.split(features)):
    print(fold, end=' ', flush=True)
    if model == 'xgboost':
        data[fold] = {'train': xgb.DMatrix(label=target.iloc[train_idx],
                                           data=features.iloc[train_idx],
                                           nthread=-1),                    #
use avail. threads
                      'valid': xgb.DMatrix(label=target.iloc[test_idx],
                                           data=features.iloc[test_idx],
                                           nthread=-1)}
    elif model == 'lightgbm':
        train = lgb.Dataset(label=target.iloc[train_idx],
                            data=features.iloc[train_idx],
                            categorical_feature=cat_cols,
                            free_raw_data=False)

        # align validation set histograms with training set
        valid = train.create_valid(label=target.iloc[test_idx],
                                   data=features.iloc[test_idx])

        data[fold] = {'train': train.construct(),
                      'valid': valid.construct()}

    elif model == 'catboost':
        # get categorical feature indices
        cat_cols_idx = [features.columns.get_loc(c) for c in cat_cols]
        data[fold] = {'train': Pool(label=target.iloc[train_idx],
                                    data=features.iloc[train_idx],
                                    cat_features=cat_cols_idx),

                      'valid': Pool(label=target.iloc[test_idx],
                                    data=features.iloc[test_idx],
                                    cat_features=cat_cols_idx)}
```

The available options vary slightly:

- `xgboost` allows the use of all available threads
- `lightgbm` explicitly aligns the quantiles that are created for the validation set with the training set
- The `catboost` implementation needs feature columns identified using indices rather than labels

How to tune hyperparameters

The numerous hyperparameters are listed in `gbm_params.py`. Each library has parameter settings to:

- Specify the overall objectives and learning algorithm
- Design the base learners
- Apply various regularization techniques
- Handle early stopping during training
- Enabling the use of GPU or parallelization on CPU

The documentation for each library details the various parameters that may refer to the same concept, but which have different names across libraries. The GitHub repository contains links to a site that highlights the corresponding parameters for `xgboost` and `lightgbm`.

Objectives and loss functions

The libraries support several boosting algorithms, including gradient boosting for trees and linear base learners, as well as DART for LightGBM and XGBoost. LightGBM also supports the GOSS algorithm which we described previously, as well as random forests.

The appeal of gradient boosting consists of the efficient support of arbitrary differentiable loss functions and each library offers various options for regression, classification, and ranking tasks. In addition to the chosen loss function, additional evaluation metrics can be used to monitor performance during training and cross-validation.

Learning parameters

Gradient boosting models typically use decision trees to capture feature interaction, and the size of individual trees is the most important tuning parameter. XGBoost and CatBoost set the `max_depth` default to 6. In contrast, LightGBM uses a default `num_leaves` value of 31, which corresponds to five levels for a balanced tree, but imposes no constraints on the number of levels. To avoid overfitting, `num_leaves` should be lower than 2^{max_depth}. For example, for a well-performing `max_depth` value of 7, you would set `num_leaves` to 70–80 rather than $2^7=128$, or directly constrain `max_depth`.

The number of trees or boosting iterations defines the overall size of the ensemble. All libraries support `early_stopping` to abort training once the loss functions register no further improvements during a given number of iterations. As a result, it is usually best to set a large number of iterations and stop training based on the predictive performance on a validation set.

Regularization

All libraries implement the regularization strategies for base learners, such as minimum values for the number of samples or the minimum information gain required for splits and leaf nodes.

They also support regularization at the ensemble level using shrinkage via a learning rate that constrains the contribution of new trees. It is also possible to implement an adaptive learning rate via callback functions that lower the learning rate as the training progresses, as has been successfully used in the context of neural networks. Furthermore, the gradient boosting loss function can be regularized using *L1* or *L2*, regularization similar to the Ridge and Lasso linear regression models by modifying $\Omega(h_m)$ or by increasing the penalty γ for adding more trees, as described previously.

The libraries also allow for the use of bagging or column subsampling to randomize tree growth for random forests and decorrelate prediction errors to reduce overall variance. The quantization of features for approximate split finding adds larger bins as an additional option to protect against overfitting.

Randomized grid search

To explore the hyperparameter space, we specify values for key parameters that we would like to test in combination. The sklearn library supports `RandomizedSearchCV` to cross-validate a subset of parameter combinations that are sampled randomly from specified distributions. We will implement a custom version that allows us to leverage early stopping while monitoring the current best-performing combinations so we can abort the search process once satisfied with the result rather than specifying a set number of iterations beforehand.

To this end, we specify a parameter grid according to each library's parameters as before, generate all combinations using the built-in Cartesian `product` generator provided by the `itertools` library, and randomly `shuffle` the result. In the case of LightGBM, we automatically set `max_depth` as a function of the current `num_leaves` value, as shown in the following code:

```
param_grid = dict(
        # common options
        learning_rate=[.01, .1, .3],
        colsample_bytree=[.8, 1],   # except catboost

        # lightgbm
        num_leaves=[2 ** i for i in range(9, 14)],
        boosting=['gbdt', 'dart'],
        min_gain_to_split=[0, 1, 5],   # not supported on GPU

all_params = list(product(*param_grid.values()))
n_models = len(all_params) # max number of models to cross-validate
shuffle(all_params)
```

We then execute cross-validation as follows:

```
GBM = 'lightgbm'
for test_param in all_params:
    cv_params = get_params(GBM)
    cv_params.update(dict(zip(param_grid.keys(), test_param)))
    if GBM == 'lightgbm':
        cv_params['max_depth'] =
int(ceil(np.log2(cv_params['num_leaves'])))
        results[n] = run_cv(test_params=cv_params,
                        data=datasets,
                        n_splits=n_splits,
                        gb_machine=GBM)
```

The `run_cv` function implements cross-validation for all three libraries. For the `light_gbm` example, the process looks as follows:

```
def run_cv(test_params, data, n_splits=10):
    """Train-Validate with early stopping"""
    result = []
    cols = ['rounds', 'train', 'valid']
    for fold in range(n_splits):
        train = data[fold]['train']
        valid = data[fold]['valid']

        scores = {}
        model = lgb.train(params=test_params,
```

```
                            train_set=train,
                            valid_sets=[train, valid],
                            valid_names=['train', 'valid'],
                            num_boost_round=250,
                            early_stopping_rounds=25,
                            verbose_eval=50,
                            evals_result=scores)

        result.append([model.current_iteration(),
                        scores['train']['auc'][-1],
                        scores['valid']['auc'][-1]])

    return pd.DataFrame(result, columns=cols)
```

The `train()` method also produces validation scores that are stored in the `scores` dictionary. When early stopping takes effect, the last iteration is also the best score. See the full implementation on GitHub for additional details.

How to evaluate the results

Using a GPU, we can train a model in a few minutes and evaluate several hundred parameter combinations in a matter of hours, which would take many days using the sklearn implementation. For the LightGBM model, we explore both a factor version that uses the libraries' ability to handle categorical variables and a dummy version that uses one-hot encoding.

The results are available in the `model_tuning.h5` HDF5 store. The model evaluation code samples are in the `eval_results.ipynb` notebook.

Cross-validation results across models

When comparing average cross-validation AUC across the four test runs with the three libraries, we find that CatBoost produces a slightly higher AUC score for the top-performing model, while also producing the widest dispersion of outcomes, as shown in the following graph:

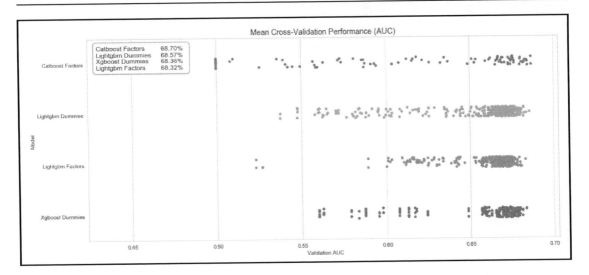

The top-performing CatBoost model uses the following parameters (see notebook for detail):

- `max_depth` of 12 and `max_bin` of 128
- `max_ctr_complexity` of 2, which limits the number of combinations of categorical features
- `one_hot_max_size` of 2, which excludes binary features from the assignment of numerical variables
- `random_strength` different from 0 to randomize the evaluation of splits

Training is a bit slower compared to LightGBM and XGBoost (all use the GPU) at an average of 230 seconds per model.

A more detailed look at the top-performing models for the LightGBM and XGBoost models shows that the LightGBM Factors model achieves nearly as good a performance as the other two models with much lower model complexity. It only consists on average of 41 trees up to three levels deep with no more than eight leaves each, while also using regularization in the form of `min_gain_to_split`. It overfits significantly less on the training set, with a train AUC only slightly above the validation AUC. It also trains much faster, taking only 18 seconds per model because of its lower complexity. In practice, this model would be preferable since it is more likely to produce good out-of-sample performance. The details are shown in the following table:

	LightGBM dummies	XGBoost dummies	LightGBM factors
Validation AUC	68.57%	68.36%	68.32%
Train AUC	82.35%	79.81%	72.12%
learning_rate	0.1	0.1	0.3
max_depth	13	9	3
num_leaves	8192		8
colsample_bytree	0.8	1	1
min_gain_to_split	0	1	0
Rounds	44.42	59.17	41.00
Time	86.55	85.37	18.78

The following plot shows the effect of different `max_depth` settings on the validation score for the LightGBM and XGBoost models: shallower trees produce a wider range of outcomes and need to be combined with appropriate learning rates and regularization settings to produce the strong result shown in the preceding table:

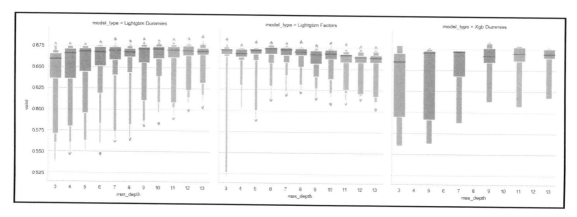

Instead of a `DecisionTreeRegressor` as shown previously, we can also use linear regression to evaluate the statistical significance of different features concerning the validation AUC score. For the LightGBM Dummy model, where the regression explains 68% of the variation in outcomes, we find that only the `min_gain_to_split` regularization parameter was not significant, as shown in the following screenshot:

```
                            OLS Regression Results
==============================================================================
Dep. Variable:                  valid   R-squared:                       0.687
Model:                            OLS   Adj. R-squared:                  0.673
Method:                 Least Squares   F-statistic:                     26.94
Date:                Wed, 24 Oct 2018   Prob (F-statistic):           7.92e-55
Time:                        14:03:45   Log-Likelihood:                 1018.7
No. Observations:                 396   AIC:                            -2001.
Df Residuals:                     378   BIC:                            -1930.
Df Model:                          17
Covariance Type:                  HC3
==============================================================================
                        coef    std err          z      P>|z|      [0.025      0.975]
------------------------------------------------------------------------------
const                 0.6145      0.005    127.970      0.000       0.605       0.624
boosting_gbtree       0.0056      0.002      2.866      0.004       0.002       0.009
learning_rate_0.1     0.0501      0.003     18.977      0.000       0.045       0.055
learning_rate_0.3     0.0516      0.003     19.150      0.000       0.046       0.057
max_depth_4           0.0060      0.005      1.094      0.274      -0.005       0.017
max_depth_5           0.0096      0.005      1.823      0.068      -0.001       0.020
max_depth_6           0.0153      0.005      3.024      0.002       0.005       0.025
max_depth_7           0.0194      0.005      3.753      0.000       0.009       0.030
max_depth_8           0.0196      0.005      3.733      0.000       0.009       0.030
max_depth_9           0.0266      0.005      5.176      0.000       0.017       0.037
max_depth_10          0.0307      0.005      5.954      0.000       0.021       0.041
max_depth_11          0.0285      0.005      5.484      0.000       0.018       0.039
max_depth_12          0.0312      0.005      6.178      0.000       0.021       0.041
max_depth_13          0.0320      0.005      6.218      0.000       0.022       0.042
colsample_bytree_0.8 -0.0112      0.003     -4.143      0.000      -0.017      -0.006
colsample_bytree_1.0 -0.0278      0.003     -8.388      0.000      -0.034      -0.021
min_gain_to_split_1  -0.0009      0.003     -0.307      0.759      -0.006       0.005
min_gain_to_split_5  -0.0016      0.002     -0.726      0.468      -0.006       0.003
==============================================================================
Omnibus:                       11.763   Durbin-Watson:                   0.856
Prob(Omnibus):                  0.003   Jarque-Bera (JB):               11.104
Skew:                          -0.361   Prob(JB):                      0.00388
Kurtosis:                       2.609   Cond. No.                         17.1
==============================================================================

Warnings:
[1] Standard Errors are heteroscedasticity robust (HC3)
```

In practice, gaining deeper insights into how the models arrive at predictions is extremely important, in particular for investment strategies where decision makers often require plausible explanations.

How to interpret GBM results

Understanding why a model predicts a certain outcome is very important for several reasons, including trust, actionability, accountability, and debugging. Insights into the nonlinear relationship between features and the outcome uncovered by the model, as well as interactions among features, are also of value when the goal is to learn more about the underlying drivers of the phenomenon under study.

A common approach to gaining insights into the predictions made by tree ensemble methods, such as gradient boosting or random forest models, is to attribute feature importance values to each input variable. These feature importance values can be computed on an individual basis for a single prediction or globally for an entire dataset (that is, for all samples) to gain a higher-level perspective on how the model makes predictions.

Feature importance

There are three primary ways to compute **global feature importance** values:

- **Gain**: This classic approach introduced by Leo Breiman in 1984 uses the total reduction of loss or impurity contributed by all splits for a given feature. The motivation is largely heuristic, but it is a commonly used method to select features.
- **Split count**: This is an alternative approach that counts how often a feature is used to make a split decision, based on the selection of features for this purpose based on the resultant information gain.
- **Permutation**: This approach randomly permutes the feature values in a test set and measures how much the model's error changes, assuming that an important feature should create a large increase in the prediction error. Different permutation choices lead to alternative implementations of this basic approach.

Individualized feature importance values that compute the relevance of features for a single prediction are less common because available model-agnostic explanation methods are much slower than tree-specific methods.

All gradient boosting implementations provide feature-importance scores after training as a model attribute. The XGBoost library provides five versions, as shown in the following list:

- `total_gain` and `gain` as its average per split
- `total_cover` as the number of samples per split when a feature was used
- `weight` as the split count from preceding values

These values are available using the trained model's `.get_score()` method with the corresponding `importance_type` parameter. For the best performing XGBoost model, the results are as follows (the *total* measures have a correlation of 0.8, as do `cover` and `total_cover`):

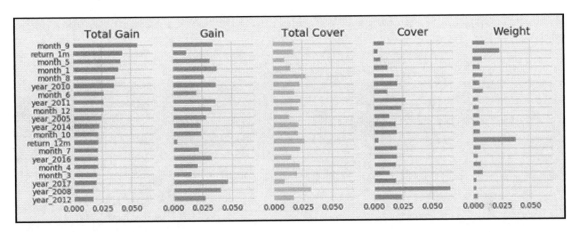

While the indicators for different months and years dominate, the most recent 1 month return is the second-most important feature from a `total_gain` perspective, and is used frequently according to the `weight` measure, but produces low average gains as it is applied to relatively few instances on average (see the notebook for implementation details).

Partial dependence plots

In addition to the summary contribution of individual features to the model's prediction, partial dependence plots visualize the relationship between the target variable and a set of features. The nonlinear nature of gradient boosting trees causes this relationship to depends on the values of all other features. Hence, we will marginalize these features out. By doing so, we can interpret the partial dependence as the expected target response.

We can visualize partial dependence only for individual features or feature pairs. The latter results in contour plots that show how combinations of feature values produce different predicted probabilities, as shown in the following code:

```
fig, axes = plot_partial_dependence(gbrt=gb_clf,
                                    X=X_dummies_clean,
                                    features=['month_9', 'return_1m',
    'return_3m', ('return_1m', 'return_3m')],
                                    feature_names=['month_9','return_1m',
```

```
'return_3m'],
                                 percentiles=(0.01, 0.99),
                                 n_jobs=-1,
                                 n_cols=2,
                                 grid_resolution=250)
```

After some additional formatting (see the companion notebook), we obtain the following plot:

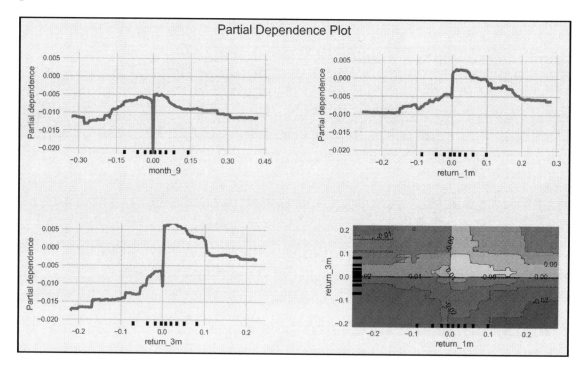

The lower-right plot shows the dependence of the probability of a positive return over the next month given the range of values for lagged 1-month and 3-month returns after eliminating outliers at the [1%, 99%] percentiles. The month_9 variable is a dummy variable, hence the step-function-like plot. We can also visualize the dependency in 3D, as shown in the following code:

```
targets = ['return_1m', 'return_3m']
target_feature = [X_dummies_clean.columns.get_loc(t) for t in targets]
pdp, axes = partial_dependence(gb_clf,
                               target_feature,
                               X=X_dummies_clean,
                               grid_resolution=100)
```

```
XX, YY = np.meshgrid(axes[0], axes[1])
Z = pdp[0].reshape(list(map(np.size, axes))).T

fig = plt.figure(figsize=(14, 8))
ax = Axes3D(fig)
surf = ax.plot_surface(XX, YY, Z,
                       rstride=1,
                       cstride=1,
                       cmap=plt.cm.BuPu,
                       edgecolor='k')
ax.set_xlabel(' '.join(targets[0].split('_')).capitalize())
ax.set_ylabel(' '.join(targets[1].split('_')).capitalize())
ax.set_zlabel('Partial Dependence')
ax.view_init(elev=22, azim=30)
```

This produces the following 3D plot of the partial dependence of the 1-month return direction on lagged 1-month and 3-months returns:

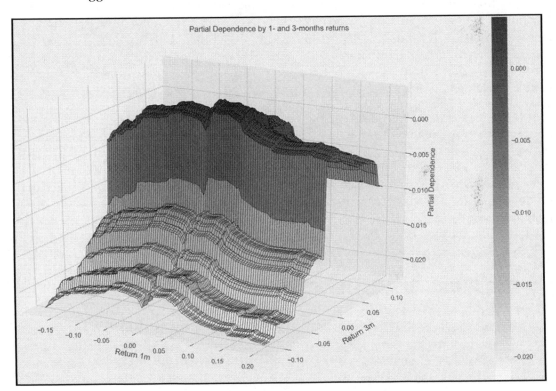

SHapley Additive exPlanations

At the 2017 NIPS conference, Scott Lundberg and Su-In Lee from the University of Washington presented a new and more accurate approach to explaining the contribution of individual features to the output of tree ensemble models called **SHapley Additive exPlanations**, or **SHAP** values.

This new algorithm departs from the observation that feature-attribution methods for tree ensembles, such as the ones we looked at earlier, are inconsistent—that is, a change in a model that increases the impact of a feature on the output can lower the importance values for this feature (see the references on GitHub for detailed illustrations of this).

SHAP values unify ideas from collaborative game theory and local explanations, and have been shown to be theoretically optimal, consistent, and locally accurate based on expectations. Most importantly, Lundberg and Lee have developed an algorithm that manages to reduce the complexity of computing these model-agnostic, additive feature-attribution methods from $O(TLD^M)$ to $O(TLD^2)$, where T and M are the number of trees and features, respectively, and D and L are the maximum depth and number of leaves across the trees. This important innovation permits the explanation of predictions from previously intractable models with thousands of trees and features in a fraction of a second. An open source implementation became available in late 2017 and is compatible with XGBoost, LightGBM, CatBoost, and sklearn tree models.

Shapley values originated in game theory as a technique for assigning a value to each player in a collaborative game that reflects their contribution to the team's success. SHAP values are an adaptation of the game theory concept to tree-based models and are calculated for each feature and each sample. They measure how a feature contributes to the model output for a given observation. For this reason, SHAP values provide differentiated insights into how the impact of a feature varies across samples, which is important given the role of interaction effects in these nonlinear models.

How to summarize SHAP values by feature

To get a high-level overview of the feature importance across a number of samples, there are two ways to plot the SHAP values: a simple average across all samples that resembles the global feature-importance measures computed previously (as shown in the left-hand panel of the following screenshot), or a scatter graph to display the impact of every feature for every sample (as shown in the right-hand panel of the following screenshot). They are very straightforward to produce using a trained model of a compatible library and matching input data, as shown in the following code:

```
# load JS visualization code to notebook
```

```
shap.initjs()

# explain the model's predictions using SHAP values
explainer = shap.TreeExplainer(model)
shap_values = explainer.shap_values(X_test)

shap.summary_plot(shap_values, X_test, show=False)
```

The scatter plot on the right of the following screenshot sorts features by their total SHAP values across all samples, and then shows how each feature impacts the model output as measured by the SHAP value as a function of the feature's value, represented by its color, where red represents high and blue represents low values relative to the feature's range:

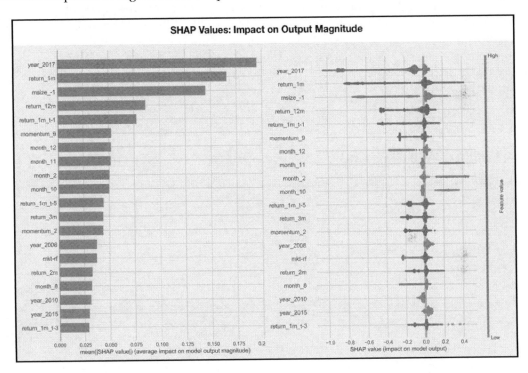

How to use force plots to explain a prediction

The following force plot shows the cumulative impact of various features and their values on the model output, which in this case was 0.6, quite a bit higher than the base value of 0.13 (the average model output over the provided dataset). Features highlighted in red increase the output. The month being October is the most important feature and increases the output from 0.338 to 0.537, whereas the year being 2017 reduces the output.

Hence, we obtain a detailed breakdown of how the model arrived at a specific prediction, as shown in the following image:

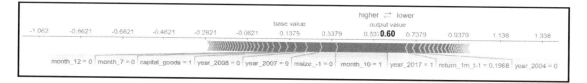

We can also compute force plots for numerous data points or predictions at a time and use a clustered visualization to gain insights into how prevalent certain influence patterns are across the dataset. The following plot shows the force plots for the first 1,000 observations rotated by 90 degrees, stacked horizontally, and ordered by the impact of different features on the outcome for the given observation. The implementation uses hierarchical agglomerative clustering of data points on the feature SHAP values to identify these patterns, and displays the result interactively for exploratory analysis (see the notebook), as shown in the following code:

```
shap.force_plot(explainer.expected_value, shap_values[:1000,:],
X_test.iloc[:1000])
```

This produces the following output:

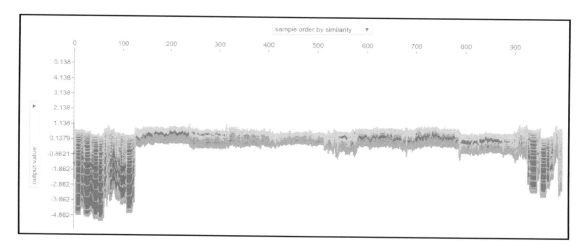

How to analyze feature interaction

Lastly, SHAP values allow us to gain additional insights into the interaction effects between different features by separating these interactions from the main effects. The `shap.dependence_plot` can be defined as follows:

```
shap.dependence_plot("return_1m", shap_values, X_test, interaction_index=2,
    title='Interaction between 1- and 3-Month Returns')
```

It displays how different values for 1-month returns (on the *x* axis) affect the outcome (SHAP value on the *y* axis), differentiated by 3-month returns:

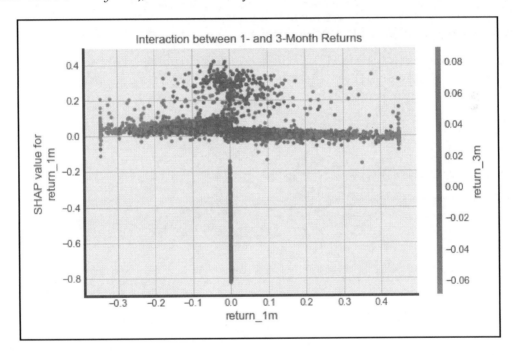

SHAP values provide granular feature attribution at the level of each individual prediction, and enable much richer inspection of complex models through (interactive) visualization. The SHAP summary scatterplot displayed at the beginning of this section offers much more differentiated insights than a global feature-importance bar chart. Force plots of individual clustered predictions allow for more detailed analysis, while SHAP dependence plots capture interaction effects and, as a result, provide more accurate and detailed results than partial dependence plots.

The limitations of SHAP values, as with any current feature-importance measure, concern the attribution of the influence of variables that are highly correlated because their similar impact could be broken down in arbitrary ways.

Summary

In this chapter, we explored the gradient boosting algorithm, which is used to build ensembles in a sequential manner, adding a shallow decision tree that only uses a very small number of features to improve on the predictions that have been made. We saw how gradient boosting trees can be very flexibly applied to a broad range of loss functions and offer many opportunities to tune the model to a given dataset and learning task.

Recent implementations have greatly facilitated the use of gradient boosting by accelerating the training process and offering more consistent and detailed insights into the importance of features and the drivers of individual predictions. In the next chapter, we will turn to Bayesian approaches to ML.

12
Unsupervised Learning

In Chapter 6, *Machine Learning Process*, we discussed how unsupervised learning adds value by uncovering structures in the data without an outcome variable, such as a teacher, to guide the search process. This task contrasts with the setting for supervised learning that we focused on in the last several chapters.

Unsupervised learning algorithms can be useful when a dataset contains only features and no measurement of the outcome, or when we want to extract information independent of the outcome. Instead of predicting future outcomes, the goal is to study an informative representation of the data that is useful for solving another task, including the exploration of a dataset.

Examples include identifying topics to summarize documents (see Chapter 14, *Topic Modeling*), reducing the number of features to reduce the risk of overfitting and the computational cost for supervised learning, or grouping similar observations, as illustrated by the use of clustering for asset allocation at the end of this chapter.

Dimensionality reduction and clustering are the main tasks for unsupervised learning:

- **Dimensionality reduction** transforms the existing features into a new, smaller set, while minimizing the loss of information. A broad range of algorithms exists that differ only in how they measure the loss of information, whether they apply linear or non-linear transformations, or the constraints they impose on the new feature set.
- **Clustering algorithms** identify and group similar observations or features instead of identifying new features. Algorithms differ in how they define the similarity of observations and their assumptions about the resulting groups.

More specifically, this chapter covers the following:

- How **Principal Component Analysis (PCA)** and **Independent Component Analysis (ICA)** perform linear dimensionality reduction
- How to apply PCA to identify risk factors and eigen portfolios from asset returns
- How to use non-linear manifold learning to summarize high-dimensional data for effective visualization
- How to use t-SNE and UMAP to explore high-dimensional alternative image data
- How k-Means, hierarchical, and density-based clustering algorithms work
- How to use agglomerative clustering to build robust portfolios according to hierarchical risk parity

The code samples for each section are in the directory of the online GitHub repository for this chapter at `https://github.com/PacktPublishing/Hands-On-Machine-Learning-for-Algorithmic-Trading`.

Dimensionality reduction

In linear algebra terms, the features of a dataset create a **vector space** whose dimensionality corresponds to the number of linearly independent columns (assuming there are more observations than features). Two columns are linearly dependent when they are perfectly correlated so that one can be computed from the other using the linear operations of addition and multiplication.

In other words, they are parallel vectors that represent the same rather than different directions or axes and only constitute a single dimension. Similarly, if one variable is a linear combination of several others, then it is an element of the vector space created by those columns, rather than adding a new dimension of its own.

The number of dimensions of a dataset matter because each new dimension can add a signal concerning an outcome. However, there is also a downside known as the **curse of dimensionality**: as the number of independent features grows while the number of observations remains constant, the average distance between data points also grows, and the density of the feature space drops exponentially.

The implications for machine learning are dramatic because prediction becomes much harder when observations are more distant; that is, different to each other. The next section addresses the resulting challenges.

Dimensionality reduction seeks to represent the information in the data more efficiently by using fewer features. To this end, algorithms project the data to a lower-dimensional space while discarding variation in the data that is not informative, or by identifying a lower-dimensional subspace or manifold on or near which the data lives.

A manifold is a space that locally resembles Euclidean space. One-dimensional manifolds include lines and circles (but not screenshots of eight, due to the crossing point). The manifold hypothesis maintains that high-dimensional data often resides in a lower-dimensional space that, if identified, permits a faithful representation of the data in this subspace.

Dimensionality reduction thus compresses the data by finding a different, smaller set of variables that capture what matters most in the original features to minimize the loss of information. Compression helps counter the curse of dimensionality, economizes on memory, and permits the visualization of salient aspects of higher-dimensional data that is otherwise very difficult to explore.

Linear and non-linear algorithms

Dimensionality reduction algorithms differ in the constraints they impose on the new variables and how they aim to minimize the loss of information:

- **Linear algorithms** such as PCA and ICA constrain the new variables to be linear combinations of the original features; that is, hyperplanes in a lower-dimensional space. Whereas PCA requires the new features to be uncorrelated, ICA goes further and imposes statistical independence—the absence of both linear and non-linear relationships. The following screenshot illustrates how PCA projects three-dimensional features into a two-dimensional space:

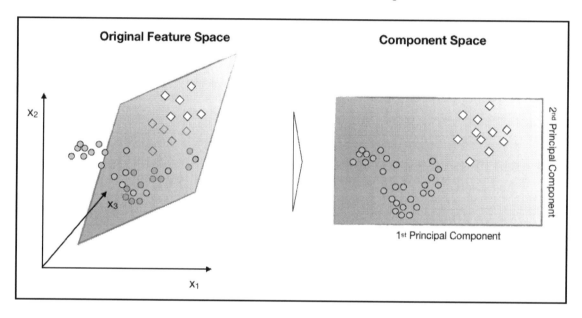

- Non-linear algorithms are not restricted to hyperplanes and can capture more complex structure in the data. However, given the infinite number of options, the algorithms still need to make assumptions to arrive at a solution. In this section, we show how **t-distributed Stochastic Neighbor Embedding (t-SNE)** and **Uniform Manifold Approximation and Projection (UMAP)** are very useful for visualizing higher-dimensional data. The following screenshot illustrates how manifold learning identifies a two-dimensional sub-space in the three-dimensional feature space (the `manifold_learning` notebook illustrates the use of additional algorithms, including local linear embedding):

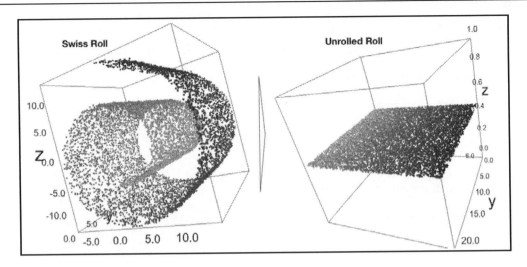

The curse of dimensionality

An increase in the number of dimensions of a dataset means there are more entries in the vector of features that represents each observation in the corresponding Euclidean space. We measure the distance in a vector space using Euclidean distance, also known as the **L2 norm**, which we applied to the vector of linear regression coefficients to train a regularized Ridge Regression model.

The Euclidean distance between two *n*-dimensional vectors with Cartesian coordinates $p = (p_1, p_2, ..., p_n)$ and $q = (q_1, q_2, ..., q_n)$ is computed using the familiar formula developed by Pythagoras:

$$d(p, q) = \sqrt{\sum_{i=1}^{n}(p_i - q_i)^2}$$

Hence, each new dimension adds a non-negative term to the sum, so that the distance increases with the number of dimensions for distinct vectors. In other words, as the number of features grows for a given number of observations, the feature space becomes increasingly sparse; that is, less dense or emptier. On the flip side, the lower data density requires more observations to keep the average distance between data points the same.

The following chart shows how many data points we need to maintain the average distance of 10 observations uniformly distributed on a line. It increases exponentially from 10^1 in a single dimension to 10^2 in two and 10^3 in three dimensions, as the data needs to expand by a factor of 10 each time we add a new dimension:

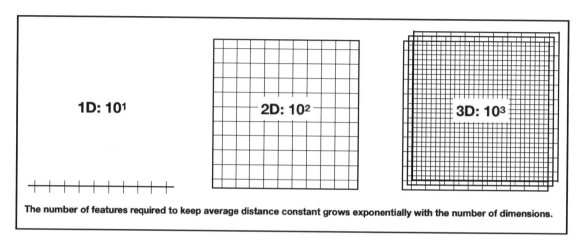

The number of features required to keep average distance constant grows exponentially with the number of dimensions.

The `curse_of_dimensionality` notebook in the GitHub repo folder for this section simulates how the average and minimum distances between data points increase as the number of dimensions grows:

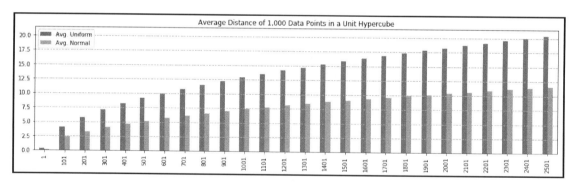

The simulation draws features in the range [0, 1] from uncorrelated uniform or correlated normal distributions, and gradually increases the number of features to 2,500. The average distance between data points increases to over 11 times the feature range for features drawn from the normal distribution, and to over 20 times in the (extreme) case of uncorrelated uniform distribution.

When the distance between observations grows, supervised machine learning becomes more difficult because predictions for new samples are less likely to be based on learning from similar training features. Put differently, the number of possible unique rows grows exponentially as the number of features increases, which makes it so much harder to efficiently sample the space.

Similarly, the complexity of the functions learned by flexible algorithms that make fewer assumptions about the actual relationship grows exponentially with the number of dimensions.

Flexible algorithms include the tree-based models we saw in `Chapter 10`, *Decision Trees and Random Forests*, and `Chapter 11`, *Gradient Boosting Machines*, and the deep neural networks that we will cover from `Chapter 17`, *Deep Learning* onward. The variance of these algorithms increases as they get more opportunity to overfit to noise in more dimensions, resulting in poor generalization performance.

In practice, features are correlated, often substantially so, or do not exhibit much variation. For these reasons, dimensionality reduction helps to compress the data without losing much of the signal, and combat the curse while also economizing on memory. In these cases, it complements the use of regularization to manage prediction error due to variance and model complexity.

The critical question that we take on in the following section then becomes: what are the best ways to find a lower-dimensional representation of the data that loses as little information as possible?

Linear dimensionality reduction

Linear dimensionality reduction algorithms compute linear combinations that translate, rotate, and rescale the original features to capture significant variation in the data, subject to constraints on the characteristics of the new features.

Principal Component Analysis (PCA), invented in 1901 by Karl Pearson, finds new features that reflect directions of maximal variance in the data while being mutually uncorrelated, or orthogonal.

Independent Component Analysis (ICA), in contrast, originated in signal processing in the 1980s, with the goal of separating different signals while imposing the stronger constraint of statistical independence.

This section introduces these two algorithms and then illustrates how to apply PCA to asset returns to learn risk factors from the data, and to build so-called eigen portfolios for systematic trading strategies.

Principal Component Analysis

PCA finds principal components as linear combinations of the existing features and uses these components to represent the original data. The number of components is a hyperparameter that determines the target dimensionality and needs to be equal to or smaller than the number of observations or columns, whichever is smaller.

PCA aims to capture most of the variance in the data, to make it easy to recover the original features and so that each component adds information. It reduces dimensionality by projecting the original data into the principal component space.

The PCA algorithm works by identifying a sequence of principal components, each of which aligns with the direction of maximum variance in the data after accounting for variation captured by previously-computed components. The sequential optimization also ensures that new components are not correlated with existing components so that the resulting set constitutes an orthogonal basis for a vector space.

This new basis corresponds to a rotated version of the original basis so that the new axis point in the direction of successively decreasing variance. The decline in the amount of variance of the original data explained by each principal component reflects the extent of correlation among the original features.

The number of components that capture, for example, 95% of the original variation relative to the total number of features provides an insight into the linearly-independent information in the original data.

Visualizing PCA in 2D

The following screenshot illustrates several aspects of PCA for a two-dimensional random dataset (see the `pca_key_ideas` notebook):

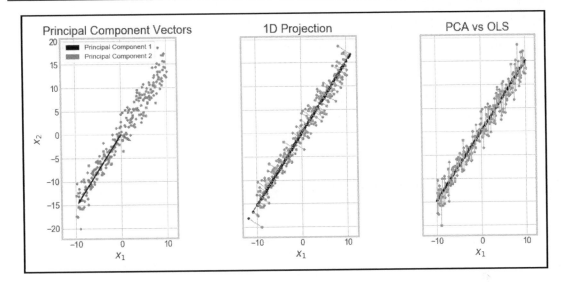

- The left panel shows how the first and second principal components align with the directions of maximum variance while being orthogonal.
- The central panel shows how the first principal component minimizes the reconstruction error, measured as the sum of the distances between the data points and the new axis.
- Finally, the right panel illustrates supervised OLS, which approximates the outcome variable (here we choose x_2) by a (one-dimensional) hyperplane computed from the (single) feature. The vertical lines highlight how OLS minimizes the distance along the outcome axis, in contrast with PCA, which minimizes the distances orthogonal to the hyperplane.

The assumptions made by PCA

PCA makes several assumptions that are important to keep in mind. These include the following:

- High variance implies a high signal-to-noise ratio
- The data is standardized so that the variance is comparable across features
- Linear transformations capture the relevant aspects of the data
- Higher-order statistics beyond the first and second moment do not matter, which implies that the data has a normal distribution

The emphasis on the first and second moments aligns with standard risk/return metrics, but the normality assumption may conflict with the characteristics of market data.

How the PCA algorithm works

The algorithm finds vectors to create a hyperplane of target dimensionality that minimizes the reconstruction error, measured as the sum of the squared distances of the data points to the plane. As illustrated above, this goal corresponds to finding a sequence of vectors that align with directions of maximum retained variance given the other components while ensuring all principal components are mutually orthogonal.

In practice, the algorithm solves the problem either by computing the eigenvectors of the covariance matrix or using the singular value decomposition.

We illustrate the computation using a randomly generated three-dimensional ellipse with 100 data points, shown in the left panel of the following screenshot, including the two-dimensional hyperplane defined by the first two principal components (see the the_math_behind_pca notebook for the following code samples):

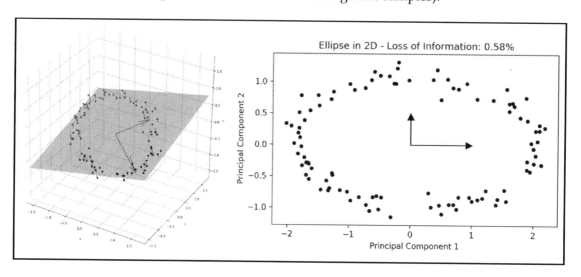

Three-dimensional ellipse and two-dimensional hyperplane

PCA based on the covariance matrix

We first compute the principal components using the square covariance matrix with the pairwise sample covariances for the features $x_i, x_j, i, j = 1, ..., n$ as entries in row i and column j:

$$cov_{i,j} = \frac{\sum_{k=1}^{N} (x_{ik} - \bar{x}_i)(x_{jk} - \bar{x}_j)}{N - 1}$$

For a square matrix M of n dimensions, we define the eigenvectors w_i and eigenvalues λ_i, $i=1, ..., n$ as follows:

$$Mw_i = \lambda_i w_i$$

Hence, we can represent the matrix M using eigenvectors and eigenvalues, where W is a matrix that contains the eigenvectors as column vectors, and L is a matrix that contains the λ_i as diagonal entries (and 0s otherwise). We define the eigendecomposition as follows:

$$M = WLW^{-1}$$

Using NumPy, we implement this as follows, where the pandas DataFrame contains the 100 data points of the ellipse:

```
# compute covariance matrix:
cov = np.cov(data, rowvar=False) # expects variables in rows by default
cov.shape
(3, 3)
```

Next, we calculate the eigenvectors and eigenvalues of the covariance matrix. The eigenvectors contain the principal components (where the sign is arbitrary):

```
eigen_values, eigen_vectors = eig(cov)
eigen_vectors
array([[ 0.71409739, -0.66929454, -0.20520656],
[-0.70000234, -0.68597301, -0.1985894 ],
[ 0.00785136, -0.28545725, 0.95835928]])
```

We can compare the result with the result obtained from sklearn, and find that they match in absolute terms:

```
pca = PCA()
pca.fit(data)
C = pca.components_.T # columns = principal components
C
array([[ 0.71409739, 0.66929454, 0.20520656],
[-0.70000234, 0.68597301, 0.1985894 ],
[ 0.00785136, 0.28545725, -0.95835928]])
np.allclose(np.abs(C), np.abs(eigen_vectors))
True
```

We can also verify the eigendecomposition, starting with the diagonal matrix L that contains the eigenvalues:

```
# eigenvalue matrix
ev = np.zeros((3, 3))
np.fill_diagonal(ev, eigen_values)
ev # diagonal matrix
array([[1.92923132, 0. , 0. ],
[0. , 0.55811089, 0. ],
[0. , 0. , 0.00581353]])
```

We find that the result does indeed hold:

```
decomposition = eigen_vectors.dot(ev).dot(inv(eigen_vectors))
np.allclose(cov, decomposition)
```

PCA using Singular Value Decomposition

Next, we'll look at the alternative computation using **Singular Value Decomposition (SVD)**. This algorithm is slower when the number of observations is greater than the number of features (the typical case), but yields better numerical stability, especially when some of the features are strongly correlated (often the reason to use PCA in the first place).

SVD generalizes the eigendecomposition that we just applied to the square and symmetric covariance matrix to the more general case of $m \times n$ rectangular matrices. It has the form shown at the center of the following diagram. The diagonal values of Σ are the singular values, and the transpose of V^* contains the principal components as column vectors:

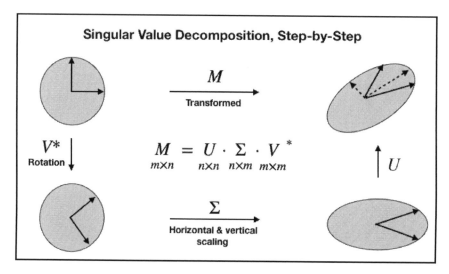

In this case, we need to make sure our data is centered with mean zero (the computation of the covariance preceding took care of this):

```
n_features = data.shape[1]
data_ = data - data.mean(axis=0
Using the centered data, we compute the singular value decomposition:
U, s, Vt = svd(data_)
U.shape, s.shape, Vt.shape
((100, 100), (3,), (3, 3))
We can convert the vector s that only contains the singular values into an
nxm matrix and show that the decomposition works:
S = np.zeros_like(data_)
S[:n_features, :n_features] = np.diag(s)
S.shape
(100, 3)
```

We find that the decomposition does indeed reproduce the standardized data:

```
np.allclose(data_, U.dot(S).dot(Vt))
True
```

Lastly, we confirm that the columns of the transpose of V^* contain the principal components:

```
np.allclose(np.abs(C), np.abs(Vt.T))
True
```

In the next section, we show how sklearn implements PCA.

PCA with sklearn

The `sklearn.decomposition.PCA` implementation follows the standard API based on the `fit()` and `transform()` methods, which compute the desired number of principal components and project the data into the component space, respectively. The convenience method `fit_transform()` accomplishes this in a single step.

PCA offers three different algorithms that can be specified using the `svd_solver` parameter:

- `Full` computes the exact SVD using the LAPACK solver provided by SciPy
- `Arpack` runs a truncated version suitable for computing less than the full number of components
- `Randomized` uses a sampling-based algorithm that is more efficient when the dataset has more than 500 observations and features, and the goal is to compute less than 80% of the components
- `Auto` uses randomized where most efficient, otherwise, it uses the full SVD

See references on GitHub for algorithmic implementation details.

Other key configuration parameters of the PCA object are as follows:

- `n_components`: These compute all principal components by passing `None` (the default), or limit the number to `int`. For `svd_solver=full`, there are two additional options: a float in the interval [0, 1] computes the number of components required to retain the corresponding share of the variance in the data, and the `mle` option estimates the number of dimensions using maximum likelihood.
- `whiten`: If `True`, it standardizes the component vectors to unit variance that, in some cases, can be useful for use in a predictive model (the default is `False`).

To compute the first two principal components of the three-dimensional ellipsis and project the data into the new space, use `fit_transform()` as follows:

```
pca = PCA(n_components=2)
projected_data = pca.fit_transform(data)
projected_data.shape
(100, 2)
```

The explained variance of the first two components is very close to 100%:

```
pca2.explained_variance_ratio_
array([0.77381099, 0.22385721])
```

The screenshot at the beginning of this section shows the projection of the data into the new two-dimensional space.

Independent Component Analysis

Independent Component Analysis (ICA) is another linear algorithm that identifies a new basis on which to represent the original data, but pursues a different objective to PCA.

ICA emerged in signal processing, and the problem it aims to solve is called **blind source separation**. It is typically framed as the cocktail party problem, in which a given number of guests are speaking at the same time so that a single microphone would record overlapping signals. ICA assumes there are as many different microphones as there are speakers, each placed at different locations so as to record a different mix of the signals. ICA then aims to recover the individual signals from the different recordings.

In other words, there are n original signals and an unknown square mixing matrix A that produces an n-dimensional set of m observations, so that:

$$\underset{n \times m}{X} = \underset{n \times n}{A} \; \underset{n \times m}{s}$$

The goal is to find the matrix $W=A^{-1}$ that untangles the mixed signals to recover the sources.

The ability to uniquely determine the matrix W hinges on the non-Gaussian distribution of the data. Otherwise, W could be rotated arbitrarily given the multivariate normal distribution's symmetry under rotation.

Furthermore, ICA assumes the mixed signal is the sum of its components and is unable to identify Gaussian components because their sum is also normally distributed.

ICA assumptions

ICA makes the following critical assumptions:

- The sources of the signals are statistically independent
- Linear transformations are sufficient to capture the relevant information
- The independent components do not have a normal distribution
- The mixing matrix A can be inverted

ICA also requires the data to be centered and whitened; that is, to be mutually uncorrelated with unit variance. Preprocessing the data using PCA as outlined above achieves the required transformations.

The ICA algorithm

FastICA, used by sklearn, is a fixed-point algorithm that uses higher-order statistics to recover the independent sources. In particular, it maximizes the distance to a normal distribution for each component as a proxy for independence.

An alternative algorithm called **InfoMax** minimizes the mutual information between components as a measure of statistical independence.

ICA with sklearn

The ICA implementation by sklearn uses the same interface as PCA, so there is little to add. Note that there is no measure of explained variance because ICA does not compute components successively. Instead, each component aims to capture independent aspects of the data.

PCA for algorithmic trading

PCA is useful for algorithmic trading in several respects. These include the data-driven derivation of risk factors by applying PCA to asset returns, and the construction of uncorrelated portfolios based on the principal components of the correlation matrix of asset returns.

Data-driven risk factors

In Chapter 7, *Linear Models*, we explored risk factor models used in quantitative finance to capture the main drivers of returns. These models explain differences in returns on assets based on their exposure to systematic risk factors and the rewards associated with these factors.

In particular, we explored the Fama-French approach, which specifies factors based on prior knowledge about the empirical behavior of average returns, treats these factors as observable, and then estimates risk model coefficients using linear regression. An alternative approach treats risk factors as latent variables and uses factor analytic techniques such as PCA to simultaneously estimate the factors and how they drive returns from historical returns.

In this section, we will review how this method derives factors in a purely statistical or data-driven way, with the advantage of not requiring ex-ante knowledge of the behavior of asset returns (see the pca and risk_factor notebook models for details).

We will use the Quandl stock price data and select the daily adjusted close prices of the 500 stocks with the largest market capitalization and data for the 2010-18 period. We then compute the daily returns as follows:

```
idx = pd.IndexSlice
with pd.HDFStore('../../data/assets.h5') as store:
stocks = store['us_equities/stocks'].marketcap.nlargest(500)
returns = (store['quandl/wiki/prices']
.loc[idx['2010': '2018', stocks.index], 'adj_close']
.unstack('ticker')
.pct_change())
```

We obtain 351 stocks and returns for over 2,000 trading days:

```
returns.info()
DatetimeIndex: 2072 entries, 2010-01-04 to 2018-03-27
Columns: 351 entries, A to ZTS
```

PCA is sensitive to outliers, so we winsorize the data at the 2.5% and 97.5% quantiles:

```
returns = returns.clip(lower=returns.quantile(q=.025),
upper=returns.quantile(q=.975),
axis=1)
```

PCA does not permit missing data, so we will remove stocks that do not have data for at least 95% of the time period, and in a second step, remove trading days that do not have observations on at least 95% of the remaining stocks:

```
returns = returns.dropna(thresh=int(returns.shape[0] * .95), axis=1)
returns = returns.dropna(thresh=int(returns.shape[1] * .95))
```

We are left with 314 equity return series covering a similar period:

```
returns.info()
DatetimeIndex: 2070 entries, 2010-01-05 to 2018-03-27
Columns: 314 entries, A to ZBH
```

We impute any remaining missing values using the average return for any given trading day:

```
daily_avg = returns.mean(1)
returns = returns.apply(lambda x: x.fillna(daily_avg))
```

Now we are ready to fit the principal components model to the asset returns using default parameters to compute all components using the full SVD algorithm:

```
pca = PCA()
pca.fit(returns)
PCA(copy=True, iterated_power='auto', n_components=None, random_state=None,
svd_solver='auto', tol=0.0, whiten=False)
```

We find that the most important factor explains around 40% of the daily return variation. The dominant factor is usually interpreted as the market, whereas the remaining factors can be interpreted as industry or style factors, in line with our discussion in Chapter 5, *Strategy Evaluation*, and Chapter 7, *Linear Models*, depending on the results of closer inspection (see the next example).

The plot on the right shows the cumulative explained variance, and indicates that around 10 factors explain 60% of the returns of this large cross-section of stocks:

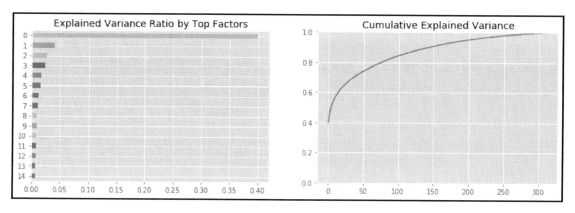

The notebook contains a simulation for a broader cross-section of stocks and the longer 2000-18 time period. It finds that, on average, the first three components explained 25%, 10%, and 5% of 500 randomly selected stocks.

The cumulative plot shows a typical elbow pattern that can help identify a suitable target dimensionality because it indicates that additional components add less explanatory value.

We can select the top two principal components to verify that they are indeed uncorrelated:

```
risk_factors = pd.DataFrame(pca.transform(returns)[:, :2],
columns=['Principal Component 1', 'Principal Component 2'],
index=returns.index)
risk_factors['Principal Component 1'].corr(risk_factors['Principal
Component 2'])
7.773256996252084e-15
```

Moreover, we can plot the time series to highlight how each factor captures different volatility patterns:

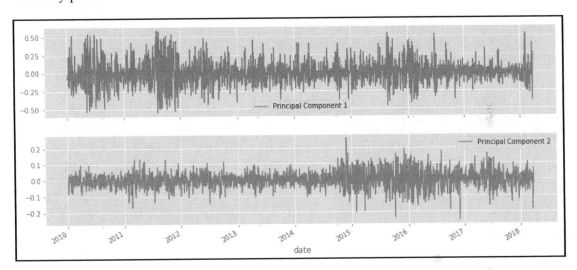

A risk factor model would employ a subset of the principal components as features to predict future returns, similar to our approach in `Chapter 7`, *Linear Models – Regression and Classification*.

Eigen portfolios

Another application of PCA involves the covariance matrix of the normalized returns. The principal components of the correlation matrix capture most of the covariation among assets in descending order and are mutually uncorrelated. Moreover, we can use standardized principal components as portfolio weights.

Let's use the 30 largest stocks with data for the 2010-2018 period to facilitate the exposition:

```
idx = pd.IndexSlice
with pd.HDFStore('../../data/assets.h5') as store:
stocks = store['us_equities/stocks'].marketcap.nlargest(30)
returns = (store['quandl/wiki/prices']
.loc[idx['2010': '2018', stocks.index], 'adj_close']
.unstack('ticker')
.pct_change())
```

We again winsorize and also normalize the returns:

```
normed_returns = scale(returns
        .clip(lower=returns.quantile(q=.025),
          upper=returns.quantile(q=.975),
          axis=1)
.apply(lambda x: x.sub(x.mean()).div(x.std()))))
```

After dropping assets and trading days as in the previous example, we are left with 23 assets and over 2,000 trading days. We estimate all principal components, and find that the two largest explain 55.9% and 15.5% of the covariation, respectively:

```
pca.fit(cov)
pd.Series(pca.explained_variance_ratio_).head()
0 55.91%
1 15.52%
2 5.36%
3 4.85%
4 3.32%
```

Next, we select and normalize the four largest components so that they sum to 1 and we can use them as weights for portfolios that we can compare to an equal-weighted portfolio formed from all stocks:

```
top4 = pd.DataFrame(pca.components_[:4], columns=cov.columns)
eigen_portfolios = top4.div(top4.sum(1), axis=0)
eigen_portfolios.index = [f'Portfolio {i}' for i in range(1, 5)]
```

The weights show distinct emphasis—for example, **Portfolio 3** puts large weights on Mastercard and Visa, the two payment processors in the sample, whereas **Portfolio 2** has more exposure to technology companies:

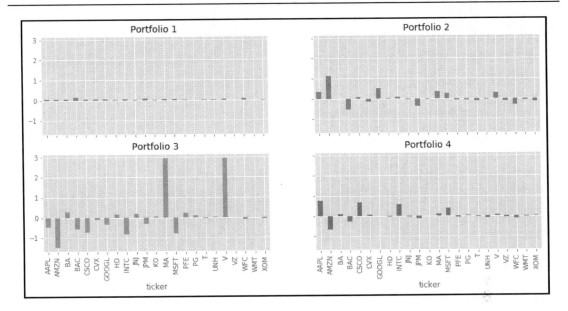

When comparing the performance of each portfolio over the sample period to **The Market** consisting of our small sample, we find that portfolio 1 performs very similarly, whereas the other portfolios capture different return patterns:

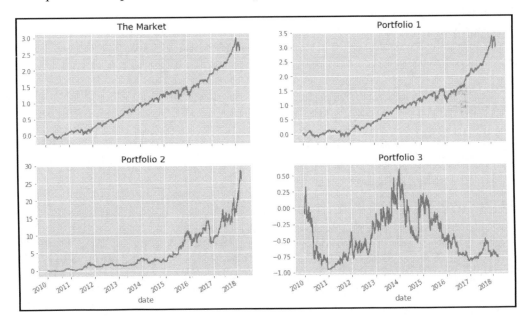

Comparing performances of each portfolio

Manifold learning

Linear dimensionality reduction projects the original data onto a lower-dimensional hyperplane that aligns with informative directions in the data. The focus on linear transformations simplifies the computation and echoes common financial metrics, such as PCA's goal to capture the maximum variance.

However, linear approaches will naturally ignore signal reflected in non-linear relationships in the data. Such relationships are very important in alternative datasets containing, for example, image or text data. Detecting such relationships during exploratory analysis can provide important clues about the data's potential signal content.

In contrast, the manifold hypothesis emphasizes that high-dimensional data often lies on or near a lower-dimensional non-linear manifold that is embedded in the higher dimensional space. The two-dimensional swiss roll displayed in the screenshot at the beginning of this section illustrates such a topological structure.

Manifold learning aims to find the manifold of intrinsic dimensionality and then represent the data in this subspace. A simplified example uses a road as one-dimensional manifolds in a three-dimensional space and identifies data points using house numbers as local coordinates.

Several techniques approximate a lower dimensional manifold. One example is **locally-linear embedding** (**LLE**), which was developed in 2000 by Sam Roweis and Lawrence Saul and used to unroll the swiss roll in the previous screenshot (see examples in the `manifold_learning_lle` notebook).

For each data point, LLE identifies a given number of nearest neighbors and computes weights that represent each point as a linear combination of its neighbors. It finds a lower-dimensional embedding by linearly projecting each neighborhood onto global internal coordinates on the lower-dimensional manifold, and can be thought of as a sequence of PCA applications.

Visualization requires the reduction to at least three dimensions, possibly below the intrinsic dimensionality, and poses the challenge of faithfully representing local and global structure. This challenge relates to the increasing distance associated with the curse of dimensionality. While the volume of a sphere expands exponentially with the number of dimensions, the space in lower dimensions available to represent high-dimensional data is much more limited.

For example, in 12 dimensions, there can be 13 equidistant points, but in two dimensions there can only be three that form a triangle with sides of equal length. Hence, accurately reflecting the distance of one point to its high-dimensional neighbors in lower dimensions risks distorting the relations among all other points. The result is the crowding problem: to maintain global distances, local points may need to be placed too closely together, and vice versa.

The following two sections cover techniques that have made progress in addressing the crowding problem for the visualization of complex datasets. We will use the fashion MNIST dataset, a more sophisticated alternative to the classic handwritten digit MNIST benchmark data used for computer vision. It contains 60,000 train and 10,000 test images of fashion objects in 10 classes (see following samples):

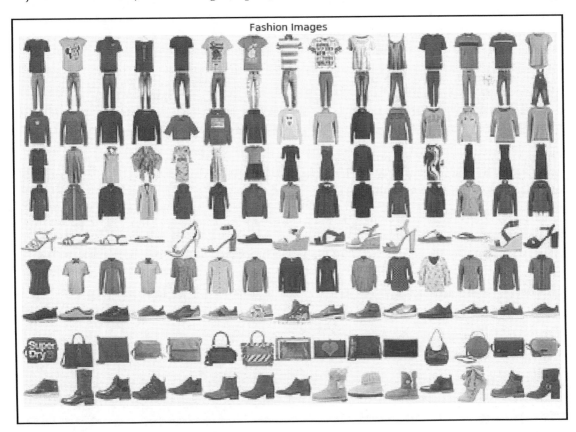

The goal of a manifold learning algorithm for this data is to detect whether the classes lie on distinct manifolds, to facilitate their recognition and differentiation.

t-SNE

The t-distributed stochastic neighbor embedding is an award-winning algorithm developed in 2010 by Laurens van der Maaten and Geoff Hinton to detect patterns in high-dimensional data. It takes a probabilistic, non-linear approach to locating data on several different but related low-dimensional manifolds.

The algorithm emphasizes keeping similar points together in low dimensions, as opposed to maintaining the distance between points that are apart in high dimensions, which results from algorithms such as PCA that minimize squared distances.

The algorithm proceeds by converting high-dimensional distances to (conditional) probabilities, where high probabilities imply low distance and reflect the likelihood of sampling two points based on similarity. It accomplishes this by positioning a normal distribution over each point and computing the density for a point and each neighbor, where the perplexity parameter controls the effective number of neighbors.

In a second step, it arranges points in low dimensions and uses similarly computed low-dimensional probabilities to match the high-dimensional distribution. It measures the difference between the distributions using the Kullback-Leibler divergence, which puts a high penalty on misplacing similar points in low dimensions.

The low-dimensional probabilities use a Student's t-distribution with one degree of freedom, as it has fatter tails that reduce the penalty of misplacing points that are more distant in high dimensions, to manage the crowding problem.

The upper panels of the following chart show how t-SNE is able to differentiate between the image classes. A higher perplexity value increases the number of neighbors used to compute local structure, and gradually results in more emphasis on global relationships:

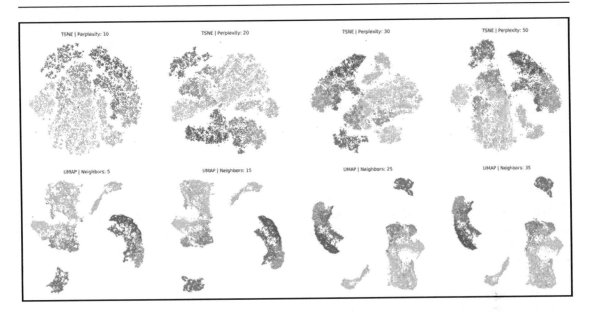

t-SNE is currently the state-of-the-art in high-dimensional data visualization. Weaknesses include the computational complexity that scales quadratically in the number n of points because it evaluates all pairwise distances, but a subsequent tree-based implementation has reduced the cost to $n \log n$.

t-SNE does not facilitate the projection of new data points into the low-dimensional space. The compressed output is not a very useful input for distance-based or density-based cluster algorithms, because t-SNE treats small and large distances differently.

UMAP

Uniform Manifold Approximation and Projection is a more recent algorithm for visualization and general dimensionality reduction. It assumes the data is uniformly distributed on a locally-connected manifold and looks for the closest low-dimensional equivalent using fuzzy topology. It uses a neighbors parameter that impacts the result similarly as perplexity above.

It is faster, and hence scales better to large datasets than t-SNE, and sometimes preserves global structure than better than t-SNE. It can also work with different distance functions, including, for example, cosine similarity, which is used to measure the distance between word count vectors.

The four charts in the bottom row of the previous figure illustrates how UMAP does indeed move the different clusters further apart, whereas t-SNE provides more granular insight into the local structure.

The notebook also contains interactive Plotly visualizations for each algorithm, which permit the exploration of the labels and identify which objects are placed close to each other.

Clustering

Both clustering and dimensionality reduction summarize the data. As just discussed in detail, dimensionality reduction compresses the data by representing it using new, fewer features that capture the most relevant information. Clustering algorithms, by contrast, assign existing observations to subgroups that consist of similar data points.

Clustering can serve to better understand the data through the lens of categories learned from continuous variables. It also permits automatically categorizing new objects according to the learned criteria. Examples of related applications include hierarchical taxonomies, medical diagnostics, and customer segmentation.

Alternatively, clusters can be used to represent groups as prototypes, using (for example) the midpoint of a cluster as the best representative of learned grouping. An example application includes image compression.

Clustering algorithms differ with respect to their strategies for identifying groupings:

- Combinatorial algorithms select the most coherent of different groupings of observations
- Probabilistic modeling estimates distributions that most likely generated the clusters
- Hierarchical clustering finds a sequence of nested clusters that optimizes coherence at any given stage

Algorithms also differ in their notion of what constitutes a useful collection of objects, which needs to match the data characteristics, domain, and the goal of the applications. Types of groupings include the following:

- Clearly separated groups of various shapes
- Prototype-based or center-based compact clusters
- Density-based clusters of arbitrary shape
- Connectivity-based or graph-based clusters

Important additional aspects of a clustering algorithm include the following:

- Whether it requires exclusive cluster membership
- Whether it makes hard (binary) or soft (probabilistic) assignment
- Whether it is complete and assigns all data points to clusters

The following sections introduce key algorithms, including k-Means, hierarchical, and density-based clustering, as well as Gaussian mixture models. The `clustering_algos` notebook compares the performance of these algorithms on different, labeled datasets to highlight their strengths and weaknesses. It uses mutual information (see `Chapter 6`, *The Machine Learning Process*) to measure the congruence of cluster assignments and labels.

k-Means clustering

k-Means is the most well-known clustering algorithm and was first proposed by Stuart Lloyd at Bell Labs in 1957.

The algorithm finds K centroids and assigns each data point to exactly one cluster with the goal of minimizing the within-cluster variance (called inertia). It typically uses Euclidean distance, but other metrics can also be used. k-Means assumes that clusters are spherical and of equal size, and ignores the covariance among features.

The problem is computationally difficult (np-hard) because there are K^N ways to partition the N observations into K clusters. The standard iterative algorithm delivers a local optimum for a given K and proceeds as follows:

1. Randomly define K cluster centers and assign points to nearest centroid.
2. Repeat as follows:
    - For each cluster, compute the centroid as the average of the features
    - Assign each observation to the closest centroid
3. Convergence: assignments (or within-cluster variation) don't change.

The `kmeans_implementation` notebook shows how to code the algorithm using Python, and visualizes the algorithm's iterative optimization. The following screenshot highlights how the resulting centroids partition the feature space into areas called **Voronoi** which delineate the clusters:

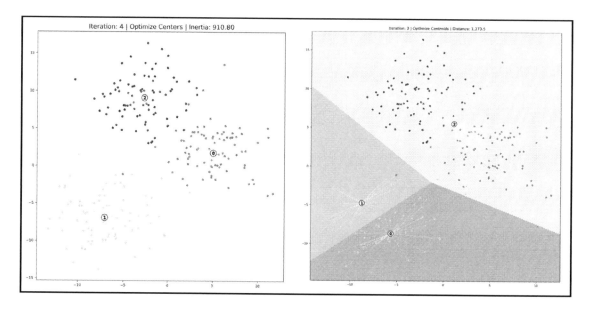

The result is optimal for the given initialization, but alternative starting positions will produce different results. Hence, we compute multiple clusterings from different initial values and select the solution that minimizes within-cluster variance.

k-Means requires continuous or one-hot encoded categorical variables. Distance metrics are typically sensitive to scale so that standardizing features is necessary to make sure they have equal weight.

The strengths of k-Means include its wide range of applicability, fast convergence, and linear scalability to large data while producing clusters of even size.

The weaknesses include:

- The need to tune the hyperparameter *k*
- The lack of a guarantee to find a global optimum
- Restrictive assumption that clusters are spheres and features are not correlated
- Sensitivity to outliers

Evaluating cluster quality

Cluster quality metrics help select among alternative clustering results.
The `kmeans_evaluation` notebook illustrates the following options:

1. The k-Means objective function suggests we compare the evolution of the inertia or within-cluster variance.
2. Initially, additional centroids decrease the inertia sharply because new clusters improve the overall fit.
3. Once an appropriate number of clusters has been found (assuming it exists), new centroids reduce the within-cluster variance by much less as they tend to split natural groupings.
4. Hence, when k-Means finds a good cluster representation of the data, the inertia tends to follow an elbow-shaped path similar to the explained variance ratio for PCA, as shown in the following screenshot (see notebook for implementation details):

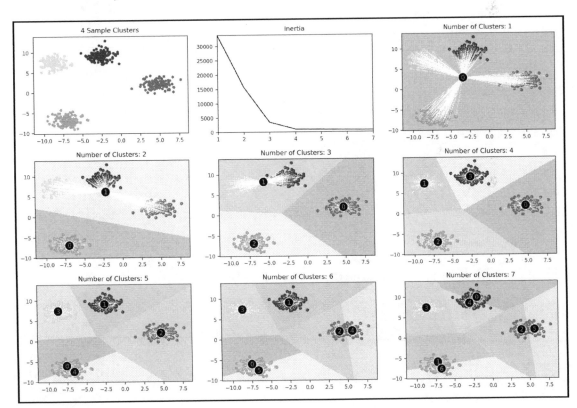

The silhouette coefficient provides a more detailed picture of cluster quality. It answers the question: how far are the points in the nearest cluster, relative to the points in the assigned cluster?

To this end, it compares the mean intra-cluster distance (a) to the mean distance of the nearest cluster (b) and computes the following score s:

$$s = \frac{b - a}{max(a, b)} \in [-1, 1]$$

The score can vary from between *-1* and *1*, but negative values are unlikely in practice because they imply that the majority of points are assigned to the wrong cluster. A useful visualization of the silhouette score compares the values for each data point to the global average because it highlights the coherence of each cluster relative to the global configuration. The rule of thumb is to avoid clusters with mean scores below the average for all samples.

The following screenshot shows an excerpt from the silhouette plot for three and four clusters, where the former highlights the poor fit of cluster *1* by sub-par contributions to the global silhouette score, whereas all of the four clusters have some values that exhibit above average scores:

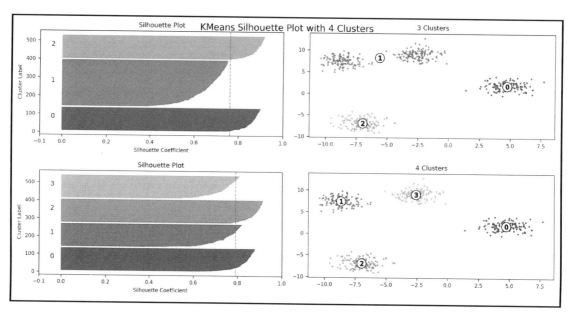

In sum, given the usually unsupervised nature, it is necessary to vary the hyperparameters of the cluster algorithms and evaluate the different results. It is also important to calibrate the scale of the features, in particular when some should be given a higher weight and should thus be measured on a larger scale.

Finally, to validate the robustness of the results, use subsets of data to identify whether particular patterns emerge consistently.

Hierarchical clustering

Hierarchical clustering avoids the need to specify a target number of clusters because it assumes that data can successively be merged into increasingly dissimilar clusters. It does not pursue a global objective but decides incrementally how to produce a sequence of nested clusters that range from a single cluster to clusters consisting of the individual data points.

There are two approaches:

1. **Agglomerative clustering** proceeds bottom-up, sequentially merging two of the remaining groups based on similarity
2. **Divisive clustering** works top-down and sequentially splits the remaining clusters to produce the most distinct subgroups

Both groups produce *N-1* hierarchical levels and facilitate the selection of a clustering at the level that best partitions data into homogenous groups. We will focus on the more common agglomerative clustering approach.

The agglomerative clustering algorithm departs from the individual data points and computes a similarity matrix containing all mutual distances. It then takes *N-1* steps until there are no more distinct clusters, and each time updates the similarity matrix to substitute elements that have been merged by the new cluster so that the matrix progressively shrinks.

While hierarchical clustering does not have hyperparameters like k-Means, the measure of dissimilarity between clusters (as opposed to individual data points) has an important impact on the clustering result. The options differ as follows:

- **Single-link**: the distance between nearest neighbors of two clusters
- **Complete link**: the maximum distance between respective cluster members
- **Group average**: the distance between averages for each group
- **Ward's method**: minimizes within-cluster variance

Visualization – dendrograms

Hierarchical clustering provides insight into degrees of similarity among observations as it continues to merge data. A significant change in the similarity metric from one merge to the next suggests a natural clustering existed prior to this point.

The dendrogram visualizes the successive merges as a binary tree, displaying the individual data points as leaves and the final merge as the root of the tree. It also shows how the similarity monotonically decreases from bottom to top. Hence, it is natural to select a clustering by cutting the dendrogram.

The following screenshot (see the `hierarchical_clustering` notebook for implementation details) illustrates the dendrogram for the classic Iris dataset with four classes and three features, using the four different distance metrics introduced precedingly:

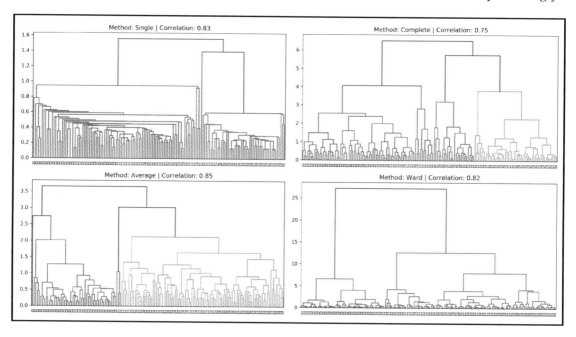

It evaluates the fit of the hierarchical clustering using the cophenetic correlation coefficient, which compares the pairwise distances among points and the cluster similarity metric at which a pairwise merge occurred. A coefficient of 1 implies that closer points always merge earlier.

Different linkage methods produce dendrograms of different appearance, so we cannot use this visualization to compare results across methods. In addition, Ward's method, which minimizes within-cluster variance, may not properly reflect the change in variance, but rather the total variance, which may be misleading. Instead, other quality metrics such as cophenetic correlation, or measures such as inertia (if aligned with the overall goal), may be more appropriate.

The strengths of clustering include:

- You do not need to specify the number of clusters
- It offers insight about potential clustering by means of an intuitive visualization
- It produces a hierarchy of clusters that can serve as taxonomy
- It can be combined with k-Means to reduce the number of items at the start of the agglomerative process

Weaknesses of hierarchical clustering include:

- The high cost in terms of computation and memory because of the numerous similarity matrix updates
- It does not achieve the global optimum because all merges are final
- The curse of dimensionality leads to difficulties with noisy, high-dimensional data

Density-based clustering

Density-based clustering algorithms assign cluster membership based on proximity to other cluster members. They pursue the goal of identifying dense regions of arbitrary shapes and sizes. They do not require the specification of a certain number of clusters but instead rely on parameters that define the size of a neighborhood and a density threshold (see the `density_based_clustering` notebook for relevant code samples).

DBSCAN

Density-based spatial clustering of applications with noise (DBSCAN) was developed in 1996, and received the *Test of Time* award at the 2014 KDD conference because of the attention it has received in both theory and practice.

It aims to identify core and non-core samples, where the former extend a cluster and the latter are part of a cluster but do not have sufficient nearby neighbors to further grow the cluster. Other samples are outliers and not assigned to any cluster.

It uses an `eps` parameter for the radius of the neighborhood and `min_samples` for the number of members required for core samples. It is deterministic and exclusive and has difficulties with clusters of different density and high-dimensional data. It can be challenging to tune the parameters to the requisite density, especially as it is often not constant.

Hierarchical DBSCAN

Hierarchical DBSCAN is a more recent development that assumes clusters are islands of potentially differing density, to overcome the DBSCAN challenges just mentioned. It also aims to identify the core and non-core samples. It uses the `min_cluster_ size` and `min_samples` parameters to select a neighborhood and extend a cluster. The algorithm iterates over multiple `eps` values and chooses the most stable clustering.

In addition to identifying clusters of varying density, it provides insight into the density and hierarchical structure of the data.

The following screenshots show how DBSCAN and HDBSCAN are able to identify very differently shaped clusters:

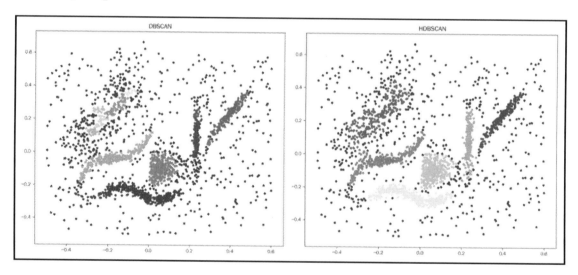

Gaussian mixture models

A **Gaussian mixture model (GMM)** is a generative model that assumes the data has been generated by a mix of various multivariate normal distributions. The algorithm aims to estimate the mean and covariance matrices of these distributions.

It generalizes the k-Means algorithm: it adds covariance among features so that clusters can be ellipsoids rather than spheres, while the centroids are represented by the means of each distribution. The GMM algorithm performs soft assignments because each point has the probability to be a member of any cluster.

The expectation-maximization algorithm

GMM uses the expectation-maximization algorithm to identify the components of the mixture of Gaussian distributions. The goal is to learn the probability distribution parameters from unlabeled data.

The algorithm proceeds iteratively as follows:

1. Initialization—Assume random centroids (for example, using k-Means)
2. Repeat the following steps until convergence (that is, changes in assignments drop below the threshold):
   - **Expectation step**: Soft assignment—compute probabilities for each point from each distribution
   - **Maximization step**: Adjust normal-distribution parameters to make data points most likely

The following screenshot shows the GMM cluster membership probabilities for the Iris dataset as contour lines:

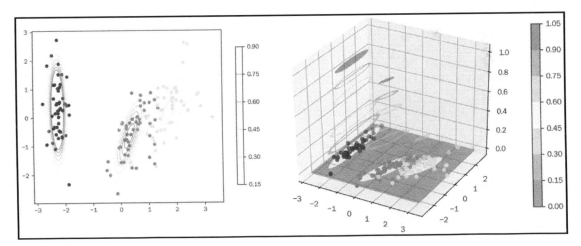

Hierarchical risk parity

The key idea of hierarchical risk parity is to use hierarchical clustering on the covariance matrix in order to be able to group assets with similar correlations together, and reduce the number of degrees of freedom by only considering similar assets as substitutes when constructing the portfolio (see notebook and Python files in the `hierarchical_risk_parity` subfolder for details).

The first step is to compute a distance matrix that represents proximity for correlated assets and meets distance metric requirements. The resulting matrix becomes an input to the SciPy hierarchical clustering function which computes the successive clusters using one of several available methods discussed so far:

```python
def get_distance_matrix(corr):
    """Compute distance matrix from correlation;
    0 <= d[i,j] <= 1"""
    return np.sqrt((1 - corr) / 2)
distance_matrix = get_distance_matrix(corr)
linkage_matrix = linkage(squareform(distance_matrix), 'single')
```

The `linkage_matrix` can be used as input to the `seaborn.clustermap` function to visualize the resulting hierarchical clustering. The dendrogram displayed by `seaborn` shows how individual assets and clusters of assets are merged based on their relative distances:

```python
clustergrid = sns.clustermap(distance_matrix,
method='single',
row_linkage=linkage_matrix,
col_linkage=linkage_matrix,
cmap=cmap, center=0)
sorted_idx = clustergrid.dendrogram_row.reordered_ind
sorted_tickers = corr.index[sorted_idx].tolist()
```

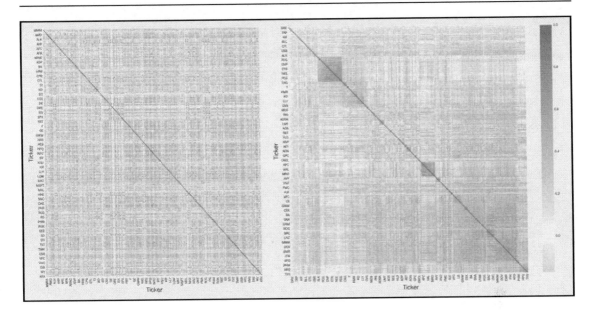

Heatmap

Compared to a `seaborn.heatmap` of the original correlation matrix, there is now significantly more structure in the sorted data (right panel).

Using the tickers sorted according to the hierarchy induced by the clustering algorithm, HRP now proceeds to compute a top-down inverse-variance allocation that successively adjusts weights depending on the variance of the subclusters further down the tree:

```
def get_cluster_var(cov, cluster_items):
    """Compute variance per cluster"""
    cov_ = cov.loc[cluster_items, cluster_items]  # matrix slice
    w_ = get_inverse_var_pf(cov_)
    return (w_ @ cov_ @ w_).item()
```

To this end, the algorithm uses bisectional search to allocate the variance of a cluster to its elements based on their relative riskiness:

```
def get_hrp_allocation(cov, tickers):
    """Compute top-down HRP weights"""

    weights = pd.Series(1, index=tickers)
    clusters = [tickers]  # initialize one cluster with all assets

    while len(clusters) > 0:
        # run bisectional search:
        clusters = [c[start:stop] for c in clusters
```

```
                    for start, stop in ((0, int(len(c) / 2)),
                                         (int(len(c) / 2), len(c)))
                    if len(c) > 1]
        for i in range(0, len(clusters), 2):  # parse in pairs
            cluster0 = clusters[i]
            cluster1 = clusters[i + 1]

            cluster0_var = get_cluster_var(cov, cluster0)
            cluster1_var = get_cluster_var(cov, cluster1)

            weight_scaler = 1 - cluster0_var / (cluster0_var +
    cluster1_var)
            weights[cluster0] *= weight_scaler
            weights[cluster1] *= 1 - weight_scaler
        return weights
```

The resulting portfolio allocation produces weights that sum to 1 and reflect the structure present in the correlation matrix (see notebook for details).

Summary

In this chapter, we explored unsupervised learning methods that allow us to extract valuable signal from our data, without relying on the help of outcome information provided by labels.

We saw how we can use linear dimensionality reduction methods, such as PCA and ICA, to extract uncorrelated or independent components from the data that can serve as risk factors or portfolio weights. We also covered advanced non-linear manifold learning techniques that produce state-of-the-art visualizations of complex alternative datasets.

In the second part, we covered several clustering methods that produce data-driven groupings under various assumptions. These groupings can be useful, for example, to construct portfolios that apply risk-parity principles to assets that have been clustered hierarchically.

In the next three chapters, we will learn about various ML techniques for a key source of alternative data, namely, natural language processing for text documents.

13
Working with Text Data

This is the first of three chapters dedicated to extracting signals for algorithmic trading strategies from text data using **natural language processing (NLP)** and **machine learning (ML)**.

Text data is very rich in content, yet unstructured in format, and hence requires more preprocessing so that an ML algorithm can extract the potential signal. The key challenge lies in converting text into a numerical format for use by an algorithm, while simultaneously expressing the semantics or meaning of the content. We will cover several techniques that capture nuances of language that are readily understandable to humans so that they can become an input for ML algorithms.

In this chapter, we introduce fundamental feature extraction techniques that focus on individual semantic units; that is, words or short groups of words called **tokens**. We will show how to represent documents as vectors of token counts by creating a document-term matrix that, in turn, serves as input for text classification and sentiment analysis. We will also introduce the Naive Bayes algorithm, which is popular for this purpose.

In the following two chapters, we build on these techniques and use ML algorithms such as topic modeling and word-vector embedding to capture information contained in a broader context.

In particular, in this chapter, we will cover the following:

- What the fundamental NLP workflow looks like
- How to build a multilingual feature extraction pipeline using `spaCy` and `TextBlob`
- How to perform NLP tasks such as **part-of-speech (POS)** tagging or named entity recognition
- How to convert tokens to numbers using the document-term matrix
- How to classify text using the Naive Bayes model
- How to perform sentiment analysis

The code samples for the following sections are in the GitHub repository for this chapter, and references are listed in the main README file.

How to extract features from text data

Text data can be extremely valuable given how much information humans communicate and store using natural language—the diverse set of data sources relevant to investment range from formal documents such as company statements, contracts, and patents, to news, opinion, and analyst research, and even to commentary and various types of social media posts and messages.

Numerous and diverse text data samples are available online to explore the use of NLP algorithms, many of which are listed among the references for this chapter.

To guide our journey through the techniques and Python libraries that most effectively support the realization of this goal, we will highlight NLP challenges, introduce critical elements of the NLP workflow, and illustrate applications of ML from text data to algorithmic trading.

Challenges of NLP

The conversion of unstructured text into a machine-readable format requires careful preprocessing to preserve valuable semantic aspects of the data. How humans derive meaning from, and comprehend the content of language, is not fully understood and improving language understanding by machines remains an area of very active research.

NLP is challenging because the effective use of text data for ML requires an understanding of the inner workings of language as well as knowledge about the world to which it refers. Key challenges include the following:

- Ambiguity due to polysemy; that is, a word or phrase can have different meanings depending on context (local high-school dropouts cut in half could be taken a couple of ways, for instance).
- Non-standard and evolving use of language, especially in social media.

- The use of idioms, such as throw in the towel.
- Tricky entity names, Where is A Bug's Life playing?
- Knowledge of the world—Mary and Sue are sisters versus Mary and Sue are mothers.

The NLP workflow

A key goal in using ML from text data for algorithmic trading is to extract signals from documents. A document is an individual sample from a relevant text data source, such as a company report, a headline or news article, or a tweet. A corpus, in turn, is a collection of documents (plural: *corpora*).

The following diagram lays out the key steps to convert documents into a dataset that can be used to train a supervised ML algorithm capable of making actionable predictions:

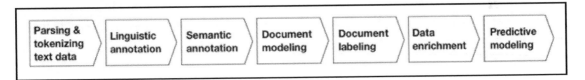

Fundamental techniques extract text features semantic units called **tokens**, and use linguistic rules and dictionaries to enrich these tokens with linguistic and semantic annotations. The **bag-of-words (BoW)** model uses token frequency to model documents as token vectors, which leads to the document-term matrix that is frequently used for text classification.

Advanced approaches use ML to refine features extracted by these fundamental techniques and produce more informative document models. These include topic models that reflect the joint usage of tokens across documents and word-vector models that capture the context of token usage.

We will review key decisions made at each step and related trade-offs in more detail before illustrating their implementation using the spaCy library in the next section. The following table summarizes the key tasks of an NLP pipeline:

Feature	Description
Tokenization	Segments text into words, punctuation marks, and so on.
POS tagging	Assigns word types to tokens, such as a verb or noun.
Dependency parsing	Labels syntactic token dependencies, such as *subject <=> object*.

Stemming and lemmatization	Assigns the base forms of words: *was => be, rats => rat.*
Sentence boundary detection	Finds and segments individual sentences.
Named entity recognition	Labels real-world objects, such as people, companies, and locations.
Similarity	Evaluates the similarity of words, text spans, and documents.

Parsing and tokenizing text data

A token is an instance of a characters that appears in a given document and should be considered a semantic unit for further processing. The vocabulary is a set of tokens contained in a corpus deemed relevant for further processing. A key trade-off in the following decisions is the accurate reflection of the text source at the expense of a larger vocabulary that may translate into more features and higher model complexity.

Basic choices in this regard concern the treatment of punctuation and capitalization, the use of spelling correction, and whether to exclude very frequent so-called **stop words** (such as *and* or *the*) as meaningless noise.

An additional decision is about the inclusion of groups of *n* individual tokens called **n-grams** as semantic units (an individual token is also called a **unigram**). An example of a 2-gram (or bi-gram) is New York, whereas New York City is a 3-gram (or tri-gram).

The goal is to create tokens that more accurately reflect the document's meaning. The decision can rely on dictionaries or a comparison of the relative frequencies of the individual and joint usage. Including n-grams will increase the number of features because the number of unique n-grams tends to be much higher than the number of unique unigrams and will likely add noise unless filtered for significance by frequency.

Linguistic annotation

Linguistic annotations include the application of **syntactic and grammatical rules** to identify the boundary of a sentence despite ambiguous punctuation, and a token's role in a sentence for POS tagging and dependency parsing. It also permits the identification of common root forms for stemming and lemmatization to group related words:

- **POS annotations:** It helps disambiguate tokens based on their function (this may be necessary when a verb and noun have the same form), which increases the vocabulary but may result in better accuracy.

- **Dependency parsing**: It identifies hierarchical relationships among tokens, is commonly used for translation, and is important for interactive applications that require more advanced language understanding, such as chatbots.
- **Stemming**: It uses simple rules to remove common endings, such as *s, ly, ing,* and *ed,* from a token and reduce it to its stem or root form.
- **Lemmatization**: It uses more sophisticated rules to derive the canonical root (lemma) of a word. It can detect irregular roots, such as better and best, and more effectively condenses vocabulary, but is slower than stemming. Both approaches simplify vocabulary at the expense of semantic nuances.

Semantic annotation

Named entity recognition (**NER**) aims to identify tokens that represent objects of interest, such as people, countries, or companies. It can be further developed into a **knowledge graph** that captures semantic and hierarchical relationships among such entities. It is a critical ingredient for applications that, for example, aim to predict the impact of news events or sentiment.

Labeling

Many NLP applications learn to predict outcomes from meaningful information extracted from text. Supervised learning requires labels to teach the algorithm the true input-output relationship. With text data, establishing this relationship may be challenging and may require explicit data modeling and collection.

Data modeling decisions include how to quantify sentiments implicit in a text document like an email, a transcribed interview, or a tweet, or which aspects of a research document or news report to assign to a specific outcome.

Use cases

The use of ML with text data for algorithmic trading relies on the extraction of meaningful information in the form of features that directly or indirectly predict future price movements. Applications range from the exploitation of the short-term market impact of news to the long-term fundamental analysis of the drivers of asset valuation. Examples include the following:

- The evaluation of product review sentiment to assess a company's competitive position or industry trends

- The detection of anomalies in credit contracts to predict the probability or impact of a default
- The prediction of news impact in terms of direction, magnitude, and affected entities

JP Morgan, for instance, developed a predictive model based on 250,000 analyst reports that outperformed several benchmark indices and produced uncorrelated signals relative to sentiment factors formed from consensus EPS and recommendation changes.

From text to tokens – the NLP pipeline

In this section, we will demonstrate how to construct an NLP pipeline using the open source Python library, spaCy. The textacy library builds on spaCy and provides easy access to spaCy attributes and additional functionality.

Refer to the nlp_pipeline_with_spaCy notebook for the following code samples, installation instructions, and additional details.

NLP pipeline with spaCy and textacy

spaCy is a widely used Python library with a comprehensive feature set for fast text processing in multiple languages. The usage of tokenization and annotation engines requires the installation of language models. The features we will use in this chapter only require small models; larger models also include word vectors that we will cover in Chapter 15, *Word Embeddings*.

Once installed and linked, we can instantiate a spaCy language model and then call it on a document. As a result, spaCy produces a doc object that tokenizes the text and processes it according to configurable pipeline components that, by default, consist of a tagger, a parser, and a named-entity recognizer:

```
nlp = spacy.load('en')
nlp.pipe_names
['tagger', 'parser', 'ner']
```

Let's illustrate the pipeline using a simple sentence:

```
sample_text = 'Apple is looking at buying U.K. startup for $1 billion'
doc = nlp(sample_text)
```

Parsing, tokenizing, and annotating a sentence

Parsed document content is iterable, and each element has numerous attributes produced by the processing pipeline. The following sample illustrates how to access the following attributes:

- `.text`: Original word text
- `.lemma_`: Word root
- `.pos_`: Basic POS tag
- `.tag_`: Detailed POS tag
- `.dep_`: Syntactic relationship or dependency between tokens
- `.shape_`: The shape of the word regarding capitalization, punctuation, or digits
- `.is alpha`: Check whether the token is alphanumeric
- `.is stop`: Check whether the token is on a list of common words for the given language

We iterate over each token and assign its attributes to a `pd.DataFrame`:

```
pd.DataFrame([[t.text, t.lemma_, t.pos_, t.tag_, t.dep_, t.shape_,
t.is_alpha, t.is_stop] for t in doc],
            columns=['text', 'lemma', 'pos', 'tag', 'dep', 'shape',
'is_alpha', 'is_stop'])
```

Which produces the following output:

text	lemma	pos	tag	dep	shape	is_alpha	is_stop
Apple	apple	PROPN	NNP	nsubj	Xxxxx	TRUE	FALSE
is	be	VERB	VBZ	aux	xx	TRUE	TRUE
looking	look	VERB	VBG	ROOT	xxxx	TRUE	FALSE
at	at	ADP	IN	prep	xx	TRUE	TRUE
buying	buy	VERB	VBG	pcomp	xxxx	TRUE	FALSE
U.K.	u.k.	PROPN	NNP	compound	X.X.	FALSE	FALSE
startup	startup	NOUN	NN	dobj	xxxx	TRUE	FALSE
for	for	ADP	IN	prep	xxx	TRUE	TRUE
$	$	SYM	$	quantmod	$	FALSE	FALSE
1	1	NUM	CD	compound	d	FALSE	FALSE
billion	billion	NUM	CD	pobj	xxxx	TRUE	FALSE

We can visualize syntactic dependency in a browser or notebook using the following:

```
displacy.render(doc, style='dep', options=options, jupyter=True)
```

The result is a dependency tree:

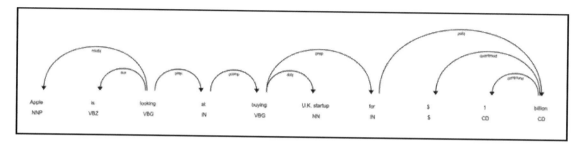

Dependency tree

We can get additional insights into the meaning of attributes using `spacy.explain()`, as here:

```
spacy.explain("VBZ")
verb, 3rd person singular present
```

Batch-processing documents

We will now read a larger set of 2,225 BBC News articles (see GitHub for data source details) that belong to five categories and are stored in individual text files. We need to do the following:

1. Call the `.glob()` method of pathlib's `Path` object.
2. Iterate over the resulting list of paths.
3. Read all lines of the news article excluding the heading in the first line.
4. Append the cleaned result to a list:

```
files = Path('..', 'data', 'bbc').glob('**/*.txt')
bbc_articles = []
for i, file in enumerate(files):
    _, _, _, topic, file_name = file.parts
    with file.open(encoding='latin1') as f:
        lines = f.readlines()
        body = ' '.join([l.strip() for l in lines[1:]]).strip()
        bbc_articles.append(body)
len(bbc_articles)
2225
```

Sentence boundary detection

We will illustrate sentence detection by calling the NLP object on the first of the articles:

```
doc = nlp(bbc_articles[0])
type(doc)
spacy.tokens.doc.Doc
```

spaCy computes sentence boundaries from the syntactic parse tree so that punctuation and capitalization play an important but not decisive role. As a result, boundaries will coincide with clause boundaries, even for poorly punctuated text.

We can access parsed sentences using the `.sents` attribute:

```
sentences = [s for s in doc.sents]
sentences[:3]
[Voting is under way for the annual Bloggies which recognize the best web
blogs - online spaces where people publish their thoughts - of the year. ,
Nominations were announced on Sunday, but traffic to the official site was
so heavy that the website was temporarily closed because of too many
visitors.,
Weblogs have been nominated in 30 categories, from the top regional blog,
to the best-kept-secret blog.]
```

Named entity recognition

spaCy enables named entity recognition using the `.ent_type_` attribute:

```
for t in sentences[0]:
    if t.ent_type_:
        print('{} | {} | {}'.format(t.text, t.ent_type_,
spacy.explain(t.ent_type_)))
annual | DATE | Absolute or relative dates or periods
the | DATE | Absolute or relative dates or periods
year | DATE | Absolute or relative dates or periods
```

textacy facilitates access to the named entities that appear in the first article:

```
from textacy.extract import named_entities
entities = [e.text for e in named_entities(doc)]
pd.Series(entities).value_counts()
year                          4
US                            2
South-East Asia Earthquake    2
annual                        2
Tsunami Blog                  2
```

N-grams

N-grams combine *N* consecutive tokens. N-grams can be useful for the BoW model because, depending on the textual context, treating something such as data scientist as a single token may be more meaningful than treating it as two distinct tokens: data and scientist.

`textacy` makes it easy to view the `ngrams` of a given length *n* occurring with at least `min_freq` times:

```
from textacy.extract import ngrams
pd.Series([n.text for n in ngrams(doc, n=2, min_freq=2)]).value_counts()
East Asia          2
Asia Earthquake    2
Tsunami Blog       2
annual Bloggies    2
```

spaCy's streaming API

To pass a larger number of documents through the processing pipeline, we can use `spaCy`'s streaming API as follows:

```
iter_texts = (bbc_articles[i] for i in range(len(bbc_articles)))
for i, doc in enumerate(nlp.pipe(iter_texts, batch_size=50, n_threads=8)):
    assert doc.is_parsed
```

Multi-language NLP

`spaCy` includes trained language models for English, German, Spanish, Portuguese, French, Italian, and Dutch, as well as a multi-language model for NER. Cross-language usage is straightforward since the API does not change.

We will illustrate the Spanish language model using a parallel corpus of TED Talk subtitles (see the GitHub repo for data source references). For this purpose, we instantiate both language models:

```
model = {}
for language in ['en', 'es']:
    model[language] = spacy.load(language)
```

We then read small corresponding text samples in each model:

```
text = {}
path = Path('../data/TED')
for language in ['en', 'es']:
    file_name = path / 'TED2013_sample.{}'.format(language)
    text[language] = file_name.read_text()
```

Sentence boundary detection uses the same logic but finds a different breakdown:

```
parsed, sentences = {}, {}
for language in ['en', 'es']:
    parsed[language] = model[language](text[language])
    sentences[language] = list(parsed[language].sents)
print('Sentences:', language, len(sentences[language]))
Sentences: en 19
Sentences: es 22
```

POS tagging also works in the same way:

```
pos = {}
for language in ['en', 'es']:
    pos[language] = pd.DataFrame([[t.text, t.pos_, spacy.explain(t.pos_)]
    for t in sentences[language][0]],
        columns=['Token', 'POS Tag', 'Meaning'])
pd.concat([pos['en'], pos['es']], axis=1).head()
```

The result is the side-by-side token annotations for the English and Spanish documents:

Token	POS Tag	Meaning	Token	POS Tag	Meaning
There	ADV	adverb	Existe	VERB	verb
s	VERB	verb	una	DET	determiner
a	DET	determiner	estrecha	ADJ	adjective
tight	ADJ	adjective	y	CONJ	conjunction
and	CCONJ	coordinating conjunction	sorprendente	ADJ	adjective

The next section illustrates how to use parsed and annotated tokens to build a document-term matrix that can be used for text classification.

NLP with TextBlob

`TextBlob` is a Python library that provides a simple API for common NLP tasks and builds on the **Natural Language Toolkit (NLTK)** and the Pattern web mining libraries. `TextBlob` facilitates POS tagging, noun phrase extraction, sentiment analysis, classification, translation, and more.

To illustrate the use of `TextBlob`, we sample a BBC sports article with the headline *Robinson ready for difficult task*. Similarly to `spaCy` and other libraries, the first step is to pass the document through a pipeline represented by the `TextBlob` object to assign annotations required for various tasks (see the `nlp_with_textblob` notebook for this section):

```
from textblob import TextBlob
article = docs.sample(1).squeeze()
parsed_body = TextBlob(article.body)
```

Stemming

To perform stemming, we instantiate `SnowballStemmer` from the `nltk` library, call its `.stem()` method on each token and display modified tokens:

```
from nltk.stem.snowball import SnowballStemmer
stemmer = SnowballStemmer('english')
[(word, stemmer.stem(word)) for i, word in enumerate(parsed_body.words)
    if word.lower() != stemmer.stem(parsed_body.words[i])]
[('Andy', 'andi'),
('faces', 'face'),
('tenure', 'tenur'),
('tries', 'tri'),
('winning', 'win'),
```

Sentiment polarity and subjectivity

`TextBlob` provides polarity and subjectivity estimates for parsed documents using dictionaries provided by the Pattern library. These dictionaries map adjectives frequently found in product reviews to sentiment polarity scores, ranging from -1 to +1 (negative ↔ positive) and a similar subjectivity score (objective ↔ subjective).

The `.sentiment` attribute provides the average for each over the relevant tokens, whereas the `.sentiment_assessments` attribute lists the underlying values for each token (see notebook):

```
parsed_body.sentiment
Sentiment(polarity=0.088031914893617, subjectivity=0.46456433637284694)
```

From tokens to numbers – the document-term matrix

In this section, we first introduce how the BoW model converts text data into a numeric vector space representation that permits the comparison of documents using their distance. We then proceed to illustrate how to create a document-term matrix using the sklearn library.

The BoW model

The BoW model represents a document based on the frequency of the terms or tokens it contains. Each document becomes a vector with one entry for each token in the vocabulary that reflects the token's relevance to the document.

The document-term matrix is straightforward to compute given the vocabulary. However, it is also a crude simplification because it abstracts from word order and grammatical relationships. Nonetheless, it often achieves good results in text classification quickly and, thus, is a very useful starting point.

The following diagram (the one on the right) illustrates how this document model converts text data into a matrix with numerical entries, where each row corresponds to a document and each column to a token in the vocabulary. The resulting matrix is usually both very high-dimensional and sparse; that is, one that contains many zero entries because most documents only contain a small fraction of the overall vocabulary:

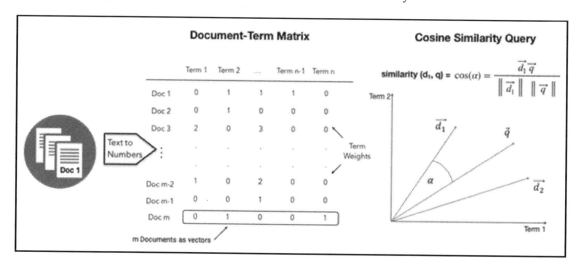

Resultant matrix

There are several ways to weigh a token's vector entry to capture its relevance to the document. We will illustrate how to use sklearn to use binary flags, which indicate presence or absence, counts, and weighted counts that account for differences in term frequencies across all documents; that is, in the corpus.

Measuring the similarity of documents

The representation of documents as word vectors assigns to each document a location in the vector space created by the vocabulary. Interpreting vector entries as Cartesian coordinates in this space, we can use the angle between two vectors to measure their similarity because vectors that point in the same direction contain the same terms with the same frequency weights.

The preceding diagram (the one on the right) illustrates—simplified in two dimensions—the calculation of the distance between a document represented by a vector d_1 and a query vector (either a set of search terms or another document) represented by the vector q.

Cosine similarity equals the cosine of the angle between the two vectors. It translates the size of the angle into a number in the range [0, 1] since all vector entries are non-negative token weights. A value of 1 implies that both documents are identical concerning their token weighs, whereas a value of 0 implies that two documents only contain distinct tokens.

As shown in the diagram, the cosine of the angle is equal to the dot product of the vectors; that is, the sum product of their coordinates, divided by the product of the lengths, measured by the Euclidean norms of each vector.

Document-term matrix with sklearn

The scikit-learn preprocessing module offers two tools to create a document-term matrix. CountVectorizer uses binary or absolute counts to measure the **term frequency** $tf(d, t)$ for each document d and token t.

TfidFVectorizer, in contrast, weighs the (absolute) term frequency by the **inverse document frequency (idf)**. As a result, a term that appears in more documents will receive a lower weight than a token with the same frequency for a given document but lower frequency across all documents. More specifically, using the default settings, tf-$idf(d, t)$ entries for the document-term matrix are computed as tf-$idf(d, t) = tf(d, t) \times idf(t)$:

$$\mathrm{idf}(t) = \log \frac{1 + n_d}{1 + \mathrm{df}(d, t)} + 1$$

Here n_d is the number of documents and $df(d, t)$ the document frequency of term t. The resulting tf-idf vectors for each document are normalized with respect to their absolute or squared totals (see the sklearn documentation for details). The tf-idf measure was originally used in information retrieval to rank search engine results and has subsequently proven useful for text classification or clustering.

Both tools use the same interface and perform tokenization and further optional preprocessing of a list of documents before vectorizing the text by generating token counts to populate the document-term matrix.

Key parameters that affect the size of the vocabulary include the following:

- `stop_words`: Use a built-in or provide a list of (frequent) words to exclude
- `ngram_range`: Include n-grams in a range for *n* defined by a tuple of (n_{min}, n_{max})
- `lowercase`: Convert characters accordingly (default is `True`)
- `min_df` / `max_df`: Ignore words that appear in less / more (`int`) or a smaller/larger share of documents (if `float` [0.0,1.0])
- `max_features`: Limit the number of tokens in a vocabulary accordingly
- `binary`: Set non-zero counts to 1 `True`

See the `document_term_matrix` notebook for the following code samples and additional details. We are again using the 2,225 BBC News articles for illustration.

Using CountVectorizer

The notebook contains an interactive visualization that explores the impact of the `min_df` and `max_df` settings on the size of the vocabulary. We read the articles into a DataFrame, set the `CountVectorizer` to produce binary flags and use all tokens, and call its `.fit_transform()` method to produce a document-term matrix:

```
binary_vectorizer = CountVectorizer(max_df=1.0,
                                    min_df=1,
                                    binary=True)

binary_dtm = binary_vectorizer.fit_transform(docs.body)
<2225x29275 sparse matrix of type '<class 'numpy.int64'>'
    with 445870 stored elements in Compressed Sparse Row format>
```

The output is a `scipy.sparse` matrix in row format that efficiently stores of the small share (<0.7%) of `445870` non-zero entries in the `2225` (document) rows and `29275` (token) columns.

Visualizing vocabulary distribution

The visualization shows that requiring tokens to appear in at least 1% and fewer than 50% of documents restricts the vocabulary to around 10% of the almost 30,000 tokens.

This leaves a mode of slightly over 100 unique tokens per document (left panel), and the right panel shows the document frequency histogram for the remaining tokens:

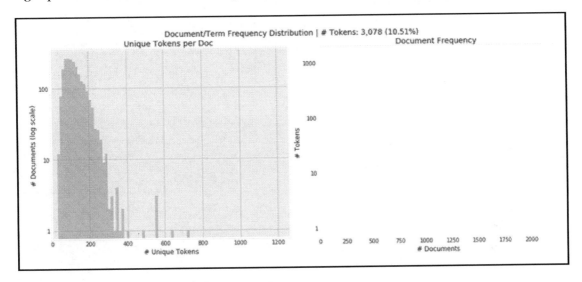

Documents/Term frequency distribution

Finding the most similar documents

The `CountVectorizer` result lets us find the most similar documents using the `pdist()` function for pairwise distances provided by the `scipy.spatial.distance` module. It returns a condensed distance matrix with entries corresponding to the upper triangle of a square matrix. We use `np.triu_indices()` to translate the index that minimizes the distance to the row and column indices that in turn correspond to the closest token vectors:

```
m = binary_dtm.todense() # pdist does not accept sparse format
pairwise_distances = pdist(m, metric='cosine')
closest = np.argmin(pairwise_distances) # index that minimizes distance
rows, cols = np.triu_indices(n_docs) # get row-col indices
rows[closest], cols[closest]
(11, 75)
```

Articles number 11 and 75 are closest by cosine similarity because they share 58 tokens (see notebook):

Topic	tech	tech
Heading	Software watching while you work	BT program to beat dialer scams
Body	Software that can not only monitor every keystroke and action performed at a PC but can also be used as legally binding evidence of wrong-doing has been unveiled. Worries about cyber-crime and sabotage have prompted many employers to consider monitoring employees.	BT is introducing two initiatives to help beat rogue dialer scams, which can cost dial-up net users thousands. From May, dial-up net users will be able to download free software to stop computers using numbers not on a user's pre-approved list.

Both `CountVectorizer` and `TfidFVectorizer` can be used with `spaCy`; for example, to perform lemmatization and exclude certain characters during tokenization, we use the following:

```
nlp = spacy.load('en')
def tokenizer(doc):
    return [w.lemma_ for w in nlp(doc)
                if not w.is_punct | w.is_space]
vectorizer = CountVectorizer(tokenizer=tokenizer, binary=True)
doc_term_matrix = vectorizer.fit_transform(docs.body)
```

See the notebook for additional details and more examples.

TfidFTransformer and TfidFVectorizer

`TfidfTransfomer` computes tf-idf weights from a document-term matrix of token counts, such as the one produced by the `CountVectorizer`.

`TfidfVectorizer` performs both computations in a single step. It adds a few parameters to the `CountVectorizer` API that controls smoothing behavior.

TFIDF computation works as follows for a small text sample:

```
sample_docs = ['call you tomorrow',
               'Call me a taxi',
               'please call me... PLEASE!']
```

We compute the term frequency as we just did:

```
vectorizer = CountVectorizer()
tf_dtm = vectorizer.fit_transform(sample_docs).todense()
tokens = vectorizer.get_feature_names()
term_frequency = pd.DataFrame(data=tf_dtm,
                              columns=tokens)
```

	call	me	please	taxi	tomorrow	you
0	1	0	0	0	1	1
1	1	1	0	1	0	0
2	1	1	2	0	0	0

Document frequency is the number of documents containing the token:

```
vectorizer = CountVectorizer(binary=True)
df_dtm = vectorizer.fit_transform(sample_docs).todense().sum(axis=0)
document_frequency = pd.DataFrame(data=df_dtm,
                                  columns=tokens)
```

	call	me	please	taxi	tomorrow	you
0	3	2	1	1	1	1

The tf-idf weights are the ratio of these values:

```
tfidf = pd.DataFrame(data=tf_dtm/df_dtm, columns=tokens)
```

	call	me	please	taxi	tomorrow	you
0	0.33	0.00	0.00	0.00	1.00	1.00
1	0.33	0.50	0.00	1.00	0.00	0.00
2	0.33	0.50	2.00	0.00	0.00	0.00

The effect of smoothing

To avoid zero division, TfidfVectorizer uses smoothing for document and term frequencies:

- smooth_idf: Add 1 to document frequency, as if an extra document contained every token in the vocabulary, to prevent zero divisions
- sublinear_tf: Apply sublinear tf scaling; in other words, replace tf with 1 + log(tf)

In combination with normed weights, the results differ slightly:

```
vect = TfidfVectorizer(smooth_idf=True,
                       norm='l2',   # squared weights sum to 1 by
                                      document
                       sublinear_tf=False,  # if True, use 1+log(tf)
                       binary=False)
pd.DataFrame(vect.fit_transform(sample_docs).todense(),
             columns=vect.get_feature_names())


    call    me  please  taxi  tomorrow   you
0   0.39  0.00    0.00  0.00      0.65  0.65
1   0.43  0.55    0.00  0.72      0.00  0.00
2   0.27  0.34    0.90  0.00      0.00  0.00
```

How to summarize news articles using TfidFVectorizer

Due to their ability to assign meaningful token weights, TFIDF vectors are also used to summarize text data. For instance, Reddit's `autotldr` function is based on a similar algorithm. See the notebook for an example using the BBC articles.

Text Preprocessing - review

The large number of techniques to process natural language for its use in machine learning models that we introduced in this section is necessary to address the complex nature of this highly unstructured data source. The engineering of good language features is both challenging and rewarding and is arguably the most important step in unlocking the semantic value hidden in text data.

In practice, experience helps us select transformations that remove noise rather than the signal, but it will likely remain necessary to cross-validate and compare the performance of different combinations of preprocessing choices.

Text classification and sentiment analysis

Once text data has been converted into numerical features using the NLP techniques discussed in the previous sections, text classification works just like any other classification task.

In this section, we will apply these preprocessing technique to news articles, product reviews, and Twitter data and teach you about various classifiers to predict discrete news categories, review scores, and sentiment polarity.

First, we will introduce the Naive Bayes model, a probabilistic classification algorithm that works well with the text features produced by a bag-of-words model.

The code samples for this section are in the `text_classification` notebook.

The Naive Bayes classifier

The Naive Bayes algorithm is very popular for text classification because low computational cost and memory requirements facilitate training on very large, high-dimensional datasets. Its predictive performance can compete with more complex models, provides a good baseline, and is best known for successful spam detection.

The model relies on Bayes' theorem (see `Chapter 9`, *Bayesian Machine Learning*) and the assumption that the various features are independent of each other given the outcome class. In other words, for a given outcome, knowing the value of one feature (such as the presence of a token in a document) does not provide any information about the value of another feature.

Bayes' theorem refresher

Bayes' theorem expresses the conditional probability of one event (for instance, that an email is spam as opposed to benign ham) given another event (for example, that the email contains certain words), as follows:

$$\underbrace{P(\text{is spam}|\text{has words})}_{\text{Posterior}} = \frac{\overbrace{P(\text{has words} \mid \text{is spam})}^{\text{Likelihood}}\overbrace{P(\text{is spam})}^{\text{Prior}}}{\underbrace{P(\text{has words})}_{\text{Evidence}}}$$

The **posterior** probability that an email is in fact spam, given it contains certain words, depends on the interplay of three factors:

- The **prior** probability that an email is spam
- The **likelihood** of encountering these word in a spam email
- The **evidence**; that is, the probability of seeing these words in an email

To compute the posterior, we can ignore the evidence because it is the same for all outcomes (spam versus ham), and the unconditional prior may be easy to compute.

However, the likelihood poses insurmountable challenges for a reasonably sized vocabulary and a real-world corpus of emails. The reason is the combinatorial explosion of words that did or did not appear jointly in different documents and that prevent the evaluation required to compute a probability table and assign a value to the likelihood.

The conditional independence assumption

The assumption that is making the model both tractable and justifiably calling it Naive is that the features are independent conditional on the outcome. To illustrate, let's classify an email with the three words *Send money now* so that Bayes' theorem becomes the following:

$$P(spam \mid send\ money\ now) = \frac{P(send\ money\ now \mid spam) \times P(spam)}{P(send\ money\ now)}$$

Formally, the assumption that the three words are conditionally independent means that the probability of observing *send* is not affected by the presence of the other terms given the mail is spam; in other words, *P(send | money, now, spam) = P(send | spam)*. As a result, we can simplify the likelihood function:

$$P(spam \mid send\ money\ now) = \frac{P(send \mid spam) \times P(money \mid spam) \times P(now \mid spam) \times P(spam)}{P(send\ money\ now)}$$

Using the naive conditional independence assumption, each term in the numerator is straightforward to compute as relative frequencies from the training data. The denominator is constant across classes and can be ignored when posterior probabilities need to be compared rather than calibrated. The prior probability becomes less relevant as the number of factors—that is, features—increases.

In summary, the advantages of the Naive Bayes model are fast training and prediction because the number of parameters is linear in the number of features, and their estimation has a closed-form solution (based on training data frequencies) rather than expensive iterative optimization. It is also intuitive and somewhat interpretable, does not require hyperparameter tuning, and is relatively robust to irrelevant features given a sufficient signal.

However, when the independence assumption does not hold, and text classification depends on combinations of features or features are correlated, the model will perform poorly.

News article classification

We start with an illustration of the Naive Bayes model for news article classification using the BBC articles that we read as before to obtain a DataFrame with 2,225 articles from five categories:

```
RangeIndex: 2225 entries, 0 to 2224
Data columns (total 3 columns):
topic 2225 non-null object
heading 2225 non-null object
body 2225 non-null object
```

Training and evaluating multinomial Naive Bayes classifier

We split the data into the default 75:25 train-test sets, ensuring that test set classes closely mirror the train set:

```
y = pd.factorize(docs.topic)[0] # create integer class values
X = docs.body
X_train, X_test, y_train, y_test = train_test_split(X, y, random_state=1,
stratify=y)
```

We proceed to learn the vocabulary from the training set and transform both datasets using CountVectorizer with default settings to obtain almost 26,000 features:

```
vectorizer = CountVectorizer()
X_train_dtm = vectorizer.fit_transform(X_train)
X_test_dtm = vectorizer.transform(X_test)
X_train_dtm.shape, X_test_dtm.shape
((1668, 25919), (557, 25919))
```

Training and prediction follow the standard sklearn fit/predict interface:

```
nb = MultinomialNB()
nb.fit(X_train_dtm, y_train)
y_pred_class = nb.predict(X_test_dtm)
```

We evaluate multiclass predictions using `accuracy` and find that the default classifier achieved almost 98%:

```
accuracy_score(y_test, y_pred_class)
0.97666068222621
```

Sentiment analysis

Sentiment analysis is one of the most popular uses of NLP and machine learning for trading because positive or negative perspectives on assets or other price drivers are likely to impact returns.

Generally, modeling approaches to sentiment analysis rely on dictionaries, such as the `TextBlob` library, or models that are trained on outcomes for a specific domain. The latter is preferable because it permits more targeted labeling; for instance, by tying text features to subsequent price changes rather than indirect sentiment scores.

We will illustrate machine learning for sentiment analysis using a Twitter dataset with binary polarity labels, and a large Yelp business review dataset with a five-point outcome scale.

Twitter data

We use a dataset that contains 1.6 million training and 350 test tweets from 2009 with algorithmically assigned binary positive and negative sentiment scores that are fairly evenly split (see the relevant notebook for more detailed data exploration).

Multinomial Naive Bayes

We create a document-term matrix with 934 tokens as follows:

```
vectorizer = CountVectorizer(min_df=.001, max_df=.8, stop_words='english')
train_dtm = vectorizer.fit_transform(train.text)
<1566668x934 sparse matrix of type '<class 'numpy.int64'>'
    with 6332930 stored elements in Compressed Sparse Row format>
```

We then train the `MultinomialNB` classifier as before and predict the test set:

```
nb = MultinomialNB()
nb.fit(train_dtm, train.polarity)
predicted_polarity = nb.predict(test_dtm)
```

The result is over 77.5% accuracy:

```
accuracy_score(test.polarity, y_pred_class)
0.7768361581920904
```

Comparison with TextBlob sentiment scores

We also obtain `TextBlob` sentiment scores for tweets and note (see the following left-hand diagram) that positive test tweets receive a significantly higher sentiment estimate. We then use the `MultinomialNB` model and the `.predict_proba()` method to compute predicted probabilities and compare both models using the respective Area Under the Curve (see the following right-hand diagram):

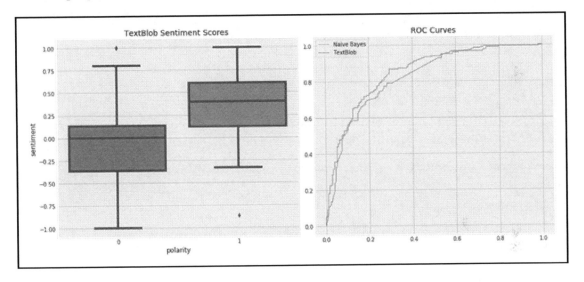

TextBlob sentiment scores

The Naive Bayes model outperforms `TextBlob` in this case.

Business reviews – the Yelp dataset challenge

Finally, we apply sentiment analysis to the significantly larger Yelp business review dataset with five outcome classes. The data consists of several files with information on the business, the user, the review, and other aspects that Yelp provides to encourage data science innovation.

We will use around six million reviews produced over the 2010-2018 period (see the relevant notebook for details). The following diagrams show the number of reviews and the average number of stars per year:

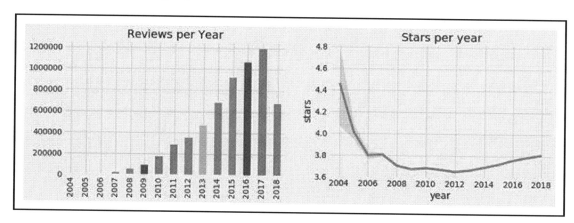

Graphs representing number of reviews and the average number of stars per year

In addition to the text features resulting from the review texts, we will also use other information submitted with the review or about the user.

We will train various models on data through 2017 and use 2018 as the test set.

Benchmark accuracy

Using the most frequent number of stars (=5) to predict the test set, we achieve an accuracy close to 52%:

```
test['predicted'] = train.stars.mode().iloc[0]
accuracy_score(test.stars, test.predicted)
0.5196950594793454
```

Multinomial Naive Bayes model

Next, we train a Naive Bayes classifier using a document-term matrix produced by CountVectorizer with default settings:

```
nb = MultinomialNB()
nb.fit(train_dtm,train.stars)
predicted_stars = nb.predict(test_dtm)
```

The prediction produces 64.7% accuracy on the test set, a 24.4% improvement over the benchmark:

```
accuracy_score(test.stars, predicted_stars)
0.6465164206691094
```

One-versus-all logistic regression

We proceed to train a one-versus-all logistic regression that trains one model per class, while treating the remaining classes as the negative class, and predicts probabilities for each class using the different models.

Using only text features, we train and evaluate the model as follows:

```
logreg = LogisticRegression(C=1e9)
logreg.fit(X=train_dtm, y=train.stars)
y_pred_class = logreg.predict(test_dtm)
```

The model achieves significantly higher accuracy at 73.6%:

```
accuracy_score(test.stars, y_pred_class)
0.7360498864740219
```

Combining text and numerical features

The dataset contains various numerical features (see the relevant notebook for implementation details).

Vectorizers produce `scipy.sparse` matrices. To combine vectorized text data with other features, we need to first convert these to sparse matrices as well; many sklearn objects and other libraries, such as LightGBM, can handle these very memory-efficient data structures. Converting the sparse matrix to a dense NumPy array risks memory overflow.

Most variables are categorical, so we use one-hot encoding since we have a fairly large dataset to accommodate the increase in features.

We convert the encoded numerical features and combine them with the document-term matrix:

```
train_numeric = sparse.csr_matrix(train_dummies.astype(np.int8))
train_dtm_numeric = sparse.hstack((train_dtm, train_numeric))
```

Multinomial logistic regression

Logistic regression also provides a multinomial training option that is faster and more accurate than the one-versus-all implementation. We use the `lbfgs` solver (see the sklearn documentation linked on GitHub for details):

```
multi_logreg = LogisticRegression(C=1e9, multi_class='multinomial',
                                  solver='lbfgs')
multi_logreg.fit(train_dtm_numeric.astype(float), train.stars)
y_pred_class = multi_logreg.predict(test_dtm_numeric.astype(float))
```

This model improves the performance to 74.6% accuracy:

```
accuracy_score(test.stars, y_pred_class)
0.7464488070176475
```

In this case, tuning the regularization parameter `C` did not lead to very significant improvements (see the notebook).

Gradient-boosting machine

For illustration purposes, we also train a LightGBM gradient-boosting tree ensemble with default settings and the `multiclass` objective:

```
param = {'objective':'multiclass', 'num_class': 5}
booster = lgb.train(params=param,
                    train_set=lgb_train,
                    num_boost_round=500,
                    early_stopping_rounds=20,
                    valid_sets=[lgb_train, lgb_test])
```

The basic settings do not improve on multinomial logistic regression, but further parameter tuning remains an unused option:

```
y_pred_class = booster.predict(test_dtm_numeric.astype(float))
accuracy_score(test.stars, y_pred_class.argmax(1) + 1)
0.738665855696524
```

Summary

In this chapter, we explored numerous techniques and options to process unstructured data with the goal of extracting semantically meaningful, numerical features for use in machine learning models.

We covered the basic tokenization and annotation pipeline and illustrated its implementation for multiple languages using spaCy and TextBlob. We built on these results to create a document model based on the bag-of-words model to represent documents as numerical vectors. We learned how to refine the preprocessing pipeline and then used vectorized text data for classification and sentiment analysis.

In the remaining two chapters on alternative text data, we will learn how to summarize text using unsupervised learning to identify latent topics (in the next chapter) and examine techniques to represent words as vectors that reflect the context of word usage and have been used very successfully to proceed richer text features for various classification tasks.

14
Topic Modeling

In the last chapter, we converted unstructured text data into a numerical format using the bag-of-words model. This model abstracts from word order and represents documents as word vectors, where each entry represents the relevance of a token to the document.

The resulting **document-term matrix (DTM)**, (you may also come across the transposed term-document matrix) is useful to compare documents to each other or to a query vector based on their token content, and quickly find a needle in a haystack or classify documents accordingly.

However, this document model is both high-dimensional and very sparse. As a result, it does little to summarize the content or get closer to understanding what it is about. In this chapter, we will use unsupervised machine learning in the form of topic modeling to extract hidden themes from documents. These themes can produce detailed insights into a large body of documents in an automated way. They are very useful to understand the haystack itself and permit the concise tagging of documents because using the degree of association of topics and documents.

Topic models permit the extraction of sophisticated, interpretable text features that can be used in various ways to extract trading signals from large collections of documents. They speed up the review of documents, help identify and cluster similar documents, and can be annotated as a basis for predictive modeling. Applications include the identification of key themes in company disclosures, or earnings call transcripts, customer reviews or contracts, annotated using, for example, sentiment analysis or direct labeling with subsequent asset returns.

More specifically, in this chapter, we will cover these topics:

- What topic modeling achieves, why it matters, and how it has evolved
- How **Latent Semantic Indexing (LSI)** reduces the dimensionality of the DTM
- How **probabilistic Latent Semantic Analysis (pLSA)** uses a generative model to extract topics

- How **Latent Dirichlet Allocation** (**LDA**) refines pLSA and why it is the most popular topic model
- How to visualize and evaluate topic modeling results
- How to implement LDA using sklearn and gensim
- How to apply topic modeling to collections of earnings calls and Yelp business reviews

 The code samples for the following sections are in the directory of the GitHub repository for this chapter, and references are listed in the main README file.

Learning latent topics: goals and approaches

Topic modeling aims to discover hidden topics or themes across documents that capture semantic information beyond individual words. It aims to address a key challenge in building a machine learning algorithm that learns from text data by going beyond the lexical level of what has been written to the semantic level of what was intended. The resulting topics can be used to annotate documents based on their association with various topics.

In other words, topic modeling aims to automatically summarize large collections of documents to facilitate organization and management, as well as search and recommendations. At the same time, it can enable the understanding of documents to the extent that humans can interpret the descriptions of topics.

Topic models aim to address the curse of dimensionality that can plague the bag-of-words model. The document representation based on high-dimensional sparse vectors can make similarity measures noisy, leading to inaccurate distance measurement and overfitting of text classification models.

Moreover, the bag of words model ignores word order and loses context as well as semantic information because it is not able to capture synonymy (several words have the same meaning) and polysemy (one word has several meanings). As a result, document retrieval or similarity search may miss the point when the documents are not indexed by the terms used to search or compare.

These shortcoming prompt this question: how do we model and learn meaning topics that facilitate a more productive interaction with text data?

From linear algebra to hierarchical probabilistic models

Initial attempts by topic models to improve on the vector space model (developed in the mid-1970s) applied linear algebra to reduce the dimensionality of the document-term matrix. This approach is similar to the algorithm we discussed as principal component analysis in `Chapter 12`, *Unsupervised Learning*, on unsupervised learning. While effective, it is difficult to evaluate the results of these models absent a benchmark model.

In response, probabilistic models emerged that assume an explicit document generation process and provide algorithms to reverse engineer this process and recover the underlying topics.

This table highlights key milestones in the model evolution that we will address in more detail in the following sections:

Model	Year	Description
Latent Semantic Indexing (LSI)	1988	Reduces the word space dimensionality to capture semantic document-term relationships by
Probabilistic Latent Semantic Analysis (pLSA)	1999	Reverse-engineers a process that assumes words generate a topic and documents are a mix of topics
Latent Dirichlet Allocation (LDA)	2003	Adds a generative process for documents: a three-level hierarchical Bayesian model

Latent semantic indexing

Latent Semantic Indexing (LSI, also called Latent Semantic Analysis) sets out to improve the results of queries that omitted relevant documents containing synonyms of query terms. It aims to model the relationships between documents and terms to be able to predict that a term should be associated with a document, even though, because of variability in word use, no such association was observed.

LSI uses linear algebra to find a given number, *k*, of latent topics by decomposing the DTM. More specifically, it uses **Singular Value Decomposition (SVD)** to find the best lower-rank DTM approximation using k singular values and vectors. In other words, LSI is an application of the unsupervised learning techniques of dimensionality reduction we encountered in `Chapter 12`, *Unsupervised Learning* to the text representation that we covered in `Chapter 13`, *Working with Text Data*. The authors experimented with hierarchical clustering but found it too restrictive to explicitly model the document-topic and topic-term relationships, or capture associations of documents or terms with several topics.

In this context, SVD serves the purpose of identifying a set of uncorrelated indexing variables or factors that permit us to represent each term and document by its vector of factor values.

The following figure illustrates how SVD decomposes the DTM into three matrices, two containing orthogonal singular vectors and a diagonal matrix with singular values that serve as scaling factors. Assuming some correlation in the original data, singular values decay in value so that selecting only the largest T singular values produces a lower-dimensional approximation of the original DTM that loses relatively little information. Hence, in the reduced version the rows or columns that had N items only have $T<N$ entries.

This reduced decomposition can be interpreted as illustrated next, where the first $M \times T$ matrix represents the relationships between documents and topics, the diagonal matrix scales the topics by their corpus strength, and the third matrix models the term-topic relationship:

The rows of the matrix that results from the product of the first two matrices, $U_T \Sigma_T$, corresponds to the locations of the original documents projected into the latent topic space.

How to implement LSI using sklearn

We will illustrate the application of LSI using the BBC article data that we introduced in the last chapter because it is small enough to permit quick training and allow us to compare topic assignments to category labels. See the `latent_semantic_indexing` notebook for additional implementation details:

1. We begin by loading the documents and creating a train and (stratified) test set with 50 articles.

2. Then, we vectorize the data using `TfidfVectorizer` to obtain weighted DTM counts and filter out words that appear in less than 1% or more than 25% of the documents, as well as generic stopwords, to obtain a vocabulary of around 2,900 words:

   ```
   vectorizer = TfidfVectorizer(max_df=.25, min_df=.01,
   stop_words='english',
   binary=False)
   train_dtm = vectorizer.fit_transform(train_docs.article)
   test_dtm = vectorizer.transform(test_docs.article)
   ```

3. We use `sklearn`'s `TruncatedSVD` class, which only computes the k largest singular values to reduce the dimensionality of the document-term matrix. The deterministic arpack algorithm delivers an exact solution, but the default randomized implementation is more efficient for large matrices.

4. We compute five topics to match the five categories, which explain only 5.4% of the total DTM variance so higher values would be reasonable:

   ```
   svd = TruncatedSVD(n_components=5, n_iter=5, random_state=42)
   svd.fit(train_dtm)
   svd.explained_varianceratio
   array([0.00187014, 0.01559661, 0.01389952, 0.01215842, 0.01066485])
   ```

5. LSI identifies a new orthogonal basis for the document-term matrix that reduces the rank to the number of desired topics.

6. The `.transform()` method of the trained `svd` object projects the documents into the new topic space that is the result of reducing the dimensionality of the document vectors and corresponds to the $U_T \Sigma_T$ transformation illustrated before:

   ```
   train_doc_topics = svd.transform(train_dtm)
   train_doc_topics.shape
   (2175, 5)
   ```

7. We can sample an article to view its location in the topic space. We draw a `Politics` article that is most (positively) associated with topics 1 and 2:

```
i = randint(0, len(train_docs))
train_docs.iloc[i, :2].append(pd.Series(doc_topics[i],
index=topic_labels))
Category Politics
Heading What the election should really be about?
Topic 1 0.33
Topic 2 0.18
Topic 3 0.12
Topic 4 0.02
Topic 5 0.06
```

8. The topic assignments for this sample align with the average topic weights for each category illustrated next (`Politics` is the leftmost). They illustrate how LSI expresses the k topics as directions in a k-dimensional space (the notebook includes a projection of the average topic assignments per category into two-dimensional space).

9. Each category is clearly defined, and the test assignments match with train assignments. However, the weights are both positive and negative, making it more difficult to interpret the topics:

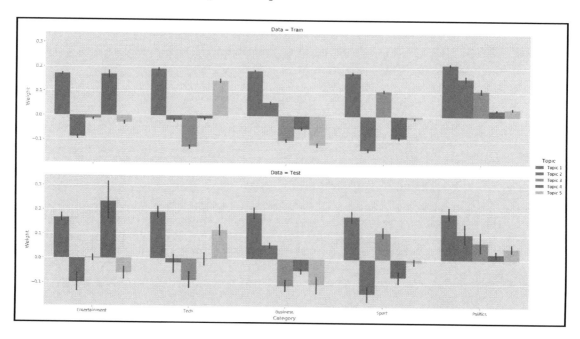

10. We can also display the words that are most closely associated with each topic (in absolute terms). The topics appear to capture some semantic information but are not differentiated:

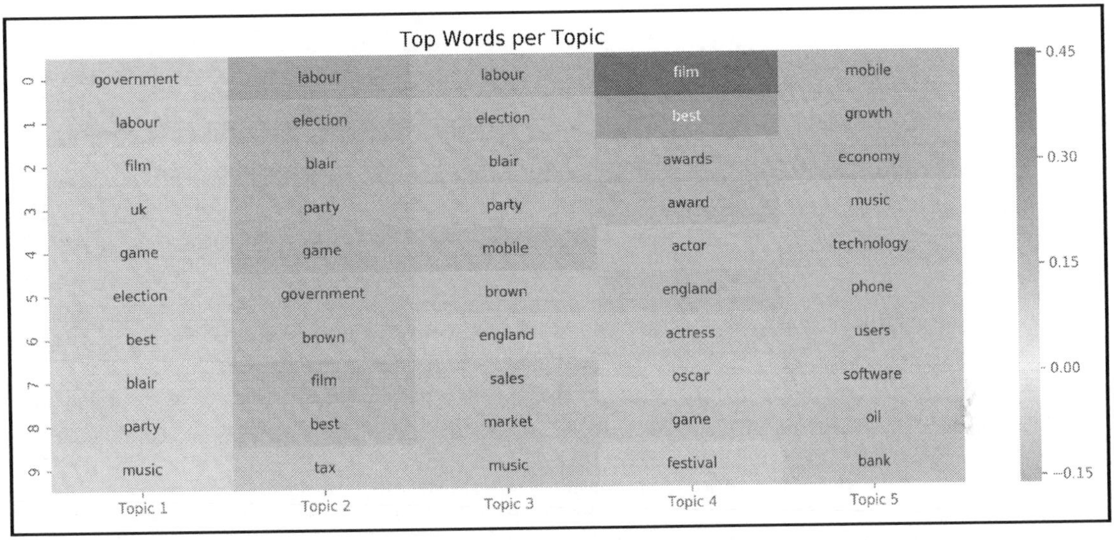

Pros and cons

The benefits of LSI include the removal of noise and mitigation of the curse of dimensionality, while also capturing some semantics and clustering both documents and terms.

However, the results of LSI are difficult to interpret because topics are word vectors with both positive and negative entries. There is also no underlying model that would permit the evaluation of fit and provide guidance when selecting the number of dimensions or topics.

Probabilistic latent semantic analysis

Probabilistic Latent Semantic Analysis (pLSA) takes a statistical perspective on LSA and creates a generative model to address the lack of theoretical underpinnings of LSA.

pLSA explicitly models the probability each co-occurrence of documents d and words w described by the DTM as a mixture of conditionally independent multinomial distributions that involve topics t.

The symmetric formulation of this generative process of word-document co-occurrences assumes both words and documents are generated by the latent topic class, whereas the asymmetric model assumes the topics are selected given the document, and words result from a second step given the topic:

$$P(w,d) = \underbrace{\sum_t P(d \mid t)P(w \mid t)}_{\text{symmetric}} = \underbrace{P(d)\sum_t P(t \mid d)P(w \mid t)}_{\text{asymmetric}}$$

The number of topics is a hyperparameter chosen before training and is not learned from the data.

Probabilistic models often use the following plate notation to express dependencies. The following figure encodes the relationships just describe for the asymmetric model. Each rectangle represents multiple items, such as **M Documents** for the outer and **N Words** for each document for the inner block. We only observe the documents and their content, and the model infers the hidden or latent topic distribution:

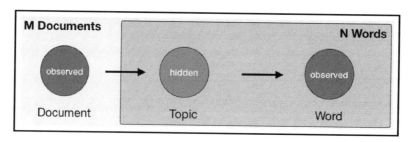

The benefit of using a probability model is that we can now compare models by evaluating the probability they assign to new documents given the parameters learned during training.

How to implement pLSA using sklearn

pLSA is equivalent to non-negative matrix factorization using a Kullback-Leibler Divergence objective (see references on GitHub `https://github.com/PacktPublishing/Hands-On-Machine-Learning-for-Algorithmic-Trading`). Hence, we can use the `sklearn.decomposition.NM` class to implement this model, following the LSA example.

Using the same train-test split of the DTM produced by the `TfidfVectorizer`, we fit pLSA as follows:

```
nmf = NMF(n_components=n_components,
random_state=42,
solver='mu',
beta_loss='kullback-leibler',
max_iter=1000)
nmf.fit(train_dtm)
```

We get a measure of the reconstruction error, which is a substitute for the explained variance measure from before:

```
nmf.reconstruction_err_
316.2609400385988
```

Due to its probabilistic nature, pLSA produces only positive topic weights that result in more straightforward topic-category relationships for the test and training sets:

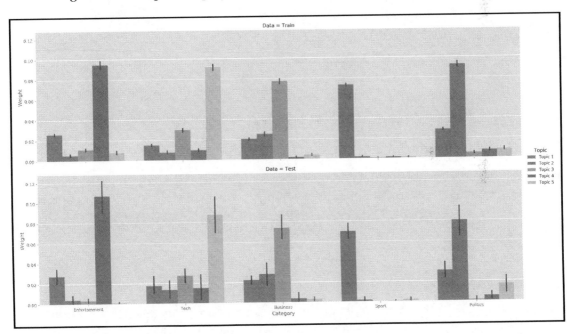

We can also see that the word lists that describe each topic begin to make more sense; for example, the **Entertainment** category is most directly associated with **Topic 4**, which includes the words **film**, **start**, and so on:

Latent Dirichlet allocation

Latent Dirichlet allocation (LDA) extends pLSA by adding a generative process for topics.

It is the most popular topic model because it tends to produce meaningful topics that humans can relate to, can assign topics to new documents, and is extensible. Variants of LDA models can include metadata such as authors, or image data, or learn hierarchical topics.

How LDA works

LDA is a hierarchical Bayesian model that assumes topics are probability distributions over words, and documents are distributions over topics. More specifically, the model assumes that topics follow a sparse Dirichlet distribution, which implies that documents cover only a small set of topics, and topics use only a small set of words frequently.

The Dirichlet distribution

The Dirichlet distribution produces probability vectors that can be used with discrete distributions. That is, it randomly generates a given number of values that are positive and sum to one as expected for probabilities. It has a parameter of positive, real value that controls the concentration of the probabilities. Values closer to zero mean that only a few values will be positive and receive most probability mass. The following screenshot illustrates three draws of size 10 for α = *0.1* (the `dirichlet_distribution` notebook contains a simulation so you can experiment with different parameter values):

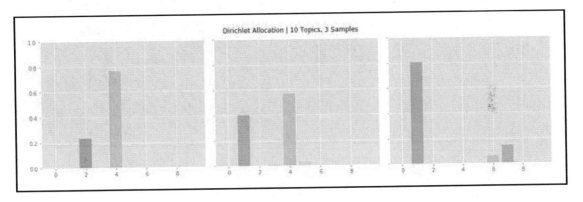

Dirichlet allocation

The generative model

The Dirichlet distribution figures prominently in the LDA topic model, which assumes the following generative process when an author adds an article to a body of documents:

1. Randomly mix a small subset of shared topics *K* according to the topic probabilities
2. For each word, select one of the topics according to the document-topic probabilities
3. Select a word from the topic's word list according to the topic-word probabilities

As a result, the article content depends on the weights of each topic and on the terms that make up each topic. The Dirichlet distribution governs the selection of topics for documents and words for topics and encodes the idea that a document only covers a few topics, while each topic uses only a small number of words frequently.

The plate notation for the LDA model summarizes these relationships:

Parameter	Description
α	Dirichlet prior: per-document topic-distribution
β	Dirichlet prior: per-topic word-distribution
θ_m	Topic distribution for document m
ϕ_k	Word distribution for topic k
z_{mn}	Topic for word n in document m

Reverse-engineering the process

The generative process is fictional but turns out to be useful because it permits the recovery of the various distributions. The LDA algorithm reverse-engineers the work of the imaginary author and arrives at a summary of the document-topic-word relationships that concisely describes the following:

- The percentage contribution of each topic to a document
- The probabilistic association of each word with a topic

LDA solves the Bayesian inference problem of recovering the distributions from the body of documents and the words they contain by reverse-engineering the assumed content generation process. The original paper uses **variational Bayes (VB)** to approximate the posterior distribution. Alternatives include Gibbs sampling and expectation propagation. Later, we will illustrate implementations using the sklearn and gensim libraries.

How to evaluate LDA topics

Unsupervised topic models do not provide a guarantee that the result will be meaningful or interpretable, and there is no objective metric to assess the result as in supervised learning. Human topic evaluation is considered the gold standard but is potentially expensive and not readily available at scale.

Two options to evaluate results more objectively include perplexity, which evaluates the model on unseen documents, and topic coherence metrics, which aim to evaluate the semantic quality of the uncovered patterns.

Perplexity

Perplexity, when applied to LDA, measures how well the topic-word probability distribution recovered by the model predicts a sample, for example, unseen text documents. It is based on the entropy $H(p)$ of this distribution p and computed with respect to the set of tokens w:

$$2^{H(p)} = 2^{-\sum_w p(w) \log_2 p(w)}$$

Measures closer to zero imply the distribution is better at predicting the sample.

Topic coherence

Topic coherence measures the semantic consistency of the topic model results, that is, whether humans would perceive the words and their probabilities associated with topics as meaningful.

To this end, it scores each topic by measuring the degree of semantic similarity between the words most relevant to the topic. More specifically, coherence measures are based on the probability of observing the set of words W that define a topic together.

We use two measures of coherence that have been designed for LDA and shown to align with human judgment of topic quality, namely the UMass and the UCI measures.

The UCI metric defines a word pair's score to be the sum of the **Pointwise Mutual Information (PMI)** between two distinct pairs of (top) topic words $w_i, w_j \in w$ and a smoothing factor ε:

$$\text{coherence}_{\text{UCI}} = \sum_{(w_i, w_j) \in W} \log \frac{p(w_i, w_j) + \epsilon}{p(w_i)p(w_j)}$$

The probabilities are computed from word co-occurrence frequencies in a sliding window over an external corpus such as Wikipedia, so that this metric can be thought of as an external comparison to a semantic ground truth.

In contrast, the UMass metric uses the co-occurrences in a number of documents D from the training corpus to compute a coherence score:

$$\text{coherence}_{\text{UMass}} = \sum_{(w_i, w_j) \in W} \log \frac{D(w_i, w_j) + \epsilon}{D(w_j)}$$

Rather than a comparison to an extrinsic ground truth, this measure reflects intrinsic coherence. Both measures have been evaluated to align well with human judgment. In both cases, values closer to zero imply that a topic is more coherent.

How to implement LDA using sklearn

Using the BBC data as before, we use `sklearn.decomposition.LatentDirichletAllocation` to train an LDA model with five topics (see the sklearn documentation for detail on parameters, and the notebook `lda_with_sklearn` for implementation details):

```
lda = LatentDirichletAllocation(n_components=5,
                                n_jobs=-1,
                                max_iter=500,
                                learning_method='batch',
                                evaluate_every=5,
                                verbose=1,
                                random_state=42)
ldat.fit(train_dtm)
LatentDirichletAllocation(batch_size=128, doc_topic_prior=None,
            evaluate_every=5, learning_decay=0.7, learning_method='batch',
            learning_offset=10.0, max_doc_update_iter=100, max_iter=500,
```

```
mean_change_tol=0.001, n_components=5, n_jobs=-1,
n_topics=None, perp_tol=0.1, random_state=42,
topic_word_prior=None, total_samples=1000000.0, verbose=1)
```

The model tracks the in-sample perplexity during training and stops iterating once this measure stops improving. We can persist and load the result as usual with sklearn objects:

```
joblib.dump(lda, model_path / 'lda.pkl')
lda = joblib.load(model_path / 'lda.pkl')
```

How to visualize LDA results using pyLDAvis

Topic visualization facilitates the evaluation of topic quality using human judgment. pyLDAvis is a Python port of LDAvis, developed in R and D3.js. We will introduce the key concepts; each LDA implementation notebook contains examples.

pyLDAvis displays the global relationships between topics while also facilitating their semantic evaluation by inspecting the terms most closely associated with each topic and, inversely, the topics associated with each term. It also addresses the challenge that terms that are frequent in a corpus tend to dominate the multinomial distribution over words that define a topic. LDAVis introduces the relevance r of the term w to topic t, to produce a flexible ranking of key terms using a weight parameter $0<=\lambda<=1$.

With ϕ_{wt} as the model's probability estimate of observing the term w for topic t, and as the marginal probability of w in the corpus:

$$r(w, k|\lambda) = \lambda log(\phi_{kw}) + (1 - \lambda)log\frac{\phi kw}{p_w}$$

The first term measures the degree of association of term t with topic w, and the second term measures the lift or saliency, that is, how much more likely the term is for the topic than in the corpus.

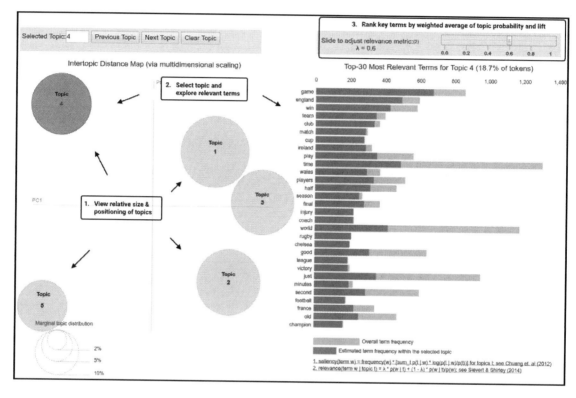

Topic 14

The tool allows the user to interactively change λ to adjust the relevance, which updates the ranking of terms. User studies have found that $\lambda=0.6$ produces the most plausible results.

How to implement LDA using gensim

`gensim` is a specialized NLP library with a fast LDA implementation and many additional features. We will also use it in the next chapter on word vectors (see the `latent_dirichlet_allocation_gensim` notebook for details).

It facilitates the conversion of DTM produced by sklearn into gensim data structures as follows:

```
train_corpus = Sparse2Corpus(train_dtm, documents_columns=False)
test_corpus = Sparse2Corpus(test_dtm, documents_columns=False)
id2word = pd.Series(vectorizer.get_feature_names()).to_dict()
```

Gensim LDA algorithm includes numerous settings, which are as follows:

```
LdaModel(corpus=None,
         num_topics=100,
         id2word=None,
         distributed=False,
         chunksize=2000, # No of doc per training chunk.
         passes=1,       # No of passes through corpus during training
         update_every=1, # No of docs to be iterated through per update
         alpha='symmetric',
         eta=None,       # a-priori belief on word probability
         decay=0.5,      # % of lambda forgotten when new doc is examined
         offset=1.0,     # controls slow down of first few iterations.
         eval_every=10,  # how often estimate log perplexity (costly)
         iterations=50,          # Max. of iterations through the corpus
         gamma_threshold=0.001, # Min. change in gamma to continue
         minimum_probability=0.01, # Filter topics with lower
                                   probability
         random_state=None,
         ns_conf=None,
         minimum_phi_value=0.01, # lower bound on term probabilities
         per_word_topics=False,  #  Compute most word-topic
                                    probabilities
         callbacks=None,
         dtype=<class 'numpy.float32'>)
```

Gensim also provides an `LdaMulticore` model for parallel training that may speed up training using Python's multiprocessing features for parallel computation.

Model training just requires instantiating the `LdaModel` object as follows:

```
lda = LdaModel(corpus=train_corpus,
num_topics=5,
id2word=id2word)
```

Topic coherence measures whether the words in a topic tend to co-occur together. It adds up a score for each distinct pair of top-ranked words. The score is the log of the probability that a document containing at least one instance of the higher-ranked word also contains at least one instance of the lower-ranked word.

Large negative values indicate words that don't co-occur often; values closer to zero indicate that words tend to co-occur more often. `gensim` permits topic coherence evaluation that produces the topic coherence and shows the most important words per topic:

```
coherence = lda_gensim.top_topics(corpus=train_corpus, coherence='u_mass')
```

We can display the results as follows:

```
topic_coherence = []
topic_words = pd.DataFrame()
for t in range(len(coherence)):
    label = topic_labels[t]
    topic_coherence.append(coherence[t][1])
    df = pd.DataFrame(coherence[t][0], columns=[(label, 'prob'), (label,
'term')])
    df[(label, 'prob')] = df[(label, 'prob')].apply(lambda x:
'{:.2%}'.format(x))
    topic_words = pd.concat([topic_words, df], axis=1)
topic_words.columns = pd.MultiIndex.from_tuples(topic_words.columns)
pd.set_option('expand_frame_repr', False)
print(topic_words.head())
pd.Series(topic_coherence, index=topic_labels).plot.bar();
```

This shows the following top words for each topic:

Topic 1		Topic 2		Topic 3		Topic 4		Topic 5	
Probability	Term	Probability	Term	Probability	Term	Probability	Term	Probability	Term
0.55%	online	0.90%	best	1.04%	mobile	0.64%	market	0.94%	labour
0.51%	site	0.87%	game	0.98%	phone	0.53%	growth	0.72%	blair
0.46%	game	0.62%	play	0.51%	music	0.52%	sales	0.72%	brown
0.45%	net	0.61%	won	0.48%	film	0.49%	economy	0.65%	election
0.44%	used	0.56%	win	0.48%	use	0.45%	prices	0.57%	united

And the corresponding coherence scores, which highlight the decay of topic quality (at least in part due to the relatively small dataset):

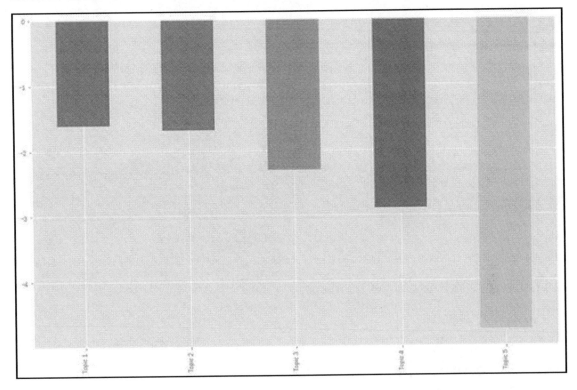

Decay of topic quality

Topic modeling for earnings calls

In `Chapter 3`, *Alternative Data for Finance*, we learned how to scrape earnings call data from the SeekingAlpha site. In this section, we will illustrate topic modeling using this source. I'm using a sample of some 500 earnings call transcripts from the second half of 2018. For a practical application, a larger dataset would be highly desirable. The `earnings_calls` directory contains several files, with examples mentioned later.

See the `lda_earnings_calls` notebook for details on loading, exploring, and preprocessing the data, as well as training and evaluating individual models, and the `run_experiments.py` file for the experiments described here.

Data preprocessing

The transcripts consist of individual statements by a company representative, an operator, and usually a question and answer session with analysts. We will treat each of these statements as separate documents, ignoring operator statements, to obtain 22,766 items with mean and median word counts of 144 and 64, respectively:

```
documents = []
for transcript in earnings_path.iterdir():
    content = pd.read_csv(transcript / 'content.csv')
    documents.extend(content.loc[(content.speaker!='Operator') &
(content.content.str.len() > 5), 'content'].tolist())
len(documents)
22766
```

We use `spaCy` to preprocess these documents as illustrated in `Chapter 13`, *Working with Text Data* (see the notebook) and store the cleaned and lemmatized text as a new text file.

Data exploration reveals domain-specific stopwords such as year and quarter that we remove in a second step, where we also filter out statements with fewer than ten words so that some 16,150 remain.

Model training and evaluation

For illustration, we will create a document-term matrix containing terms appearing in between 0.5% and 50% of documents for around 1,560 features. Training a 15-topic model using 25 passes over the corpus takes a bit over two minutes on a four-core i7.

The top 10 words per topic identify several distinct themes that range from obvious financial information to clinical trials (topic 4) and supply chain issues (12):

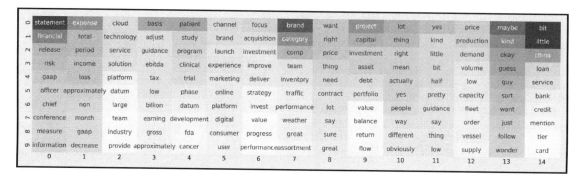

statement	expense	cloud	basis	patient	channel	focus	brand	want	project	lot	yes	price	maybe	bit
financial	total	technology	adjust	study	brand	acquisition	category	right	capital	thing	kind	production	kind	little
release	period	service	guidance	program	launch	investment	comp	price	investment	right	little	demand	okay	china
risk	income	solution	ebitda	clinical	experience	improve	team	thing	asset	mean	bit	volume	guess	loan
gaap	loss	platform	tax	trial	marketing	deliver	inventory	need	debt	actually	half	low	guy	service
officer	approximately	datum	low	phase	online	strategy	traffic	contract	portfolio	yes	pretty	capacity	sort	bank
chief	non	large	billion	datum	platform	invest	performance	lot	value	people	guidance	fleet	want	credit
conference	month	team	earning	development	digital	value	weather	say	balance	way	say	order	just	mention
measure	gaap	industry	gross	fda	consumer	progress	great	sure	return	different	thing	vessel	follow	tier
information	decrease	provide	approximately	cancer	user	performance	assortment	great	flow	obviously	low	supply	wonder	card
0	1	2	3	4	5	6	7	8	9	10	11	12	13	14

Using pyLDAvis' relevance metric with a 0.6 weighting of unconditional frequency relative to lift, topic definitions become more intuitive, as illustrated for topic 14 about sales performance:

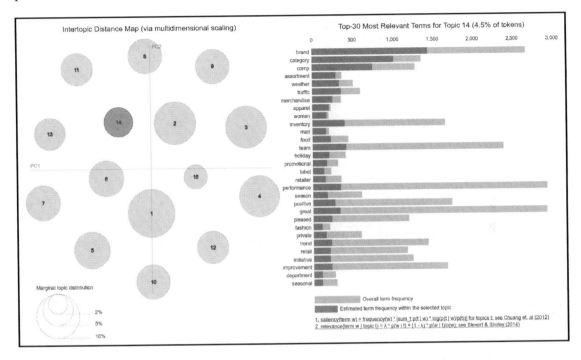

Sales performance for Topic 14

The notebook also illustrates how to look up documents by their topic association. In this case, an analyst can review relevant statements for nuances, use sentiment analysis to further process the topic-specific text data, or assign labels derived from market prices.

Running experiments

To illustrate the impact of different parameter settings, we ran a few hundred experiments for different DTM constraints and model parameters. More specifically, we let the `min_df` and `max_df` parameters range from 50-500 words and 10% to 100% of documents, respectively using alternatively binary and absolute counts. We then trained LDA models with 3 to 50 topics, using 1 and 25 passes over the corpus.

The following chart illustrates the results in terms of topic coherence (higher is better), and perplexity (lower is better). Coherence drops after 25-30 topics and perplexity similarly increases:

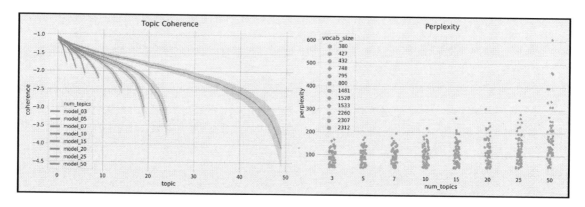

The notebook includes regression results that quantify the relationships between parameters and outcomes. We generally get better results using absolute counts and a smaller vocabulary.

Topic modeling for Yelp business reviews

The `lda_yelp_reviews` notebook contains an example of LDA applied to six million business review on Yelp. Reviews are more uniform in length than the statements extracted from the earnings call transcripts. After cleaning as before, the 10th and 90th percentiles range from 14 to 90 tokens.

We show results for one model using a vocabulary of 3,800 tokens based on *min_df=0.1%* and *max_df=25%* with a single pass to avoid a lengthy training time for 20 topics. We can use the `pyldavis topic_info` attribute to compute relevance values for *lambda=0.6* that produce the following word list (see the notebook for details):

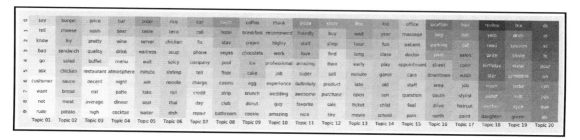

Gensim provides a `LdaMultiCore` implementation that allows for parallel training using Python's multiprocessing module and improves performance by 50% when using four workers. More workers do not further reduce training time though, due to I/O bottlenecks.

Summary

In this chapter, we explored the use of topic modeling to gain insights into the content of a large collection of documents. We covered Latent Semantic Analysis, which uses dimensionality reduction of the DTM to project documents into a latent topic space. While effective in addressing the curse of dimensionality caused by high-dimensional word vectors, it does not capture much semantic information. Probabilistic models make explicit assumptions about the interplay of documents, topics, and words that allow algorithms to reverse engineer the document generation process and evaluate the model fit on new documents. We saw that LDA is capable of extracting plausible topics that allow us to gain a high-level understanding of large amounts of text in an automated way, while also identifying relevant documents in a targeted way.

In the next chapter, we will learn how to train neural networks that embed individual words in a high-dimensional vector space that captures important semantic information and allows us to use the resulting word vectors as high-quality text features.

15
Word Embeddings

In the two previous chapters, we applied the bag-of-words model to convert text data into a numerical format. The results were sparse, fixed-length vectors that represent documents in a high-dimensional word space. This allows evaluating the similarity of documents and creates features to train a machine learning algorithm and classify a document's content or rate the sentiment expressed in it. However, these vectors ignore the context in which a term is used so that, for example, a different sentence containing the same words would be encoded by the same vector.

In this chapter, we will introduce an alternative class of algorithms that use neural networks to learn a vector representation of individual semantic units such as a word or a paragraph. These vectors are dense rather than sparse, and have a few hundred real-valued rather than tens of thousands of binary or discrete entries. They are called **embeddings** because they assign each semantic unit a location in a continuous vector space.

Embeddings result from training a model to relate tokens to their context with the benefit that similar usage implies a similar vector. Moreover, we will see how the embeddings encode semantic aspects, such as relationships among words by means of their relative location. As a result, they are powerful features for use in the deep learning models that we will introduce in the following chapters.

More specifically, in this chapter, we will cover the following topics:

- What word embeddings are and how they work and capture semantic information
- How to use trained word vectors
- Which network architectures are useful to train Word2vec models
- How to train a Word2vec model using Keras, gensim, and TensorFlow
- How to visualize and evaluate the quality of word vectors
- How to train a Word2vec model using SEC filings
- How `Doc2vec` extends Word2vec

How word embeddings encode semantics

The bag-of-words model represents documents as vectors that reflect the tokens they contain. Word embeddings represent tokens as lower dimensional vectors so that their relative location reflects their relationship in terms of how they are used in context. They embody the distributional hypothesis from linguistics that claims words are best defined by the company they keep.

Word vectors are capable of capturing numerous semantic aspects; not only are synonyms close to each other, but words can have multiple degrees of similarity, for example, the word driver could be similar to motorist or to cause. Furthermore, embeddings reflect relationships among pairs of words such as analogies (Tokyo is to Japan what Paris is to France, or went is to go what saw is to see) as we will illustrate later in this section.

Embeddings result from training a machine learning model to predict words from their context or vice versa. In the following section, we will introduce how these neural language models work and present successful approaches including Word2vec, `Doc2vec`, and fastText.

How neural language models learn usage in context

Word embeddings result from training a shallow neural network to predict a word given its context. Whereas traditional language models define context as the words preceding the target, word-embedding models use the words contained in a symmetric window surrounding the target. In contrast, the bag-of-words model uses the entirety of documents as context and uses (weighted) counts to capture the cooccurrence of words rather than predictive vectors.

Earlier neural language models that were used included nonlinear hidden layers that increased the computational complexity. Word2vec and its extensions simplified the architecture to enable training on large datasets (Wikipedia, for example, contains over two billion tokens; see `Chapter 17`, *Deep Learning*, for additional details on feed-forward networks).

The Word2vec model – learn embeddings at scale

A Word2vec model is a two-layer neural net that takes a text corpus as input and outputs a set of embedding vectors for words in that corpus. There are two different architectures to learn word vectors efficiently using shallow neural networks depicted in the following figure:

- The **Continuous-Bag-Of-Words (CBOW)** model predicts the target word using the average of the context word vectors as input so that their order does not matter. A CBOW model trains faster and tends to be slightly more accurate for frequent terms, but pays less attention to infrequent words.
- The **Skip-Gram (SG)** model, by contrast, uses the target word to predict words sampled from the context. It works well with small datasets and finds good representations even for rare words or phrases:

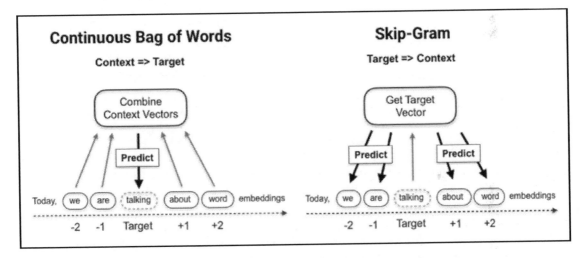

Hence, the Word2vec model receives an embedding vector as input and computes the dot product with another embedding vector. Note that, assuming normed vectors, the dot product is maximized (in absolute terms) when vectors are equal, and minimized when they are orthogonal.

It then uses backpropagation to adjust the embedding weights in response to the loss computed by an objective function due to any classification errors. We will see in the next section how Word2vec computes the loss.

Training proceeds by sliding the context window over the documents, typically segmented into sentences. Each complete iteration over the corpus is called an **epoch**. Depending on the data, several dozen epochs may be necessary for vector quality to converge.

Technically, the SG model has been shown to factorize a word-context matrix that contains the pointwise mutual information of the respective word and context pairs implicitly (see references on GitHub).

Model objective – simplifying the softmax

Word2vec models aim to predict a single word out of the potentially very large vocabulary. Neural networks often use the softmax function that maps any number of real values to an equal number of probabilities to implement the corresponding multiclass objective, where h refers to the embedding and v to the input vectors, and c is the context of word w:

$$p(\ w\ |\ c) = \frac{exp(h^T v'_w)}{\sum_{w_i \in V} exp(h^T v'_{w_i})}$$

However, the softmax complexity scales with the number of classes, as the denominator requires the computation of the dot product for all words in the vocabulary to standardize the probabilities. Word2vec models gain efficiency by using a simplified version of the softmax or sampling-based approaches (see references for details):

- The **hierarchical softmax** organizes the vocabulary as a binary tree with words as leaf nodes. The unique path to each node can be used to compute the word probability.
- **Noise-contrastive estimation** (**NCE**) samples out-of-context "noise words" and approximates the multiclass task by a binary classification problem. The NCE derivative approaches the softmax gradient as the number of samples increases, but as few as 25 samples can yield convergence similar to the softmax, at a rate that is 45 times faster.
- **Negative sampling** (**NEG**) omits the noise word samples to approximate NCE and directly maximizes the probability of the target word. Hence, NEG optimizes the semantic quality of embedding vectors (similar vectors for similar usage) rather than the accuracy on a test set. It may, however, produce poorer representations for infrequent words than the hierarchical softmax objective.

Automatic phrase detection

Preprocessing typically involves phrase detection, that is, the identification of tokens that are commonly used together and should receive a single vector representation (for example, New York City, see the discussion of n-grams in `Chapter 13`, *Working with Text Data*).

The original Word2vec authors use a simple lift scoring method that identifies two words w_i, w_j as a bigram if their joint occurrence exceeds a given threshold relative to each word's individual appearance, corrected by a discount factor δ:

$$score(w_i, w_j) = \frac{count(w_i, w_j) - \delta}{count(w_i)count(w_j)}$$

The scorer can be applied repeatedly to identify successively longer phrases.

An alternative is the normalized point-wise mutual information score that is more accurate, but also more costly to compute. It uses the relative word frequency *P(w)* and varies between +1 and -1:

$$NPMI = \frac{ln(P(w_i, w_j)/P(w_i)P(w_j))}{-ln(P(w_i, w_j))}$$

How to evaluate embeddings – vector arithmetic and analogies

The bag-of-words model creates document vectors that reflect the presence and relevance of tokens to the document. **Latent semantic analysis** reduces the dimensionality of these vectors and identifies what can be interpreted as latent concepts in the process. **Latent Dirichlet allocation** represents both documents and terms as vectors that contain the weights of latent topics.

The dimensions of the word and phrase vectors do not have an explicit meaning. However, the embeddings encode similar usage as proximity in the latent space in a way that carries over to semantic relationships. This results in the interesting properties that analogies can be expressed by adding and subtracting word vectors.

The following figure shows how the vector connecting Paris and France (that is, the difference of their embeddings) reflects the capital of relationship. The analogous relationship, London: UK, corresponds to the same vector, that is, the UK is very close to the location obtained by adding the capital of vector to London:

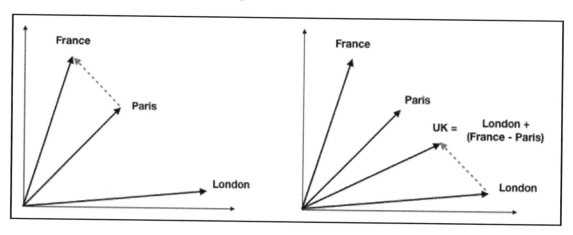

Just as words can be used in different contexts, they can be related to other words in different ways, and these relationships correspond to different directions in the latent space. Accordingly, there are several types of analogies that the embeddings should reflect if the training data permits.

The Word2vec authors provide a list of several thousand relationships spanning aspects of geography, grammar and syntax, and family relationships to evaluate the quality of embedding vectors. As illustrated above, the test validates that the target word (UK) is closest to the result of adding the vector that represents an analogous relationship (Paris: France) to the target's complement (London).

The following figure projects the 300-dimensional embeddings of the most closely related analogies for a Word2vec model trained on the Wikipedia corpus, with over 2 billion tokens, into two dimensions using **principal component analysis (PCA)**. A test of over 24,400 analogies from the following categories achieved an accuracy of over 73.5% (see notebook):

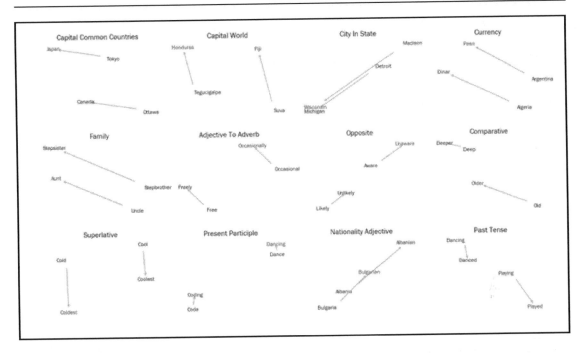

Working with embedding models

Similar to other unsupervised learning techniques, the goal of learning embedding vectors is to generate features for other tasks such as text classification or sentiment analysis.

There are several options to obtain embedding vectors for a given corpus of documents:

- Use embeddings learned from a generic large corpus such as Wikipedia or Google News
- Train your own model using documents that reflect a domain of interest

The less generic and more specialized the content of the subsequent text modeling task is, the more preferable is the second approach. However, quality word embeddings are data-hungry and require informative documents containing hundreds of millions of words.

How to use pre-trained word vectors

There are several sources for pretrained word embeddings. Popular options include Stanford's GloVE and spaCy's built-in vectors (see the notebook `using_trained_vectors` for details).

GloVe – global vectors for word representation

GloVe is an unsupervised algorithm developed at the Stanford NLP lab that learns vector representations for words from aggregated global word-word co-occurrence statistics (see references). Vectors pretrained on the following web-scale sources are available:

- Common Crawl with 42B or 840B tokens and a vocabulary or 1.9M or 2.2M tokens
- Wikipedia 2014 + Gigaword 5 with 6B tokens and a vocabulary of 400K tokens
- Twitter using 2B tweets, 27B tokens and a vocabulary of 1.2M tokens

We can use gensim to convert and load the vector text files into the KeyedVector object:

```
from gensim.models import Word2vec, KeyedVectors
 from gensim.scripts.glove2Word2vec import glove2Word2vec
glove2Word2vec(glove_input_file=glove_file, Word2vec_output_file=w2v_file)
 model = KeyedVectors.load_Word2vec_format(w2v_file, binary=False)
```

The Word2vec authors provide text files containing over 24,000 analogy tests that gensim uses to evaluate word vectors.

The word vectors trained on the Wikipedia corpus cover all analogies and achieve an overall accuracy of 75.5% with some variation across categories:

Category	Samples	Accuracy	Category	Samples	Accuracy
capital-common-countries	506	94.86%	comparative	1,332	88.21%
capital-world	8,372	96.46%	superlative	1,056	74.62%
city-in-state	4,242	60.00%	present-participle	1,056	69.98%
currency	752	17.42%	nationality-adjective	1,640	92.50%
family	506	88.14%	past-tense	1,560	61.15%
adjective-to-adverb	992	22.58%	plural	1,332	78.08%
opposite	756	28.57%	plural-verbs	870	58.51%

The Common Crawl vectors for the 100,000 most common tokens cover about 80% of the analogies and achieve slightly higher accuracy at 78%, whereas the Twitter vectors cover only 25% with 62% accuracy.

How to train your own word vector embeddings

Many tasks require embeddings or domain-specific vocabulary that pretrained models based on a generic corpus may not represent well or at all. Standard Word2vec models are not able to assign vectors to out-of-vocabulary words and instead use a default vector that reduces their predictive value.

For example, when working with industry-specific documents, the vocabulary or its usage may change over time as new technologies or products emerge. As a result, the embeddings need to evolve as well. In addition, corporate earnings releases use nuanced language not fully reflected in GloVe vectors pretrained on Wikipedia articles.

We will illustrate the Word2vec architecture using the Keras library that we will introduce in more detail in the next chapter and the more performant gensim adaptation of the code provided by the Word2vec authors. The notebook Word2vec contains additional implementation detail, including a reference of a TensorFlow implementation.

The Skip-Gram architecture in Keras

To illustrate the Word2vec network architecture, we use the TED Talk dataset with aligned English and Spanish subtitles that we first introduced in Chapter 13, *Working with Text Data*.

The notebook contains the code to tokenize the documents and assign a unique ID to each item in the vocabulary. We require at least five occurrences in the corpus and keep a vocabulary of 31,300 tokens.

Noise-contrastive estimation

Keras includes a `make_sampling_table` method that allows us to create a training set as pairs of context and noise words with corresponding labels, sampled according to their corpus frequencies.

The result is 27 million positive and negative examples of context and target pairs.

The model components

The *Skip-Gram* model contains a 200-dimensional embedding vector for each vocabulary item, resulting in 31,300 x 200 trainable parameters, plus two for the sigmoid output.

In each iteration, the model computes the dot product of the context and the target-embedding vectors, passes the result through the sigmoid to produce a probability and adjusts the embedding based on the gradient of the loss.

Visualizing embeddings using TensorBoard

TensorBoard is a visualization tool that permits the projection of the embedding vectors into three dimensions to explore the word and phrase locations.

Word vectors from SEC filings using gensim

In this section, we will learn word and phrase vectors from annual US **Securities and Exchange Commission (SEC)** filings using gensim to illustrate the potential value of word embeddings for algorithmic trading. In the following sections, we will combine these vectors as features with price returns to train neural networks to predict equity prices from the content of security filings.

In particular, we use a dataset containing over 22,000 10-K annual reports from the period 2013-2016 that are filed by listed companies and contain both financial information and management commentary (see Chapter 3, *Alternative Data for Finance*). For about half of the 11-K filings for companies, we have stock prices to label the data for predictive modeling (see references about data sources and the notebooks in the sec-filings folder for details).

Preprocessing

Each filing is a separate text file and a master index contains filing metadata. We extract the most informative sections, namely, the following:

- **Items 1 and 1A**: Business and Risk Factors
- **Items 7 and 7A**: Management's Discussion and Disclosures about Market Risks

The notebook preprocessing shows how to parse and tokenize the text using spaCy, similar to the approach taken in Chapter 14, *Topic Modeling*. We do not lemmatize the tokens to preserve the nuances of word usage.

Automatic phrase detection

We use `gensim` to detect phrases as previously introduced. The `Phrases` module scores the tokens and the `Phraser` class transforms the text data accordingly. The notebook shows how to repeat the process to create longer phrases:

```
sentences = LineSentence(f'ngrams_1.txt')
phrases = Phrases(sentences=sentences,
                  min_count=25,  # ignore terms with a lower count
                  threshold=0.5,  # only phrases with higher score
                  delimiter=b'_',  # how to join ngram tokens
                  scoring='npmi')  # alternative: default
grams = Phraser(phrases)
sentences = grams[sentences]
```

The most frequent bigrams include `common_stock`, `united_states`, `cash_flows`, `real_estate`, and `interest_rates`.

Model training

The `gensim.models.Word2vec` class implements the SG and CBOW architectures introduced previously. The Word2vec notebook contains additional implementation detail.

To facilitate memory-efficient text ingestion, the `LineSentence` class creates a generator from individual sentences contained in the provided text file:

```
sentence_path = Path('data', 'ngrams', f'ngrams_2.txt')
sentences = LineSentence(sentence_path)
```

The `Word2vec` class offers the configuration options previously introduced:

```
model = Word2vec(sentences,
                 sg=1,      # 1=skip-gram; otherwise CBOW
                 hs=0,      # hier. softmax if 1, neg. sampling if 0
                 size=300,    # Vector dimensionality
                 window=3,    # Max dist. btw target and context word
                 min_count=50,  # Ignore words with lower frequency
                 negative=10,  # noise word count for negative sampling
                 workers=8,    # no threads
                 iter=1,      # no epochs = iterations over corpus
                 alpha=0.025,  # initial learning rate
                 min_alpha=0.0001 # final learning rate
                 )
```

The notebook shows how to persist and reload models to continue training, or how to store the embedding vectors separately, for example, for use in ML models.

Model evaluation

Basic functionality includes identifying similar words:

```
model.wv.most_similar(positive=['iphone'],
                      restrict_vocab=15000)
              term  similarity
0          android    0.600454
1       smartphone    0.581685
2              app    0.559129
```

We can also validate individual analogies using positive and negative contributions accordingly:

```
model.wv.most_similar(positive=['france', 'london'],
                      negative=['paris'],
                      restrict_vocab=15000)

              term  similarity
0   united_kingdom    0.606630
1          germany    0.585644
2      netherlands    0.578868
```

Performance impact of parameter settings

We can use the analogies to evaluate the impact of different parameter settings. The following results stand out (see detailed results in the `models` folder):

- Negative sampling outperforms the hierarchical softmax, while also training faster
- The Skip-Gram architecture outperforms CBOW given the objective function
- Different `min_count` settings have a smaller impact, with the midpoint of 50 performing best

Further experiments with the best performing SG model, using negative sampling and a `min_count` of 50, show the following:

- Smaller context windows than five lower the performance
- A higher negative sampling rate improves performance at the expense of slower training
- Larger vectors improve performance, with a size of 600 yielding the best accuracy at 38.5%

Sentiment analysis with Doc2vec

Text classification requires combining multiple word embeddings. A common approach is to average the embedding vectors for each word in the document. This uses information from all embeddings and effectively uses vector addition to arrive at a different location point in the embedding space. However, relevant information about the order of words is lost.

By contrast, the state-of-the-art generation of embeddings for pieces of text such as a paragraph or a product review is to use the document-embedding model `Doc2vec`. This model was developed by the Word2vec authors shortly after publishing their original contribution.

Similar to Word2vec, there are also two flavors of `Doc2vec`:

- The **distributed bag of words (DBOW)** model corresponds to the Word2vec CBOW model. The document vectors result from training a network in the synthetic task of predicting a target word based on both the context word vectors and the document's doc vector.
- The **distributed memory (DM)** model corresponds to the Word2vec Skip-Gram architecture. The doc vectors result from training a neural net to predict a target word using the full document's doc vector.

Gensim's `Doc2vec` class implements this algorithm.

Training Doc2vec on yelp sentiment data

We use a random sample of 500,000 Yelp (see Chapter 13, *Working with Text Data*) reviews with their associated star ratings (see notebook yelp_sentiment):

```
df = (pd.read_parquet('yelp_reviews.parquet', engine='fastparquet')
        .loc[:, ['stars', 'text']])
stars = range(1, 6)
sample = pd.concat([df[df.stars==s].sample(n=100000) for s in stars])
```

We apply use simple pre-processing to remove stopwords and punctuation using NLTK's tokenizer and drop reviews with fewer than 10 tokens:

```
import nltk
nltk.download('stopwords')
from nltk import RegexpTokenizer
from nltk.corpus import stopwords
tokenizer = RegexpTokenizer(r'\w+')
stopword_set = set(stopwords.words('english'))

def clean(review):
    tokens = tokenizer.tokenize(review)
    return ' '.join([t for t in tokens if t not in stopword_set])

sample.text = sample.text.str.lower().apply(clean)
sample = sample[sample.text.str.split().str.len()>10]
```

Create input data

The gensim.models.doc2vec class processes documents in the TaggedDocument format that contains the tokenized documents alongside a unique tag that permits accessing the document vectors after training:

```
sentences = []
for i, (_, text) in enumerate(sample.values):
    sentences.append(TaggedDocument(words=text.split(), tags=[i]))
```

The training interface works similar to word2vec with additional parameters to specify the Doc2vec algorithm:

```
model = Doc2vec(documents=sentences,
                dm=1,              # algorithm: use distributed memory
                dm_concat=0,       # 1: concat, not sum/avg context vectors
                dbow_words=0,      # 1: train word vectors, 0: only doc
                                   #    vectors
                alpha=0.025,       # initial learning rate
```

```
                    size=300,
                    window=5,
                    min_count=10,
                    epochs=5,
                    negative=5)
    model.save('test.model')
```

You can also use the `train()` method to continue the learning process and, for example, iteratively reduce the learning rate:

```
for _ in range(10):
    alpha *= .9
    model.train(sentences,
                total_examples=model.corpus_count,
                epochs=model.epochs,
                alpha=alpha)
```

As a result, we can access the document vectors as features to train a sentiment classifier:

```
X = np.zeros(shape=(len(sample), size))
y = sample.stars.sub(1) # model needs [0, 5) labels
for i in range(len(sample)):
 X[i] = model[i]
```

We will train a `lightgbm` gradient boosting machine as follows:

1. Create `lightgbm Dataset` objects from the train and test sets:

```
    train_data = lgb.Dataset(data=X_train, label=y_train)
    test_data = train_data.create_valid(X_test, label=y_test)
```

2. Define the training parameters for a multiclass model with five classes (using defaults otherwise):

```
    params = {'objective'   : 'multiclass',
                'num_classes': 5}
```

3. Train the model for 250 iterations and monitor the validation set error:

```
    lgb_model = lgb.train(params=params,
                            train_set=train_data,
                            num_boost_round=250,
                            valid_sets=[train_data, test_data],
                            verbose_eval=25)
```

4. Lightgbm predicts probabilities for all five classes. We obtain class predictions using `np.argmax()` to obtain the column index with the highest predicted probability:

```
y_pred = np.argmax(lgb_model.predict(X_test), axis=1)
```

5. We compute the accuracy score to evaluate the result and see an improvement of more than 100% over the baseline of 20% for five balanced classes:

```
accuracy_score(y_true=y_test, y_pred=y_pred)
0.44955063467061984
```

6. Finally, we take a closer look at predictions for each class using the confusion matrix:

```
cm = confusion_matrix(y_true=y_test, y_pred=y_pred)
cm = pd.DataFrame(cm / np.sum(cm), index=stars, columns=stars)
```

7. And visualize the result as a `seaborn` heatmap:

```
sns.heatmap(cm, annot=True, cmap='Blues', fmt='.1%')
```

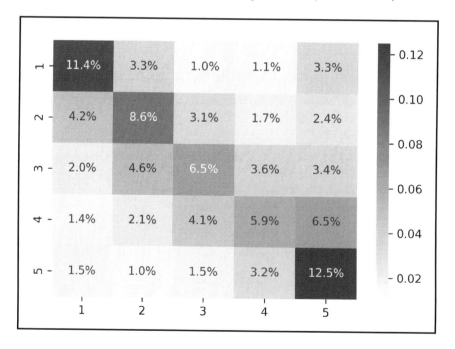

In sum, the `doc2vec` method allowed us to achieve a very substantial improvement in test accuracy over a naive benchmark without much tuning. If we only select top and bottom reviews (with five and one stars, respectively) and train a binary classifier, the AUC score achieves over 0.86 using 250,000 samples from each class.

Bonus – Word2vec for translation

The notebook translation demonstrates that the relationships encoded in one language often correspond to similar relationships in another language.

It illustrates how word vectors can be used to translate words and phrases by projecting word vectors from the embedding space of one language into the space of another language using a translation matrix.

Summary

This chapter started with how word embeddings encode semantics for individual tokens more effectively than the bag-of-words model that we used in `Chapter 13`, *Working with Text Data*. We also saw how to evaluated embedding by validating if semantic relationships among words are properly represented using linear vector arithmetic.

To learn word embeddings, we use shallow neural networks that used to be slow to train at the scale of web data containing billions of tokens. The `word2vec` model combines several algorithmic innovations to dramatically speed up training and has established a new standard for text feature generation. We saw how to use pretrained word vectors using `spaCy` and `gensim`, and learned to train our own word vector embeddings. We then applied a `word2vec` model to SEC filings. Finally, we covered the `doc2vec` extension that learns vector representations for documents in a similar fashion as word vectors and applied it to Yelp business reviews.

Now, we will begin part 4 on deep learning (available online as mentioned in the Preface), starting with an introduction to feed-forward networks, popular deep learning frameworks and techniques for efficient training at scale.

16
Next Steps

The goal of this book was to enable you to apply **machine learning (ML)** to a variety of data sources and the extract signals useful for the design and execution of an investment strategy. To this end, we introduced ML as an important element in the trading strategy process. We saw that ML can add value at multiple steps in the process of designing, testing, executing, and evaluating a strategy.

It became clear that the core value proposition of ML consists of the ability to extract actionable information from much larger amounts of data more systematically than human experts would ever be able to. On the one hand, this value proposition has really gained currency with the explosion of digital data that made it both more promising and necessary to leverage computing power for data processing. On the other hand, the application of ML still requires significant human intervention and expertise to define objectives, select and curate data, design and optimize a model and make appropriate use of the results.

In this concluding chapter, we will briefly summarize the key tools, applications, and lessons learned throughout the book to avoid losing sight of the big picture after so much detail. We will then identify areas that we did not cover but would be worthwhile to focus on as you aim to expand on the many ML techniques we introduced and become productive in their daily use. We will highlight skill sets that are valuable for individual productivity.

In summary, in this chapter, we will go through the following topics:

- Review key takeaways and lessons learned,
- Point out the next steps to build on the techniques in this book,
- Suggest ways to incorporate ML into your investment process.

Key takeaways and lessons learned

Important insights to keep in mind as you proceed to the practice of ML for trading include:

- Data is the single most important ingredient
- Domain expertise helps realize the potential value in the data, especially in finance
- ML offers tools for many use cases that should be further developed and combined to create solutions for new problems using data
- The choice of model objectives and performance diagnostics are key to productive iterations towards an optimal system
- Backtest overfitting is a huge challenge that requires significant attention
- Transparency around black-box models can help build confidence and facilitate adoption

We will elaborate a bit more on each of these ideas.

Data is the single most important ingredient

The rise of ML in trading and everywhere else largely complements the data explosion that we covered in great detail. We illustrated in Chapter 2, *Market and Fundamental Data* how to access and work with these data sources, historically the mainstay of quantitative investment. In Chapter 3, *Alternative Data for Finance*, we laid out a framework with the criteria to assess the potential value of alternative datasets.

A key insight is that the state-of-the-art ML techniques like deep neural networks are successful because their predictive performance continues to improve with more data. On the flip side, model and data complexity need to match to balance the bias-variance trade-off. Managing data quality and integrating datasets are key steps in realizing the potential value.

Quality control

Just like oil, a popular comparison these days, data passes through a pipeline with several stages from its raw form to a refined product that can fuel a trading strategy. It is critical to pay careful attention to the quality of the final product to get the desired mileage out of it.

Sometimes, you get data in raw form and control the numerous transformations required for your purposes. More often, you deal with an intermediate product and should get clarity about what exactly the data measures at this point.

Different from oil, there is often no objective quality standard as data sources continue to proliferate. Instead, the quality depends on its signal content, which in turn depends on your investment objectives. The cost-effective evaluation of new datasets requires a productive workflow, including appropriate infrastructure that we will address in the following section.

Data integration

The value of data for an investment strategy often depends on combining complementary sources of market, fundamental and alternative data. We saw that the predictive power of ML algorithms like tree-based ensembles or neural networks is in part due to their ability to detect non-linear relationships, in particular, interaction effects among variables.

The ability to modulate the impact of a variable as a function of other model features thrives on data inputs that capture different aspects of a target outcome. The combination of asset prices with macro fundamentals, social sentiment, credit card payment, and satellite data will likely yield significantly more reliable predictions throughout different economic and market regimes than each source on its own (provided there the data is large enough to learn the hidden relationships).

Working with data from multiple sources increases the challenges of proper labeling. It is vital to assign accurate timestamps to avoid a lookahead bias by testing an algorithm with data before it actually became available. Data, for example, may have timestamps assigned by a provider that require adjustments to reflect the point in time when they would have been available for a live algorithm.

Domain expertise helps unlock value in data

We emphasized that data is a necessary driver of successful ML applications, but that domain expertise is also crucial to inform strategic direction, feature engineering and data selection, and model design.

In any domain, practitioners have theories about the drivers of key outcomes and relationships among them. Finance stands out by the amount of relevant quantitative research, both theoretical and empirical. Marcos López de Prado and others (see GitHub for references `https://github.com/PacktPublishing/Hands-On-Machine-Learning-for-Trading`) criticize most empirical results given pervasive data mining that may invalidate the findings. Nonetheless, a robust understanding of how financial markets work exists and should inform the selection and use of data as well as the justification of strategies that rely on machine learning. We outlined key ideas in `Chapter 4`, *Alpha Factor Research* and `Chapter 5`, *Strategy Evaluation*.

On the other hand, novel ML techniques will likely uncover new hypotheses about drivers of financial outcomes that will inform ML theory and should then be independently tested.

Feature engineering and alpha factor research

More than the raw data, feature engineering is often the key to making signal useful for an algorithm. Leveraging decades of research into risk factors that drive returns on theoretical and empirical grounds is a good starting point to prioritize data transformations that are more likely to reflect relevant information.

However, only creative feature engineering will lead to innovative strategies that can compete in the market over time. Even for new alpha factors, a compelling narrative that explains how they work, given established ideas on market dynamics and investor behavior, will provide more confidence to allocate capital.

The risks of false discoveries and overfitting to historical data make it even more necessary to prioritize strategies prior to testing rather than *let the data speak*. We covered how to deflate the Sharpe ratio in light of the number of experiments.

ML is a toolkit for solving problems with data

ML offers algorithmic solutions and techniques that can be applied to many use cases. Parts 2, 3, and 4 of the book (as mentioned in `Chapter 1`, *Machine Learning for Trading*) have presented ML as a diverse set of tools that can add value to various steps of the strategy process, including:

- Idea generation and alpha factor research,
- Signal aggregation and portfolio optimization,
- Strategy testing

- Trade execution, and
- Strategy evaluation

Even more so, ML algorithms are designed to be further developed, adapted and combined to solve new problems in different contexts. For these reasons, it is important to understand key concepts and ideas underlying these algorithms, in addition to being able to apply them to data for productive experimentation and research as outlined in Chapter 6, *The Machine Learning Process*.

Furthermore, the best results are often achieved by combining human experts with ML tools. In Chapter 1, *Machine Learning for Trading*, we covered the quantamental investment style where discretionary and algorithmic trading converge. This approach will likely further grow in importance and depends on the flexible and creative application of the fundamental tools that we covered and their extensions to a variety of data sets.

Model diagnostics help speed up optimization

In Chapter 6, *The Machine Learning Process*, we outlined some of the most important concepts. ML algorithms learn relationships between input data and a target by making assumptions about the functional form. If the learning is based on noise rather than signal, predictive performance will suffer.

Of course, we do not know today how to separate signal and noise from the perspective of tomorrow's outcomes. Model diagnostics, for example, using learning curves and the optimization verification test can help alleviate this fundamental challenge and calibrate the choice or configuration of an algorithm to the data or task at hand. This task can be made easier by defining focused model objectives and, for complex models, distinguishing between performance shortcomings due to issues with the optimization algorithm or the objective itself.

Making do without a free lunch

No system—computer program or human—has a basis to reliably predict outcomes for new examples beyond those it observed during training. The only way out is to have some additional prior knowledge or make assumptions that go beyond the training examples. We covered a broad range of algorithms from Chapter 7, *Linear Models* and Chapter 8, *Time Series Models*, to non-linear ensembles in Chapter 10, *Decision Trees and Random Forest* and Chapter 11, *Gradient Boosting Machines* as well as neural networks in various chapters of part 4 of this book.

We saw that a linear model makes a strong assumption that the relationship between inputs and outputs has a very simple form, whereas the models discussed later aim to learn more complex functions. While it's probably obvious that a simple model will fail in most circumstances, a complex model is not always better. If the true relationship is linear but the data is noisy, the complex model will learn the noise as part of the complex relationship that it assumes to exist. This is the basic idea behind the *No Free Lunch Theorem* that states no algorithm is universally superior for all tasks. Good fit in some instances comes at the cost of poor performance elsewhere.

The key tools to tailor the choice of the algorithm to the data are data exploration and experiments based on an understanding of the assumptions the model makes.

Managing the bias-variance trade-off

A different perspective on the challenge of adapting an algorithm to data is the trade-off between bias and variance that cause prediction errors beyond the natural noisiness of the data. A simple model that does not adequately capture the relationships in the data will underfit and exhibit bias, that is, make systematically wrong predictions. A model that is too complex will overfit and learn the noise in addition to any signal so that the result will show a lot of variance for different samples.

The key tool to diagnose this trade-off at any given iteration of the model selection and optimization process is the learning curve. It shows how training and validation errors depend on the sample size. This allows us to decide between different options to improve performance: adjust the complexity of the model or get more data points.

The closer the training error is to human or other benchmarks, the more likely the model will overfit. The low validation error tells us that we are lucky and found a good model. If the validation error is high, we are not. If it continues to decline with the training size, however, more data may help. If the training error is high, more data is unlikely to help and we should instead add features or use a more flexible algorithm.

Define targeted model objectives

One of the first steps in the machine learning process is the definition of an objective for the algorithm to optimize. Sometimes, the choice is simple, for example, in a regression problem. A classification task can be more difficult, for example, when we care about precision and recall. Consolidating conflicting objectives into a single metric like the F1 score helps to focus optimization efforts. We can also include conditions that need to be met rather than optimized for. We also saw that reinforcement learning is all about defining the right reward function to guide the agent's learning process.

The optimization verification test

Andrew Ng (see references on GitHub: `https://github.com/PacktPublishing/Hands-On-Machine-Learning-for-Algorithmic-Trading`) emphasizes the distinction between performance shortcomings due to a problem with the learning algorithm or the optimization algorithm. Complex models like neural networks assume non-linear relationships and the search process of the optimization algorithm may end up in a local rather than a global optimum.

If, for example, a model fails to correctly translate a phrase, the test compares the scores for the correct prediction and the solution discovered by the search algorithm. If the learning algorithm scores the correct solution higher, the search algorithm requires improvements. Otherwise, the learning algorithm is optimizing for the wrong objective.

Beware of backtest overfitting

We covered the risks of false discoveries due to overfitting to historical data repeatedly throughout the book. `Chapter 5`, *Strategy Evaluation* lays out the main drivers and potential remedies. The low noise-to-signal ratio and relatively small datasets (compared to a web-scale image or text data) make this challenge particularly serious in the trading domain. Awareness is critical because the ease of access to data and tools to apply ML increase the risks exponentially.

There is no escape because there is no method of prevention. However, we presented methods to adjust backtest metrics to account for repeated trials such as the deflated Sharpe ratio. When working towards a live trading strategy, stage paper-trading and closely monitored performance during execution in the market need to be part of the implementation process.

How to gain insights from black-box models

Deep neural networks and complex ensembles can raise suspicion when they are considered impenetrable black-box models, in particular in light of the risks of backtest overfitting. We introduced several methods to gain insights into how these models make predictions in `Chapter 11`, *Gradient Boosting Machines*.

In addition to conventional measures of feature importance, the recent game-theoretic innovation of **SHapley Additive exPlanations (SHAP)** is a significant step towards understanding the mechanics of complex models. SHAP values allow for exact attribution of features and their values to predictions so that it becomes easier to validate the logic of a model in the light of specific theories about market behavior for a given investment target. Besides justification, exact feature importance scores and attribution of predictions allow for deeper insights into the drivers of the investment outcome of interest.

On the other hand, there is some controversy to which extend transparency around model predictions should be a goal in itself. Geoffrey Hinton, one of the inventors of deep learning, argues that human decisions are also often obscure and machines should similarly be evaluated by their results, as we expect from investment managers.

ML for trading in practice

As you proceed to integrate the numerous tools and techniques into your investment and trading process, there are numerous things you could focus your efforts on. If your goal is to make better decisions, you should select projects that are realistic yet ambitious given your current skill set. This will help you to develop an efficient workflow underpinned by productive tools and gain practical experience.

We will briefly list some of the tools that are useful to expand on the Python ecosystem covered in this book and refer to the links listed on GitHub to dive deeper. These include big data technologies that will eventually be necessary to implement ML for trading strategies at scale. We will also list some of the platforms that allow you to implement trading strategies using Python, often with access to data sources and ML algorithms and libraries.

Data management technologies

The central role of data in the ML process requires familiarity with a range of technologies to store, transform, and analyze data at scale, including the use of cloud-based services such as Amazon Web Services, Azure, and Google Cloud.

Database systems

Data storage implies the use of databases, historically dominated by **relational database management systems (RDBMS)** that use SQL to store and retrieve data in a well-defined table format with commercial providers like Oracle and Microsoft and open-source implementations like PostgreSQL and MySQL. More recently, alternatives have emerged that are often collectively labeled NoSQL but are quite diverse, namely:

- **Key-value storage**: Fast read/write access to objects. We covered the HDF5 format in `Chapter 2`, *Market and Fundamental Data* that facilitates fast access to a pandas DataFrame.
- **Columnar storage**: Capitalizes on the homogeneity of data in a column to facilitates compression and faster column-based operations such as aggregation. Used in the popular Amazon Redshift data warehouse solution, Apache Parquet, Cassandra, or Google's Big Table.
- **Document store**: Designed to store data that defies the rigid schema definition required by an RDBMS. Popularized by web applications that use JSON or XML format that we encountered in `Chapter 4`, *Alpha Factor Research*. Used, for example, in MongoDB.
- **Graph database**: Designed to store networks that have nodes and edges and specializes in queries about network metrics and relationships. Used in Neo4J and Apache Giraph.

There has been some conversion towards the conventions established by the relational database systems. The Python ecosystem facilitates the interaction with many standard data sources and provides fast HDF5 and Parquet formats as demonstrated throughout the book.

Big Data technologies – Hadoop and Spark

Data management at scale, that is, hundreds of GB and beyond, require the use of multiple machines that form a cluster to conduct read, write and compute operations in parallel, that is, it is distributed over various machines.

The Hadoop ecosystem has emerged as an open-source software framework for distributed storage and processing of big data using the MapReduce programming model developed by Google. The ecosystem has diversified under the roof of the Apache Foundation and today includes numerous projects that cover different aspects of data management at scale. Key tools within Hadoop include:

- **Apache Pig**: Data processing language to implement large-scale **extract-transform-load (ETL)** pipelines using MapReduce, developed at Yahoo
- **Apache Hive**: The defacto standard for interactive SQL queries over petabytes of data developed at Facebook
- **Apache HBASE**: NoSQL database for real-time read/write access that scales linearly to billions of rows and millions of columns, and can combines data sources using a variety of different schemas.

Apache Spark has become the most popular platform for interactive analytics on a cluster. The MapReduce framework allowed for parallel computation but required repeated read/write operations from disk to ensure data redundancy. Spark has dramatically accelerated computation at scale due to the **Resilient Distributed Data (RDD)** structure that allows for highly optimized in-memory computation. This includes iterative computation as required for optimization, for example gradient descent for numerous ML algorithms.

ML tools

We covered many libraries of the Python ecosystem in this book. Python has evolved to become the language of choice for data science and ML and the set of open-source libraries continues to both diversify and mature, built on the robust core of scientific computing libraries NumPy and SciPy. The popular pandas library that has contributed significantly to popularizing the use of Python for data science is planning its 1.0 release. The scikit-learn interface has become the standard for modern ML libraries like `xgboost` or `lightgbm` that often interface with the various workflow automation tools like `GridSearchCV` and `Pipeline` that we used repeatedly throughout the book.

There are several providers that aim to facilitate the ML workflow:

- H2O.ai (`https://www.h2o.ai/`) offers the H2O platform that integrates cloud computing with ML automation. It allows users to fit thousands of potential models to their data to explore patterns in the data. It has interfaces in Python as well as R and Java.

- DataRobot aims to automate the model development process by providing a platform to rapidly build and deploy predictive models in the cloud or on-premise.
- Dataiku is a collaborative data science platform designed to help the analysts and engineers explore, prototype, build, and deliver their own data products

There are also several open-source initiatives led by companies that build on and expand the Python ecosystem:

- The quantitative hedge fund Two Sigma contributes quantitative analysis tools to the Jupyter Notebook environment under the `beakerx` project
- Bloomberg has integrated the Jupyter Notebook into its terminal to facilitate the interactive analysis of their financial data

Online trading platforms

The main options to develop trading strategies that use machine learning are online platforms that often look for and allocate capital to successful trading strategies. Popular solutions include Quantopian, Quantconnect, QuantRocket, and the more recent Alpha Trading Labs that focuses on high-frequency trading.

In addition, **Interactive Brokers (IB)** offers a Python API that you can use to develop your own trading solution.

Quantopian

We introduced the Quantopian platform and demonstrated the use of its research and trading environment to analyze and test trading strategies against historical data. Quantopian uses Python and offers lots of educational material.

Quantopian hosts ongoing daily competitions to recruit algorithms for its crowd-sourced hedge fund portfolio. Quantopian provides capital to the winning algorithm. Live-trading was discontinued in September 2017, but the platform still provides a large range of historical data and attracts an active community of developers and traders that is a good starting point to discuss ideas and learn from others.

QuantConnect

QuantConnect is another open source, community-driven algorithmic trading platform that competes with Quantopian. It also provides an IDE to backtest and live-trade algorithmic strategies using Python and other languages.

QuantConnect also has a dynamic, global community from all over the world, and provides access to numerous asset classes, including equities, futures, forex, and cryptocurrency. It offers live-trading integration with various brokers such as IB, OANDA, and GDAX.

QuantRocket

QuantRocket is a Python-based platform for researching, backtesting, and running automated, quantitative trading strategies. It provides data collection tools, multiple data vendors, a research environment, multiple backtesters, and live and paper trading through IB. It prides itself on support for international equity trading and sets itself apart with its flexibility.

QuantRocket supports multiple engines—its own Moonshot, as well as third-party engines chosen by the user. While QuantRocket doesn't have a traditional IDE, it is integrated well with Jupyter to produce something similar. QuantRocket is not free, however, and pricing starts at 19 USD/month at the time of writing.

Conclusion

We started by highlighting the explosion of digital data and the emergence of ML as a strategic capability for investment and trading strategies. This dynamic reflects global business and technology trends beyond finance and is much more likely to continue than to stall or reverse. Many investment firms are just getting started to leverage the range of artificial intelligence tools, just as individuals are acquiring the relevant skills and business processes are adapting to these new opportunities for value creation, as outlined in the introductory chapter.

There are also numerous exciting developments for the application of ML to trading on the horizon that are likely to further propel the current momentum. They are likely to become relevant in the coming years and include the automation of the ML process, the generation of synthetic training data, and the emergence of quantum computing. The extraordinary vibrancy of the field implies that this alone could fill a book and the journey will continue to remain exciting.

Other Books You May Enjoy

If you enjoyed this book, you may be interested in these other books by Packt:

Machine Learning Algorithms - Second Edition

Giuseppe Bonaccorso

ISBN: 9781789347999

- Study feature selection and the feature engineering process
- Assess performance and error trade-offs for linear regression
- Build a data model and understand how it works by using different types of algorithm
- Learn to tune the parameters of Support Vector Machines (SVM)
- Explore the concept of natural language processing (NLP) and recommendation systems
- Create a machine learning architecture from scratch

Building Machine Learning Systems with Python - Third Edition
Luis Pedro Coelho, Willi Richert, Matthieu Brucher

ISBN: 9781788623223

- Build a classification system that can be applied to text, images, and sound
- Employ Amazon Web Services (AWS) to run analysis on the cloud
- Solve problems related to regression using scikit-learn and TensorFlow
- Recommend products to users based on their past purchases
- Understand different ways to apply deep neural networks on structured data
- Address recent developments in the field of computer vision and reinforcement learning

Leave a review - let other readers know what you think

Please share your thoughts on this book with others by leaving a review on the site that you bought it from. If you purchased the book from Amazon, please leave us an honest review on this book's Amazon page. This is vital so that other potential readers can see and use your unbiased opinion to make purchasing decisions, we can understand what our customers think about our products, and our authors can see your feedback on the title that they have worked with Packt to create. It will only take a few minutes of your time, but is valuable to other potential customers, our authors, and Packt. Thank you!

Index